Counselling Skills

Second Edition

Second Edition

Counselling Skills

A Practical Guide for Counsellors and Helping Professionals

John McLeod
and Julia McLeod

McGraw Hill

Open University Press

Open University Press
McGraw-Hill Education
McGraw-Hill House
Shoppenhangers Road
Maidenhead
Berkshire
England
SL6 2QL

email: enquiries@openup.co.uk
world wide web: www.openup.co.uk

and Two Penn Plaza, New York, NY 10121-2289, USA

First published 2007
Reprinted 2010, 2011
First published in this second edition 2011

A catalogue record of this book is available from the British Library

ISBN-13: 978-0-33-524426-3
ISBN-10: 0-33-524426-2
eBook: 978-0-33-524227-0

Library of Congress Cataloging-in-Publication Data
CIP data applied for

Typesetting and e-book compilations by
RefineCatch Limited, Bungay, Suffolk
Printed in the UK by Bell & Bain Ltd, Glasgow

Fictitious names of companies, products, people, characters and/or data that may be used
herein (in case studies or in examples) are not intended to represent any real individual,
company, product or event.

The *McGraw·Hill* Companies

Dedication

For Kate, Emma and Hannah

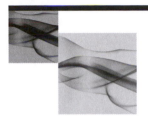

Contents

Preface

A previous edition of this book was published in 2006, with the title *Counselling Skill*. This current edition offers a significantly enhanced and expanded account of the same territory, with a stronger emphasis on practical methods and strategies for helping people struggling to deal with problems in living.

We have written this book to meet the learning needs of two groups of people:

1 Practitioners such as doctors, nurses, teachers, clergy, and those who work in social services, human resources, trades unions, community projects, the criminal justice system, advice centres and many other contexts, who are called upon by the people with whom they are dealing to provide emotional support around coping with pressing personal concerns. We use the term *embedded counselling* to describe the counselling activities undertaken by such practitioners – their counselling role is embedded within wider professional responsibilities;

2 Those who are at an early stage of foundation training in counselling and psychotherapy. The book offers a comprehensive account of a set of practical skills for establishing and maintaining collaborative counselling relationships and facilitating change. At the beginning stages of training to be a professional counsellor, participants are unlikely to be working with therapy clients, and find it necessary to draw on their experience of counselling relationships in previous or other concurrent work roles as a source of reflection and learning.

It may be helpful to comment on the way in which this book has been written. We have tried, as far as possible, to present what we have had to say in a straightforward and direct manner as possible, with relatively few references to sources being cited within the main body of the text. For the most part, key sources have been signalled through recommendations for further reading provided at the end of sections and chapters. We have also used boxes to highlight the relevance of research studies and key concepts. At regular intervals, readers will find self-reflection tasks that are designed to ground the material in personal experience, and encourage exploration of implications for practice. Each chapter is preceded by an excerpt of the story of Donald, his wife Anita and his nurse-counsellor Sally. We hope that the unfolding drama of Donald's use of counselling to help him come to terms with life-threatening illness will assist readers in making connections between the various themes that are discussed in different chapters. Donald, Anita and Sally are not, of course, actual people, but instead are composite characters, based on the experiences of several individuals with whom we have worked.

We make no apology for making reference to research evidence throughout the book. In our view, the majority of people who study counselling skills are undertaking degree-level programmes, or are already graduates. Practitioners of both embedded counselling and specialist stand-alone counselling operate in professional environments in which research evidence informs all aspects of policy and practice, and if counselling skills and emotional support are to be taken seriously in these settings it is essential for more and better studies of the processes and outcomes of the use of counselling skills be carried out.

We would like to record our appreciation to the many friends and colleagues whose ideas and conversations have deepened and maintained our interest in counselling: Joe Armstrong, Bud Baxter, Ronen Berger, Tim Bond, Julia Buckroyd, Anne Chien, Kitt Coomber, Mick Cooper, Edith Cormack, Elaine Craig, Wendy Drewery, Robert Elliott, Brent Gardner, Kim Etherington, Anjali Goswami, Colin Kirkwood, Elke Lambers, Steve Lang, Noreen Lillie, Thomas Mackrill, Mhairi Macmillan, Catherine Marriott, Lynsey McMillan, Dave Mearns, Ann Moir-Bussy, Denis O'Hara, Fiona O'Hara, Moira Pollock, Steve Quince, Brian Rodgers, Alison Rouse, Alison Shoemark, Salma Siddique, Mhairi Thurston, Dot Weaks, William West, Sue Wheeler, Mark Widdowson and Jeannie Wright. We are grateful to Monika Lee at the Open University Press for her generous encouragement and sensible advice, and to her colleagues Richard Townrow and Mandy Gentle for their efficient and timely practical assistance throughout the process of writing and production. We would also like to record our appreciation for all that we have learned from our students on the Certificate in Counselling Skills programme at the University of Abertay Dundee.

Our greatest debt is to our daughters Kate, Emma and Hannah, whose lives remain a source of joy and wonder to us both.

CHAPTER 1

An invitation to counselling

I don't know what is going to happen to me
I don't know where to turn
Collapsing at home
The pain
Thinking it was the end
Waiting for the paramedics
Then in the hospital
The doctors and nurses
Cautiously hopeful
In a reserved kind of way
The family
Stiff upper lips
Being strong
And all that
But me?
My life has changed completely
It's not real
I'm now living in a different world to the rest of them

Introduction

This book is intended for people who are involved in working with people in any kind of helping, managing or facilitative role; for example, teaching, social work, the health professions, clergy, advice work, training, human resources (HR) and the justice system. Anyone who does such a job is required to be skilled in many different forms of interpersonal contact, such as communicating information, interviewing to gather information, shared decision-making and counselling. The particular form of interpersonal contact that is known as 'counselling' refers to any interaction where someone seeks to explore, understand or resolve a problematic or troubling *personal* aspect of a practical issue that is being dealt with. Counselling is what happens when a person consults someone else around a *problem in living* – a conflict or dilemma that is getting in the way; that is, preventing people from living their lives in the way in which they would wish. Teachers, social workers and nurses, and those who work in other 'people' roles, frequently encounter such requests from their clients or service users.

The following chapters provide a framework for making sense of episodes of counselling that are *embedded* in other activities and roles. The book is about counsell*ing*, rather than being a counsell*or*. It is intended for people who already possess professional knowledge and training in a field such as nursing or teaching, and who recognize the value of developing better strategies for responding constructively and effectively to moments when the person with whom they are working *needs to talk*. The key aim of the book is to make it clear what can be done at such moments, and how to do it. The book will also be useful to 'specialist' counsellors, people who deliver counselling on a stand-alone basis, typically structured around weekly one-hour meetings with a 'client', and have no other involvement with that person outside the counselling hour, or their counselling role. The value of this book for such specialist counsellors is that it seeks to explain some of the fundamental elements of their craft.

It is taken for granted in this book that a useful counselling conversation can take place within about 8–10 minutes. This length of time represents a typical window of opportunity that a teacher, doctor or manager may have to allow someone to talk through something that is troubling them. Of course, there are many situations in which longer periods of time may be available, or where sequences of separate 10-minute talks may be linked together. But it is nevertheless important to recognize that a 10-minute talk can make a difference. Time pressure should not be used as an excuse for avoiding to listen to clients' stories, or allowing them to talk things through.

Throughout this book, the terms 'counsellor' and 'person' are used to refer to the one who seeks counselling (the person) and the one who offers it (the counsellor). This use of the term counsellor is *not* intended to imply 'professionally qualified and accredited as a stand-alone counsellor'. Rather, it refers to someone engaged in offering an episode of counselling *at that moment* – someone who is fulfilling the function of counsellor for another person who needs to talk through a matter that is concerning them. On the whole, the term person is employed in preference to client because episodic or embedded counselling rarely involves the kind of formal contracting and role definition ('I am a counsellor with an office and diploma on my wall') that would justify the use of this word. The examples that are used in this book encompass a wide spectrum of work settings, many of which do not routinely refer to people as clients. For example, users of educational institutions such as schools and colleges are rarely described as clients. Other terms, such as service user, patient and client are used where the context requires.

Exercise 1.1: *Images of counselling*

As you begin to read this book, what prior assumptions about counselling do you hold? What are your images of counselling? What is your own critical stance in relation to counselling – what do you believe at this point is beneficial or good about counselling, and where are your points of scepticism and reservation?

A narrative approach

This book takes a broadly narrative approach to making sense of how counselling helps people. The idea of a narrative approach refers to a significant movement within the social and health sciences, and psychology, in recent years (Greenhalgh and Hurwitz, 1998; McLeod, 1997a, b). The enormous success of engineering, technology and the physical sciences in the nineteenth and twentieth centuries lead to a situation in which it became commonplace to view human beings as mechanisms, as objects, machines or organisms that might break down and require fixing. It began to be clear to many people that such an attitude, while valuable in some respects, brought with it the danger of dehumanization, of eroding or even losing the essential quality of what makes us human. The concept of narrative provides a succinct and yet powerful means of reminding ourselves of our human qualities, and bringing emphasis to these qualities in our thinking and practice.

Narrative is concerned with the human capacity to tell stories. We use stories to communicate to each other the important or memorable things that happen to us on an everyday basis. Within our heads, and in our own lives, each of us lives out a story or stories, and construct our identity and sense of self through creating a story of our life, our autobiography. Culturally, the beliefs, values and world view of a set of people are carried through narrative in the form of myth, scripture, literature and 'news'.

Box 1.1: *Help is where you find it*

Cowen (1982) carried out interviews into the kind of help provided around emotional and interpersonal problems to their clients by hairdressers, lawyers specializing in family issues, factory supervisors and bartenders. He found that moderate to serious personal problems were raised with all groups, but particularly with hairdressers and lawyers. A range of different ways of handling these helping conversations were reported – some of the strategies used by these informal helpers were much the same as those employed by professional therapists. In this, and other research studies, hairdressers have been found to be particularly resourceful in terms of responding to the personal problems of their clients (Cowen *et al.*, 1979; Milne and Mullin, 1987). In a study that looked at the value of informal help from the perspective of the person seeking assistance, McLennan (1991) conducted a survey of university students who reported themselves as having experienced emotional and interpersonal difficulties. Some of them had consulted counsellors, while others had spoken to their friends or informal helpers about their difficulties. When asked about the quality of their relationship with their professional counsellor or informal helper, there was no difference between the two groups in terms of the amount of time they received, helper/counsellor availability, or the extent to which they felt understood or accepted. Hart (1996) surveyed specialist student counsellors, and academic tutors who carried out pastoral work with students, and found that there was a high degree of overlap between the two groups in the use of skills such as listening, understanding feelings and promoting self-esteem. The findings of these studies, and many other investigations into the role of non-professional counselling-type help, suggest that a lot of informal and 'embedded' counselling takes place in a wide variety of community settings. Almost certainly, a much higher proportion of problems in living are handled informally than are ever seen by a professional counsellor or psychologist – while around 35 per cent of the population experience mental health problems at any one time, only 3 per cent of the population seek professional help.

Narrative simultaneously embraces the individual and the social. Stories are told by individual persons, yet draw in some way on a stock of cultural narratives, and, once told, become a shared product that can be retold. Stories embrace consistency and change in life. Although a story that is told by a person may have a consistent structure and content, every telling is different – the performance of a story always includes some aspect of improvization in response to a specific listener or audience. Any coherent story conveys information about an event that unfolds over time, involves intention and purpose, reveals the relationship between the protagonist or central figure of the story and other people, and communicates feeling and emotion. Stories also have an evaluative element – events are placed in a moral landscape.

A narrative approach to counselling is therefore one that takes seriously all of the dimensions of humanness (intention, relationship, temporality, feeling and morality) that are involved in a process of storytelling. More specifically, a narrative approach draws attention to the ways in which people use language and talk to construct their lives. A narrative approach to counselling is one that promotes sensitivity to the use of language on the part of the person seeking help, and the counsellor who supplies that help. A key idea here is that some ways of talking can position the person, in relation to an issue or concern, in a way that there can seem no possible movement forward. A different way of talking, by contrast, can open up new possibilities for feeling and action. A narrative approach also recognizes the value of the basic human process of storytelling. From such a perspective, it is possible to see that what many people want when they seek counselling is merely an opportunity to tell their story and have it received and affirmed. The conditions of modern life mean that many people are walking around with stories of huge personal significance that they cannot tell, because there is no one willing to listen to them. These people are therefore alone with the pain that may be woven through their story, are unable to enlist social support and solidarity from other people, and have limited opportunity to reflect on, and learn from, what has happened for them. This is where counselling fits in.

Box 1.2: *Being able to be an important person in someone else's life*

There are few more troubling circumstances for any parent than falling into a pattern of conflict and disconnection with one's children. In a study carried out in Sweden by Kerstin Neander and Carola Skott (2006), parents who had success-fully come through this kind of episode were interviewed about the people who had exerted a decisive positive influence on the child and the family during that period. These key figures included nurses, social workers, teachers, a youth leader and a school principal. What were the characteristics of these important people? Their specific professional role and training did not seem to matter. What made a difference was the development of mutual trust, genuine feelings of warmth and acceptance, a sense of being treated as worthwhile and 'special', a clear focus on what was best for the child, making progress through a series of small everyday events, and developing a new and more positive story about the child. At the heart of this process was a perception that 'these people . . . were able to create new situations in which the children and parents could feel comfortable and do well' (p. 309). The aim of this book is to explore what makes it possible for practitioners in these kinds of educational and caring roles to be important people in the lives of their clients.

Making a space to talk it through

At the heart of any form of counselling is *making a space to talk it through*. This phrase is offered as a kind of touchstone throughout the book, and operates as a reminder of what the role of counselling actually is in relation to the troubles that people experience. It is a phrase that carries a great deal of meaning:

●   'Making a space . . .'. The idea of *making* implies that counselling is an intentional, purposeful activity. It is not something that 'just happens' – it has to be 'made'. This 'making' is an activity that is carried out by both partici-pants working together. The person cannot make a counselling space in the absence of the willingness and involvement of the counsellor, and vice versa. The notion of 'making a space' also invites consideration of similar concepts, such as 'creating', 'building' and 'constructing', all of which are valuable in terms of understanding this process: counselling can be understood as an activity that is 'co-constructed'. The use of these terms in turn introduces the question: what are the materials that are being used in this making or building process? There are several personal 'powers' or abilities that are brought into service in the making of a counselling space: attention, physical posture and proximity, language, the arrangement of seating, control of time, and so on. What can be made will depend on the materials that are available in any specific situation.

●   'Making a *space* to talk. . . .'. What is meant by a 'space' in the context of counselling? What kind of space is this? It is a space that exists both in the life of the person who wishes to talk about a problem, and in the relation-ship between that person and their counsellor. One of the main themes of this book is that it is important to understand people as living their lives within a personal niche that they have made for themselves within their society and culture. This niche, or personal world, can at times be hard to live in – things go wrong. Counselling is a space outside of the person's everyday life in which they can stand back from their routine and reflect on what they might wish to do to change things to make them better. A counselling space is like a 'bubble', 'haven' or place of emotional safety into which the person can step for a period of time, and to which they can return when necessary. A counselling space is also a space in the relationship between the person and the counsellor. There are many aspects to the relationship between a person and someone who takes the role of counsellor to them: making arrangements to meet (next week at the same time?), other roles, gender/age/ethnic similarity or difference, shared experiences outside of the counselling room (bumping into each other in the supermarket). However, if counselling is to happen, there needs to be a time when these other facets of the relationship fade into the background to allow a different kind of conversation to develop. The idea of a space implies boundary – there is an edge to a space. A space is surrounded by other things, but within the space there is nothing – it is a *space*. In counselling, while various structures may be brought in from outside ('let's use this problem-solving format to work through the difficulty you are having in making a decision on your career options. . . .'), the basic premise of counselling is that it starts with an empty space where the person is offered the possibility of talking about (or not talking about) anything they like. The notion of space invites reflection on the nature of other spaces in which meaningful personal and emotional learning can occur. There are ways in which a counselling space is similar to, as well as different from, the space that a person enters when they read a good novel, the space created on the stage of a theatre, or the space experienced when walking in the hills.

- '. . . a space *to talk* it through . . .'. Counselling is essentially about talking. Putting something into words, or bringing it into language, can be a very powerful healing experience. Language incorporates an infinite number of ways of making meaning. Words, phrases and discourses reflect the meaning-making activity of multiple generations of people. There is always another way to talk about something, and each way of talking is associated with a different position in relation to the topic, and a different set of things that might be done. Finding the words to say it, naming, differentiating – these accomplishments of talk bring an issue or concern into a space where it can be examined by talker and listener together. It also makes it possible for the talker to hear themself – talking opens up possibilities for reflection. The talker can observe the impact of their words on the hearer. The shift from monologue (this problem has been rattling around in my head) to dialogue dissolves isolation and social exclusion, and introduces the possibility of sharing and support. Talking invites laughter. Joining together all the separate bits of things that might be said about something to arrive at the whole story provides a sense of coherence.

- '. . . to talk *it* through . . .'. The significance of 'it' lies in the fact that the issue or concern that a person wishes to talk about is rarely clearly defined. Usually, there is a vague sense of something being wrong, a painful feeling, a need to talk. The task of counselling typically involves activities that can be described as 'mapping', 'exploring' or 'naming' the issue, or 'getting a handle on it'. The act of finding the right words to capture the sense of 'it' can lead to a sense of relief ('*that's* what it's about'). Mapping the shape and contours of 'it' opens up possibilities for what can be done about 'it'. This process can also be understood in terms of finding a *focus* for a counselling conversation.

- '. . . to talk it *through* . . .'. To talk something through implies that a conversation aims to be comprehensive and thorough, encompassing all relevant aspects of an issue. It also implies the possibility of resolution, of talk that reaches a point where nothing more needs to be said. When a person is talking about a significant personal issue, there is a sense of a story unfolding. The person has the experience of being on a 'track', with an awareness of 'nextness' in their talk – there is something else to be said. This something else is rarely preplanned on the part of the person, but instead arises from being in a situation of being given permission to talk. Talking it through also invokes a sense of movement through a landscape to arrive at another place.

The idea of 'making a space to talk it through' defines the central purpose of counselling – this is what counselling is essentially about. It represents an understanding of counselling that places an emphasis on the existence of a relationship within which such a space can be created, and the role of language, storytelling and conversation as the medium through which two people can work together to make a difference.

Exercise 1.2: *Opportunities to be known*

What kinds of opportunities do you have in your own life to talk to someone else about issues that concern you? How satisfactory are these opportunities in enabling you to gain a sense that you have been fully able to 'talk through' the issue? What are the characteristics of these situations (e.g. the attitude and qualities of the listener) that either help or hinder this process for you? What have been the consequences for you of times in your life where you have *not* had access to these opportunities?

Learning counselling skills

The material included in this book can be used to support the teaching of counselling courses at various levels. It may be useful, therefore, to give some consideration to what is involved in developing skill in counselling. There are many counselling training courses available, and an extensive literature around models of training, and research. There are also codes of practice published by professional associations that recommend standards for training programmes. The general consensus is that there are four main areas that should be addressed in this kind of training. First, any person offering a counselling relationship to others should possess an ability to make sense of what they are doing in the form of a model or theoretical framework. Second, training should involve an extensive period of reflective practice in which the person develops methods and strategies for face-to-face work. This 'skill' training characteristically involves observing expert counsellors (live or on video), practising methods with and on other members of a training group, and possibly recording and discussing counselling sessions with actual people seeking help. Third, training in counselling requires development of self-awareness. If effective counselling depends on the quality of the relationship between person and counsellor, then it is essential that the counsellor has an understanding of what they bring to that relationship in terms of their own relationship needs and patterns, and capacity to respond constructively to the type of relationship that is preferred by the person seeking their help. On training courses, the development of self-awareness is typically facilitated through such activities as: reflective group discussion; workshops on difficult relationship issues such as sexuality, difference and control; the experience of being a user or client of counselling;

and keeping a personal learning journal. Finally, training courses need to cover professional and ethical issues, such as maintaining confidentiality and using supervision or consultative support.

In the context of this book, it is important to be clear that what it offers is a framework for understanding the skill of counselling, and not the skill itself. Becoming skilful in a counselling role is something that comes about through working with a group of people over a period of time in a setting that encourages honest support and challenge. While counselling courses are generally experienced by participants as personally rewarding and valuable, this kind of learning can be uncomfortable at times; for example, when other members of a learning group point out one's avoidance and self-protection strategies in interpersonal situations. There is little point of engaging in such training unless one is ready to offer a commitment to this type of personal learning.

Box 1.3: *What do people want?*

There have been many research studies that have explored the question of what people find helpful in counselling and other forms of professional care. However, it can also be instructive to investigate what people *don't* want. In Sweden there is a national organization to which patients and their relatives can report dissatisfaction with the health care they have encountered. In an analysis of complaints received by this agency Jangland *et al.* (2009) found that the largest category of dissatisfaction referred to lack of empathy, respect and acknowledgement. Examples of statements from patients and relatives included:

> Since there was a patient next to us separated only by a curtain, we had no private sphere for our conversation with the doctor. We could hear when the doctor gave the other patient information about his diagnosis . . .

> I was told 'there's nothing we can do'. The information was given without feeling and with a complete lack of empathy and concern . . .

> The doctor came into the room without shaking hands or greeting me and didn't make eye contact at any time during the conversation.

> They answered our questions reluctantly and showed no sympathy for our situation.

In these cases, an absence of human consideration and caring from doctors and nurses was sufficient to make individuals want to write and complain. These people were not aggrieved because medical errors had been perpetrated on them – they were hurt because basic emotional support had not been provided.

Conclusions

This chapter has sought to introduce some of the ideas that are developed in more detail throughout the rest of the book. Counselling is described as a particular kind of conversation, which takes place within relationships where the person can feel sufficiently safe to openly explore difficulties and painful areas of life experience. Counselling is a process that can occur in many situations, not just in the office of a specialist counsellor or psychotherapist. This book represents an invitation to counselling to practitioners in such fields as social and health care and education, whose counselling role is embedded within other professional responsibilities. In order to provide counselling that is ethical, effective and tailored to the needs and preferences of those who are seeking help, it is necessary to make use of research and critical inquiry to question existing assumptions and develop new frameworks for practice.

Suggested further reading

There has been very little critical debate around the development of counselling skills training, and the models that inform it. A powerful article by Deborah Cameron argues that current models of communication skills and interpersonal skills have been developed without sufficient attention to the ways in which, in reality, people in organizations actually relate to each other:

Cameron, D. (2004) Communication culture: issues for health and social care. In M. Robb, S. Barrett, C. Komaromy and A. Rogers (eds) *Communication, Relationships and Care: A Reader*. London: Routledge. (The other chapters in this book also present a variety of valuable critical perspectives.)

An amusing and informative book, that captures the spirit of counselling:

De Board, R. (2007) *Counselling for Toads: A Psychological Adventure*. London: Routledge.

A model of embedded counselling

On the bus to the hospital. Traffic. The same streets. Donald looks out of the window. Just a couple of weeks to the 60th birthday. The big one. They are planning something, but they won't say what. Months of feeling unwell. Heart attack. Tests. Diagnosis. Physiotherapy. Pills. Every week, a visit from the nurse from the heart clinic just 'to see how you are getting along'. More tests. Like a dream. This can't be real. Sleep-walking through it all. 'Isn't he coping well'. Behind the front, a different kind of pain.

Introduction

Offering a counselling relationship to a person who is looking for assistance in talking through a personal issue carries a burden of responsibility. It is not a commitment to be undertaken casually. Being in the role of counsellor often involves learning about, and responding to, areas of sensitivity, pain and confusion in a person's life. It is essential, therefore, to possess a robust framework for practice, and to be prepared. While it is necessary for anyone offering counselling to be willing to make a genuine, personal response, it is also important to be able to refer back to a map, or model of the counselling process, as a means of reflecting on what is happening, and as a basis for explaining to the person or service user what to expect and why.

The model of embedded counselling that is introduced in this chapter is intended to apply to any occasion when a person asks or invites someone in a professional role to help them to talk through a personal issue. The duration of episodes of embedded counselling can range from brief (five-minute) micro-counselling conversations through to lengthy conversations that stretch over periods of several months or even years. The purpose of the present chapter is to provide an initial outline of the ideas and assumptions that inform the practice of embedded counselling. Subsequent chapters focus on the application of these principles in practice.

A model of embedded counselling

The model of embedded counselling used in this book is based on a set of assumptions about the person seeking help, the helper or counsellor, the organizational context within which they meet, and the process of counselling.

The person seeking help

Each of us exists within a society in culture, which shapes the way we think and feel. However, in modern societies, there is not a monolithic cultural system that completely determines each person's life. Instead, each individual constructs a personal niche in society, within which they seek to live a satisfying and meaningful life (Willi, 1999). Counselling episodes are triggered when a person experiences a *problem in living* – a blockage, conflict or absence within their life – that they cannot resolve by using resources that are immediately available to them. One of the main aims of counselling is to help the person to activate the personal, social and cultural resources that they require in order to resolve their current problem in living – effective counselling helps people to become more *resourceful*.

Exercise 2.1: *Mapping your personal niche*

Get a piece of paper and some coloured pens or crayons, and draw your personal niche. Include real and imagined people, places, activities, objects and anything else that is important in constituting your 'world'. What have you learned about yourself by doing this? What are the areas of your life space or niche that are most troubling for you? What are the areas that represent your sources of personal strength? Which areas of your niche might you open up to a counsellor, and which might remain hidden?

This way of thinking about people who seek help differs from the ideas that inform the majority of counselling textbooks. In the main, current writing about counselling is dominated by an approach that characterizes the problems that people bring to counselling as being essentially *psychological* in nature. From a psychological perspective, problems can be viewed in terms of malfunctioning psychological 'mechanisms' or 'deficits' that need to be fixed. For example, from a psychological point of view a person may be regarded as suffering from low self-esteem, irrational thinking, unprocessed emotions, intrusive memories, and so on

(Gergen, 1990). In contrast to these ideas, this book takes the view that it is more helpful to understand people as *social* beings, who co-construct the human reality within which we live through the way we interact and talk, and the stories we tell, and who can work together to resolve problems that arise in the course of everyday life. The advantage of a social perspective is that it highlights the connectedness and solidarity between people, and the cultural traditions within which we live. The key point here is that counselling, as envisaged within this model, is not a matter of addressing deficits that are hypothesized to exist within the individual. Counselling is not a matter of repairing or fixing a faulty mechanism within the 'self' or 'psyche' of a person. The 'problem' is not in the person's mind. Instead, counselling is the business of working with the person to deal with real difficulties in the actual social world in which they live, and to locate the resources from within that world that they can use to make a difference.

Box 2.1: *How we talk about how to deal with personal troubles*

We live in a culture which sustains a wide variety of ways of making sense of emotional problems and relationship issues. There is a strand of thought in contemporary society that promotes the idea that such issues are best seen as 'mental health' issues, and addressed through medication. Another strand draws on long-standing religious ideas about the right way to live. People who are influenced by this way of thinking often feel guilty for having deviated from the way they 'ought' to behave, and are looking for guidance on how to restore themselves to the 'right' path. A further powerful way of thinking about personal troubles is to view them as psychological problems arising from early childhood events (psychoanalysis), a failure to accept oneself (humanistic) or the persistence of faulty ways of thinking (cognitive-behavioural). In constructing a personal niche, each of us tends to select the ideas from these (and many other) cultural discourses that fit into the life we are seeking to create for ourselves. As a result, when we may eventually seek counselling, we tend to have definite preferences for the kinds of strategies and processes that we believe will help us.

Implicit in this perspective is that the person who seeks help is active and purposeful in seeking to resolve their problems and live a more satisfying life. In counselling, it is never a good idea to 'objectify' the person, to regard someone seeking help as a passive victim of events or fate. People always make sense of what has happened to them, and devise ways of coping and surviving. We all live in a world that encompasses a rich variety of strategies and ideas about how to deal with problems in living, and we each possess our own repertoire of theories and methods for getting through life. The idea of human *agency*, the capacity of people to be intentional and active in constructing (in concert with others) the reality in which they live, is one of the basic assumptions that informs the counselling framework presented in this book.

On a day-to-day basis, it is inevitable that a constant series of *problems in living* will arise in anyone's life. These problems in living comprise dilemmas and challenges around the negotiation of personal needs and desires, and can take the form of personal issues such as conflicts in relationships with others, uncertainty or confusion around life choices, fear or avoidance of people and situations, and loss of clarity and hope over the future. Most of the time, a person deals with such issues by employing any one of a range of problem-solving resources; for example, taking advice from a family member, going for a walk in the hills to think the matter through, praying, reading a book or newspaper article on the topic, and so on. The most frequently used type of informal personal problem-solving probably occurs through everyday conversation, storytelling and gossip, where people share their experiences of how they have dealt with the challenges that life has presented them with. Occasionally, however, a problem will emerge that cannot be resolved through the use of the resources that are immediately to hand for the person. There can be many reasons why a problem may become intractable. The person may lack people and relationships with whom to share the problem; for example, because they have moved to a new city, or because people with whom they have been close have died. Alternatively, the person may have access to a social network, but is reluctant to talk to anyone in that network because of the nature of the problem. This may happen if the person perceives the problem in living as being embarrassing or shameful. For example, a person may find their job stressful, but may work in a high achievement environment where the implicit 'rules' of the organization may make it very hard to admit vulnerability to a colleague. Another factor that may contribute to a problem building up, and reaching a point where friends and family and other immediate resources are not enough, is the use by the person of strategies for self-care and coping that are based on avoidance. If a person deals with an issue by 'trying not to think about it' or by self-medicating through drugs and alcohol, they can quite quickly get to a point where it is too big to talk about, or it is too embarrassing to admit that they had allowed it to get to the point it had reached. For example, a college student gets a bad mark for an assignment and worries about failing the course, and deals with these pressures by skipping classes, and staying in bed watching TV and eating chocolate.

Box 2.2: *The social roots of problems in living*

It can be valuable for those in counselling roles to make use of some of the ideas developed by contemporary sociologists. The key writer in this area is probably

Anthony Giddens, who analyses the ways in which the conditions of modern life make it hard for people to sustain a secure identity or sense of who they are, and argues that the emergence of the counselling profession can be understood as a cultural response to this growing uncertainty: counselling becomes the place where we can stand back from the details of our everyday life and gain some sense of who we are (Giddens, 1991). These ideas have been further articulated by other socio-logical writers. For example, Richard Sennett (1998) has studied the ways that changing patterns of employment, brought about by the global economy, have resulted in the loss of a secure identity as a worker. As people shift from one tempo-rary job to another, are allocated to ever-changing teams within an organization, or work from home, it becomes harder to develop deep relationships with colleagues. Zygmunt Bauman (2004) suggests that the global capitalist economy and depletion of planetary resources has been responsible for a vast number of what he calls 'wasted lives' – people such as immigrants, refugees, the unemployed, the disabled, who are surplus to the requirements of the economic system, and who therefore cease to matter. A theme that runs through these sociological accounts of modern life is the extent to which people feel *excluded* from full participation in a mean-ingful social life.

The 'problems in living' that lead people to seek counselling can be viewed as operating at two levels. One level consists of practical dilemmas that can be resolved by 'moving the furniture around' in the sense of making strategic but relatively minor adjustments to the way life is lived. However, some people who seek help are also troubled from what can be defined as *existential* challenges that reflect more fundamental tensions in their relationships with the world around them. These existential challenges are linked to some basic dimensions of well-being:

- being in relationships with others and having a sense of mutuality, belonging and involvement in caring
- constructing and maintaining a coherent and valued sense of identity or capacity to answer the question 'who am I?'
- discovering, nourishing and aligning with sources of meaning and purpose that provide a sense of well-being, fulfilment and generativity.

It is important for counsellors to acknowledge these different types of problem in living, and to be open to working with clients at the right level. Although embedded counselling conversations are typically triggered by emotional reactions to practical situations, sometimes these everyday dilemmas reflect bigger issues around connectedness and belonging, identity and fulfilment.

The counsellor

Embedded counselling is provided by people who are employed as teachers, nurses, social workers or in any other profession whose work involves interacting with people, and whose role incorporates a counselling dimension. Usually, such practitioners are not described or titled within their organizations as 'counsellors', because the counselling aspect of their work is secondary to their main functions. To some extent, in principle, all practitioners in such occupations fulfil some kind of counselling role simply through their front-line contact with people who are troubled. However, members of these occupational groups tend to differ in terms of the level of their interest in counselling, and in their willingness to engage in counselling conversations with their clients. This is similar to what happens in many other areas of role specialization within occupations. For example, a teacher may develop considerable knowledge and expertise around 'subsidiary roles' such as being a trade union representative, serving on the school council, organizing international student visits, or being involved in school–university liaison. None of these activities actually involves *teaching*, which is what teachers are trained for and paid to do, but they are all necessary elements in the effective functioning of a school. Likewise, some teachers (and members of other professions) may develop a particular niche for themselves within their organization as the person to go to for counselling.

Some of the key characteristics of successful practitioners of embedded counselling include:

- self-awareness
- curiosity about how people cope
- cultural sensitivity
- values that affirm the worth of other people
- interest in relationships
- realistic appreciation of what is possible in their particular work context.

These attributes are grounded in life experience. Counselling training can help participants to reflect on these themes, and can offer theoretical perspectives for making sense of what their counselling role is. However, good counsellors are not made by training courses – they are made by life.

A capacity for self-awareness is a crucial element of any counselling role, and is central to a counsellor's ability to relate to the experiences of the person who is seeking help. The person may be struggling with personal difficulties around such themes as loss, being out of control, hopelessness, despair, powerlessness and confusion. A counsellor is better able to provide a rounded, human response if they have previously explored their own experiences of these issues, and are familiar with the contours of the territory that the person is entering. Self-awareness also gives the counsellor an appreciation of their own areas of vulnerability. When a counsellor allows themself to listen fully to the difficulties of another person, they are inevitably opening themself up to the other person's pain. It is useful for any counsellor to be familiar with the aspects of their life around which they are sensitive or vulnerable at, and work out some strategies for dealing with these areas, rather than discovering these issues during an actual session when they are trying to be there for the other person. Finally, self-awareness helps the counsellor to know that the person seeking help is similar to them in some ways, and different in others. It is only by consciously knowing one's own reactions and patterns in sufficient detail that a counsellor is able to avoid falling into the trap of assuming that everyone else must think and feel the same as they do.

There are many ways in which this kind of self-awareness can be cultivated – keeping a journal, writing an autobiography, talking to friends and family, visiting people and places for earlier chapters of your life, and receiving personal counselling. The common thread across all of these activities is that they involve systematic, ongoing *reflection* on personal experience. While it is helpful for a person who is in the role of counsellor to have had a rich experience of life, it is not enough merely to have undergone difficult times – to be able to use these events to inform a counselling response, it is necessary to have gone at least some way to put these experiences into words, and make sense of them. A counsellor is not primarily a role model – someone who has survived crises and who therefore acts as an example to be followed – but instead is someone who is better seen as a co-worker. In working alongside a person seeking help, to resolve problems in living through talking about them and finding solutions, it is necessary for a counsellor already to have done some of this in their own life.

Exercise 2.2: *Developing self-awareness*

What have you done over the last 10 years to develop your own self-awareness? In what ways have you reflected on your life, and documented what you have learned? To what extent are you able to explain and understand the origins of your own strengths and limitations as a helper or counsellor in your own upbringing and in the culture(s) within which you have lived? What is your current and future self-awareness agenda – what are the aspects of your life that you want to explore further?

Developing sensitivity to the huge range of beliefs that exist about learning, change and 'healing' is an important element in preparation for a counselling role (see Box 2.1). A person who is seeking help inevitably has their own ideas about how their problem has developed, and what needs to be done to sort it. For example, a person who has always tended to solve problems by action-planning and goal-setting, and never looks back, is likely to be frustrated and turned off by a counsellor who persistently asks questions such as 'does this remind you of anything?' or 'can you think of the first time this happened?' Beliefs about learning and change, and how to deal with problems in living, are linked in complex ways to demographic factors such as gender, ethnicity and social class. Sensitivity to the person's 'helping belief system' lies at the heart of competence in working effectively with *difference*.

Case examples of sensitivity to the client's beliefs about learning and change

As a cardiac care health adviser in a primary care clinic, with a key responsibility to work with patients seeking to accomplish lifestyle changes around issues of smoking cessation and obesity, Manjit looks for leverage in relation to long-standing patterns of unhealthy behaviour by mobilizing his patients' beliefs about what will help. After he has met them and come to an agreement about their commitment to change, he says to them 'I'm wondering about whether you have tried to stop smoking/reduce your weight in the past. Have you? Can you tell me about what has worked for you in the past?' At every subsequent meeting with a patient, he always asks them whether they believe that the approach they are taking is effective, how it can be approved, and what the person thinks that Manjit could do differently that might be more helpful to them.

Ian is a community psychiatric nurse who believes that the people with whom he works have an illness that can best be treated through the administration of drugs, and that his job is to help his clients to understand this, and to work together to find the right dosage and develop strategies for dealing with side-effects. One of his patients, Donald, is a member of a mental health user group, which espouses and promotes a philosophy of survival and recovery based on social solidarity and political action. Ian is frustrated that Donald will only take medication at times of crisis. Donald is frustrated because he does not think that Ian ever takes his views seriously, and does his utmost to limit the frequency of their meetings.

Eva is a family support worker who is fascinated by the different strategies that the people with whom she works can find in order to resolve their problems. Much of her job involves assisting families with school-age children who have behavioural problems, such as hyperactivity and aggression, and who are difficult to manage both at home and in school. Eva believes that 'different things work for different people – these families have so much on their plate that they won't commit themselves to anything that doesn't make sense to them'. One of the families that she helps has evolved a routine based on outdoor pursuits such as hillwalking and riding. Another family has devoted a great deal of time to working out their own methods for consistently rewarding certain types of behaviour in their son. Yet another family places great emphasis on diet.

Beliefs about learning and change inform much of what happens in counselling. However, few people have a very clear idea about what they believe in these areas, because there is usually little requirement to think about these questions in the course of everyday life. Preparation for fulfilling a counselling role involves developing a sensitivity to beliefs about problems and how they can be resolved, and strategies for inviting people to articulate these assumptions.

Exercise 2.3: *How do you deal with troubles in your own life?*

What ideas and strategies do you use when you are confronted by your own problems in living? What is your preferred coping style? Take some time to reflect on and make notes about two or three recent episodes in your life when you have been troubled or under stress. For the purpose of this exercise, your focus should not be on the actual situation itself, but on what you personally *thought* and *did* in order to resolve the situation. Once you have mapped out at least some of your favoured coping strategies, go through each of them in turn and identify the underlying cultural assumptions and discourses (e.g. religious, medical, psychological, philosophical) that they are drawn from. It can be valuable to carry out this learning activity in a small group as a means of becoming aware of the diversity of assumptions and strategies that people use. Finally, in relation to your counselling role: how do you react when you have a client whose ideas about dealing with personal troubles are different from your own?

There are some additional characteristics of people who are drawn towards counselling roles. Typically, such people are interested in relationships, and have a strong commitment to the idea that quality of well-being relies on quality of relationships. This does not mean that people who are drawn to counselling have had untroubled relationships – sometimes people who have come through abusive childhoods and difficult marriages have learned a great deal about the importance of relationships and how good relationships operate. It is usual for the average age of participants on counselling training programmes to be in the 30–40-year band, and for most of them to have either had troubled relationship histories in their own lives, or to have previously worked in jobs where they have learned at close hand about the costs of relationship failure. Another key characteristic of people who become counsellors is a commitment to a set of values that affirms the worth of individual persons, and the capacity of individuals to fulfil themselves and make a contribution to the common good. A pessimistic world view, or a tendency to label or criticize people, is likely to undermine the counselling process.

A final attribute of people who seek to expand their embedded counselling roles is that they are competent in their primary work task. Quite often, nurses, teachers, social workers and others who seek counselling training have reached a point in their careers where they are confident about what they do, and therefore feel able to extend and deepen the counselling that they offer their clients or service users. They possess a good enough understanding of the organizations in which they work in order to appreciate what is possible in respect of counselling, and what is not possible. They also know where to find relevant emotional and practical support within their organization, and about the ethical framework of their profession. It is quite hard for students or trainees in these professions to respond to the counselling needs of service users unless they have a supportive mentor. Embedded counselling can be a balancing act that requires making moment-by-moment judgements around how much time can be spent with each client, and whether you are the best person to be having this conversation with them. It is not helpful for clients if the person to whom they are looking for counselling help is caught up in their own anxieties; counselling works best when it is the client who is anxious, and the counsellor who is the one who is emotionally grounded and secure.

This discussion of the characteristics of the counsellor reflects an observation that some people are better at counselling than others. There is no disgrace in not being interested in wanting to listen to the troubles of other people. Complex organizations need all kinds of people: those who manage and strategize; those who have highly advanced technical knowledge; and those who just do their job and live their lives. Some people are good at emotional care and counselling, and it is important that human service organizations in areas such as education, health care and social work should find ways of valuing their contribution and create opportunities for them to apply their skills in practice.

Box 2.3: *The origins of counselling skills*

Counselling skills, such as attending, challenging, listening and immediacy, are based on ways of relating to other people that are within the interpersonal repertoire of most people, even before they commence counselling training. Anyone who is able to sustain mutually satisfying relationships with others is already using most of the skills that are involved in counselling. What happens during counselling training is that the person learns how to use their existing interpersonal skills and awareness in a particular way in order to be able to facilitate the person seeking help to 'talk things through'.

The organizational setting

There are many different kinds of organization within which embedded counselling is practised. Some health care organizations, such as the National Health Service (NHS) in the UK, are massive entities that employ many thousands of people. By contrast, there are small voluntary sector welfare and training organizations that employ only a small group of personnel. Even within large organizations, the ethos of care that exists may vary greatly across different departments and units. For example, in a school system, the importance given to counselling may depend a great deal on the attitude of the head teacher or principal in each specific school. Despite these differences, it seems reasonable to suggest that the counselling role of front-line teachers, nurses, social workers and other practitioners has been steadily eroded over the last 20 years in response to the introduction of increasing competitiveness and external accountability within the human service sector. Essentially, human service professionals are expected to do more with less, and what they do is defined and audited to a high degree. As a result, the space for human contact and caring has been reduced. Despite the wishes and best efforts of those who work within these agencies, the effect of wider trends within society has been to dehumanize, bureaucratize and technologize the process of teaching and caring.

What all this means is that in many organizations there are significant challenges faced by practitioners who want to respond to the wishes of their clients to enter into counselling conversations. Some of these challenges are physical and tangible, such as access to spaces where people can talk privately, and having enough control over time scheduling to take the risk of inviting a client to 'say more' about how they are feeling at that moment. Other challenges are associated with the organizational culture within which the practitioner has to function. For example, does the organizational culture acknowledge the validity of emotions, and does it encourage staff to seek support from colleagues if they have been affected by client stories that they have heard? There are also challenges that arise from legal, regulatory and supervisory protocols. For example, what are the limits to the confidentiality that a practitioner can offer a client in respect of what they are told – what needs to be recorded in notes, what needs to be immediately reported to a supervisor or manager, and what happens to this information? There are also aspects of the structure and reward system of organizations that have a bearing on the extent to which counselling conversations take place. Do staff get financial support and time off to attend counselling courses, or to receive counselling supervision? Does being good at counselling contribute positively or negatively to promotion prospects?

There are few organizations that wholeheartedly support counselling, and few that entirely prohibit it. The situation in most human service organizations is that there are pockets of support for counselling, and creative ways of adapting systems and procedures so that some kind of counselling may be possible. In this, counselling is no different from many other activities that do not easily sit within the core objectives of an organization. For example, there are multiple challenges faced by colleagues in organizations who wish to promote anti-discriminatory practice, work–life balance, environmental consciousness and sustainability, social responsibility, and so on.

Organizational factors shape the capacity to create spaces for counselling. The organization largely determines the kind of buildings that are constructed, and the use of space and time within these buildings. The organization also exerts considerable control around how staff relate to each other, and what they do on an hour-by-hour basis. Alongside this kind of 'top-down' control, there are usually mechanisms through which staff in turn can exert some influence on decision-making and policy around these issues. The organization also tends to have a strong impact on clients and service users in terms of making it clear to them what they can expect, and what they are there for. Although client feedback is elicited in most agencies, it is rare that this is manifested in the possibility that individual clients can decide on the treatment they themselves actually receive.

One of the key features of the embedded counselling model that is presented in this book is that it places a great deal of emphasis on the importance of organizational context. The counselling literature includes a huge number of good ideas about how to work with people to help them to resolve problems in living. What the literature tends to ignore, unfortunately, is that these ideas are always applied in specific contexts, and that particular organizational contexts make some things possible and other things not possible. For example, most models of counselling assume that there is continuity of contact between one client and one counsellor – in some health care settings it is just not possible to guarantee that this will happen.

The process of embedded counselling

For practitioners whose counselling function is embedded in another professional role, such as health worker or teacher, it can be difficult to know whether a client or service user is actually looking for a chance to talk about a personal issue, or whether they are happy enough to continue with the primary task such as nursing care or learning. In recent years, some researchers in the area of doctor–patient interaction have developed a useful approach to deciding whether the use of a counselling intervention might be appropriate. These researchers have been exploring the idea that in a consultation patients may present their doctors with a series of *empathic opportunities*. Within an interview with a doctor, the main focus of a patient's talk concentrates on reporting relevant medical information, usually in response to questions asked by the physician. From time to time, however, the patient may signal an area of personal concern or worry. The question then is whether the doctor acknowledges this 'empathic opportunity' and whether they are able to follow it up. The example below is taken from a study carried out by Eide *et al.* (2004) into consultations between cancer patients and oncologists:

Patient: I heard quite badly before (*gives medical information*) but now my hearing is much reduced (*gives medical information*), so that I find it hard to function if they say something to me (*potential empathic opportunity*).

Doctor: A lot of sound . . . .

Patient: I walk with a watch that supposedly makes a noise (*gives medical information*). And I have boys at home who make a lot of noise, but I can't hear them at all (*gives medical information*).

Doctor: No, I hear that (*laughter*).

Patient: Yes, of course you hear well, but I don't hear it at all, so that is my biggest handicap (*potential empathic opportunity*).

Doctor: Yes, it may be that it will get a bit better. I don't know if it will return to normal, but I think it's a bit early to say, so soon after the operation . . .

Patient: Yes, I had it before as well, due to the chemo (*gives medical information*).

Doctor: Yes, the chemo, and not the operation, but the chemo . . . How do you feel . . . something in your feet?

Patient: Yes, I feel as if my feet are tight, that they . . . (*gives medical information*).

Doctor: Well, I think this will improve. It will never be completely as it was, but it can be better.

Patient: That's in my feet and in my hands. I can live with that (*gives psychosocial information*) . . . But then there's the sound in my ear (*gives medical information*) . . . If I sit in a meeting, I have to concentrate enormously, and when I come home, then . . . Then I am so tired (*empathic opportunity*).

In this excerpt, the researchers have made a distinction between potential empathic opportunities, defined as 'patient statement(s) from which a clinician might infer underlying emotion that has not been explicitly expressed' and actual empathic opportunities, defined as 'direct and explicit expression of emotion by a patient' (Eide *et al.*, 2004: 292). In this case, the doctor has not acknowledged the potential empathic opportunities provided by the patient early in the conversation, choosing to focus only on medical matters. Towards the end of the conversation, the patient returns to the emotional issue that concerns her in a more explicit manner. Further research on empathic opportunities, and how practitioners respond to the expression of emotions and personal concerns by clients, has been carried out by Bylund and Makoul (2002), Gallacher *et al.* (2001), Jansen *et al.* (2010) and Laron and Yeo (2005).

The concept of empathic opportunities represents a central aspect of embedded counselling, because it describes the main ways in which a practitioner can shift from their practical involvement with a client (around tasks associated with their primary role as teacher, nurse or social worker) into a counselling role. A key skill of embedded counselling consists of being able to negotiate this transition effectively by checking out with the client that they do in fact wish to talk about what is concerning them, and then creating an appropriate space within which a counselling conversation can take place. A further essential skill is associated with the capacity to close the space in a satisfactory manner, to make the transition back to the underlying work of being a nurse, social worker or other type of practitioner. Within the counselling space, the process of counselling that takes place will draw on counselling skills and methods that are well established, and are introduced in later chapters of this book. However, the pressure of time that usually accompanies embedded counselling means that it is important for practitioners to be able quickly to identify a focus for the counselling in terms of a specific counselling task that can be accomplished within the time that is available. A list of counselling tasks is introduced in Chapter 4.

Finally, it is worth noting that the idea of *empathic opportunities* is also relevant in situations of specialist counselling where counselling is the only basis for the contact between practitioner and client. In specialist or stand-alone counselling, clients often talk in general terms about the issues and difficulties in their life, and in effect supply the counsellor with background knowledge without getting close to their real concerns. Just as in embedded counselling situations, the moment when a client in stand-alone counselling expresses what they *feel* in a direct manner can be viewed as an implicit invitation to get closer, and to explore issues in a deeper way.

Box 2.4: *Embedded counselling in action: taking advantage of empathic opportunities*

Expert practitioners of medicine, nursing and other professionals are able to incorporate powerful moments of counselling within their work with clients or patients. In a study carried out by Branch and Malik (1993), video recordings were made of 20 doctor–patient consultations conducted by experienced and highly regarded physicians. The length of these consultations ranged from 12 to 20 minutes. Within this series of doctor–patient clinical interviews, the researchers were able to identify five episodes in which patients discussed their concerns about personal, emotional and family issues. These 'windows of opportunity' lasted for between three and seven minutes each. Typically, the doctor would begin the interview by addressing current medical issues. After a few minutes, in response to a felt sense that the patient was worried or concerned in some way, the practitioner would ask an open question, such as 'anything more going on?' or 'what else?' The patient's response to this question would be accompanied by what the researchers described as a 'change of pace' on the part of the doctor – they would listen, speak more slowly and softly, be silent, and lean forward. These physicians were skilled in ending these counselling episodes, which they did by expressing understanding, empathically summarizing key themes, and making suggestions for further action (e.g. making a referral to a specialist counsellor). Although these doctors did not use a counselling approach throughout their interviews with patients, they were able to do so within the context of specific, focused micro-episodes. Branch and Malik (1993) concluded that: '. . . the patients seemed satisfied that they had adequately expressed themselves. We think that seasoned clinicians have learned through practice to employ brief but intense windows of opportunity to deal with their patients' concerns, and yet to remain time-efficient' (p. 1668). This study provides evidence for the potential value of brief counselling conversations that are embedded within other practitioner relationships. It also illustrates the relative infrequency of such encounters – even in this group of expert physicians, such encounters only took place in 25 per cent of consultations, despite psychosocial issues being brought up by patients in the majority of these meetings.

Exercise 2.4: *Reflecting on your experience as a client*

Think about situations where you have interacted with a practitioner such as a nurse, doctor, social worker or teacher, who has been helping you with a practical matter related to their area of professional expertise. In any of these interactions, did you express any emotions or personal concerns? If so, did the practitioner working with you seem to be aware of what you were feeling, and how adequately did they respond to your concerns? Finally, what have you learned from this exercise that can inform your practice as a counsellor?

A summary of key ideas

The key ideas within the model presented in this chapter can be summarized in terms of a series of propositions around the core elements of effective counselling:

(a) Background

    1 *Espousing a world view that emphasizes human resourcefulness and strengths.* People who seek help are viewed as actively and purposefully collaborating with others to find ways to resolve problems in living. In doing so, they draw on a range of ideas within their culture around how to make sense of problems and how best to address them. In general, people seek assistance from professional sources as a late or last resort, and continue to make use of their personal or private coping strategies alongside any professional assistance that is offered.

2 *Possessing a genuine interest in helping.* Practitioners who effectively engage in embedded counselling are people whose lives exhibit an ongoing curiosity and interest in making sense of their own lives, a commitment to the importance of relationships, identification with life-affirming values, and a caring approach to others. Ultimately, the counselling skills and methods used in embedded counselling are grounded in and arise from life experience.

3 *Taking account of organizational realities.* The practice of embedded counselling is informed by a systematic, critical analysis of the organizational context within which the practitioner is employed. Counselling is informed by an appreciation of what is possible and appropriate within the particular organizational context within which it occurs. Practitioners of embedded counselling actively seek to construct suitable arrangements for counselling within their workplaces.

(b) The process of counselling

4 *Responding to empathic opportunities.* When engaged in routine educational or caring activities with a client or service user, the practitioner of embedded counselling is sensitive to the occurrence of 'windows of opportunity', or 'empathic opportunities', understood as moments when the client expresses emotion or in some other way refers to a problem in living that is troubling them.

5 *Gaining consent for counselling.* The practitioner responds to such opportunities by reporting what they have observed, and inquiring about whether the client would like to discuss what is happening in more detail;

6 *Making a space.* If the client wishes to explore the matter further, the counsellor seeks to establish a counselling space, defined in terms of time, location and confidentiality boundaries.

7 *Finding a focus.* Given that it is unlikely that there is, or could be, a contract for long-term work, the counsellor seeks to establish a focus for the conversation in terms of what the client wants to achieve in the time available (goals) and the immediate task or tasks that might be accomplished that could assist the client in making progress to that goal.

8 *Flexible use of counselling methods that make sense to the client.* Given that clients have different preferences around the type of activity that they regard as helpful, and that the practitioner does not have time to socialize the client into a predetermined therapy approach, it is essential that the counsellor is flexibly capable of using their counselling skills to facilitate a range of methods of task completion.

9 *Collaboratively checking out that what is happening is acceptable to the client at all stages.* The counsellor routinely and regularly invites the client to provide feedback on whether the approach that is being taken to their problem is helpful, and if they have other ideas about what else might be helpful.

10 *Monitoring the interaction in terms of risk.* The counsellor pays attention to anything that arises that indicates a risk of harm to the client or other people, and if necessary invites the client to shift the focus of the conversation in the direction of how such risks might be managed. One important area of risk is associated with the possibility that successful resolution of the client's problem may require the involvement of other expertise in addition to, or other than, that of the practitioner.

11 *Closing the space.* The counsellor is aware of the time available, and the undesirability of leaving the client in a state of increased vulnerability. The counsellor is responsible for managing time, and exploring arrangements (if necessary) for further meetings or alternative sources of help.

12 *Using supervision.* What have you learned from each counselling episode in which you have been involved? What did you do well? What might you have done better? What are the lessons for the future? An effective counsellor uses supervision or consultation to explore these questions, and as a source of emotional support.

When such a sequence is carried out effectively, clients or service users are able to return to their everyday lives with new understandings or strategies that they are able to use to deal with the problem in living that had been troubling them in the first place.

Compared to specialist counselling, there are several ways in which embedded counselling can potentially be more effective for clients. The client is in a position to make an informed decision about who they want as a counsellor. For example, a school student may know several teachers fairly well, and from among this list may be able to choose the one who seems most trustworthy or sympathetic. What this means is that the client does not need to spend time during counselling in a process of testing out their counsellor, and making up their mind whether they think that their counsellor is OK. It is also likely that the counsellor will already know something about the client, and so does not need to go through a whole process of collecting information. Beyond this, it is probably the case that people talk to (or try to talk to) professionals who are within their immediate orbit, before they take the step of making an appointment to see a counsellor, and then waiting until they receive an appointment time. What this means is that practitioners of embedded counselling are likely to hear about problems earlier at a point where they are perhaps more readily dealt with. The flexible, 'grass-roots' nature of embedded counselling means that there is little opportunity for the counsellor to seek to inculcate the client into a therapy theory or methodology that is alien or harmful to them – the counsellor needs to stick pretty closely to what fits with the client's common sense. Finally, the fact that embedded counselling is oriented towards activating the client's strengths and resources means that there is a good chance that whatever the client learns in the counselling session will be applicable in their everyday life.

At the same time, the structure of weekly contracted 'specialist' counselling or psychotherapy represents a powerful means through which people can come to terms with problems in living. In some cases, the outcome of an embedded counselling encounter may be that the client decides to enter therapy.

Conclusions

The model of embedded counselling that has been outlined in this chapter reflects the reality of contemporary professional life where the possibility of human contact and caring is in conflict with demanding work schedules. The model suggests that it is essential for practitioners with an embedded counselling role to engage in appropriate *preparation* by thinking carefully and consulting with others around the question of how counselling conversations can be sustained within their particular organizational context. It also suggests that it is helpful to view clients, patients and service users as existing in networks of social relationships. What the person wants to talk about will almost certainly arise from some kind of crisis in their relational network. Within the busy schedules of nurses, teachers, social workers and other human service professionals, the possibility of engaging in a counselling conversation arises when the practitioner is open to *empathic opportunities*, or moments in the interaction where the person makes reference to a problem in living that is currently bothering them. The role of the counsellor at this point is to check out whether the person wants to talk further about the problem, and if they do, then to create an environment in which a counselling conversation can take place. The value of that conversation for the client will depend on the counsellor's ability to find a focus in respect of what can usefully be discussed in what is likely to be a relatively brief period of time, and on the counsellor's capacity to find a way of working together that fits well enough with the client's pre-existing assumptions and expectations about how people help each other.

The embedded counselling model is also informed by *ethical* considerations. Any counselling carried out by a teacher, nurse, social worker or other practitioner needs to be consistent with the ethical guidelines that exist within their profession; for example, in relation to duty of care. The process of counselling that is outlined in the model incorporates the essential ethical dimension of informed consent, by specifying that practitioners should always check with their client whether they wish to explore an issue in more depth. The focus on specific counselling tasks represents a further means of ensuring ethical practice – the safety of the client is maintained by breaking the counselling agenda into manageable chunks, rather than trying to open up all aspects of their problem for exploration at the one time.

Another way of looking at all this is to think about what it is that people want or need when they are troubled. On the whole, people want:

- to get on with their lives
- to talk to someone when they get stuck in their lives
- to have a space where they can safely talk things through with someone they trust
- to be treated as resourceful and worthwhile human beings
- to be in control, and have their ideas about what is helpful (or otherwise) taken seriously
- to deal with problems step by step.

A skilled counsellor is a person who is able to respond adequately to these needs. The key factor in a counsellor's capacity to respond in a helpful way is not technical expertise and competence, but values and heart. If a counsellor consistently can act on the basis of values that affirm the worth and potential of the person, then there is a good chance that between them they will be able to achieve something that is useful. Technical expertise, in the form of knowledge of psychological theories, and methods of therapy, that is delivered in the wrong spirit, is in the end likely to compound a person's problems.

These ideas and the kinds of practical strategies that enable them to be put into action are explored in more detail in the chapters that follow. Chapters 4 and 5 consider the nature and characteristics of the counselling skills that comprise the basic ingredients of embedded counselling. Chapter 6 then returns to the model of embedded counselling in terms of a counselling 'menu' through which these ingredients can be combined in order to address the problems in living (the 'hunger') of clients.

Suggested further reading

A comprehensive account of how counselling skills and ideas can enrich all aspects of social work practice:

Seden, J. (2005) *Counselling Skills in Social Work Practice*, 2nd edn. Maidenhead: Open University Press.

CHAPTER 3

Counselling skills: basic building blocks of embedded practice

'That nurse is really easy to talk to'.
'In what way?'
'I don't know. She just is. I find that I'm saying things that I never planned to talk about. Its like she's able to really get on my wavelength. I don't know how she does it. She's just got the knack'.

Introduction

In the previous chapters, a broad-brush understanding was offered of the nature of embedded counselling, and where it fits into professional roles in fields such as nursing, social work and education. The focus of the discussion, in this chapter and the chapters that follow, now shifts to a more concrete level, to a consideration of what actually happens in effective conversations and interactions between those who are seeking help for problems in living and those professionals to whom they turn for assistance. In this chapter, the aim is to provide an appreciation of the concept of *counselling skills* as a means of making sense of how facilitative people in any walk of life make a difference to the lives of others. The idea that the complex activity of counselling can be broken down into a set of discrete skills has proved to be a useful means for thinking about counselling training and practice: counselling skills can be viewed as the basic building blocks of a facilitative relationship.

This chapter seeks to provide a framework for making sense of counselling skills by reviewing the background to the emergence of a skill-oriented perspective in counselling. The discussion then moves to an exploration of the concept of 'skill' – what assumptions are we making when we use this term? Some influential counselling skills models are then explored in detail, leading to a summary of the main counselling skills that are involved in everyday helping practice. The chapter concludes with a summary that discusses counselling skills in the context of embedded counselling theory and practice.

The emergence of a skills perspective

The idea that psychological processes and interpersonal behaviour can be viewed as 'skills' can be traced back to the 1950s. During World War II, psychologists employed by the British armed forces had been given the task of analysing the kinds of tasks performed by soldiers and aircrew, such as assembling and firing a weapon, with the aim of making suggestions regarding how these tasks could be performed more effectively and accurately, and the best ways in which training could be provided for people carrying them out. These psychologists came up with the idea of breaking down each task or function into a set of component skills, which could be learned separately and then built up into the final complete task sequence. The model of skill that emerged emphasized the sequence of actions that the operator needed to go through, and the operator's attention to feedback around whether each operation had been effective in achieving its intended goals. In the immediate post-war years, the concept of skill proved to be valuable as a means of analysing task performance in a variety of areas. In particular, the concept of skill was embraced by social psychologists, such as Michael Argyle, who were interested in understanding the way that people interacted with each other (Argyle and Kendon, 1967). Interesting and important advances in applied social psychology were made in respect of interpersonal and social skills, which established the idea that the concept of 'skill' could usefully be applied to the analysis of social interaction and performance. By the 1970s, under the leadership of the British clinical psychologist, Peter Trower, the concept of social skill that had been developed by Argyle was being applied in work with people reporting a variety of mental health difficulties (Trower et al., 1978; Twentyman and McFall, 1975). One of the key ideas within this approach was that instead of viewing intervention for mental health problems as a form of treatment, it was now regarded as a form of training in which the patient could be guided through a series of learning or skill-acquisition activities.

In the USA, a parallel development was taking place. Within the field of counselling, the late 1940s and early 1950s saw a vast expansion of the psychological therapies in the USA, largely stimulated by the need to respond to mental health problems in returning service personnel. A great deal of investment at that time was directed into the development of client-centred therapy, an approach to counselling and psychotherapy developed in the 1940s by Carl Rogers. Motivated by the pressure to train counsellors effectively and quickly, some of Rogers' students and colleagues, including Charles Truax and Robert Carkhuff, came to the conclusion that it would be sensible to treat the core concepts of client-centred therapy, such as non-directiveness, empathy and unconditional positive regard, as skills. These psychologists then developed training programmes in which students were taught, and practised a set of counselling skills. This approach became known as the human resources development model (Carkhuff, 1969a, b; Cash, 1984). In the 1960s, a large number of counselling and helping skills programmes were developed by influential figures in the counselling and psychology professions in the USA, such as Allen Ivey (Ivey and Galvin, 1984), Thomas Gordon (1984), Norman Kagan (1984), Bernard Guerney (1984) and Gerald Goodman (1984).

All of these skills programmes were inspired by the original work by Truax and Carkhuff, and, like them, broke down the activity of counselling into a series of component skills. The scientifically proven principles of therapeutic change, as identified in research originally carried out by Carl Rogers and others, were now to be made available to paraprofessionals, non-psychologists and members of peer support groups (Gendlin, 1984a; Boukydis, 1984).

Within the field of counselling, a skills perspective has generated a technology of counselling training that has been widely adopted by universities, colleges and training institutions around the world. Typically, students or trainees listen to an explanation of the skill, and observe a demonstration, live or on video. They then practise the skill in small groups, and receive feedback. Reviews of research into the effectiveness of this kind of training model can be found in Baker *et al.* (1990) and Hill and Lent (2006). An understanding of the historical emergence of a skills approach in psychology and counselling makes it possible to begin to appreciate why this way of thinking about human interaction has been so influential: the distinctive value of a skills perspective is that it is highly practical, and focuses on fairly brief sequences of behaviour that can be taught and learned without needing to think about deeper theoretical issues.

Exercise 3.1: *Reflecting on your personal experience of learning a practical skill*

Think about a practical skill that you have recently acquired or developed. This could be work-related, arising from your involvement in sport, or concerned with some aspect of domestic life. Examples could be: learning to use a new application on your phone or PC; a sporting accomplishment such as being able to make a top-spin serve in tennis; changing a baby's nappy; and being able to prune fruit trees properly. Once you have decided on a specific skill that has been meaningful for you, take some time to reflect on the following questions:

- What were the pre-existing skills that you already had that you had to develop further or bring together in order to master this new skill (e.g. necessary elements of making a top-spin serve in tennis are the more basic skills of *throwing a ball* and *holding a racket*)?
- What was the *process* of acquiring this new skill? What stages did you go through?
- What types of assistance and tuition from other people were helpful or unhelpful?

- What are the implications of what you discovered about the experience of learning a practical skill for your learning and development in relation to counselling skills?

  If possible, it is helpful to meet with others to share and discuss the insights triggered by this exercise.

The experience of learning and using skills

There are some aspects of skill acquisition and usage that have significant implications for the way that counselling skills are learned and applied. First, it is important to acknowledge that any complex skill always consists of a combination of pre-existing simpler skills. For people who are learning to be counsellors, or to enhance their counselling competence within another professional role, the counselling skills that they are taught are always in some sense already there. From an early age, babies learn how to observe others, how to smile, how to detect emotional signals, and how to take turns in conversation or other kinds of interaction. Later in life, we learn how to empathize with others, and how to be supportive and helpful when another person is in distress. These are some of the core interpersonal skills that are required in order to be able to carry out counselling skills such as paraphrasing the meaning of a statement that the client has made, or using an open-ended question to encourage a client to explore what their feelings are around an issue. Counselling skills are therefore grounded in life experience. Someone who is being trained in counselling skills should not be learning anything they did not know already – what they should be learning is how to apply what they already know in a more purposeful and aware manner to achieve a particular result. This is why effective counselling skills training involves self-reflection on the part of trainees as a means of allowing the learner to be more in touch with their own personal experiences of helping and being helped, which in turn heightens their awareness of the basic skills to which they were exposed, or which they were able to use, in these situations.

Another crucial aspect of counselling skills is that they almost always have a physical, *embodied* dimension to them. It is possible to envisage skills that are purely cognitive (e.g. doing a complex multiplication calculation in your head). However, most practical skills involve actual physical activity. This is certainly true for counselling, which is more like learning to dance than like learning to do sums in one's head. So, a book such as this one, which offers a verbal explanation of counselling skills, can never function as a sufficient basis for learning these skills. It is always essential to be able to see how someone else does the skill, and to get feedback on one's own performance of a skill.

A further element of the application of any skill is that it involves using *feedback* on the effect of each action that the person takes, and using that information to make adjustments to the next action that forms part of the skill sequence. For example, making a serve in tennis begins by throwing the ball in the air. The server needs to watch the ball. At a very basic level, they need to detect whether they have thrown it high enough and straight enough to hit it, or whether the throw has been too unbalanced to make the ball hittable (in which case the intended serve is not followed through). The requirement in effective skill use to make use of feedback introduces another embodied dimension to the process: a skilful person is someone who has learned what to look at, listen to, and viscerally sense, and who knows what to do with this information. As a result, careful and accurate *observation* is intrinsic to skill use – an accomplished skill user is able to observe the impact of their use of a skill (has it achieved the result that was expected?) and is a keen observer of how other people use skills (and how they themselves use them).

An additional critical aspect of any skill is that it involves a *sequence* of activity. As a person becomes more skilful, they make sense of what they are doing in terms of longer sequences. For example, a novice chess player may only be capable of thinking one or two moves ahead: 'if I move this rook, it will avoid it being captured by my opponent's Queen'. By contrast, expert chess players call upon conceptual strategies that involve an appreciation of complex possibilities that may occur over a lengthy sequence of moves. This phenomenon underlies one of the paradoxes of counselling skills training – experienced counsellors do not tend to think in terms of specific skills. When *learning* about counselling, it tends to be useful to pay attention to specific, discrete skills such as 'listening'. Eventually, though, the aim is to be able to take these specific skills for granted, and, for example, to be able to think instead about the work with a client in terms of the degree to which a suffi- cient degree of empathic attunement is being maintained. 'Empathic attunement' is a more abstract concept that encompasses complex sequences of basic skills such as listening, reflecting, and so on.

A final facet of the experience of skill acquisition is the phenomenon of *awkwardness*. Most people have a baseline of practical and interpersonal skills with which they feel comfortable – they know how to use them, and feel confident when they are using them. Invariably, moving on and becoming more skilled involves some degree of awkwardness, because it requires that the person try something that they do not yet know how to do properly. Sometimes, learning a skill may involve *unlearning* other skills. For example, it is possible to produce a perfectly acceptable tennis serve from a square-on stance, but if a player wants to learn how to make a top-spin serve they need to change their stance so that they are at right angles to the baseline – this can feel very awkward!

Taken together, these aspects of skill use underscore the fact that skill acquisi- tion involves active *practice* – receiving instruction, watching how someone else does it, trying it out yourself, getting feedback, trying again, and so on. This process inevitably incorporates lots of mistakes as the learner tries out different skills in different sequences. Counselling training therefore usually includes lots of oppor- tunities for practice in an environment in which it is acceptable to make mistakes.

Usually, at least at the start, counselling trainees practise their skills on each other to minimize the negative impacts of their errors, before moving on to 'real' clients.

Counselling skills models

These ideas have been developed and applied in the field of counselling by a number of leading figures in the counselling profession. There have been two broad approaches to understanding counselling skills – the *microskills* model associated with Allen Ivey, and a variety of *three-stage* models, developed by Robert Carkhuff, Gerard Egan, Clara Hill, and others.

The microskills approach

The *microskills* model, developed by the American psychologist, Allen Ivey, and his colleagues (Ivey *et al.*, 2010), has been widely adopted within counselling skills training programmes, and is supported by an extensive programme of research. The microskills model has been around since the 1960s, with new ideas being added on a regular basis. As a result, recent versions of the model are highly complex and multidimensional. However, the basic ideas that inform this approach are that: (a) there are some core skills that are essential in all helping situations; and (b) there are certain interaction sequences that tend to be useful for clients. In addition, the microskills approach places a strong emphasis on the idea that affective helpers are *intentional* in the way that they work with clients. In other words, the helper is aware of what they are trying to achieve, and is able to select appropriate responses and strategies at the right moment from a broad repertoire of skills and ideas:

> . . . intentionality is acting with a sense of capability and deciding from among a range of alternative actions. The intentional individual has more than one action, thought, or behaviour to choose from in responding to changing life situations. The intentional individual can generate alternatives in a given situation and approach a problem from multiple vantage points, using a variety of skills and personal qualities, adapting styles to suit different individuals and cultures
>
> (Ivey *et al.*, 2010: 21)

The concept of intentionality represents an important and distinctive element within the microskills model, because it functions as a reminder that it is not helpful to assume that there is any single fixed counselling formula that will be appropriate for all clients. One of the hallmarks of Ivey's writing over several decades has been a commitment to the acknowledgement of cultural diversity, and the notion of intentionality is his way of emphasizing that it is essential to be flexible in the face of different needs, and different assumptions about helping and healing, that are associated with people from different backgrounds and life experience.

Within the microskills model, the core skills that underpin all forms of helping are *attending* skills. These skills encompass eye contact, a warm and interested tone of voice, 'verbal tracking' (willingness to stick with the client's story rather than changing the subject) and appropriate body language (e.g. facing the person, leaning forward, using encouraging gestures). These characteristics are summarized by Ivey *et al.* (2010) as comprising 'the three Vs + B: visuals, vocals, verbals, and body language'.

A further level of the microskills framework involves integrating basic attending skills into a 'well-formed interview'. Ivey *et al.* (2010: 209–11) suggest that, from the perspective of the client, an effective interview or counselling session typically consists of the following sequence:

- *Developing a relationship*. Initiating the session, offering structure and establishing rapport.
- *Story and strengths*. Gathering data about the person's story, and their concerns and issues.
- *Goals*. Identifying what the client wants to happen.
- *Restorying*. Exploring alternatives and confronting incongruities in the story.
- *Action*. Acting on new stories and understandings. Ending the session.

If the counsellor and client are able to meet on a number of occasions, this sequence is repeated in respect of different aspects of the client's issue or problem, as it evolves in response to the client's previous attempts to resolve it. A key assumption that informs this aspect of the model is that a failure to complete the sequence within a meeting runs the risk of leaving the client frustrated or with a sense of hopelessness, whereas completing the sequence produces a sense that progress is being made.

Although this interview sequence can be accomplished with the application of basic attending skills, in some situations the sequence calls for a capacity to make use of more advanced *influencing skills*. These advanced skills include: identifying contradictions and mixed messages in the client's story; challenging the client in a supportive manner; clarifying issues; looking at the issue from multiple perspectives; reframing or reinterpreting the client's experience; and working with the immediate, here-and-now responses of the client.

Ivey *et al.* (2010) view these skills as fitting together into a hierarchy, which they visualize as being like a pyramid. At the apex of the pyramid is the integration of different layers of microskills into the counsellor's *personal style*, which reflects their individual strengths and weaknesses, cultural context and values. The microskills model provides a powerful resource for organizing training programmes, because it specifies basic skills that represent a starting point for training, and then offers a framework that explains how and why these core skills can be combined (into an interview sequence), augmented (by advanced influencing skills and interventions) and finally can be personalized by the trainee.

Three-stage models of counselling skill

There are a number of theorists who suggest that the process of helping a person to deal with a problem can be broken down into three stages. The original version of this type of approach probably began in the work of Carkhuff (1969a, b), who was a student and then a colleague of Carl Rogers. More recently, the most influential three-stage models are associated with the writings of Clara Hill, and Gerard Egan.

The Helping Skills Model

The *Helping Skills Model* developed by Clara Hill (2004) suggests that the helping or counselling process consists of three stages: *exploration, insight* and *action*. The main counsellor skills and tasks at each stage are:

1 *Exploration*

   Skills: using open questions, attending, listening, restatements, reflection of feelings, self-disclosure of insight and silence as means of:
   ● establishing rapport and developing a therapeutic relationship
   ● encouraging clients to tell their stories
   ● encouraging clients to share their thoughts and feelings
   ● facilitating arousal of emotions
   ● learning about the client's own perspective on their problem.

2 *Insight*

   Skills: using challenges, interpretation, self-disclosure of insight and immediacy in order to:
   ● work with clients to construct new insight
   ● encourage clients to determine their role in their thoughts, feelings and actions
   ● work with clients to address issues in the relationship (e.g. misunderstandings).

3 *Action*

   Skills: offering information, feedback and guidance, homework assignments, and techniques such as relaxation and role-play for the purpose of:
   ● encouraging clients to explore possible new behaviours
   ● assisting clients in deciding on actions
   ● facilitating the development of skills for action
   ● providing feedback about attempted changes
   ● assisting clients in evaluating changes and modifying action plans.

For Hill (2004: 25), the underlying process that takes place through these stages can be summarized as: 'the helping process involves taking clients "down and into" understanding themselves more and the "up and out" into the world, better able to cope with problems.'

Hill (2004) argues that it is important for helpers to have an appreciation of the theoretical principles underlying each of these stages. The *exploration* stage is informed by the person-centred theory of Carl Rogers. The *insight* stage draws on psychoanalytic concepts developed by Freud and others. Finally, the *action* stage is an expression of ideas from cognitive-behavioural theory (CBT). Throughout these three stages, it is essential for the counsellor to work with the client to maintain an agreed *focus* for their work together. The *Helping Skills Model* is informed by research into the characteristics of helpful and unhelpful interventions (Hill, 2001).

The Skilled Helper Model

The Skilled Helper Model, devised by Gerard Egan (2004), proposes a three-stage approach to facilitating change which is similar to the Hill (2004) framework:

Stage 1   Helping the client to tell their story

- tuning-in – empathic presence
- listening to verbal and non-verbal communication
- communicating back to the client what you have understood
- highlighting core issues in the client's story
- probing and summarizing
- identifying problems and opportunities
- identifying contradictions in the story and challenging the client.

Stage 2   Helping the client to determine what they need and want

- goal-setting
- decision-making
- identifying possibilities for a better future
- moving from possibilities to choices
- making a commitment to change.

Stage 3   Implementing action strategies to help the client to get what they need and want

- identifying and evaluating strategies
- making an action plan
- making change happen.

The strengths and weaknesses of three-stage models

The idea that the counselling process can be organized into three stages (exploration–insight–action) makes a lot of sense to a lot of people, both clients and practitioners. A three-stage model offers a sense of direction and momentum to counselling. It helps trainees to appreciate the aim and purpose of specific skills that they are using. For many helpers who have been socialized into a controlling, advice-giving, 'fix-it' style of interacting with others, three-stage models make it clear that a problem needs to be described and understood before it can be resolved. At the same time, the model emphasizes that just talking about an issue is not enough – at some point the person needs to make changes in their life and move on.

There are, however, also some limitations associated with three-stage models. In practice, with many clients the process of counselling is far from tidy. The person may get to a stage of taking action, find that these changes are not effective, and loop back into the exploration stage. There are also occasions when clients just want assistance in making changes that they have worked out for themselves, and are not interested in insight or exploration. Possibly the most significant weakness of any three-stage model is that it implies that effective counselling *should* involve progress through these three domains. This expectation can result in counsellors pushing their clients through the stages before they are ready. In deference to the counsellor, the client may then accede to a false resolution of their issues.

Exercise 3.2: *Reflecting on your experience as a client*

Take a few moments to reflect on your experience as a client, either in formal counselling/psychotherapy or in an embedded counselling situation. To what extent did the process of counselling correspond to the kinds of stages described by Carkhuff and other theorists?

Conclusions

Counselling skills represent the basic building blocks of counselling practice. In this chapter, the development of different counselling skills models has been explored. In the chapter that follows, the skills that are incorporated into these models are described in more detail. The present chapter has had two main aims. There has been an attempt to introduce the ideas of important figures in this field, such as Robert Carkhuff, Gerard Egan, Allen Ivey and Clara Hill. There has also been an intention to encourage a questioning stance in relation to these models. On the whole, the models described in this chapter were devised to simplify complex human capabilities so that they could be taught to young people undergoing training in psychology, nursing, medicine, social work, and other fields, and could provide a basis for assessment of competence in these students. In taking this path, a certain amount of over-simplification has been inevitable. Specifically, it can be argued that the skills models that are currently used do not take sufficient account of three essential factors: the personal awareness of the practitioner, the relationship between practitioner and client, and the organizational context within which counselling and helping takes place. In addition, skills models have not paid enough attention to the purpose of this kind of work in respect of the goals of clients, and the step-by-step tasks that are required in order to accomplish these goals. The model of embedded counselling, introduced in Chapter 2 and developed in more detail in Chapter 5, offers a contextualized approach that takes account of the organizational and practical realities of using counselling skills in real-life settings.

Suggested further reading

A classic book, which provides a context for understanding the development of counselling skills theory and practice over the last three decades is as follows:

Larson, D. (1984) *Teaching Psychological Skills: Models for Giving Psychology Away*. Monterey, CA: Brooks/Cole.

CHAPTER 4

An A–Z of counselling skills

The previous chapter provided an introduction to the idea that counselling can be viewed based on the application of a set of skills and discussed the ideas of important counselling skills theorists such as Carkhuff, Egan, Hill and Ivey. The aim of the present chapter is to explore a set of core counselling skills that represent basic competences for anyone involved in offering a counselling relationship. These skills are introduced in alphabetical order to reflect a position that they are of equal importance. Although it is possible to separate out these skills, for purposes of training and research, in practice they are all interconnected and form part of a general way of being with a person that is characteristic of all approaches to counselling.

The material in this chapter is not intended to supply a sufficient basis in itself for acquiring the counselling skills that are being discussed. Developing skilfulness in counselling situations requires observing how other people use these skills, trying out the skills in practice, and receiving feedback and coaching around how effective this practice has been. In addition, it is valuable to read about how different writers describe the same skills – there are always more aspects to a practical skill than can be captured in words, and different authors tend to highlight contrasting aspects of skill use. At the end of the chapter there is a list of sources of recommended further reading on the nature of counselling skills.

Box 4.1: *What are counselling skills for?*

It is always important to keep in mind that counselling skills are used for a purpose. It does not matter how elegantly a counsellor empathizes with the client – if the counsellor's response is not facilitative, and does not make a difference to the client, then it is of little value. Conversely, some counsellor responses that may appear to observers to be awkward or idiosyncratic may be experienced by the client as very helpful. How can we know that a counselling skill is being used effectively? In training sessions, and in actual practice, it is essential to get some sense of the impact that a counsellor response has had on a client. There are several kinds of impact that can be observed. Counselling skills may be used to:

● Help the client to *tell their story*: what the counsellor says and does has the effect of enabling the person to continue talking in a deeper and more personally meaningful manner.

● *Develop the relationship*: the counsellor's response has the effect of building connection between counsellor and client, or conveying to the client that the counsellor is interested and caring, and believes in the client's capacity to resolve the issues that are being explored.

● *Enable reflection and choice*: what the counsellor says or does may open up a space for the client to be more aware of what they are experiencing, or to consider alternative courses of action.

● *Create a new experience*: sometimes a client can be invited to engage in an experience that they may have rarely undergone before – for example, a withdrawn person may engage in eye contact, a highly talkative person may sit in silence for a few moments.

When practising counselling skills; for instance, in the context of a training course, it is useful to evaluate skill use in terms of what Sachse and Elliott (2002) have characterized as *triples*: a sequence of interaction that starts with a client statement, followed by a counsellor statement, and ending with a further client response. At this 'micro'-level of analysis, effective use of counselling skills can be observed as resulting in small but meaningful shifts in the client in the direction of exploring an issue more fully, or being more connected to the counsellor. By contrast, ineffective counselling skills can be observed as having an opposite effect – the client may lose track of what they were talking about, or may withdraw from contact with the counsellor.

Exercise 4.1: *Reflecting on your own counselling skills*

Before reading any further in this chapter, take a few moments to make a list of the counselling skills that you use a lot in interaction with other people, and feel confident or competent about, and another list of counselling skills that are more problematic for you.

An A–Z of counselling skills

TABLE 4.1 Core counselling skills

Attending	Observing
Attunement	Offering feedback
Bodily awareness	Process monitoring
Boundary management	Providing information
Caring	Questioning
Challenging	Reflecting/restating
Checking out/clarifying	Reframing
Giving advice	Remembering
Immediacy	Self-disclosure
Listening	Self-monitoring
Making sense	Structuring
Naming	Using silence
	Witnessing

Attending

In a counselling relationship, the person seeking help should be the focus of attention. It can be distracting for the client if they are trying to talk about an issue and they start to think that their counsellor is not really paying attention. There are therefore two sides to the skill of *attending* – internal and external. At an internal level, the counsellor needs to be genuinely focused on the client, rather than preoccupied with other matters. At an external level, the quality of the counsellor's attention needs to be conveyed to the client. Some of the ways in which attending can be conveyed are through a slight forward lean, facial expression and gestures that are responsive to the client, appropriate eye contact, and what Allen Ivey has described as 'minimal encouragers' – noises or brief statements such as 'mmm' or 'yes'. As with any skill, trying too hard or doing too much can be counterproductive. For example, too much eye contact can be embarrassing or shaming for some clients. There are important cultural differences in acceptable styles of attending: Northern Europeans mainly prefer a more distanced style, while many other cultural groups expect a more animated response.

Attunement

An effective counsellor seeks to tune in to what the client is experiencing, and to the client's way of expressing these experiences. *Attunement* refers to a wide range of ways in which this kind of person-to-person alignment can take place. For example, at an emotional level, an attuned counsellor may feel, within their own body, emotions that are present for the client. Attunement also refers to using the same words as the client (e.g. if a client states that they were 'down', it may be discordant for the counsellor to respond by using the term 'depressed'). In addition, it can be helpful for the counsellor to follow the pace and rhythm with which the client speaks, and even to mirror the client's body language. When the process of attunement works well, the client will tend to have a sense that the counsellor is 'with' them. When it is absent, the counselling process may have a stop–start quality, marked by a failure to develop topics, and the client (and counsellor) becoming self-conscious around a sense that things are not going well between them. In the longer term, failure of attunement makes it hard for the counsellor to know what tasks and methods are right for a particular client, and to evaluate whether the counselling is being helpful.

Bodily awareness

There does not appear to be a suitable word to describe this skill. It refers to a capacity to make use of information from non-verbal cues and the physical presence of both client and counsellor. Most counselling takes place in face-to-face interactions in which the emphasis is on verbal expression. But these words are produced by bodies, and are accompanied by multiple bodily cues. It is valuable for counsellors to have some exposure to modes of therapy that involve physical activity, such as adventure therapy, dance therapy or psychodrama, or to watch video recordings of face-to-face therapy sessions with the sound turned off. Even minimal experience of any of these activities will make it clear that a great deal of meaning is expressed through body posture and movement, and that the quality of a relationship is conveyed through an interpersonal 'dance' that takes place between two people. Skilled counsellors are able to observe bodily phenomena in themselves ('I am aware that I am sitting hunched up and with my legs crossed – what could that mean?') and in their clients, integrate these data into the verbal and aural information they are receiving, and use it to inform the process of counselling.

Boundary management

If counselling can be defined as 'making a space to talk it through' (Chapter 1), then it is the responsibility of the counsellor to ensure that the boundary of the space is secure enough to 'contain' whatever the 'it' might be that a person needs to explore. A large part of the skill of boundary managing is practical: appropriate seating, a private confidential place to meet, no interruptions and an agreed start and finish time. Another element of boundary managing is contractual; for example, in respect of issues such as frequency of meetings, or information (e.g. of illegal activity, self-harm or abuse) that would need to be reported to an authority. A more subtle aspect of boundary management is concerned with the emotional or psychological meaning of the counsellor–client relationship. For example, either the client or the counsellor may desire to pull the relationship out of a counselling 'space' and into a different kind of interpersonal space, such as the territory of friendship, business or sexual intimacy. A boundary issue that can emerge for practitioners of nursing, social work, teaching and other professions who are engaging in embedded counselling is the extent to which they are willing to share their own experience with the client. Typically, such practitioners have been trained to remain in a fairly distanced 'professional' role in relation to patients and clients. However, within a counselling relationship, there can be times when self-disclosure on the part of the counsellor can be very helpful for the client. Part of the skill of boundary management involves the development of strategies for how to deal with this kind of situation.

Caring

From the point of view of the person receiving counselling, one of the most valued aspects of the process is a feeling that the counsellor genuinely cares (Bedi et al., 2005; Levitt et al., 2006). Caring can be expressed in a variety of ways. Small acts of caring can involve responding to the person's physical needs, such as for a more comfortable chair, or a glass of water. Caring can be conveyed through remembering information that is significant for a client, such as their birthday, or the date when a loved one died. For some clients, the active involvement of the counsellor is experienced as caring; for instance, rather than passively reflecting back what the person has said, the counsellor cares enough to make suggestions, or initiate activities or exercises. An essential facet of caring is bound up in anticipating how certain events might have an impact on a person; for example, looking ahead to emotionally difficult holiday periods, such as Christmas. Satisfied clients sometimes refer to this factor when they describe their counsellor as not being bound by a professional role, treating them as someone 'special', or being willing to 'go an extra mile' for them (Neander and Skott, 2006). For a counsellor, the skill of caring starts with a genuine interest in a client, which in turn is built around a capacity to resist burnout and emotional distancing through effective professional self-care. Conveying caring involves keeping in mind the question: 'what is it that *this* particular person might need from me to believe that I care about them?'

Challenging

Someone who is seeking help will usually want their counsellor to be 'on their side', to be a supportive, safe relationship. However, clients also want their counsellor to be honest with them to point out when they seem to be not making sense, contradicting themselves, avoiding things, or indulging in self-destructive behaviour. The skill of *confronting* or *challenging* is hard for many counsellors, who tend to be people who avoid conflict and hold a preference for harmonious, close relationships. Counsellors often believe that to challenge a client runs the risk of undermining the therapeutic relationship. There is of course some validity in adopting caution around the use of challenging – a high proportion of people who seek counselling do so because they have been exposed to critical and demeaning responses from other people in their lives, and are therefore highly sensitive to any hint of judgementalism on the part of their counsellor. It is important for counsellors to keep a hold of the idea that what they are doing when they challenge a client is not only potentially useful in itself, as a means of stimulating new understanding or new behaviour, but also represents an opportunity for the client to learn about *supportive* challenging that arises from a position of empathic caring. There are three key principles involved in supportive challenging. First, the counsellor signals that they are concerned about some aspect of what the client is doing or saying, and would like to challenge the client. The counsellor asks if this would be a good point at which to share these concerns, or whether doing so would interrupt the flow of whatever else the client wanted to explore at that moment. Second, the challenge or confrontation is framed in terms of a tentative statement around a possible contradiction between different statements that the client had made. For example: 'you mentioned that you wanted to use the counselling to deal with the arguments you have with your spouse, but we have met twice and you haven't mentioned this issue again . . .'; 'you say you feel OK and relaxed, and yet you sound angry . . .'; 'you want to be more honest with your mother, and yet it seems to me that you have just described a conversation with her where you did everything in your power to hide information about . . .'. The crucial aspect of this kind of formulation is that it is grounded in evidence, and is specific to a particular issue rather than being generalized ('totalizing' or general statements such as 'you are resistant to looking at your own behaviour' are rarely facilitative, because they merely trigger either an avoidance response or angry and resentful fighting back). The third principle of challenging or confronting a client is to observe what happens next and to be willing to work with whatever process then ensues. Does the client openly engage with the issue, or do they change the topic? If the latter, it would usually be necessary for the counsellor to point out that this is what the client seems to have done. By being tentative, the counsellor allows the client to correct the counsellor's formulation. For example, a client who seems to be avoiding talking about their spouse might say 'I have been holding back because I thought that *you* were uncomfortable with this issue', or 'yes, but it's not argument so much as a feeling that they do not support me in dealing with the stress I feel about my work situation'.

Checking out/clarifying

It is clear to anyone who knows anything about counselling that at its core the role of counsellor hinges on a capacity for *listening* to someone who needs to talk through an issue. However, although listening is fundamental and essential, it is more helpful when combined with a willingness to check with the speaker that what is being heard and understood is accurate. One of the least helpful counselling responses in the long run is to react to a client by saying 'I know how you feel', or making some variant of that statement. Can the client believe that you know how they feel, if you have not attempted to put into words what you believe their feeling state consists of? Further, how sure can a counsellor be that they really grasp what the client is feeling, rather than misunderstanding or misinterpreting the emotional signals that are being sent? It is only when the counsellor regularly checks out with the client that their understanding is accurate that both of them can proceed in the confidence that they are on the same wavelength. Sometimes, checking out requires little more than reflecting or restating what the person has said, or summarizing the main meanings that have been gleaned from what has been said. This kind of minimal checking out has the advantage of reassuring the client that they are being understood, while not interrupting the flow of what they are talking about. However, it can also be facilitative from time to time to make longer checking-out statements that seek to encompass the connections between experiences or events, or convey the counsellor's understanding of the client's whole story. A basic reflective checking out might take the form 'my sense is that what you are feeling is a sense of frustration and anger, and maybe also a little sadness that it had to come to this . . . is that the way it is for you?' A more complex or 'narrative' type of checking out would tend to add a further layer of cause-and-effect sequencing: 'I'd like to just check with you that I'm understanding what you are feeling. It's as though when your brother behaves in this self-destructive way, as he did last week, that you have a sense of frustration and anger, and maybe also a little sadness that it had to come to this, and then when you feel like that you just want to withdraw from him and have nothing to do with him, which then leads to feeling depressed and guilty – is that about right?' An important aspect of checking out can involve seeking to *clarify* the meaning of what the client has said. If a coun-sellor feels confused when a client is talking, or has a sense that there are things that are not being said, then it can be helpful to follow this up through a process of checking out. For example: 'I can see in the way you are talking about what happened that you are angry. But I'm not quite sure where the sadness fits with that. Could you say a bit more about that feeling of being sad?' There are several key component skills that contribute to effective checking out: *timing* (finding the right moment to interrupt the flow of the client's self-expression), *observing* how the person responds to the checking-out statement (particularly for signs that the statement was not fully accurate), and *phrasing* (conveying the nuanced complexity of what the client has said while remaining succinct). Good checking out also encompasses *non-verbal* aspects of what the client has conveyed (e.g. voice quality, gesture and posture) as well their actual words.

Giving advice

Everyone knows that counsellors do not offer advice. The position that most coun-sellors take on advice is that they are not there to tell the client what to do, but to facilitate them in a process where they can arrive at their own solutions. The wisdom of this position is reinforced by an appreciation of the futility of advice-giving in everyday life. Many (or most) friends or family members respond to the problems of those close to them by offering well-meaning advice ('why don't you

. . .?'), only for the troubled one to say 'yes, but . . .'. (The intricate dynamics of the 'why don't you . . . yes but' game were first documented by Eric Berne in 1964 in his best-selling book *Games People Play*.) On the other hand, clients can some-times ask for advice, and may do so on the basis of knowing that the counsellor is in possession of knowledge and experience around the issue for which they seek advice, or may have an inkling that the counsellor does have a position on the issue. In this kind of situation, the client may be puzzled and may feel rejected ('I am not important enough for him to tell me what he really thinks I should do . . .') if the counsellor does not respond to a request for advice. The skill of offering advice when in a counsellor role therefore hinges on an appreciation of the pros and cons and implications of advice-giving. It is seldom helpful in a counselling role to offer unsolicited advice. Usually, all this does is give the counsellor a false sense that they are doing something useful, while distracting the client from talking about what they need to talk about. When a person explicitly asks their counsellor for advice on a matter, it may be valuable to take the opportunity to acknowledge the person's own resources in relation to the matter in hand ('I'm happy to suggest what I think you might do, but I feel sure that you have thought a lot about this yourself – what are the options that you have been looking at yourself?') and their capacity to enlist the help of other people in their life ('. . . and I was wondering who else you have talked to about this, and what they have said'). This kind of preamble has the effect of placing the counsellor's advice in the context of other advice, and thus defusing any notion that what the counsellor might suggest has any special authoritative status – it keeps the client in the driving seat. It can then also be useful to *hedge* the advice that is offered ('you need to be aware that what I'm going to say comes from my perspective – there are definitely other ways of approaching this issue'). Once the advice is offered, it is good to be curious about what the client has made of it ('how does that sound to you . . . is there something there that you think you can use, or not?'). Throughout the whole process of advice-giving, the counsellor should not imply that they have any investment in whether or not the client follows their advice, and might even wish to applaud any indica-tion that the client is being selective around which elements of the advice are of practical value to them.

Immediacy

A lot of what is discussed in counselling refers to what is or has happened 'out there' in the client's life. Occasionally, it can also be useful to focus on what is happening right here and now in the counselling room. The skill of being able to make use of here-and-now processes is generally discussed in terms of the concept of *immediacy*. There are two broad types of immediacy. The first involves paying attention to something that the client is doing right now (e.g. 'you said that you agreed with my analysis of the situation, but when you spoke you clenched your fist and looked away . . . I'm wondering if there is something else that you are maybe finding hard to say? Could you maybe just stay with that feeling for a moment, and try to find words for it?'). The second type of immediacy occurs when the counsellor describes their personal response to the client. This second form of immediacy is sometimes described as counsellor *self-involvement*. An example might be: 'when you say that you agree with me and then look away and act sort of angry then I have a sense of being dismissed, as though I'm a little boy who doesn't get to hear what the grown-ups are talking about'. Or: 'I don't know if this is relevant, but I just felt scared there, as if I had said the wrong thing and was in trouble'. A key element in all counsellor training is about enabling students to feel confident about using the skill of immediacy. This is because the rules of 'normal' or 'polite' conversation generally proscribe this kind of bluntness or honesty, and also because immediacy is scary – once you open the door to this kind of statement, who knows where the conversation might go? Despite these difficulties, counselling trainers tend to push the value of immediacy, because it can deepen the level of intimacy or connectedness in the client–counsellor relationship, and can also help the client to begin to move beyond a cautious or 'safe' account of their troubles, and to begin to talk in a more emotionally honest manner about the things that really matter to them.

Listening

The art of listening lies at the heart of counselling – good counsellors are good listeners. A crucial dimension of listening involves letting the other person know that you are listening. This skill was described earlier in the chapter in the section on *attending*. It can be disconcerting and disturbing for a person to start to talk about something that is meaningful for them, and to have a sense that their interlocutor is not paying attention to them. Effective attending therefore functions as a means of communicating to the client that their counsellor is still listening. However, the appearance of attending is not much help to the client if real listening is not taking place. Genuine listening involves making an effort to grasp the *whole* of what a person is saying (or expressing through their voice quality and non-verbal cues such as posture). Genuine listening involves suspending or bracketing-off any assumptions about the meaning of what a person is saying, and instead being open to what is actually there. Effective listening requires switching off one's internal dialogue in order to tune in to the other person's story. It calls for a willingness to be there in the moment. None of this is easy. In everyday conversations, we listen to each other, but only up to a point – at least some of the time, we are rehearsing what we intend to say when our turn comes round. In many professional situations, we are trained to listen *for* specific types of information. For example, a doctor or nurse learns to listen for symptoms and for information that will confirm a particular diagnosis. A police officer may be trained to listen for evasions and contradictions in the story told by a suspect or witness. The listening that counsellors do is more open-ended than this. It is more like listening for the person behind the story. Also, as they listen to the person, a skilled counsellor also listens to themself (see below: *self-monitoring*). There are perhaps at least two observable manifestations of counsellor listening. First, when a counsellor is sufficiently tuned in to the client's story, they may begin to finish the client's sentences, or seamlessly make links between what is being said now and what was said in previous conversations. This comes across to observers as a conversation that is *flowing* with each speaker in synchrony with the other.

A second observable feature of good listening is the occurrence of pauses and silences. Because a counsellor is listening in this kind of holistic manner, they may find it hard to formulate an immediate response when the time comes for them to speak. Typically, if a counsellor has been listening well enough, they may need a few moments to reflect on what has been said, before they begin to speak. What this kind of deep listening makes possible is for the counsellor to gain a sense of the many facets of whatever issue the person is exploring. It can be very powerful for the client if as much as possible of this complexity can then be reflected back to them in the counsellor's response, because it subtly invites the possibility that an issue or problem can be viewed in different ways. As with other counselling skills, developing a capacity to listen effectively is something that can only be acquired through practice and experiment with other people who are willing to provide honest constructive feedback. Also, for any counsellor, reflection on one's ability to listen is likely to lead to the identification of personal issues and vulnerabilities: no matter how good a listener someone is, there are always some topics that cause the shutters to come down.

Box 4.2: *When counselling skills are used inappropriately*

The discussion of counselling skills in this chapter concentrates on how these ways of interacting with people can have beneficial effects. However, it is also important to be aware that counselling skills can have *negative* effects: anything that is powerful enough to do good can also do harm. A useful model of ineffective and harmful uses of counselling skills has been developed by John Heron (2001: particularly ch. 13). He identifies four types of error: *unsolicited* use of skills; *manipulative* interventions; *compulsive* behaviour by the counsellor (e.g. they persist with an approach that is not helping the client); and *unskilled* interventions (where the counsellor is trying to do the right thing but is just not very good at it). These are all examples of situations where the counsellor is genuinely trying to help, but is failing to do so. Beyond these errors, for Heron, lies the territory of *perverted* interventions, where the 'helper' is deliberately seeking to damage someone who is vulnerable.

Making sense

One of the most common triggers for seeking help from a counsellor is the experience of not being able to make sense of some aspects of one's life. The person may be frightened, overwhelmed or confused by experiences that they are having. Making sense of these experiences allows the person to gain some control over events, or 'get a handle' on what is happening. Gaining understanding also tends to reduce the emotional pressure on a person, because they are more able to see things in perspective and as a result acquire some distance from their feelings. The skill of being able to work with a client to make sense of a problem therefore represents a crucial area of competence for any counsellor. There are three broad sense-making strategies that are typically used by counsellors. The first strategy is to invite the person to explain how they personally make sense of the problem or issue that is bothering them, possibly by using an open question such as 'this is clearly a big issue for you, and I'm sure that you must have really thought deeply about why it is happening . . .'. A variant on this approach is to listen for explanatory accounts that are implicit in the way the person talks about a problem (e.g. 'as I'm listening to you, it seems to me that you think that you can't give up smoking because you are weak-willed – is that the way you make sense of it?'). A further variant is to ask the person how they make sense of similar situations (e.g. 'you mentioned to me that you have already changed your lifestyle in the area of taking more exercise – how do you understand how you were able to do that?'). Tapping into the sense-making frameworks that the person already espouses is always a good idea, because it avoids the awkwardness of trying to persuade the person of the validity of ideas that may be strange or alien to them. A second sense-making strategy is to create a space for developing understanding by listing or displaying the events or experiences that are puzzling for the person. Visual diagrams can be very useful in this kind of work. For example, when a person can see the sequence of events that leads to a crisis laid out in front of them on a flipchart page, then it may be much easier for them to find a meaningful pattern that allows them to make sense of what has been happening. The third strategy is for the counsellor to offer the client an explanatory framework that is based on some kind of pre-existing theory or model. This kind of approach has an educative dimension, because the counsellor is trying to teach the client some new ideas. The dangers associated with this strategy are that the client can become confused by the new ideas, or can defer to what they perceive as the greater wisdom of the counsellor (while in truth not regarding the counsellor's explanation as credible or useful). A lot of the time, clients who are baffled by a counsellor's theories will not say so to the therapist for fear of being impolite or ungrateful. These risks are exacerbated by the fact that offering a client an explanatory framework can feed into a counsellor's self-aggrandizing desire to appear knowledgeable, wise and clever. Having said all that, there are times when a counsellor-supplied theory can make a huge difference to a client: all of us draw on ideas and theories to help us to make sense of various aspects of life, and we learned these ideas from somewhere.

Naming

A really lovely skill, which some counsellors are able to use to powerful effect, is that of finding the right word to describe an experience. This skill applies in situations where there is some aspect of a person's life that is implicit and unsaid. For example, a counsellor working with a woman who was consistently self-critical struggled to find a way of referring to the client's positive qualities, and eventually struck on the word 'feisty'. This concept had a lot of meaning for the client, and the two of them were then able to talk about 'that feisty side of you' or 'the feistier option' – conversational possibilities that were not available up until that point.

Observing

Being observant is a skill that tends not to get sufficient recognition in the counsel-ling literature. Where a person sits, how they move, what they do with their hands, where they look, how they dress, how these and other characteristics change from day to day or moment to moment (and what triggers such changes) – these are all valuable sources of information for a counsellor. The purpose of observation in counselling is not to collect information for the purpose of diagnosis, but instead to use every means possible to enter the personal world of the client, and to create opportunities for reflection and learning. It can be useful for clients to share the outcomes of observation: 'I noticed that when you started to talk about your father you bit your lip and hunched up in your chair . . . I don't know if that means anything, but it somehow struck me as significant . . .'. A particularly important time to observe the client is in the moment following a statement or intervention made by the counsellor – does the client look as though what you said has deepened their process of exploration and meaning-making, or do they look confused or frustrated? A standard learning exercise around the development of observation skills is to watch a video of a counselling session with the sound turned off. It is usually possible to understand a lot of what is happening, even in the absence of words.

Offering feedback

There is an aspect of counselling that is like being a mirror for the person who is seeking help. It is as though the person is caught up in the complexity and stuckness of their problem, and needs to be able to ask someone external to the situation a question such a 'what does this look like to you?' or even 'what (or who) do *I* look like to you?' Responding to this kind of question involves a process of providing feedback to a person. Giving feedback is therefore potentially very important for some clients, but can be a risky business. There are probably three main risks. There is a danger of making what can be categorized as a *totalizing* statement, or blanket description of a person's actions. For example, a client is talking about a situation that is hard to handle, and asks the counsellor how his behaviour comes across to her. The counsellor says: 'well, what I see is someone who is avoiding facing up to something'. Client interprets this as: 'she thinks I am being a *complete coward*'. This example illustrates a second risk associated with feedback that is generalized rather than anchored in observations of specific behav-iour. What might have been better for this counsellor to have said might have been 'when you spend the evening with your wife and don't mention this issue, that looks to me as if you are avoiding it, and yet I also know that you are spending a lot of time talking to your best friend, and to me, about how to face up to it'. This statement is explicit about where the avoiding is happening (and implicitly is opening up the possibility of a conversation about how that pattern might be changed) and also balances different items of feedback against each other (thus not falling into the trap of totalizing). A third form of unhelpful feedback is when the statement made by the counsellor is too *bland* (e.g. 'what I see is someone who is struggling with some really difficult choices in his life' – a statement that could be made at almost any time to almost any client). Bland or empty feedback can make the client wonder whether the counsellor really cares, or has really been paying attention, or perhaps even suspect that the counsellor has chosen to conceal the awfulness of what they have observed ('she thinks I am pathetic but she can't bring herself to say it'). Effective feedback is timely, specific, nuanced, comprehensive and owned ('what I see is X' rather than 'you are X'). In some situations the activity of providing feedback overlaps with the skill of *immediacy*; for instance, when the feedback refers to how the counsellor feels when a client says or does some particular thing. On counselling skills training courses, participants usually gain a lot of experience in giving and receiving feedback to and from each other, and thereby gain essential first-hand experience around the types of feedback that can be facilitative or otherwise.

Process monitoring

What happens in a counselling session unfolds and changes from moment to moment. These phenomena can be understood as comprising the *process* of counselling. There are processes that occur on many different levels within the thoughts and feelings of each participant and within the relationship between them. A detailed discussion of theory and research on the process of counselling can be found in McLeod (2009: ch. 15). A skilled counsellor needs to be aware of, or monitor, this process as a means of keeping track of what is happening. Some examples of types of information that may be relevant to an understanding of the counselling process are as follows:

- topic shifts (the client or the counsellor suddenly stops talking about one issue, and changes tack)
- change in interpersonal connectedness ('I feel a lot closer to/distant from the client compared to a few minutes ago')
- change in depth of emotional processing (the client moves from superficial discussion of a topic to exploring his deepest feelings around it – or vice versa)
- shift in client self-concept (a month ago, all he talked about was how useless he was, and now he is starting to acknowledge his own strengths).

Remaining aware of these (and other) types of information can help the counsellor to identify what works for each individual client, what kinds of intervention may be counterproductive (e.g. a clumsy interpretation may lead to the client shifting from exploring deep feelings to a more superficial or distanced account of their problems), and how well the client and counsellor are working together. The skill of process monitoring involves paying attention to process factors while retaining a primary focus on the content of what the person is actually talking about. Most of the time, process monitoring feeds into fine-tuning and minor adjustments to the counsellor's approach to the client. Sometimes, however, process monitoring can identify a crisis in the counselling. For example, if the client seems to be disengaged from the conversation, it may be necessary to return to first principles and review whether the client is getting what they want or need from the counselling.

Providing information

A person in the role of counsellor is a potential source of information for the person seeking help. Some of this information may relate to the counsellor themself – when they are available, the limits to the confidentiality that they can offer, and their training and experience. Other information may relate to alternative sources of help – specialist counselling and psychotherapy services that may be available, clinics, support groups, and so on. There are information sources that in themselves constitute forms of therapeutic assistance, such as self-help books and websites. There are also information sources that address health and social care issues that the client may be experiencing, from how to support a family member with dementia, through how to claim housing benefits. These information sources may be suggested and supplied by the counsellor, or the client may find information that they then wish to check out or discuss with the counsellor. All of these types of information can be regarded as resources that have the potential to assist the person in working through their difficulties and moving on in their life. A key counsellor quality that contributes to skilled use of information sources is *curiosity*. We live in a culture in which hard-pressed health care systems try to reduce the burden on health professionals by providing patients with leaflets, websites and call centres where they can acquire information about how they can take care of themselves. All this can be very useful, but it can also result in people having a sense of being 'fobbed off' with a leaflet rather than being allowed to talk to a person who is an enduring caring presence in their life. It can also result in mountains of unread leaflets. Skilfully providing information in counselling therefore requires that the counsellor finds ways to include the information within the counselling conversation and therapeutic relationship, rather than just suggesting or supplying information and expecting the client to assimilate it on their own. In this process, it is sensible to keep in mind the fact that information is never neutral. There are some information sources, such as pro-anorexia websites, that most sensible people would regard as scary and dangerous. But even mainstream self-help books, leaflets and websites are likely to include ideas and examples that range across a spectrum, from extremely helpful through to confusing and irrelevant. It is therefore essential for counsellors to read and think about the information sources they recommend to clients, or those that clients recommend to them.

Questioning

Questions comprise one of the basic elements of language use. Human beings have evolved language as a means of communication, and questions represent a linguistic form that has obvious survival value: asking another person for information or assistance. Question-and-answer sequences comprise a large part of the discourse that occurs between people who are close to each other: 'what did you do at the weekend?', 'do you like my new haircut?' For many students, one of the hardest parts of counsellor training is associated with the process of learning *not* to ask questions, or to learn how to ask particular types of questions for particular purposes. Being a counsellor involves putting to one side one's 'natural' or taken-for-granted way of asking questions, and to acquire instead a more consciously intentional approach to the art of questioning. Why is this? There are two main problems with the unreflective use of questions in counselling. First, in many counselling situations, the aim is to help the client to tell their story in their own words. Asking questions runs the risk that the ongoing flow of the client's story will be broken – they lose the thread of what they are trying to put into words by having to break off and answer the counsellor's questions. In other words, there is the possibility that questions will alter the client's process in an unhelpful manner. Second, a question tends to be formulated from the frame of reference of the questioner, and subtly convey the questioner's assumptions about the topic that is being discussed. This aspect of questioning is summed up in the idea that 'behind every question is a statement'. For example, if a client is talking about feeling anxious in social situations, their counsellor might respond by posing a question such as: 'when did this anxiety start . . . what was the first time you were aware of being affected in this way?' The statement behind this question could be summed up as: 'I believe that it is important for us to look at how this all started, because that is the best way to find out what needs to be done to change it'. However, it may be that the client either does not see the relevance of thinking about how it all started, or is puzzled by why the counsellor might want to know that specific piece of information at that particular point in the story. Further discussion around the skill of using questions in counselling can be found in Chapter 9.

Reflecting/restating

As a person seeking help talks about the issues that are bothering them, it can be helpful for their counsellor to simply reflect back to them the main gist of what they have been saying. This allows the person to know that the counsellor is listening, following and understanding, and it enables the counsellor to know that their own understanding of the client's story is broadly in tune with what the client is intending to convey. A reflection or restatement is typically a brief statement, which does not interrupt the flow of the client's narrative. In addition to the basic function of confirming a basic level of contact and shared meaning between client and counsellor, the skill of reflection can serve further important therapeutic purposes. It can be useful for a client to hear their inner concerns and feelings being articulated by another person. Quite often, a person who seeks counselling help may have never previously spoken about that issue to anyone else, or may never have voiced particularly embarrassing, shameful or emotionally painful facets of the issue. As a result, their dilemma or problem may have been played in their mind over and over again as a repetitive inner monologue. In this kind of situation, it can make a huge difference to speak the words out loud, and then to hear these words being said by another person. Even this simple act can allow the person a certain amount of emotional relief and perspective. Another potentially valuable aspect of simple restatement is that it serves to slow down the flow of the person's talk. If a person is talking about an issue that is emotionally painful or embarrassing, they may well talk quickly as a means of keeping their feelings at a distance, or to avoid having to think more deeply about the issue. Reflection or restatement offers the person brief moments of pause or reflection that allow the beginnings of a process of assimilating and coming to terms with their problematic experience. With some clients, the opposite may occur – the topic is so hard to speak about that they go quiet, or there are long gaps in their discourse. Here, a brief restatement can function as a gentle nudge ('I am interested, and here is what I have picked up so far . . .') that encourages the person to continue their story. Making reflective statements can also be useful for the counsellor as a way of staying focused. If a client talks for a long time, their counsellor can become overwhelmed with information. Occasional brief restatements or reflections can operate as a strategy for organizing the client's story into more memorable 'chunks'. For all these reasons, reflection or restatement is a routine counselling skill that has wide applicability. Done well, the act of reflection can carry a great deal of meaning. Mechanical repetition of the last words the client has said is likely to have a negative impact on the client–counsellor relationship. Sensitive reflection, by contrast, is carefully timed and uses words or images that resonate with the client, communicated with a voice quality that subtly conveys a sense of caring and active engagement, and emotional attunement with the client's feeling state.

Reframing

All approaches to counselling make creative use of a distinction between feelings and behaviour on the one side, and on the other side the way that the person interprets or makes sense of these experiences. It is certainly possible to construct massive theoretical debates and research programmes around the nature and implications of this distinction. In terms of counselling skills, however, the action/ emotion versus cognition split has a straightforward application in the use of *reframing*. This skill involves two steps. The first step is to find out how the person makes sense of a problematic experience (behaviour pattern or emotional state), and for the counsellor to let the person know that they understand and appreciate the client's point of view. The second step is to invite the client to consider an alternative way of making sense of the problematic experience. Some examples are as follows:

Joe is terrified about speaking in public at an important conference; his counsellor asks him whether it might be possible that his *fear* could be viewed in a different light, as *excitement* about being able to influence other people with his ideas.

Sheila believes that she is a *failure* because she has not been able to achieve some important life goals; her counsellor responds by listing the many ways that Sheila has been successful in her life, and suggests that a different way to look at these problematic life goals might be to regard them as *incomplete* or ongoing.

Alison fails an exam, and berates herself for not being intelligent enough to pass her degree; her counsellor agrees that a lack of intelligence can be a factor in poor academic performance, but goes on to add that, from what she has heard about Alison's approach to exam revision, a lack of effective study skills and planning might offer a more accurate explanation.

In each of these examples, the counsellor is not dismissing the client's definition of the situation, but is offering a reframed understanding that can be backed up with reference to information that the client has already provided. The underlying manoeuvre that is involved in the skill of reframing is a shift from seeing an event from a standpoint of 'I am worthless and stupid' to a standpoint of 'I am a resourceful person with positive strengths and attributes'. For this intervention to be effective, the counsellor needs to believe in the alternative perspective that she is offering, and be willing and able to explain why she thinks that it represents a valid way of thinking about the situation. Typically, a client will not buy into a reframe straight away, but may need to try it on for size or be reminded about it at regular intervals. What can also happen is that the act of reframing can trigger further conversation and exploration of the more general issue of how, why, where and when the person self-sabotages themself, or is dominated by their 'inner critic'.

Remembering

Another skill that does not receive nearly enough attention and acknowledgement in the counselling world is the ability to *remember* what the client has said and done. A big part of what a counsellor does is to be able to stay with the client in the present moment; for example, by reflecting back what has been said, or being willing to sit in silence. However, another vital aspect of counselling involves helping the client to make connection between different chapters of their life story, or different areas of their experience. An underlying difficulty that influences many people to seek counselling is a sense of a lack of coherence in their life, as if they are in possession of different pieces of a jigsaw that do not fit together. In a counselling session, a client may start off by talking about one issue, and then move on to another issue, or begin by stating a particular goal and then start exploring something that does not seem relevant to that goal. In these scenarios it is part of the job of the counsellor to hold the first bit of information in the back of their mind and then at what seems an appropriate point to reintroduce it into the conversation. For example: 'I'm aware that for the past few minutes you have been talking about your conflict with one of your work colleagues, yet at the start of the session you said that what you wanted to really focus on what you are feeling about the results of your medical tests . . . I'm wondering if there might be a connection between these things, and I was also remembering how you said to me once that when you are scared about something you start a fight . . .'. The skill of remembering can involve practical strategies such as keeping notes, reading notes before a counselling session, or writing down key phrases during a session. Some of what is being remembered is information (e.g. how many children a person has, and their ages and names), but most of it takes the form of a map of the emotional and relational world of the person. New counsellors may often worry about whether they will be able to remember what the client has said to them, and may try to deal with this fear by taking detailed notes during sessions. This is seldom effective, because it can turn a counselling session into a fact-finding interview in which lots of data are collected but nothing changes in the client's life. In the end, a counsellor needs to trust themself to be capable of remembering whatever needs to be remembered. A training exercise that can be illuminating is to make a recording of a counselling session, and at the end of the session to make notes of the information and themes that have been conveyed by the client. If the session is then transcribed and read carefully, it will be apparent that the post-session notes have missed a great deal of valuable information. This phenomenon occurs not because the counsellor lacks competence, but because clients always say more than we hear – our memories are always partial.

Self-disclosure

Self-disclosure refers to the act of sharing personal information with another individual. In counselling, it is taken for granted that the client will engage in a great deal of self-disclosure. Usually, in order to allow the client the maximum space in which to talk, and to be clear about who is the one who is helping and who is the recipient of help, a counsellor will engage in little or no self-disclosure. This arrangement is fundamentally different from most social interaction in which disclosure by one person tends to lead to parallel disclosure by the other. For example, if two friends are talking and one of them tells a story about 'the best restaurant I have ever visited', then it is highly probable that the other person will follow with their own restaurant story. By contrast, in counselling if a client tells a story of 'how I feel overweight and disgusted by how I look', then there is a very low probability that the counsellor will respond by talking about her own body-image issues, because she knows that her role is to assist the person in exploring the unique challenges in *their* life. However, there are times when this 'rule' may be threatened. For example, a client who is talking about dieting may look at their counsellor (who appears to be 'sorted' in this respect) and ask: 'do you really understand what I am talking about? Have you ever had to watch your calories?' What should the counsellor say? Alternatively, a counsellor may be listening to a client, and thinking to themself, 'I have been there, I know exactly what that feels like . . . would it be helpful for me to tell this client what it was like for me?' In the past, most counselling training strongly emphasized the idea that counsellor self-disclosure was unhelpful, and that a counsellor should resist any temptation to disclose and deflect back to the client and request for disclosure ('I sense that it might be reassuring for you if you knew that I had experienced similar issues around my weight . . .').

More recently, practical experience and research evidence suggests that careful counsellor self-disclosure can in fact be highly facilitative for some clients. What does 'careful' mean in this context? A key factor in helpful counsellor self-disclosure is that it is *in the service of the client* – that it does not create a situation in which the client feels that they need to take care of the counsellor, or the session starts to focus on the counsellor's problems at the expense of the client's agenda. A further factor is that the counsellor includes some kind of statement along the lines that people are different, and that her experience of, say, body-image issues may be quite different from the situation being faced by the client. Finally, *how* the disclosure is handled will determine whether it is ultimately helpful for the client. For example, a counsellor might acknowledge something of their own battle with binge eating in a manner that conveys a sense of superiority ('I have dealt with this when I was a teenager – there must be something seriously wrong with you if you haven't been able to deal with it after all this time'), or in a manner that encourages and invites the client to engage in further dialogue and exploration ('yes, it has been a challenge for me at different points in my life, and has really made me think about the meaning of food in my own life and in our culture as a whole'). For a counsellor, skilful use of self-disclosure arises from having worked through personal issues to a point of being able to use personal life experience in a selective and intentional manner, rather than sharing personal information that is still raw and unresolved. It should be noted that there is an important distinction to be made between self-disclosure (sharing biographical information from life outside the counselling room) and *immediacy* (sharing one's response to what is happening in the here-and-now counselling interaction). Both skills involve the counsellor talking about themself, but in different ways and for different purposes.

Self-monitoring

In a counselling relationship, the person in the role of counsellor is doing their best to be with the client and focus on the client's concerns and their story. During this activity, the counsellor does everything possible to lay aside or 'bracket-off' the issues in their own life. In this situation, any feelings, emotions, action tendencies, images or fantasies that arise in the counsellor may represent vital pieces of information about the client's world and the way that the client relates to other people. A key counsellor skill therefore consists of a capacity to engage in ongoing *self-monitoring* throughout the process of a counselling interaction. A good counsellor listens to their client, and at the same time listens to themselves listening to the client. Examples of the potentially relevant types of counsellor experience that can arise in response to clients include:

- *Feelings:* general sense that something is being left unsaid; a sense of hopelessness or despair.
- *Specific emotions*: anger, sadness, sexual arousal, boredom, fear.
- *Physical reactions*: tummy rumbling, itchiness, yawning, pain.
- *Action tendencies:* running away, moving closer, holding.
- *Images*: the client as a child in school, counsellor as an interrogator.
- *Fantasies*: we are in a chess match, it is like a scene from *Little Red Riding Hood*.

There are basically three sources of these phenomena. First, the response can arise purely from something that is happening in the counsellor's life. For instance, the counsellor may already be feeling sad before the counselling session begins, because of the death of a family member, or may have recently watched a film where a therapist acted like a police interrogator. It is important for counsellors to be sufficiently self-aware to be able to differentiate between reactions to clients that arise from their own personal 'stuff', and reactions that represent some kind of capacity to 'resonate' to the reality of the client. The fact that a counsellor is attending to 'own stuff' is of course of some interest – if a counsellor's attention is drifting towards images from recent movies, it may mean that they are avoiding really listening to the client, perhaps because what the client is saying is in some way threatening to hear. A second source of feelings, images and other internal phenomena experienced by a counsellor may be that these experiences reflect aspects of what the client is experiencing. It is as though at that moment the counsellor is sensitively 'tuned in' to the client, and picking up some hidden or unspoken facets of what the client is feeling and thinking. For example, a client may be talking about positive hopes for the future – if the counsellor at that point feels sadness it may indicate that for the client there is also some sense of loss involved in making a decision to move on in their life. A third way of making sense of these reactions is that the counsellor may be reacting to the client in a similar fashion to the ways that other people react. For example, a client's life may be full of contradictions and unkept promises with the result that their friends and family get frustrated and angry with them. When their counsellor also feels frustrated and angry, they can perhaps begin to explore in the present moment how this kind of response is triggered, and what it might mean. Effective counselling skills training and practice creates opportunities for trainees to experiment with different ways of engaging in self-monitoring and productively bringing these inner experiences into the counselling conversation. It should also provide opportunities for observing how other counsellors make use of self-monitoring, and being on the receiving end of this kind of intervention. When offering clients the fruits of self-monitoring, it is essential to be tentative and to invite the client to consider the *possibility* that what the counsellor is feeling, or the image that has jumped into her head, may have some meaning for the client. To *assume* or *insist* that these counsellor experiences *must* be relevant for the client is oppressive.

Structuring

In any counselling encounter, part of the role of the counsellor is to be mindful of the time that is available, and to take responsibility for initiating collaborative discussion around how that time might be used. Although clients are free to make suggestions or requests about the use of time (for example, by saying that they have had enough for today, or asking for more time), an important implicit dimension of a counselling session usually consists of a tacit agreement that the client has the freedom to 'let go' and 'just talk', while the counsellor takes care of time boundaries. A key aspect of the skill of *structuring* therefore consists of an awareness of the use of time, and a willingness to check out with the client and make suggestions regarding how long a session might last, how often meetings might occur, and the length of time remaining in a session. Typically, counsellors try to avoid situations where the client is in full flow and the session just comes to an abrupt end. It is better in most situations to seek to build in a few minutes to review what has been discussed, and look at what might be done next. The other aspect of structuring consists of organizing the work that needs to be done. For example, if the client identifies several goals, which of these will be tackled first? If the client wants to work on a specific problem, what are the step-by-step tasks that might need to be accomplished in order to resolve that problem, and in what order would it be best to take them? Agreeing time structures and task structures helps both the client and the counsellor to be confident that they are working together in an effective manner. Knowing that there is a clear structure for the work that is being done (even if it is a structure that can be renegotiated if necessary) helps clients to have a sense of safety and security, at a point where some areas of their lives may feel as though they are out of control and unmanageable.

Using silence

The spaces between words are highly significant in any counselling conversation. In these spaces a client may be engaged in a process of experiencing an unfolding of feelings or memories, they may be reflecting on the meaning or implications of something that has just been said or felt, or they may be desperately struggling to find some way to avoid talking about something that is in their awareness but which is too hard to put into words at that precise moment. There are also times when a counsellor may wish to take some moments to reflect on how they have understood what has been said. There are times when a counsellor may decide to wait for the client to speak, rather than initiating conversation, as a way of enacting the idea that the client is in charge of the agenda. These are all constructive uses of silence. There are also less positive uses of silence; for example, where the counsellor emotionally withdraws from the client, or conveys a signal that a particular topic is not something that they are willing to talk about. And clients may 'clam up' because they are annoyed or disappointed with their counsellor and do not feel safe enough to mention it. The skill of *using silence* therefore involves being sufficiently comfortable with silence to allow it to occur, and being sensitive to the possible meanings associated with different types of silence.

Witnessing

The final skill in this list consists of the act of *witnessing*. It is a mistake in counselling to assume that when a person talks about an issue that is important or painful for them that they necessarily want the counsellor to help them to 'do something' about that issue. Obviously, many clients want to change aspects of their lives, and want their counsellor to help them to achieve this. But just being able to talk about an issue is in itself a potentially powerful experience. When they talk about an issue in counselling, many clients are telling their story, or certain elements of their story, for the first time. In this kind of situation, just to know that someone is fully present and listening can be a healing experience. There can also be a sense of relief at putting words to emotions and memories that may have been a source of repetitive internal rumination for months or years. By being a witness to someone else's suffering, a counsellor has the possibility of affirming the essential humanity of that person. If a person tells a painful or shameful story, and has an experience of being accepted by their counsellor, they take a step out of aloneness into connectedness and mutual support.

Exercise 4.2: *Analysing your use of counselling skills*

Make an audio recording of a counselling session where you are the counsellor. For reasons of confidentiality it may be necessary to record a session where a colleague or fellow trainee is your client, rather than a real-life counselling encounter. Select a 10-minute section of the recording, and make a written transcript of what was said, including information about pauses and expressions of emotion such as laughter or tears. Take notes during the transcribing process of your immediate reactions to listening to the recording – what surprised you? Once you have constructed a transcript, go through it line by line indicating (a) the counselling skills you used at each point, and (b) the effectiveness with which you used each skill (what else might you have done or said that might have been more appropriate?). If possible, listen to the recording with other people and ask them about their perception of which skills you have used, and how well you have used them. The feedback of the client is particularly valuable in this respect. This is a learning and assessment exercise that is almost universally employed (in various formats) in counselling training programmes, and provides an invaluable opportunity to become more aware of the skills that you use (and do not use) and how well you use them. Examples of this kind of skills analysis can be found in Ivey *et al.* (2010).

Using theory to develop a broader perspective on how skills fit together

The list of counselling skills outlined in the previous section offer a framework for microanalysis of what happens during the process of counselling. It is important for counsellors to be aware of the skills they are using, because they represent the 'basics' of how to work with clients. However, it is also essential to be able to make sense of how skills fit together to form longer sequences of interaction directed towards some specific purpose. In Chapter 3, several models of counselling skills application were discussed that suggested that skills can be viewed as fitting together around distinct *stages* in the problem-solving process. Another way of making sense of how skills fit together is through Heron's (2001) *six-category model*, which proposes that there are six fundamental types of intervention used by counsellors: *prescriptive, informative, confrontative, cathartic, catalytic* and *supportive*. This theory is based on the view that counsellors need to be competent in offering all of these interventions, and to appreciate what is the right moment to use each of them when working with a client. Successful application of any of the different types of intervention involves making use of a range of core skills. Beyond the six-category model, there are also a substantial number of more abstract therapy concepts that represent particular 'bundles' of skills. For example, *empathy* is a theoretical construct that refers to the use of listening, attunement, attending and clarifying. Achieving *insight* is a process that can draw on core skills such as naming, making sense, self-disclosure and reframing. *Metacommunication* is a concept that encompasses such basic skills as clarifying, challenging, self-monitoring, process monitoring and questioning. It is vital for counsellors to be able to make use of higher-level concepts such as empathy, insight and metacommunication (and many other ideas) because these ideas make it possible to see the bigger picture, and to gain access to decades of theoretical writings that represent the distillation of the wisdom of some truly wonderful and gifted practitioners. At the same time, it is important to keep in mind that, in the end, what these concepts are referring to are combinations of basic skills – the things that we do.

In the context of the model of embedded counselling presented in this book, counselling skills are viewed as being brought together in different configurations to enable the accomplishment of the step-by-step *tasks* that provide a focus for counselling. For example, a counsellor seeking to work with a client around the task of *behaviour change* might use listening and checking out to determine how the client wished to change, might challenge the client around unreasonable goals for change, and might introduce a structure to their meetings that would allow change initiatives to be reviewed and revised as necessary. Similarly, a counsellor would draw on counselling skills when implementing counselling *methods* or interventions described in the counselling and psychotherapy literature. For example, in using a narrative therapy technique such as *externalizing the problem* (Morgan, 2001), a counsellor might in fact employ a similar skill set. Tasks and methods can be seen as defining the *purpose* or end point of skill use. The counsellor has an idea of what they might wish to achieve, and then automatically or unconsciously just do what they can to make this outcome happen. This concept is similar to the use of skills in other walks of life. For example, a carpenter draws on the same basic repertoire of woodworking skills whether they are intending to build a table or a house.

Box 4.3: *Learning skills: getting worse before you get better*

An experience that often occurs in participants on counselling skills training courses is that they feel as though their counselling gets worse before it gets better. This phenomenon is probably inevitable. Learning a skill always involves a certain amount of un-learning as habits that are not optimal are changed or dropped in order to allow more complex sequences of skills and action to be constructed. Another way of looking at this issue is that by reading books about counselling skills and observing skilled practitioners at work trainees become more aware of the subtle aspects of particular skills, and as a result may go through a phase of being quite critical about their own performance. The sense of getting worse before you get better should therefore be regarded as a sign of meaningful learning.

Conclusions

Skilled performance of a counselling role relies on a sufficient degree of competence in a broad set of component skills. The main counselling skills have been outlined in this chapter. The importance of these skills has been established through several decades of training, research and practice. The approach that has been taken in this chapter has been to regard *all* of these skills as equivalent in importance. They are not viewed as existing on different levels of sophistication or complexity, or as being activated only at certain stages in the counselling process. Instead, the position that is recommended is that a counsellor should be poised at any moment to use any skill that may be required, and may be at hand. This sounds impossibly demanding. However, in practice counsellors rarely pay much attention to the skills they are using. Being in a counselling relationship requires paying a lot of attention to the client, and then paying enough attention to what lies ahead: where are we going with this issue? As with skills learning in any domain of life, training in counselling skills involves going through a phase of awkward self-consciousness around one's performance. But this passes. From time to time counsellors go back to the practice ground or rehearsal room and revisit their skills. Occasionally they may attend master classes to be re-energized in their work through exposure to deep expertise and craftsmanship. And being able to review one's skills use in these ways is built on having put in the work, during initial training, to acquire a repertoire of skills and a vocabulary for talking about skills.

Suggested further reading

Counselling skills are multifaceted, and as a result hard to define and describe in words. Anyone interested in understanding the nature of different skills is advised to consult more than one source of information. Excellent descriptions of counselling skills can be found in the following classic texts:

Egan, G. (2004) *The Skilled Helper: A Problem Management and Opportunity Development Approach to Helping*, 8th edn. Belmont, CA: Wadsworth.

Hill, C.E. (2004) *Helping Skills: Facilitating Exploration, Insight and Action*, 2nd edn. Washington, DC: American Psychological Association.

Ivey, A.E., Ivey, M.B. and Zalaquett, C.P. (2010) *Intentional Interviewing and Counseling: Facilitating Client Development in a Multicultural Society*, 4th edn. Pacific Grove, CA: Brooks/Cole.

In order to avoid any risk that this chapter might become overcomplex, the research evidence that supports the role of particular skills, and the way they are applied, has not been addressed. A good starting point for readers interested in this research literature is:

Hill, C.E. (ed.) (2001) *Helping Skills: The Empirical Foundation*. Washington, DC: American Psychological Association.

The counselling menu: goals, tasks and methods

You asked me there about what's in the leaflet — about the counselling. Well, basically, it's just a chance for you to talk about anything that might be bothering you. Sometimes people with your condition get worried about what is going to happen to them, or find that the way that people in their family see them has changed, or get worn out by the stress of coming to the hospital every week, or even maybe they get angry with the attitudes of some of the doctors. It could be any of these things, or even things that are quite different. Some people don't seem to need to talk to me about what's happening, and others do. Everyone is different. What I try to do is to be flexible in terms of whatever it is you need. Like if it was just to check out a few things, or whether you wanted more time to talk things through. One of the things I sometimes do for people who are interested is suggest books and leaflets they can read, and websites, written by people who have had the same illness as you. Some people just use me as a shoulder to cry on — that's all right too. It's whatever will help you get through it. I would never force this on you. It's up to you to use the counselling or not.

Introduction

Throughout this book people are understood as being actively engaged in responding to the challenges that life presents them. A person seeking help is an active agent, a constructor or creator (in collaboration with others) of their world, someone with choice and responsibility. While it is obvious that events may take place that are outside of the control, or awareness of a person, the position adopted by a counsellor is always that a person has the capacity to decide what they make of these events, and to shape how they incorporate what happens into their personal niche or life space. People can be understood as carrying out their everyday lives within a personal niche assembled from the immense richness and complexity of the culture, society and nature that is known to them. As discussed in earlier chapters, the cultural resources available to both the person seeking help and their counsellor, in the form of ideas, beliefs, practices, rituals, narratives, and tools for thinking and feeling and decision-making, form the backdrop to any counselling relationship. An essential element of the skill of counselling therefore involves finding the right approach for each individual. There are huge differences between individuals in terms of what they need, or find helpful. For example, some people resolve issues by expressing their feelings and emotions, while others prefer a more cognitive approach. Some people look for a helper to take the lead, while for other people the sense of being in personal control may be of paramount importance within a counselling relationship.

The concept of the counselling menu

A useful way of thinking about how all these possibilities can be incorporated into a counselling relationship is to use the concept of the *counselling menu*. We are all familiar with restaurant menus, which list the various dishes and beverages that may be available. However, that kind of menu implies an order or structure – starter, followed by main course, followed by dessert – that is typically associated with the expectation that a diner will partake of a full meal (even though some people may decide to opt for only one item – visiting a restaurant merely to sample its chocolate cake). By contrast, the kind of micro-counselling that takes place when counselling is embedded in other work roles is necessarily more flexible, time-limited and improvizational, often more like a snack than a full meal. A more appropriate menu image for embedded counselling, therefore, is the kind of drop-down menu that is universally used in PC and internet applications – a set of options is revealed, which are not in any particular order, and clicking on one of these options may reveal another set of sub-options, and so on. Within this chapter, an imaginary counselling drop-down menu is proposed which incorporates three levels of decision-making. First, the person seeking help and the counsellor agree on the aims or *goals* of their work together. Second, having agreed the ultimate desired end point or goal, they identify what can be done now to make progress in relation to achieving that goal (the *task*). Finally, they need to decide on the best *method* for tackling that task.

Exercise 5.1: *Finding the right way to talk about preferences and choices*

In this chapter, the image or metaphor of the counselling menu is used to characterize a situation in which a client has a capacity to choose, and the person providing a service needs to be clear about what is on offer. There are other metaphors that might equally well be employed. The options for counselling could be described as on display in a shop window. The counsellor might talk in terms of using different modes of transport to take a journey. What other images or metaphors can you identify? Each metaphor that might be used introduces certain underlying or hidden assumptions. For example, a menu may imply nourishment, a show window may imply payment, and so on. So, which images or metaphors feel right to you in terms of conversations that you might conduct with clients? It can be instructive to carry out this exercise in a group – a greater number of images are likely to be generated.

Clarity about goals, tasks and methods is particularly important in embedded counselling situations. A specialist counsellor may have the scope to meet with a client over several weekly sessions, and to allow an agreement over goals, tasks and methods to emerge gradually from their preliminary conversations. Such a counsellor may also have enough time to coach the client in using the methods which are specifically favoured within their theoretical approach. In micro-counselling, by contrast, typically there is not enough time to get sidetracked on irrelevant goals, tasks or unproductive methods, and then to renegotiate a more productive way of working. Also, crucially, there are powerful ethical issues associated with deciding on which goals and tasks are appropriate to micro-counselling, and which may be too risky to attempt within this kind of relationship. Some problems or therapeutic goals require more time, and more specialist expertise, than may be available from a practitioner who is offering counselling alongside another helping role, and would therefore be unlikely to be included in a typical 'menu' offered by a practitioner whose counselling was embedded within another professional role.

The purpose of the counselling menu is to maximize the possibility that a counselling conversation has an appropriate *focus*, so that the person is given every opportunity to talk about what they need to talk about in a way that is most effective for them. An additional purpose is to open up a space for engaging in dialogue around goals, tasks and methods that may *not* be suitable for counselling, or for the actual counselling relationship that is on offer, and the question of where and how these aspirations might be pursued.

Some of the ways in which a counselling menu may be applied in practice are illustrated in the following scenarios:

Sandro is highly fearful of dental treatment. One of the nurses at the surgery has had some training in working with phobic patients, so arranges a consultation a few days before his scheduled treatment. She begins by asking him what he wants to achieve. He says he is not sure. 'Well,' she replies 'some people who worry about going to the dentist believe that it's something that is really big for them. For example, they may be afraid of other similar situations such as going to the doctor, and so they want to look at the whole issue of what is happening for them in these situations. Other people are just looking for a strategy that will help them to cope better with seeing their dentist'. Sandro indicated that he was just looking for a way of dealing with his fear of being in the dentist's chair. The nurse then asked whether he had any idea of what might help. 'Yes, I think I basically need to learn how to relax – I just get myself so wound up'. The nurse then outlined methods that could be used to manage fear and anxiety, including relaxation techniques on tape, cognitive reframing training, and a valium prescription. Together, they discussed what would be best for him.

Agnes is a social worker who works in a centre that offers support to families. Inez is a single mother, with three young children, who has been struggling with a number of issues around controlling her children's behaviour, as well as ongoing financial problems. Inez comes to trust Agnes, and asks if they can have some time together on their own to talk about 'stuff I need to get off my chest'. When they meet and begin to talk, Inez breaks down and begins to talk in a confused way about her experience of being sexually abused as a child, and how seeing her own children 'just brings it all back' and 'paralyses me'. As they talk, Agnes begins to sense that Inez is ready to face these memories and find ways of moving beyond them. She asks 'I am wondering is what you are talking about, this stuff, been around for a while, but now is something you want to really look at and put behind you?' Inez agrees: 'I want to sort it all out and put my life on a different track'. Agnes explains that she does not think that it would be a good idea for her to offer to do this with Inez: 'I haven't had the right kind of training to feel that I could give you what you need – also, as you know, with my caseload it would be very hard to guarantee that we could meet like this regularly enough'. They explore the other resources that might be available to Inez in terms of long-term therapy, especially a specialist counselling service and a survivors of sexual abuse group offered by a women's co-operative. They then agreed on the 'bits that I might be able to help you with myself', such as support for making an appointment with one of these services, and 'looking at how the therapy might make a difference to the way you are with the kids'.

What is being described in these examples is not a formal system of assessment and contracting, but an approach to practice in which the counsellor is mindful of the fact that the person seeking help has their own ideas about what they need, and is aware that there are many possible ways of meeting these needs. It is important to recognize that for anyone involved in offering counselling embedded with another role, such as that of teacher, doctor, social worker or nurse, facilitating a discussion of goals, tasks and methods does not necessarily require a high degree of training and theoretical knowledge, but can rely on a basic common-sense understanding of life. In the example of Inez, for instance, the social worker had not received much training in counselling or psychotherapy, but was able to make use of her gut response to her client, which was along the lines of 'this would be too much for me to handle'. She was also able to recognize that, within the very broad life goal that Inez had identified ('put my life on a different track'), it was possible to isolate one sub-task ('looking at the effect on the kids') that was clearly within her competence to deliver. In the case of Sandro, by contrast, the nurse responding to his fear of dental treatment had received specific training in relation to this type of problem, and was prepared to explore a sophisticated menu of possible sub-tasks and alternative methods with her patient.

The rest of this chapter provides a framework of a counselling menu that may be applicable in many counselling settings. The precise menu that is on offer in any particular counselling situation will, of course, depend on the counsellor and the organizational setting in which they are based.

Clarifying the client's goals

It is essential to recognize that a person seeking help always has an aim, or a *goal*, in entering a counselling relationship. A counselling goal can be defined as a preferred state of affairs, or outcome, that the person seeking help and their counsellor have agreed to work towards. There is always something that a person *wants* or desires, some area of discomfort with life that they wish to change, that brings a person into a counselling situation. The question 'why now?' is potentially one of the most useful things for a counsellor to keep in mind, as a person begins to talk about their troubles. Similarly, when the person has resolved the issue, has received enough of what they want or need, when they have achieved enough of their goals, then they know that they have had enough counselling and that it is time to stop.

The concept of *goal* can be used to refer to aims and objectives that may be all-encompassing, or quite specific. *Life goals* are overarching issues or existential questions that give shape to a person's life. Examples of life goals are:

- Can I move beyond the memory of the abuse I received in childhood to the point where I can believe in my own value as a person?
- What do I need to do to prove that I am good enough to satisfy my mother or father?
- My Mum and Dad are Sikh through and through, but I grew up in England – how do I define who I am as a person?

Life goals reflect personal issues that permeate all aspects of a person's life or social niche. For instance, 'moving beyond the memory of abuse' may be associated with difficulties and tensions in intimate and work relationships in the capacity to be alone, and in the capacity to make plans for the future. *Specific* goals, by contrast, refer to more limited situations or scenarios. Examples of specific goals include:

- How can I feel less anxious in interviews?
- What can I do to convey to my doctor that I don't need to take this medication any longer?
- I am caught between wanting to retire and feeling that I should continue to bring home a salary – how can I make a decision?

For practitioners whose counselling function is embedded within other work roles and responsibilities, it is much easier to respond effectively to specific goals than to more global issues. The latter tend to be associated with a massive personal agenda of beliefs, dilemmas and concerns that may need to be explored: to tackle life issues in a satisfactory manner requires plenty of time. Psychotherapists and specialist counselling agencies are in a better position to work with life goals than are counsellors whose practice is embedded in other professional roles. On the other hand, specific or situational goals may be addressed very effectively within one or two brief conversations. It is important to keep in mind that not everyone who seeks counselling wants to deal with issues at the 'life goal' level – a person who has identified a specific goal may prefer to focus on that one issue, rather than being expected to open out all aspects of their life, as might happen in psychotherapy. Nevertheless, when working with specific goals, it is important to keep in mind that ultimately they can always be understood as reflecting broader life goals, and are nested within these wider goals. For example, a person who starts off by wanting to talk about 'telling my doctor that I don't want medication' may end up realizing that such a goal represents part of a broader personal agenda that they come to describe as 'moving beyond the memory of the abuse I received in childhood to the point where I can believe in my own value as a person and stand up for what I want with people who I perceive as powerful and dominant'.

Exercise 5.2: *Reflecting on your own experience of goals*

Take a few minutes to reflect on occasions in your life where you have been a client in some kind of counselling. How clear were you about what you wanted from counselling – what your goals were? To what extent, and in what ways, did these goals shift over the course of counselling? What did your counsellor do to help you to clarify your goals, and to check whether they understood what your goals were? Finally, what have you learned from this exercise that is relevant for your practice as a counsellor?

It is important to be clear about the difference between the concept of *goal*, and the similar concept of *problem*. A personal goal is always phrased in an *active* and *positive* way, whereas problem language talks of burdens and inadequacies. A goal can be regarded as similar to a personal quest – a question that the person is trying to explore and answer. It can be useful, therefore, for a counsellor who is talking with a person about their goals to try to use active, positive language which reinforces the person's strengths, so that counselling goals are not perceived as indicators of failure but as opportunities for development and connection. For instance, Sheila was a participant in a project that was designed to help women return to work after having been carers. She described herself as crippled by fear at interviews, and not able to tell those interviewing her about her relevant experience and qualities. In a consultation session with one of the project tutors, Sheila was asked what she would like to talk about. She replied that 'I have a problem with interviews. I am wracked with nerves. I am just so anxious all the time'. The tutor responded by saying, 'Is this something that we could look at more closely? From what you have told me before about this, I'm thinking that what you want to be able to do is to make sure that you can give these interviewers every chance to know about your experience and qualities, and that the nervousness gets in the way. Would that be a reasonable way to describe what we might aim to be able to work on together?' If the tutor had accepted Sheila's initial formulation of the issue, as 'something that is wrong with me and needs to be fixed', he would have reinforced a way of describing the situation that portrayed Sheila as deficient and passive. Rephrasing the issue in active and positive language has the effect of allowing Sheila's desired positive outcome to be more clearly acknowledged ('letting the interviewers know about your good qualities') and enables the status of anxiety to be diminished from a totalizing entity to being something that merely 'gets in the way'. This use of language on the part of the tutor immediately opened up a space for different kinds of things to happen within their conversation.

In some forms of psychotherapy and specialist counselling, the therapist may spend quite a lot of time negotiating a contract with the client, which includes targets or treatment goals. It is seldom either necessary or possible to undertake this kind of formal contracting in embedded micro-counselling situations. What is helpful is to invite the person to talk about their goals. It is essential to be on the alert for whatever the person might say about what they want (their goals), whenever this might take place in a counselling conversation, and to reflect back and check out that what the counsellor has picked up is accurate.

There are many ways of encouraging a conversation about goals. Some potentially useful counsellor statements include:

> 'I can hear from what you are saying that . . . However, in an ideal scenario, if everything was just as you wanted it to be, how would it be different? How do you want things to be?'
>
> 'Can you say what it is you would like to gain from talking to me about . . .?'

'You have described your problem . . . Are you able to tell me what you would hope to happen, if we can sort this problem out? What are you aiming for?'

(At the end of a counselling session): 'I was wondering – have you got what you needed from our discussion? Is there anything else you need?'

Much of the time, however, the specific goals that a person may have are implicit in the way that they talk about the problem for which they are seeking help. It is up to the counsellor to 'listen for goals', and then check out what they have heard, rather than paying attention only to problems.

It is essential to acknowledge that people who seek counselling may have enormous difficulties in explicitly articulating what their goals are. They may *know*, at a feeling or gut level, what they want, but they may not readily be able to put this into words.

There are at least three reasons why a person may not be able to explain clearly what their goals are. First, the goal or purpose may be associated with a vague feeling – 'I'm just exhausted all the time and I don't know what it's about', or 'there's a big empty space inside me'. In these cases, it is as though the person's body has a sense of purpose and direction in somehow using tiredness or the sense of an empty space to indicate that something is wrong. In these circumstances, all the person can do is to be willing to follow where their body is leading – the end point is far from clear. A second difficulty that some people have in talking about what they want is that they know what their goal is, but are afraid or ashamed to acknowledge it. For example, Danny knew full well that he needed help to talk about his sexuality and 'come out' as gay, but would not say this until he was fully convinced that his chosen 'counsellor' (for him, a youth worker based at the local community centre) would respond in a non-critical and sympathetic manner. It was only when he felt safe enough with his counsellor that Danny was able to articulate his goals. A third type of difficulty that some people have in expressing their goals for counselling is that they may never have had the opportunity to reflect on what they want, so they can only convey a confusing jumble of reasons. To return to an example used earlier in this chapter, Sunita had a sense that she had never been able to belong, or to have a sense of fitting in, but it was only when she attended a counselling skills evening class, and took part in personal development exercises, that this vague awareness crystallized into a desire to explore and define her cultural identity.

In situations where a person has difficulty being clear about their goals, it is important for a counsellor to be willing to work with the person around the best mutual understanding of their aims that is possible, rather than wait until a fully crystallized goal statement can be formulated. What is important is for the person seeking help, and the person offering counselling, to have a sufficient level of agreement over the goals they are working together to pursue, so that they are 'on the same wavelength'.

To summarize: the idea of *goal* is important in counselling because it provides a way of structuring and organizing what happens in a counselling session. It is the ultimate reference point for whatever happens in counselling. A person seeking help will gauge whatever is being discussed in counselling against the touchstone of whether it is helping them to move closer to their goals. The concept of goal also provides a way of making a link between the immediate reason the person gives for seeking counselling ('I need to talk to someone about getting into fights with my Dad', 'I feel sad a lot of the time') and the broader direction of the person's life ('can I accept myself as a person in my own terms?') – specific goals are always linked to broader existential questions of meaning, purpose and identity, even if these bigger questions tend to remain firmly in the background in the majority of micro-counselling encounters. The notion of the person's goal acts as a reminder that the counselling space exists for a purpose – it is a kind of 'time out' to enable a person to repair their personal niche. It is also a reminder that the person seeking help is an active participant in life, a person who has purposes rather than problems and symptoms.

Counselling tasks

Although agreement over goals is essential as a way of ensuring that the person and counsellor are working towards the same ends, it is very difficult to do anything in counselling that will directly impact on a goal. What is necessary instead is to identify specific *tasks* whose completion can allow the person to take a step nearer their goal.

The model of counselling suggested in this book assumes a process through which a person who is troubled in some way by tensions within their relationships or life space, and has a sense of wanting to do something about it (goals), seeks out a counsellor and negotiates the construction of a safe space within which they can talk through their problem. But what happens next? What does 'talking through' mean in practice? Within the model of counselling skill, the specific business of counselling is understood as being based on the engagement in, and completion of, a set of distinctive counselling *tasks*. A counselling task can be defined as a sequence of actions carried out by a person in collaboration with a counsellor in order to be able to get on with their life. A task is something that the person and the counsellor undertake together. For any specific counselling task, there are a potentially infinite number of different *methods* that can be used to complete it. The safest and most helpful practice occurs when the person and their counsellor *decide together* the task in which they are engaged, and agree on the method that they will use to tackle the task.

The concepts of *task* and *method* are central to the framework for counselling practice that is introduced in this book. In the following chapters, a range of basic counselling tasks are discussed, including:

- talking though an issue in order to understand things better
- making sense of a puzzling or problematic personal reaction to a situation
- problem-solving, planning and decision-making
- changing behaviour
- dealing with difficult feelings and emotions
- finding, analysing and acting on information
- undoing self-criticism and enhancing self-care
- negotiating a life transition
- dealing with difficult or painful relationships.

The precise labels and definitions given to these tasks are inevitably fairly arbitrary. Experienced counsellors evolve their own ways of describing tasks. In practice, a counselling episode may focus on a single facet of one of these tasks (e.g. concentrating on understanding barriers to change, rather than working through a whole behaviour change sequence). Sometimes, an episode may encompass two or three interlocking tasks which are pursued at the same time (e.g. *exploring* how I *feel* in relation to a *life transition*).

Being able to work with these tasks represents a set of basic competences for anyone involved in offering counselling relationships. These tasks reflect competences that are firmly based in an everyday, common-sense ability to cope with life. We are all able to hold meaningful conversations, make sense of puzzling reactions to situations, solve problems, and so on. Being a good counsellor involves being willing to examine one's own individual strengths and weaknesses in relation to being able to carry out these tasks, developing flexibility and sensitivity in relation to engaging with other people around the tasks, and being open to learning new methods and strategies for task resolution. A good counsellor is someone who knows the 'ins and outs' of the kinds of tasks that arise in their practice, and are able to adapt or improvize methods of task completion that are appropriate to the individual with whom they are working.

Box 5.1: *An example of a task model: counselling in dementia*

Within the last decade, new methods for the early diagnosis of dementia, and the availability of drug treatments that can slow down the development of Alzheimer's disease, mean that there is an increasing number of people who have received a diagnosis of dementia yet may expect to live with their families, at a relatively good level of functioning, for many years. The diagnosis of dementia raises strong feelings, and evokes powerful negative images, not only in people with dementia but also within their surrounding family and community. In addition, it may be difficult to cope with the gradual memory loss that is associated with the disease. For these reasons, increasing attention is being given to the potential role of counselling at the time of diagnosis as a means of helping people with dementia, and their families deal with this event. In some research carried out by Weaks *et al.* (2006), people with dementia and their families were interviewed regarding their experience of the diagnosis, and the issues with which they had been confronted in the first six months following the diagnosis. Analysis of these interviews lead to the identification of a set of psychotherapeutic tasks that seemed particularly relevant to people in this situation:

- exploring the possibility of life as normal
- evaluating the usefulness of different sources of information
- understanding the changing roles within their families and wider social network
- understanding and dealing with the emotional process
- addressing deep philosophical questions, such as the possibility of loss of identity
- embracing and coping with social stigma
- creating a new and different identity
- telling and retelling their story
- find a way through the health system.

These tasks could be fulfilled using a variety of methods including formal/specialist counselling, embedded counselling from doctors, community nurses and clergy, participation in self-help groups and reading. The identification of these tasks makes it possible to design appropriate care systems, train and supervise staff, and enable people with dementia and their families to know what to expect.

Methods

Any counselling task can be carried out using a number of different *methods*. People can learn, or change, or reconstruct their personal niche, in a variety of ways, depending on their upbringing, cultural background, and temperament, and on their awareness of change resources and methods that are available within their social world. Theories of counselling, psychotherapy and psychology, religious teachings and practices, and self-help books, as well as everyday common sense, afford a vast repertoire of ways of dealing with problems in living. In any counselling situation, it is up to the person and the counsellor to decide together what they can do to complete a task.

Although the range of task-resolution methods that can be employed is potentially limitless, and continually being expanded as a result of human inventiveness and creativity, the toolkit of methods used by most counsellors can be categorized in terms of five very broadly defined types of method:

- *Conversation*. The counsellor and the person seeking help talk about the issue or task, and allow solutions and new understandings to emerge from their

TABLE 5.1 Sources of information on counselling methods

- Burns, G.W. (ed.) (2010) *Happiness, Healing, Enhancement: Your Casebook Collection for Applying Positive Psychology in Therapy*. New York: Wiley.
- Carrell, S.E. (2001) *The Therapist's Toolbox*. Thousand Oaks, CA: Sage Publications.
- Greenberg, L.S., Rice, L.N. and Elliott, R. (1993) *Facilitating Emotional Change: The Moment-by-moment Process*. New York: Guilford Press.
- Hall, E., Hall, C., Stradling, P. and Young, D. (2006) *Guided Imagery: Creative Interventions in Counselling and Psychotherapy*. London: Sage Publications.
- Hecker, L.L. and Deacon, S.A. (eds) (2006) *The Therapist's Notebook: Homework, Handouts, and Activities for Use in Psychotherapy*. New York: Routledge.
- Hecker, L.L. and Sori, C.F. (eds) (2007) *The Therapist's Notebook, Volume 2: More Homework, Handouts, and Activities for Use in Psychotherapy*. New York: Routledge.
- King, A. (2001) *Demystifying the Counseling Process: A Self-help Handbook for Counselors*. Needham Heights, MA: Allyn & Bacon.
- Leahy, R.L. (2003) *Cognitive Therapy Techniques: A Practitioner's Guide*. New York: Guilford Press.
- Seiser, L. and Wastell, C. (2002) *Interventions and Techniques*. Maidenhead: Open University Press.
- Sori, C.F. and Hecker, L.L. (eds) (2008) *The Therapist's Notebook, Volume 3: More Homework, Handouts, and Activities for Use in Psychotherapy*. New York: Routledge.
- Timulak, L. (2011) *Developing your Counselling and Psychotherapy Skills and Practice*. London: Sage Publications.
- Yalom, I. (2002) *The Gift of Therapy: Reflections on Being a Therapist*. London: Piatkus.

dialogue. This method relies on the vast richness of language, and its potential for redescribing and reconceptualizing events. Conversation, or 'just talking' is almost certainly the most frequently used method in any counselling relationship. To return to the metaphor of the software menu employed earlier in this chapter – conversation is the 'default setting' for a counselling relationship.

- *Specific interventions developed by counsellors and physiotherapists.* Either the counsellor or the person seeking help may suggest or devise activities or routines that can be applied to resolve the issue. Within the counselling world, cognitive-behaviour therapy (CBT) in particular represents a rich resource of activities, such as relaxation training, homework assignments, initiating rewards for preferred behaviour, identifying and challenging irrational beliefs, and much else. However, there is also a wide range of interventions that have been devised within other therapy approaches (see Table 5.1).

- *Arts-based creative activities.* There are many counselling tasks that can be resolved by drawing, painting, imaginative writing and enactment. For example, a person struggling to come to terms with difficult and painful emotions may find it very helpful to express their feelings in a picture, or write a letter to someone with whom they feel angry.

- *Cultural resources.* Drawing on the everyday practices that are used within the person's cultural world to express feelings, maintain connectedness and maintain a sense of personal identity. For instance, many cultural resources that can potentially make a difference to someone who may be depressed and lacking in hope and purpose, including physical exercise such as jogging, voluntary work, walking in the countryside, spiritual practices such as meditation and prayer, and attending the cinema or theatre. The role of the counsellor in relation to these methods is not to implement them within a counselling session, but to help the person to explore and find the cultural resources that are most personally meaningful, to provide support and guidance during the stage of starting to get involved, and then if necessary to help the person to get the maximum value out of the cultural activities they have undertaken in terms of making an impact on their initial problem in living.

● *The personal resources of the counsellor*. Underpinning all of these other methods is the capacity of the counsellor to apply their experience of life, and personal accomplishments and learning, to address the needs of the person seeking help.

Further ideas about counselling methods can be found in the sources listed in Table 5.1.

The key skill to using the counselling menu: shared decision-making

Having described the nature of goals, tasks and methods, and the various possibilities associated with each of these types of counselling activity, it may be worth while at this point to review briefly the basic assumptions about counselling and helping that underpin this approach. These are:

● The person who seeks help is already actively engaged in trying to resolve their problems.

● Whatever the counsellor does, the person seeking help will modify and adapt what is offered to meet their needs – the person is far from being a passive recipient of 'expert help'.

● There is no one process or mechanism of learning and change that is right for everyone – there are a multiplicity of potentially helpful learning/change processes, and each individual who seeks help will have their own preferences among them.

● There is not a counsellor alive who is competent to work with all the possible therapeutic methods and strategies that exist – each practitioner has their own knowledge base, and strengths and weaknesses.

The reality of any counselling situation, therefore, is that there are multiple possibilities on both sides. There are many things that the person seeking help definitely wants, definitely does not want, and may be willing to try out. There are other things that the counsellor is either able or not able to offer. It is the job of the counsellor to be able to mediate between these two sets of possibilities. The idea of the *counselling menu* represents a way of arriving at a decision within the shortest possible time concerning what to do and where to start.

A key competence for any counsellor, therefore, is to be able to create opportunities for discussion about the range of choices that are on offer. This competence is based on two important areas of counsellor self-awareness. The first is an awareness of the values that inform their practice, and the second is an awareness of the use of language (discussed in Chapter 9 and in other places throughout this book).

The values dimension of negotiating around goals, tasks and methods is associated with the act of positioning the person as someone who is worthwhile, who knows what is best for them, and whose views are worth knowing. Each opening that the counsellor makes, to invite the person to say what they want, is affirming these values, and at the same time expressing the genuine interest, caring and curiosity that the counsellor holds towards that person. By contrast, every time that the counsellor pre-empts a decision about what is to happen in the counselling session, no matter how sensitively and 'nicely' this is done, places the counsellor in a 'I know best' position, which negates these values.

At one level, it does not matter what words a counsellor uses, as long as these words reflect the core values and spirit of counselling. At another level, the words matter as well, because it is all too easy to slip into using the language of the 'expert', particularly when the person seeking help may be feeling vulnerable and uncertain. Some examples of language use that can contribute to shared decision-making are:

- Explaining how you work as a counsellor. For example: 'I'd like to say a few words about the way I work as a counsellor. Would it be OK to do that now – I don't want to interrupt anything you might be going to say? The main thing for me is that we are on the same wavelength, that we agree on what you are wanting to get from counselling, and what's the best way to go about achieving what you want. Does that make sense? What I need to do, therefore, is sometimes I need to just check out with you that we both understand what we are doing at that point. Would that be OK?'

- Explaining basic principles: 'In my experience as a counsellor, I have found that different people need different things from me. Some people want me to listen, other people want me to give them feedback, and so on. It's really important for me that this counselling is right for you. At any time, if you feel that what we're doing is not helping, then I would want you to let me know. So we can change what we're doing, and get things right for you'.

- Asking the person about how they perceive goals, tasks and methods. For example: 'You have told me a bit about your problems. I'd like to ask you – what is it that you want to get from counselling? What's your aim or goal?'; 'I feel I have a pretty good idea of what you want to get from counselling. To get there, we need to take things step by step. At this point, do you have an idea of what you feel you need to do first?'; 'You've talked quite a lot about feeling angry. Would that be something we could spend a bit of time looking at now? I guess that there are different ways we could look at this. Do you want to shout, or hit that cushion, or something else – what do you feel would be the best way for us to approach this right now?'

- Checking out that the person's goal, task or method statement has been understood. For example: 'Can I just check this out, what you are saying is that what you want to do now is . . .'.

- Inviting the person to identify what has worked for them in the past: 'When you have felt stuck with an angry feeling before, is there anything that has helped you to deal with it? Is that something that is relevant for what we might do now?'

- Following the completion of a task, checking whether what happened was helpful: 'We have spent a few minutes now talking through that issue about getting closer to people. We seem to have reached an end point of that, at least for the moment. Before we go on to look at some of the other issues you mentioned earlier, I'd just like to ask – was the way we approached it that helpful? Is there anything that I could have done, or that you could have done, that would be more helpful?'

These strategies serve to punctuate the ongoing flow of the counselling conversation with brief opportunities where the person seeking help and their counsellor can reorient themselves in relation to the person's goals, and remain on track. The sentences and phrases used in the examples given above should not, of course, be regarded as a fixed 'script' to be followed by all counsellors – as with everything else in counselling, it is important for the practitioner to develop a style in which principles and competences are integrated with their own personal and cultural identity.

An example of goals, methods and tasks in practice: Joey's emotional journey

Joey is a long-term prisoner nearing the end of a sentence for violent robbery. During his time in prison, Joey has experienced several episodes of what the medical officer has termed 'depression', and has made several attempts to take his own life. In his current prison, there is a well-established peer counselling service in which prisoners can be trained to provide emotional support to others. Joey has formed a good relationship with one of the peer helpers, who has spent many hours listening to Joey's story of a childhood lacking in love, care and consistency. It has been very important to Joey to learn that there could be someone who was able to accept him, and like him, even when they knew about some of the things he had done. Although Joey and his peer counsellor had never explicitly agreed on the goals of their work, each of them knew that what Joey wanted was to know that he could be acceptable as a person, particularly in respect of his emotions and feelings. After many of these sessions, the helper observed that Joey seemed to talk in a way that was 'just full of pain'. There was an extended silence, broken eventually by Joey's admission that he felt an emotional pain all the time, but believed that it was not what 'a man' would do to admit this, or even worse to express it: 'I can't afford to lose control – look what can happen when I do'. The helper responded by saying 'this is where we have got to – I'm wondering whether this pain is the next thing for us to look at'. Over their next meetings, Joey and his helper worked together to find some ways that Joey could express his pain within their counselling sessions. Once they had made some progress with this, Joey announced that he could see that he needed to figure out how to let his wife know about his pain: 'She knows there is something wrong, but I never tell her what it is – it's keeping us apart – when she visits, sometimes I just sit there in silence because I can't speak – who knows what she thinks is going on?' This triggered a new focus for the next counselling sessions – how Joey communicated with his wife, and what he could do differently.

Having decided that 'the pain' was something that they would look at together, Joey and his helper talked about how to set about this difficult and demanding task. At first, Joey could not think of anything at all that he could do to express what he felt. His helper made a list of activities that he had personally tried himself, and some that he had read about. These included: finding the part of the body where the feeling was located; making a drawing; writing a poem; working through a self-help book about emotions; keeping an emotion diary; and 'just talking about it'. Joey was worried about any activity that involved writing things down on paper, because he did not think he had the capacity to keep pieces of paper private. He was worried that any overt expression of emotion could lead to him being sent to the psychiatric unit. He said he would think about the suggestions between sessions. At the next meeting with his helper, he brought a piece of paper and a pencil and began, silently, to write from his pain: 'I am inside. I am crushed . . .'. At the end of their meeting he carefully tore the piece of paper into very small pieces. At the next session he talked about how he had allowed the pain to be in control during a workout in the prison gym. Some weeks later, he enrolled for an art class, and made clay sculptures of pain. Gradually, he found his own way to do what he needed to do.

This example emphasizes the improvizational nature of counselling. Joey and his peer helper were not operating in an ideal environment in terms of the level of privacy that was available to them. In addition, the peer helper was aware that he had relatively little training and experience in working with the type of issue that Joey was presenting. Nevertheless, between them they were able to talk about what they could do, and find a way forward. The case therefore also exemplifies the basic resourcefulness of people. The counselling that Joey received was life-changing for him (and possibly also life-saving) in spite of the limited training and experience of his counsellor: he and the counsellor had a relationship that was strong enough to hang in together until they could discover a method that would work for them.

This example illustrates two of the specific counselling tasks that are discussed more fully in later chapters – *dealing with feelings and emotion*, and *changing behaviour* – and describes a range of different methods that were used to achieve these tasks. Each of the tasks undertaken by Joey involved using the secure space provided by the relationship with a counsellor to deal with an issue arising from a difficulty within the person social niche or life space. For instance, the world that Joey lived in had silenced him in relation to a bundle of emotions that he came to describe as his 'pain'. And the way that he had learned to communicate with his wife no longer reflected the values that he wished to espouse in his family life. His discussions with his helper-counsellor allowed him an opportunity to reflect on what was happening in his life in relation to these issues, and develop strategies for doing things differently in future.

Being on the alert for things going wrong

In an 'ideal' counselling conversation, which rarely happens, a person will explore an issue with the help of the counsellor, will arrive at a new understanding or plan of action, will learn something useful about themselves, and will leave happy. Alas, there are many things that can happen to disrupt this ideal script. For example, there can be a breakdown, rupture or falling-out in the counselling relationship, the person may become suicidal or a risk to others, the person may have a panic attack, or other situations may arise that cut across any attempt to make progress around basic counselling tasks. An important competence in any counselling situation, therefore, involves routinely *monitoring* what is happening, and knowing what to do if some kind of crisis occurs. At such moments, the counsellor may need to interrupt the ongoing flow of the counselling dialogue; for example, to check on issues of client safety. An ongoing task of counselling, therefore, involves monitoring the interaction and conversation in order to become aware of any possible threats to the integrity of the counselling space. If any such threats come to light, it is necessary for the person and the counsellor to review the situation together, and decide what action might be needed to change, strengthen or repair the space, or to look for sources of help outside of the counselling relationship that might be called upon. These issues are discussed further in Chapter 19.

Exercise 5.3: *Reviewing your competence as a counsellor*

What is on your menu – what can you offer as a counsellor? Make a list of the counselling goals, tasks and methods that you are familiar with, and have had experience of, at this point in your career as a counsellor. This list can include goals, tasks and methods that you have used in a counselling role, as well as those that you have encountered when seeking help yourself. What are the 'special' items on your menu – with which goals, tasks and methods do you feel most comfortable? What are the gaps on your menu? What are the goals, tasks and methods that you would like to know more about?

Conclusions

The model of counselling goals, tasks and methods described in this chapter is particularly appropriate to counselling that is embedded in other practitioner roles, where the helper and person may have a relatively short period of time in which to talk through a problem. If a practitioner is only able to offer 10 or 20 minutes to a person, it may still be perfectly possible to complete, or make substantial progress on a counselling task within that timescale. Also, if there can only be a relatively brief contact, it is much safer for a person to agree or 'contract' to engage in a specific task ('let's look at what these feelings are telling you', 'would it be useful to try to get a sense of all the information that might be relevant to making a decision about this issue?') than to attempt to engage in a discussion around major life goals.

The process of identifying and agreeing goals, tasks and methods within a counselling session provides a series of opportunities for dialogue and joint decision-making between the counsellor and the person seeking help. It is definitely *not* the intention of this chapter to imply that the counsellor should adopt an expert stance in which they diagnose and then prescribe the goals, tasks and methods that they deem appropriate to an individual client. Not at all! As far as possible, the person seeking help should take the lead. Key skills of any counsellor lie in being able to 'hit the pause button', to suspend the ongoing flow of what the client is saying at the right moments, so that goals, tasks and methods can be discussed and agreed, and in having a sufficiently wide repertoire of methods (and awareness of how they can be applied to particular counselling tasks) to allow the maximum degree of client choice. It is essential to keep in mind also that all this takes place in the context of a relationship between the counsellor and the person with whom they are working. The counselling relationship, and the tasks of counselling, need to be viewed as two sides of the same coin. For example, it is possible to define the strength and quality of the relationship between the counsellor and the person in terms of the extent to which they are able to communicate effectively with each other around goals, tasks and methods, their capacity to arrive at a shared agreement over which goals, tasks and methods to pursue, and their joint resourcefulness and creativity in imagining possible methods that might be helpful.

The following chapters explore the nature of some of the most commonly occurring counselling tasks, and suggest some methods that may be applicable to the resolution of these tasks. When reading these chapters, it is important to remember that the methods that are discussed are intended only as examples of what is possible, and certainly do not claim to represent a comprehensive list of all the counselling methods that might be envisaged. The idea of the counselling menu implies flexibility and diversity – there are as many different menus as there are counsellors, and the items on the menu can change according to the ingredients that are available, and the requirements of guests.

Suggested further reading

The general approach to counselling that is being recommended in this chapter has been strongly influenced by the writings of the American psychotherapist, Art Bohart, around his image of the 'active client'. In a series of important papers, Bohart and Tallman (1996) and Bohart (2000, 2006) have argued that it is essential to recognize that the person seeking help is highly purposeful and active in deciding what they want from a counselling session to the extent they will often covertly reinterpret suggestions or activities suggested by the counsellor to bring them in line with what they want to happen in counselling. The key source is:

Bohart, A.C. and Tallman, K. (1999) *How Clients Make Therapy Work: The Process of Active Self-healing*. Washington, DC: American Psychological Association.

Another valuable set of ideas about how to practise counselling in a manner that fits in to what the person seeking help believes will be most helpful for them, or has found to work for them in the past, lies in the writings of the 'common factors' group of therapy theorists, trainers and researchers, such as Scott Miller, Barry Duncan and Mark Hubble. Particularly relevant to this chapter is their way of using the 'client's theory of change' as the basis for collaboratively deciding on which methods to use in an individual case:

Duncan, B.L., Miller, S.D., Wampold, B.E. and Hubble, M.A. (eds) (2009) *The Heart and Soul of Change: Delivering What Works in Therapy,* 2nd edn. Washington, DC: American Psychological Association.

The ideas in this chapter are explored in more detail in:

Cooper, M. and McLeod, J. (2010) *Pluralistic Counselling and Psychotherapy*. London: Sage Publications.

CHAPTER 6

Negotiating organizational realities

It's really different seeing you when you come to my house, compared to when we've met in the hospital. I know your room in the clinic is quiet and private and all that. But there's still that feeling that someone might pop their head round the door with some test results or something. I feel more relaxed at home, more open. I guess the bottom line is that the hospital is a scary place. At least it is for patients like me.

Introduction

For anyone whose counselling work is embedded in another work role, such as nurse or social worker, preparation for counselling requires dealing with organizational factors that may either facilitate the possibility of effective counselling, or stand in the way. There are some aspects of embedded counselling that can be an advantage compared to counselling in a specialist agency. Practitioners providing embedded counselling may find that people seeking help already know them and trust them, by virtue of their previous professional relationship. Another advantage when counselling is embedded within other roles is that the helper or counsellor may be readily accessible to the person seeking help; for example, a community nurse may routinely visit a patient two or three times a week, or a teacher sees a student every day. On the other hand, there are also disadvantages to offering counselling that is embedded in another professional role; for example, the lack of suitable rooms in which to meet, and pressures on time.

The purpose of this chapter is to explore the organizational factors that shape and influence the kind of counselling that can be carried out. The chapter will focus both on ways of making sense of organizational realities, and ways of negotiating a path through these realities in order to allow meaningful and effective counselling to take place.

An overview of organizational issues in counselling

It is important to emphasize that counselling and psychotherapy are *always* influenced by the organizational context in which they take place. Many practitioners have an image of private practice therapy, or a therapist working in an NHS clinic, as operating in an environment in which some kind of 'pure' therapy can unfold. This is far from being the case. For example, private practice therapy is powerfully influenced by money – there may be a tendency for the therapist to want to do long-term therapy as a means of income maintenance. The experiences of clients receiving counselling or psychotherapy in the NHS or other health care systems is typically shaped by such factors as waiting lists and limits on the number of therapy sessions that can be offered. These are just some of the organizational factors that operate in these 'specialist' counselling settings. Rather than imagining that it is possible to practise counselling with no regard for organizational factors, it is more accurate to adopt a position that theories of counselling (such as the model of collaborative pluralistic counselling introduced in earlier chapters of this book) describe a set of *principles* that always need to be adapted and modified to operate in particular *contexts*. In this respect, the difference between specialist counsellors and practitioners of embedded counselling is that the former can disregard the organizational context while the latter are engaged in a constant struggle to create a satisfactory counselling niche within their organization. The difference is that in the former situation the fit between principles and context is worked out before the agency opens its doors, whereas in the situation of embedded counselling (at least at present) the negotiation of organizational realities tends to need to be conducted on a day-to-day basis by each practitioner.

Whenever counselling is to be offered to clients, there are a number of organizational or environmental issues that need to be sorted out in advance to enable a safe and productive counselling relationship to be possible. These include:

- Time – how much time is available for counselling, and how often might counselling take place?
- Space – can a suitable, comfortable private space be found?
- Confidentiality – who will know about what the person talks about? What are the limits of confidentiality?
- Freedom to express emotion – what happens if the person starts to cry, or shouts out loud in an angry voice?
- Voluntariness – to what extent is the person an informed user of counselling? Do they know what they are being offered? How do they learn this? Do they feel free to refuse an offer of counselling?
- Attitudes to counselling – what do service users, colleagues, and managers think and feel about counselling? Do they understand or approve of it, or is counselling a furtive activity?

Each of these factors can have a major impact on the ability to offer a counselling relationship. In addition, there are also organizational factors that relate to the capacity of the counsellor to be effective in their work on a sustained basis:

- The level of support that is available to the counsellor – are arrangements for supervision, consultation and peers' support in place? How acceptable is it to seek out a colleague for support following a demanding counselling session?
- Procedures for referring people in need to other practitioners and services. What happens if it emerges during a counselling conversation that the person would be better served by a specialist service, or an agency that could offer a greater amount of time or support? Are referral networks in place, and information available for clients (such as leaflets) about alternative sources of help? What happens if a person mentions suicidal intent during a counselling session?

This list of organizational factors indicates the extent to which careful planning is necessary before offering counselling within other helping roles. Specialist counselling agencies and clinics, who deliver counselling and nothing else, tend to devote a great deal of care and attention to developing protocols that address these issues. In general, practitioners whose counselling is embedded within other work roles tend to be given little time or encouragement to think through these issues, and carry out this kind of preparatory work. However, the cost to the person seeking help, and to the counsellor, of failing to do the organizational groundwork, can be substantial.

Where counselling is embedded in other practice roles, it is essential to develop mechanisms for both conveying to clients and service users that practitioners are open to talking about problems in living and feelings *and* signalling that in some instances the practitioner may recommend specialist sources of psychological or other help. There are many ways that this can be done, including written materials such as leaflets, posters and websites, face-to-face contact, and using other service users (e.g. peer support groups) as intermediaries. The ideal situation is for the person seeking counselling to be an informed consumer of this kind of service – to know what they want and how to get it.

Exercise 6.1: *The possibilities for counselling in your place of work*

Take a few moments to think about the counselling that you do, or would like to do, in your organizational setting. Make notes about the ways in which organizational factors impact on the following issues:

- the amount of time that you can spend with clients
- access to private spaces where you can talk without being overheard
- access to spaces that are comfortable and nicely decorated

- how acceptable it is to cry or express anger
- how acceptable it is to talk to a colleague about how upset you feel after speaking with a client
- the limits of confidentiality
- support for you to engage in counselling training
- support for you to get counselling supervision
- recognition and praise when you do good counselling work.

Finally, look through this list again and note down any possibilities that come to mind around how you can exert influence within different levels and areas of the organization to enhance the counselling that you do.

Building a personal and professional support network

A major limitation of many counselling skills textbooks and training courses is that they fail to give sufficient attention to the *systemic* dimension of providing counselling that is embedded within other organizational roles and responsibilities. Systems theory suggests that within any social group such as a family or organizational unit, the actions of individuals are mutually interconnected in a state of balance. Any shift within the pattern of connections can unbalance the system as a whole, and to prevent this the system develops mechanisms for counteracting or damping down changes that threaten the status quo. These ideas are important for practitioners involved in offering counselling embedded in other work roles, because they act as a reminder that being able to operate effectively as an embedded counsellor is not merely a matter of being able to respond sensitively to the needs of people who seek counselling, but additionally requires setting up a system of emotional care.

Alison was a nurse who had always had an interest in counselling, and had completed a substantial amount of counsellor training. She was appointed to a post of senior nurse within a haemodialysis unit for patients who had experienced kidney failure. Knowing that living with renal disease presented individuals with significant problems and stress, she anticipated that she would be able to give expression to her counselling skills in her new job. Over her first few months in post, Alison developed a counselling relationship with several patients, and felt satisfaction at being able to help some of them work through difficult life issues. Gradually, other staff on the unit recognized Alison's skills, and directed any patients with emotional and interpersonal difficulties in her direction. She began to be overloaded. When she made a request for protected time for this area of her work, and funding to pay for access to a counselling supervisor, she was accused of being 'elitist' and 'promising patients a service that we can't deliver'. She felt increasingly isolated in the unit, and began to look for another job.

Henry was one of the patients who was helped by Alison. His illness had resulted in loss of his job, bodily changes that made him feel physically unattractive and lethargic, and in time a deteriorating relationship with his wife, who was increasingly required to take on a role as carer. Henry felt that Alison understood what was happening to him, and helped him to talk through his problems in a non-judgemental manner to the point where he was beginning to be able to develop a more hopeful and constructive attitude towards his situation. He was 'devastated' when Alison said that she would not be able to continue with their occasional half-hour 'chats'. Temporarily encouraged by the suggestion that he might be able to see a clinical psychologist, he described himself as 'shattered' by the news that there was a nine-month waiting list for psychology.

This nursing example illustrates some of the issues that can emerge when practitioners begin to respond to the counselling needs of service users, without engaging in sufficient planning and organizational groundwork. In this medical unit, there existed a well-organized system which prioritized physical care, while giving limited time to the emotional and psychological needs of patients. The introduction of counselling (more attention to emotional and personal issues) unbalanced the system. Colleagues felt both appreciative and envious of the counselling that was taking place. Patients' expectations began to shift, which placed demands on the staff group as a whole. Either the system had to change (to accommodate counselling as an integral part of the nursing service) or the 'experiment' needed to come to an end to allow the system as a whole to resume its previous state of balance.

The support network that is required for embedded counselling to take place includes three main elements:

- *Managerial:* an understanding on the part of management of the role of counselling, the resources (time, money, space) that are required to be able to offer high-quality counselling help, and the nature of confidentiality (e.g. not expecting the details of every counselling conversation to be recorded in case notes).

- *Collegial:* acceptance by co-workers of how counselling operates and what it can achieve, potential demands on time and space, and the limitations of what can be provided (not expecting 'the counsellor' to be able to deal with everything).

- *External*: suitable arrangements for access to supervision and consultation, and avenues for referral of people who require more specialized services.

It can require a substantial investment of time and resourcefulness in order to build a personal and professional support network. Rather than attempting to achieve such a network through individual effort alone, it may be more effective, if at all possible, to find a group of colleagues who share an interest in the development of counselling within an organizational setting, and then work together towards these goals.

Developing a database of resources

Ethical practice in embedded counselling (as in any other area of professional activity) means being aware of the limitations of one's competence. In a situation where a practitioner in a field such as social work, nursing or education may only offer limited or intermittent parcels of time to people seeking counselling, or has received only limited training in responding to problems in living, it is essential to be prepared to refer people seeking help to specialized services whenever this is necessary. To be able to do this effectively requires assembling information about the services that are available locally, what they offer, and how to access them. In addition, some people who may benefit from engaging in embedded counselling with their nurse or teacher may also benefit from additional concurrent help that runs alongside this counselling relationship. There is a wide variety of activities that are potentially therapeutic for people in relation to resolving problems in living; self-help groups and websites, reading, faith community groups, community action groups, environmental groups, involvement in learning and education, voluntary work, and so on. It is important to keep in mind that effective counselling does not mean that the person's problem can only be resolved through a conversation or relationship with a counsellor – in many instances, effective counselling can involve supporting the person to find other resources within their community or personal niche that may be of assistance. Good counsellors (whether practitioners in embedded counselling roles or stand-alone counsellors) are informed about the resources that are available for the client group with whom they work, and where appropriate will act as a gateway to these resources.

Exercise 6.2: *Referral pathways and alternative sources of support for clients*

One of the things that inhibits many practitioners from responding to empathic opportunities presented by their clients is the worry that they will get in 'over their heads' – they will be overwhelmed by the severity and/or complexity of their client's difficulties, and perhaps even make things worse by doing the wrong thing. These are real fears. In embedded counselling scenarios, to work ethically within one's zone of competence involves developing practical knowledge about alternative sources of help that are available to your clients, and how these resources can be accessed. Take a few moments to make (a) a list of referral pathways and alternative sources of support in your area that might be relevant to your clients, and (b) a list of people you can consult for advice and guidance if you feel that your client might need more than you can offer them. Reflect on the adequacy of these lists – is there more that you need to do to strengthen your embedded counselling 'back-up' system?

Making sense of organizations

There are two perspectives from contemporary organizational theory that are valuable for counsellors who are endeavouring to make sense of the impact of organization factors on the process of counselling. Ideas about organizational *structure* refer to the way that an organization is arranged in terms of hierarchies of authority and access to knowledge. Ideas about organizational *climate* address questions around the 'feel' of an organization – what is it like to work there, or to be a user of its services?

Most large public-sector organizations, such as education and social service departments, and Health Trusts, operate in terms of a formal hierarchical management structure with clearly defined lines of responsibility. Typically, the work done by employees who actually interact with client, or with the public, is defined in terms of protocols, manuals and guidelines, which are intended to ensure that everyone engages in best practice. Also, the activities of front-line workers may be closely monitored in respect of use of time, and audited in respect of adherence to quality standards. These aspects of organizational structure may mitigate against the provision of counselling, if counselling has not been defined at a higher management level as a sufficiently important activity to be incorporated into protocols or time allocation systems. On the other hand, when the need for counselling has been acknowledged by senior management, then these same structures can be used to ensure that training and supervisory support is in place, and that time for counselling is factored into workload planning. The implications of organizational structure for the provision of embedded counselling are therefore complex. It is inevitable that most state-funded health, education and social cases will be delivered within large organizational units that require military-style discipline and accountability in order to function properly. In such environments, local or grassroots counselling initiatives may be hard to set up and sustain. A lot will depend on the extent to which senior managers and policy-makers are aware of the potential value of counselling. A further consideration is that not all education and health/ social care is provided by large bureaucratic organizations. A certain proportion of this work is done by smaller organizations in the commercial sector or third (voluntary) sector that may operate with more of a flat hierarchy, and where it may be easier to be innovative.

The idea of organizational *culture* encompasses a wide range of processes. 'Culture' is a holistic concept that includes the history of a group, the way that people relate to each other, beliefs and myths, language, values, attitudes to leadership, what people wear, norms for expressing emotions, use of physical space and 'territory', and much else (Schein, 2004). In relation to the role of counselling in an organizational setting, one of the most significant aspects of organizational culture is concerned with the expression of emotion. In many organizations, the expression of emotions is not encouraged. For example, staff are not supposed to acknowledge the feelings and emotions that are stirred up for them through their interaction with clients and service users, and are not meant to discuss these experiences with their colleagues. In some organizations, the only acceptable emotion is *anger*. For example, anger can be channelled in a positive sense in the form of feedback to colleagues who have made mistakes. Less positively, anger can be expressed through bullying and domination by managers towards employees, or at a colleague-to-colleague level. Neither emotion-denying organizations, nor 'blame culture' organizations are fertile territory for counselling to thrive, because counselling involves creating spaces in which people have permission to feel whatever emotions are around for them at that moment. Many organizations seek to develop a 'rational' culture in which every decision is informed by statistical information, research evidence and logical decision-making. Within such environments, counselling may take root as a 'counter-culture' through which some staff seek to create enclaves of more 'humanizing' forms of interaction.

Exercise 6.3: *A narrative perspective on organizational culture*

From a narrative perspective, the culture of an organization is transmitted through the stories that are told around key events in organizational life. Take a few moments to think about recent events in your own organization that represented genuine 'water-cooler' moments – things that happened where everyone gathered round the water cooler (or equivalent) to hear the latest news. To what extent did the events described in these stories exemplify counselling values? Did the protagonists of these dramatic stories exhibit high levels of congruence, acceptance and empathy towards each other? If not, then what values were expressed through their actions? Finally – what do these stories suggest to you about the place of counselling within your organization?

A useful way of thinking about the difference between organizational structure and culture is that the former is based on a rational analysis of how authority and information flow through an organization, while the latter is concerned with a much less tangible set of unwritten rules that are driven by emotional needs rather than rational planning. A great deal of what can be considered as 'cultural' factors in organizations occur at an unconscious level, and seem to operate in much the same manner as unconscious processes in individuals. The analysis of organizational life in terms of unconscious processes was originally developed by the psychoanalyst and organizational consultant, Isabel Menzies Lyth, and her colleagues at the Tavistock Institute (Menzies, 1959; Menzies Lyth, 1988, 1989; Obholzer and Roberts, 1994). One of the key ideas that was developed by this group was the concept of *institutional defence mechanisms*. The notion of individual defence mechanisms refers to the process through which a person protects themself against painful and threatening memories and emotions by keeping these contents out of conscious awareness through mechanisms such as *projection, splitting, denial* and *repression*. Menzies Lyth and her co-workers observed that similar processes also occurred at an organizational level. For example, in an organizational setting such as a hospital, where staff deal with pain, loss and death, it can be unbearable for a nurse or a doctor to allow themself to be emotionally affected by what is going on – to do so would make it hard to continue with their work. In a hospital, however, there is usually an institution-wide defence against emotion in the form of *splitting* – the nurses and doctors are rational and distanced at all times with the result that emotions are separated off and are expressed somewhere else, such as in the presence of the hospital chaplain, or when the patient's family comes to visit. This can create problems for nurses or other health care staff who wish to adopt a counselling approach, because their actions threaten and challenge the existing system of cultural defences. One of the ways that the validity of counselling approaches is diminished in such organizational settings is to describe them in derogatory terms such as 'touchy-feely'. There may also be anger and resentment directed towards colleagues who try to use counselling methods – they may be seen as wasting time and resources. Counselling practitioners can perpetuate this kind of splitting when they view themselves as the 'caring' ones and management as 'unfeeling insensitive bureaucrats'.

Another aspect of the unconscious dynamics of organizational culture is captured in the concept of *parallel process* (McNeill and Worthen, 1989). The idea of parallel process refers to a process through which a pattern of feeling and relating that exists in one situation is unconsciously reproduced by the person in a different situation. This concept was originally developed as a means of understanding some of the things that can happen in supervision; for example, when the counsellor acts out in a session with their supervisor some of the behaviour and emotions that were earlier expressed to them by their client. Another type of parallel process is when the counsellor behaves to the client in a similar way that their supervisor behaved towards them. Crandall and Allen (1981) suggest that there can often be significant parallels between counselling issues and organizational issues, and that parallel processes occur at an organizational level. In other words, what happens between counsellor and client is influenced by what happens between the counsellor and the organization. For example, a social worker might be under pressure to prioritize risk assessment in their work with clients to avoid any possibility that a crisis might occur that would be reported in the media. When the social worker and client then agree to take a whole hour to explore the meaning of a personal issue that is bothering the client, the social worker may be subtly responding to their client in ways that serve to 'keep the lid on' any emotions. A teacher may work in a school where the staff operate on the basis of two categories of students: 'hard workers' who deserve help, and 'troublemakers' who need to be controlled. When a teacher develops a counselling relationship with one of their students who is known as a 'troublemaker', they may project this image onto the young person, and create a barrier between them. It is important to realize that the theory of parallel process does not suggest that these attitudes are consciously held by social workers or teachers – it is more that aspects of the underlying emotional ethos of the organization permeate their way of being with clients and subvert their counselling skills and values.

The aim of this section has been to explore some of the ways in which organizational factors can influence the effectiveness of the work that counsellors do, and the way that they think and feel about themselves. In organizations that function well, considerable effort is devoted, in the form of support structures, team-building and other activities, to making sure that the organization functions as well as it can, and that there is a sufficient degree of conscious reflection on how the organization operates as an entity. Effective leadership, which demonstrates an appreciation of the importance of emotions and relationships, is an essential element in all of this.

Creating a space for counselling

A counselling conversation is different from other types of conversational interaction. What makes a counselling relationship helpful is that it allows the person to step back from the action of everyday life for the purpose of reflecting on that action and possibly deciding to do things differently. In the theatre, sometimes the main character will step to the side of the stage, away from the 'scene', and speak reflectively, honestly and personally to the audience. The main scene is in darkness and the character may be lit just by one spotlight. A good counselling session has some of this quality. It takes place in a bubble or special space, out of the action. Within that space, the person may well talk and act differently from the way they perform elsewhere.

A counselling space requires two key features:

- A boundary – it must be clear when the space has been entered, who can enter it, and when it is exited.
- Rules for what can happen inside the space.

In specialist counselling and psychotherapy centres, a great deal of work is done to set the scene in terms of boundaries and rules well in advance of a client arriving. The client may receive a leaflet explaining how the agency operates, what to expect from a counselling session, and the nature of confidentiality. They will be given appointment information that makes it explicit that the counselling session will begin and end at certain times. When a counselling relationship occurs in a different kind of organizational setting, such as a hospital ward or in the person's own home, boundaries and rules need to be negotiated in such a way as to create the best possible space given the circumstances that prevail. To return to the theatre analogy, there are similarities here to street theatre companies, who are able to stage compelling dramas in all kinds of situations. However, even in a formal counselling or psychotherapy agency or clinic, the counsellor can never take it for granted that at the outset the client or patient will fully understand the counselling 'contract' – it is always good practice to give the client an opportunity to ask questions, or to revisit key points, particularly if the person has never received counselling before.

A counselling space can be regarded as a place where people go in order to look back on, and reflect on, what has been happening in their everyday life. In counselling relationships that take place outside of specialist counselling agencies, a key task for the counsellor or helper is to set the scene – to assemble a space within which a meaningful counselling conversation can take place. Part of this task involves verbally agreeing and checking out that both participants are agreed that they have now moved away from whatever other tasks they have been involved in, and are now focusing on exploring the problem in living that the person has brought up. Another aspect of the task is to attend to the physical space within which the conversation is being conducted; for example, can other people overhear? A third part of the task of making a space is to do whatever is necessary to construct a boundary by agreeing the limits of confidentiality, the length of the session, the possibility of further meetings, and the role of the helper. Competence in making a space also involves knowing how to close the space at the end of the conversation.

Exercise 6.4: *Your own experience of personally meaningful places*

What are the spaces in your own life in which you find meaning and strength? What are the factors that make these spaces possible?

Once there is agreement with a client that they wish to talk, it is helpful to provide some indication of the length of time that is available. This may involve a statement such as 'we could talk about this for few minutes now, if you like' or 'I have about 15 minutes until my next appointment – would that be enough time to begin to look at what's happening for you?' In some circumstances it may be necessary to ask the person about how much time is available to themself: 'Would it be possible to keep going for a few minutes so I could hear more about the situation you are in?' What is essential is to avoid a situation where the person in the role of counsellor begins to get distracted by the fact that they are running way behind schedule, or they abruptly bring the conversation to an end because they have run out of time. Another useful way of signalling time boundaries is to indicate that 'we only have a couple of minutes left', or to use a phrase such as 'we need to finish soon for today', and then offer a brief summary of what has been said, or the action that has been agreed. An enormous amount can be covered in a few minutes if the person talking knows that the space is there for them. People know that professional helpers such as doctors, nurses, teachers and social workers are operating under time pressures, and will usually accept the realities of what can be offered in terms of time.

Box 6.1: *Counselling spaces can be found in the most unlikely places: the healing fields*

It is a mistake to think that a nicely decorated room with two armchairs is the only, or even necessarily the best, environment for conducting a counselling session. In a profoundly moving and informative book, Sonja Linden and Jenny Grut (2002) describe the psychotherapeutic work carried out in London under the auspices of the Medical Foundation for the Care of Victims of Torture. Over a period of two decades, this group has worked with dozens of families who have been exiled from their home countries, and have been subjected to unbelievable cruelties. For the majority of these people, sitting in a room and being asked to talk about their experiences to a therapist from a different culture would have been a difficult thing to do for many reasons. Instead, the Medical Foundation secured the use of a set of garden allotments. In these spaces, people who had been exiled worked with their families to clear ground and cultivate plants, some of which came from their home country, and some from England. Together, the participants created a remembrance garden for all of their friends, colleagues and family members who had not been able to escape. As they worked in their fields, counsellors would work with them, and find moments to begin conversations about their old life that had been destroyed, and their new one that was gradually growing. The experience of gardening made possible moments of peace and reflection, as well as a wealth of shared metaphors associated with activities such as clearing the ground, planting seed, keeping fences in good order, seasons, light and darkness, putting down roots, death, and much else. This work shows how spaces for counselling can be built into another activity in a way that deepens the possibilities for relationship, connection and meaning-making.

Another practical consideration in relation to establishing a workable space for counselling is to be mindful of the physical space. Seating arrangements, proximity, ensuring that the sound of voices does not travel to others, and the availability of drinking water and tissues, all make an important contribution to creating the right kind of space. Counsellors and psychotherapists in private practice go beyond these basic material considerations, and give a great deal of thought to developing the right kind of emotional ambience, using lighting, soft furnishing and art. This kind of environmental control is seldom possible in situations where the counsellor is also performing another role, such as that of teacher or nurse. Nevertheless, part of the preparation for being willing to offer a counselling relationship needs to involve identifying the best spaces within a school or clinic where private, emotional conversations can safely take place. An issue that confronts many practitioners of embedded counselling is that of seeing a client in their home, and finding some way to make an appropriate space in a household where the TV is on, other people are around, and there may be a budgie flying about in the room. In such a situation, it may well be necessary to explain to the person why it is necessary to create a space in which there is some privacy and quiet. Similarly, in an organizational setting such as a school, it may be hard to find a quiet private place to meet.

Box 6.2: *Finding a space to be: creating stillpoints*

There is an understandable tendency when operating in the role of counsellor to seek to arrive at a resolution or answer to the problem being presented by the person. The idea of counselling as a *space* reflects an assumption that it may be helpful at times for the person to have access to a space in which there is no pressure to do or achieve anything. Ronna Jevne (1987) describes such moments as *stillpoints*, and has written about their importance in her experience of working with people who have cancer. She describes her goal as a counsellor as enabling the person to 'experience a sense of calm and strength in the midst of threat' (p. 1) in which they are aware of their resources, and has the 'strength to handle whatever is necessary' (p. 12). Jevne suggests a number of questions that may help a person to identify their own potential for finding a stillpoint, such as 'can you recall a time when you felt a greater sense of being still inside?' and 'what would be necessary for you to have a stillpoint in the future?' She adds that in her experience, 'the process is substantially dependent on the helper's capacity to achieve a stillpoint' (p. 8) for themselves. Jevne (1987) argues that the creation of a stillpoint is essentially a *non-rational* activity, which draws upon the person's connection with art, literature, spirituality and nature. In a later article, Jevne *et al.* (1998) have described stages in cancer counselling where moments of 'calm and strength' may be helpful. However, the image of the stillpoint has implications for all forms of counselling in revealing an important function of the counselling space. It is likely that most people who make use of counselling have times when all they are looking for, or needing, is some assistance to be still.

Exercise 6.5: *Creating a suitable space for counselling*

How satisfactory is the physical setting in which you work in terms of providing spaces for counselling relationships to occur? What improvements would you like to make to the physical environment in which you see people?

Conclusions

This chapter has introduced some ideas about how to make sense of what goes on in organizations, and has highlighted some of the issues that need to be considered in terms of ensuring that counselling that is carried out is supported by the organization in which it takes place, and not undermined by it. The chapter has raised more questions that is has provided answers, because at the present time there is a lack of theory and research around the topic of the organizational context of counselling. Other aspects of organizational dimensions of counselling are discussed in later chapters. For example, dealing with ethical dilemmas that can arise around reconciling the different priorities of the counselling relationship and the objectives of an organization is explored in Chapter 7, and the challenges associated with surviving in organizations and coping with stress or burnout are examined in Chapters 19 and 21. The key message of this chapter is that there are significant organizational factors that need to be taken into account when preparing to offer *any* form of counselling relationship. Some of these factors are covered in training courses, but many are not. Being well prepared is a crucial element of effective counselling, because it is through careful preparation that a person offering counselling can feel sufficiently emotionally and morally secure. This is important – after all, who wants to share their problems with someone who seems unsure of the ground on which they stand?

Box 6.3: *Adopting a strategic approach to ensure that good-quality emotional support is delivered across an organization*

It is difficult to sustain the delivery of good-quality counselling to clients within the context of a busy health care organization in which practitioners are required to juggle multiple roles and pressures. A paper by Stein et al. (2005) describes the development of a programme within Kaiser Permanente, one of the biggest health providers in the USA, which was devised to ensure that doctors engaged empathically, effectively, and in a culture-sensitive manner with the emotional and clinical needs of patients. The programme evolved over a 17-year period, and included training workshops designed to be accessible to doctors and relevant to their needs, the use of patient satisfaction surveys to collect data on the use of communication skills by practitioners, and the creation of a group of 'communication consultants' – physicians or psychologists selected on the basis of their outstanding interpersonal skills who provided a supervisory and coaching role with colleagues. A particularly innovative feature of the programme was the adoption of a memorable phrase that captured the key elements of the Kaiser Permanente approach: 'the four habits model'. Practitioners were trained in interpersonal competences related to good practice with regard to four main areas of interaction with patients:

invest in the beginning, elicit the patient's perspective, demonstrate empathy and invest in the end. Taken together, these four 'habits' encapsulated the dimensions of counselling skill that were considered to be most relevant to the role of a primary care physician within that specific organizational setting. The 'habits' model provided a readily understood language that all the doctors across the organization were able to use to discuss and reflect on their practice, and explained what was needed in practical terms that helped to address the criticism of many physicians that such issues were irrelevant. The article by Stein et al. (2005) gives a detailed account of the strategies that were used by the champions of this approach within Kaiser Permanente to maximize its chances of being taken seriously, such as building on success, enlisting the support of senior managers, using research evidence to convince tough-minded clinicians that interpersonal skills made a difference to health outcomes, and linking salary increases to ratings of patient satisfaction.

Suggested further reading

The issues associated with the delivery of counselling in various organizational settings are discussed by:

Moore, J. and Roberts, R. (eds) (2010) *Counselling and Psychotherapy in Organisational Settings*. London: Learning Matters.

Reid, M. (ed.) (2004) *Counselling in Different Settings: The Reality of Practice*. London: Palgrave Macmillan.

Stokes, A. (2001) Settings. In S. Aldridge and S. Rigby (eds) *Counselling Skills in Context*. London: Hodder & Stoughton.

Ethical principles for embedded counselling

Do you remember
The first time we met
You told me about confidentiality
And you asked me if I had ever
Felt

At risk, you said
Of harming myself.
You know
Once and for all

Well
I can tell you
Now
That of course I do
I think about it a lot

Doesn't everyone?
In my situation?

Introduction

The ethical and moral basis of professional practice represents an area of inquiry and debate that is massively significant in health and social care, education, and other professional contexts. In all of these settings, practitioners hold confidential information about clients and service users, and have the power to make decisions or recommendations that can fundamentally change a person's life. At the same time, service user groups, sections of the legal profession, some politicians, and some insurance companies, can be vigorous and unrelenting in pursuing the claims of clients who have been treated negligently or unfairly. Over and above the application of professional power and control, and client resistance to that power, there is the complexity of moral discourse in contemporary society. At times it appears as though there is hardly any agreed basis for making decisions about what is right or wrong – almost all moral judgement seems to be open to argument.

A counselling relationship can be viewed as an arena that calls for continuous vigilance around ethical issues. By definition, the client in a counselling conversation is speaking from a place of vulnerability. Implicit in the way that the client describes their problem, or the counsellor formulates a potential solution to that problem, are multiple assumptions around values and how the 'good' life is understood. On the whole, counselling theory, research and practice has been reticent about exploring ethical and moral issues. All counselling professional associations have produced their own ethical codes, which specify rules of conduct for counselling practitioners. Those who are teachers, nurses or social workers, and whose counselling is embedded in such a primary role, are similarly guided by their own professional codes. It is assumed that practitioner readers of this book will be broadly familiar with such codes. The aim of the present chapter, therefore, is not to revisit what is already known, or can be readily accessed through relevant websites, but to concentrate instead on the ethical dilemmas that arise in the course of applying counselling skills in what might be regarded as a border area between the territory of primary professions such as nursing or social work, and the territory of specialist professional counselling.

To some extent, counselling presents ethical issues that are particularly challenging for practitioners. In professions such as nursing, medicine and social work, ethical decisions may be linked to life or death issues such as taking a child into care, or withholding treatment from a patient. However, in these contexts ethical dilemmas can usually be discussed within a team over a period of time. By contrast, ethical issues in counselling can often arise in the moment, and in a situation in which other colleagues cannot have access to the same amount of information about the client. Also, making the wrong call around an ethical issue can utterly undermine the counselling relationship. For these reasons, it is essential for any kind of counselling training to take ethical issues seriously in ways that facilitate trainee awareness and competence around ethical decision-making.

The chapter approaches the nature of ethical issues in embedded counselling from different perspectives. Following a brief exploration of some examples of ethical dilemmas, there is an overview of ethical principles that inform practice in this area. A series of specific ethical issues are discussed. Finally, some practical decision-making strategies for practitioners of embedded counselling are outlined.

Examples of ethical dilemmas in embedded counselling

Grania is a nurse who has been providing counselling for some time to James, a patient who has a long-term problem, and who has needed to talk about how the illness has affected his image of himself as someone who takes care of others in his family. He brings in an expensive gift. He knows that this is something that Grania would like. In responding to her patient, Grania is open about her pleasure in being offered this gift, and also her difficulty as a practitioner bound by health service rules in being able to accept the gift without consulting her line manager and supervisor. She encourages James to share his feeling around the gift-giving, and her response. They agree that Grania will consult on the question of the gift, and that they will discuss it further at their next meeting. In the meantime, Grania is aware that the gift may be an expression of a strong wish on the part of James to be the caretaker and provider, and reflects on how and when (and whether) it would be useful to explore that idea with him.

Ian is a community support worker who has been counselling someone for six months who has a serious medical condition. He has a similar medical problem himself. At the start of his contact with this person, Ian decided not to mention his own health problem to the client. However, he is now finding it extremely difficult to carry on with the counselling, because what the client is talking about reminds him of his own pain and despair, and he keeps wanting to cry during sessions. Ian imagines that it would be overwhelming for his client if he now began to share his own condition, and manufactures a rationale for handing the care of this person over to a colleague. The client is mystified about what has happened, and feels rejected.

Miranda is a youth worker attached to a secondary school. The school has a specialist counsellor, and has a rule that any child under 16 needs to have parental permission to receive counselling. Miranda has just finished a group workshop for a class of 15-year-old children on relationship skills. At the end one of the students, Kaya, comes up to her and launches into the story of her problems. When asked about whether she has considered using the specialist school counsellor, Kaya says that her parents had not given her permission to see the actual school counsellor, 'so I chose to speak to you instead'. Miranda acknowledges the difficult situation that Kaya finds herself in, and talks for a few moments about the reason why parental approval is necessary. She asks Kaya if she would be willing to tell her what happened when she asked for her parents' approval, and whether it would be helpful if Miranda perhaps met with her parents and Kaya together to review the situation.

These dilemmas illustrate the potential complexity of situations that may be ethically problematic in embedded counselling. In each case, the person seeking help was trying to get what they needed, but did so in a way that placed the counsellor in a difficult position. The task for these counsellors was to acknowledge the dilemma, while remaining focused on maintaining an ongoing counselling relationship with the person. The story of Ian exemplified the importance of *anticipating* potentially difficult situations – Ian chose to ignore an aspect of the counselling relationship (his own health status) that had the potential to undermine his capacity to provide a safe space for counselling. The longer that time went on, the harder it became for him to do anything about the situation.

Core ethical principles

The moral basis for the practice of counselling can be expressed in different ways. At one level, the ethics of counselling is grounded in a *common-sense* appreciation of what is the 'right' thing to do. From a more reflective perspective, it is clear that counselling is informed by a set of core *values*, such as respect for the person, and belief in a person's capacity to develop and learn. These values are reflected in an array of personal *virtues*, such as honesty and integrity, that characterize practitioners who aspire to the highest standards. Finally, the moral basis of practice is also informed by *ethical principles*, which are largely similar to the ethical codes found in all health and caring professions. An important statement of the core ethical principles that inform counselling practice was made by Karen Kitchener (1984), who proposed that ethical decision-making in any counselling situation should be based on five fundamental moral constructs:

- *Autonomy*: people are understood as individuals who have the right to freedom of action and freedom of choice insofar as the pursuit of these freedoms does not interfere with the freedoms of others.
- *Non-maleficence*: the injunction to all helpers or healers that they must 'above all do no harm'.
- *Beneficence*: the intention to promote human welfare.
- *Justice*: the fair distribution of resources and services.
- *Fidelity*: being loyal and reliable, and acting in good faith.

There is an excellent discussion of these principles, and their application within counselling, available on the Ethical Guidelines pages of the British Association for Counselling and Psychotherapy (website: www.bacp.co.uk).

Box 7.1: *Relational ethics: integrating ethical principles into counselling practice*

At the heart of effective counselling is the establishment of a collaborative, trusting relationship between client and counsellor. In recent years, there has been a growing appreciation that it is helpful for counsellors to be able to interpret ethical principles within a relational context. As a result Gabriel and Casemore (2009) and others have begun to develop a framework for understanding *relational ethics*. The nature of relational ethics is exemplified in a study by Jennings *et al.* (2005) in which experienced psychotherapists were interviewed about the values that informed their work with clients. The themes that emerged for analysis of these interviews illustrate the extent to which a relational ethos permeates the ethical thinking of these practitioners. They reported that their responsibility to their clients could only be fulfilled if they continued to maintain and build their knowledge, skills and competence. Two further values that were particularly important for these practitioners were:

- *Relational connection* referred to a commitment to relationships with clients, colleagues, family and friends, and members of the community: 'to maintain competence and build expertise, they must continually be in relationships with others in the field, whether in supervision or consultation or purely for collegial support and friendship' (Jennings *et al.*, 2005: 37).

- *Humility* referred to an appreciation of their limitations as practitioners and as human beings.

This study demonstrates some of the ways in which, in practice, adherence to ethical and moral principles depends on an underlying capacity for connectedness and relationship.

The ethical principles identified by Kitchener (1984) form the basis for everything that happens in counselling, and represent a general moral horizon within which all counselling conversations take place. In practice, however, the application of these principles tends to be focused on a set of key domains:

- working within the law
- negotiating informed consent
- confidentiality
- competence (being aware of your limits as a counsellor)
- taking care around dual relationships
- sensitivity to cultural differences in moral standpoint
- dealing with risk and self-harm
- using touch.

These topics are discussed in the following sections.

Working within the law

Within any domain of professional practice, as well as within everyday life, it is important to be aware of the ways in which the legal system defines and sets limits around certain areas of conduct. In counselling, two of the issues around which practitioners may find themselves involved in legal considerations are *confidentiality* and *duty of care*. There have been many cases where counselling clients have either requested that their case notes are made available to their lawyer or the police, or prosecuting lawyers or courts have demanded access to notes. For example, if a client has made a claim for retirement on health grounds, which is contested by their employer or pension provider, the counsellor's notes may be used to corroborate the severity of the client's condition. Similarly, if a client with a drug or alcohol problem is mandated by the court to attend counselling, then in some situations the counsellor may be called on to testify whether the client has attended, and has made a serious attempt to engage with their problems. In these scenarios, counsellor confidentiality has no special legal status, and counsellors are required to place the wider social good (as represented by the legal system) over and above their commitment to their client, or even to what they might view as the well-being of their client.

Duty of care refers to situations where there is a risk of harm to the client, or to another person. The area of risk to the client through self-harm or suicide is discussed more fully in a later section of this chapter. There are also situations in which the client themself may be a risk to others. For example, in a counselling session a client may talk about how enraged they are by someone who has mistreated them to the extent that they intend to hurt them. Finally, a client may report information that indicates harm being committed by a third party; for example, someone who has sexually abused them, or someone who comes to work under the influence of drugs or alcohol. There can be ethical dilemmas for counsellors in these situations around how to respond to the information they have received. For instance, to what extent is an angry client just letting off steam, or are they actually planning to commit a crime of violence?

The issue of working within the law is heightened in many embedded counselling contexts because practitioners such as nurses, social workers and teachers may be operating within legal or quasi-legal professional guidelines that are specific to their occupational group. For example, while a private-practice psychotherapist or counsellor has some discretion in whether to report a case of sexual abuse, a social worker, nurse or teacher is *always* required to report on any suspicion of abuse that they might come across.

Exercise 7.1: *Legal considerations within your own practice*

What are the legal considerations or specific professional or organizational codes that are most relevant for your own counselling practice? To what extent, and in what ways, do you need to address these considerations in your everyday work with clients; for example, by explaining to them that if they talk about certain issues you would be required to take certain types of action? In what ways does the organization provide you with support around these issues; for example, in the form of supervision, consultation and training?

Negotiating informed consent

When someone is seeking help, before the actual counselling commences it is the responsibility of the counsellor to ensure that the person is sufficiently informed about what is on offer, and what might happen.

Examples of conversations around informed consent

Alicia, aged 15, attends a youth club and likes and trusts the community education worker who runs the club. One evening, when the club is quiet, she starts to talk about her problems at school. The youth worker says that she is very happy to talk about these issues, but that Alicia needs to know that she is only around one evening each week, and so she cannot guarantee that they could talk every week. She checks out how Alicia feels about this, and whether she might prefer it if the youth worker helped her to make an appointment at a local young person's counselling service.

His GP suspects that Mike, an unemployed man who has visited regularly with a variety of physical ailments, is bottling up a lot of feelings about how his life has worked out, but is afraid that other people might see how vulnerable he is. At one consultation, he suggests to Mike that it might be helpful if they took a bit more time to look at what was going on in his life that might be making him feel bad. He adds: '. . . of course, there could be things that are upsetting to talk about. Maybe you would want to think about whether you want to go into these things right now. Sometimes it can be better to make an appointment at the end of my afternoon clinic, when the place is quiet and we can have more time. What do you think? It's up to you'.

Elsa starts to tell her social worker about why she has taken her children out of the family home, and moved in with her mother. Before Elsa gets into her stride, the social worker intervenes to say: 'I know you know this, but I'm just reminding you that if you tell me anything that's around harm to any of the children, I would have to do something. I don't have any choice about that. I'm really happy to talk all this through with you – we've got at least an hour if we need it – but any abuse or harm has to be reported. Is that OK?'

In these examples, the person in the role of counsellor is providing the person seeking help with the information that they need in order to make an autonomous decision about whether they want to proceed, or not. In these particular examples, the counsellor was acting on the basis of an assumption that the person already possessed a reasonably good understanding of counselling, and knew what they were looking for. There are some occasions where this would not be the case, and a counsellor might need to take more time to tell a person what was involved in counselling to the point where that person was capable of making a truly informed choice.

Exercise 7.2: *Setting the scene for informed consent*

What do you say to prospective clients about what is involved in counselling? When do you say it? Is this information backed up by written materials? How adequate is this information as a basis for the client to consent to what will follow? If you have been a client yourself, what kind of consent procedure was conducted? As a result of the information you were given did you have a sense of actively giving consent for counselling to take place?

Confidentiality

Confidentiality is a central aspect of counselling. The counselling process depends on the client feeling sufficiently safe to be able to talk openly and honestly about whatever it is that is bothering them. By contrast, if someone believes that what they say will end up as a topic for gossip, or will be used against them in some way, they are unlikely to engage in much meaningful self-disclosure. However, confidentiality can never be absolute. Ethical practice requires counsellors to make use of supervision and consultation as a means of maintaining and ensuring effectiveness. In addition, in exceptional circumstances the legal system has the right to require counsellors to pass on information that they have acquired within a counselling relationship.

There are two main practical ways in which counsellors can ensure that confidentiality is dealt with in an appropriately ethical manner. First, counsellors should always behave with respect, care and tact around client information. Being a counsellor involves developing a capacity to store client information in separate 'boxes' in one's mind, and only to open each of these boxes when required to do so. It can be tempting, and sometimes even emotionally necessary to retell vivid or disturbing client stories to friends or colleagues. This kind of behaviour is always risky, because even small or incidental aspects of a story may allow the client to be identifiable. The 'default mode' for any counsellor is a state of extreme carefulness and sensitivity around passing on any client information. This aspect of the role of counsellor can be problematic in embedded counselling situations, where colleagues and organizational systems may operate on an expectation that all information about a client will be shared across a team or in a central file. The practice of embedded counselling therefore involves coming to a working agreement with colleagues and managers around what kinds of information need to be shared and kept on file, and what can remain confidential to the counsellor. For example, in many embedded counselling situations it may make sense for colleagues to know that a client is using a particular worker as a person to talk to, or even to know that certain issues are being talked about. But it may not be necessary for them to know the precise content of these talks.

A second dimension of confidentiality is associated with the client's under-standing of confidentiality, and how the counsellor negotiates this understanding. The ethical principle of autonomy is particularly relevant here – if the client is fully informed about the limits of confidentiality, then they are in a position to decide about whether or not to disclose certain areas of information. It is a mistake to assume that a client will inevitably want everything that they say in counselling to be treated as confidential. For example, a college student who uses their tutor to explore the impact of a bereavement may assume that other tutors on the course would be told about this issue and would as a result be sensitive to their emotional vulnera-bility at that time. Part of the skill of being a counsellor includes being able to choose the right moment to check out with the client around confidentiality boundaries. If time is tight, it can seem awkward and unhelpful to deflect the client from their trou-bles by initiating a discussion of confidentiality. It can be useful in some situations to have written information about confidentiality, in a leaflet or on a website, to which the client can be directed. But even if such information is available, it is still neces-sary to ask the client if they have read and understood it, and has any questions. Brief discussions around confidentiality can contribute to a strengthening of the counsel-ling relationship and counsellor–client 'alliance' if the client gains an appreciation of the professionalism of the counsellor, and a sense of being cared about. These discussions also have a preventative value – misunderstandings about confidentiality for perceived breaches that arise later in counselling can be very destructive.

Exercise 7.3: *Negotiating confidentiality*

What is the counselling confidentiality framework that you operate within in your own workplace? How do you inform people who look to you for counselling about the limits of confidentiality? How satisfactory are the confidentiality structures within which your counselling takes place? How might they be enhanced or clarified?

Being aware of your limits as a counsellor

The ethical injunctions to do good and avoid harm are closely linked to the ques-tion of counsellor competence. For example, there are many people who work in educational, health and social services jobs who get to know clients who have had experiences of sexual or emotional abuse in childhood. Sometimes, the practitioner may feel a strong urge to help the person by listening to their story, and perhaps trying to help them to come to terms with what has happened. This is a very caring response, but there are times when it may not represent the best possible course of action. If a person has been assaulted in childhood, the resulting sense of lack of trust, and perhaps self-hatred, may permeate many aspects of their life. Talking through all of that may take a long time, may involve strong emotions, and requires a great deal of persistence and consistency on the part of the helper or counsellor. Any nurse or other practitioner faced with such a situation needs to consider whether they are capable, in terms of the time they can give, and their confidence and competence as a counsellor, to accompany their client on such a journey. Starting on such a journey, and then pulling back, clearly has the potential for hurt. At the same time, ignoring what the client has said about their abuse for fear of 'getting in over my head' also has the potential for hurt or harm. What will be appropriate will depend on the circumstances. For instance, in one situation it may be best to work with the person to find a psychotherapist. In another situation, a nurse or social worker might be able to get sufficient supervisory back-up to offer supportive counselling for a period of time. Another set of issues around counsellor competence arise from what might be described as *temporary impairment*. For example, a counsellor who has recently experienced the loss of a close family member is unlikely to be much help to someone with a bereavement issue. A counsellor who is burnt out, stressed or tired is unlikely to be in a good position to offer ongoing help to someone. Being aware of one's limits as a counsellor is much easier when the practitioner has been using regular supervision or consultancy support, and there is someone who is close enough to the counsellor to challenge their attempt to be 'heroic' rather than helpful.

Exercise 7.4: *The limits of your competence*

What are the types of client, or presenting issue, that you regard as being beyond your competence at the present time? What would you do if you came across such a client or issue in your current counselling practice? How would you take care of (a) your needs and (b) the client's needs in this kind of situation? What kind of supervisory or consultative support is available to you in relation to dealing with such events?

Taking care around dual relationships

Much of the theory, literature and training that informs contemporary counselling practice is based on an assumption that the counsellor, and the person seeking help are, or should be, strangers. The assumption behind this view is that the quality of the relationship in terms of trust and confidentiality is of paramount importance, and that any contamination of that relationship with other kinds of ties should be avoided at all costs. This approach has the advantage of creating a pure kind of counsellor–client relationship in which all that the counsellor knows about the person is what they say during their weekly session, and the person can feel secure that whatever they say in counselling is safely and securely insulated from the rest of their life. Although this kind of formulation is neat and elegant, it flies in the face of several different types of 'dual relationship' situations where counselling appears to thrive:

- rural communities where everyone knows everyone else
- self-contained sub-cultures within urban areas (e.g. lesbian, gay, bisexual and transgender communities) where people choose to see counsellors who share their own values and lifestyle within a relatively restricted social group
- various types of therapeutic communities where counsellors and clients may live and work together.

However, although there are plentiful examples of counselling being delivered effectively within a dual role relationship, anyone with experience of providing counselling within such a setting knows that taking care around role boundaries is absolutely essential. After all, there would be no one who would claim that counselling could reasonably take place between close family members, such as a husband and wife, or parent and child. The crucial moral and ethical factor that represents the biggest challenge for any counselling dual relationship lies in the principle that counselling must be *in the interests of the person/client*. When the counsellor has some other kind of involvement with the person, it is necessary to be alert to any possibility that the counsellor might be responding on the basis of what would be right *for them*, rather than what would be right for the person. The recognition that it is feasible to carry out ethical and effective therapy in the context of a dual relationship has resulted in a reappraisal of this issue in recent years (Gabriel, 2005; Lazarus and Zur, 2002; Moleski and Kiselica, 2005). Moleski and Kiselica (2005) have introduced the useful concept of a *continuum* of dual/complex client–counsellor relationships, ranging from the therapeutic to the destructive.

The issue of dual relationships is of particular importance in embedded counselling where there is always a dual relationship, and where significant tensions may exist between the two types of relationship. For example, a probation officer may have the task of monitoring the behaviour of an offender living in the community, which could lead to re-imprisonment, and at the same time trying to help the person to talk about their history of abuse or sexual identity issues. A nurse on a busy hospital ward may be under pressure to administer medication to 20 patients while knowing that one of these patients needs more of their time to talk about their fear of dying. The issue is further complicated by the fact that the patient or client may become confused about where they stand in relation to the helper: 'is this a time when I can talk about how I feel, or is it just another ward round?'

In embedded counselling, it is therefore essential to take care around the dual relationships that are involved, and to be as clear as possible about what is happening at different times as different roles are activated. The ethical principle of autonomy requires that clients should be informed at all times, and able to make choices. The principle of avoidance of harm requires that shifting back and forward between roles does not frustrate or disappoint the client, or result in breaches of confidentiality ('I thought that when I said these things, it was part of the counselling, and no one else would need to know . . .'). Addressing these issues effectively involves being open to discussing and reviewing them with clients on a regular basis, being willing to be flexible around the kind of boundaries and contracts that are appropriate in each case, and making use of supervision and consultation.

When considering the issue of dual relationships in embedded counselling, it is obviously necessary to be mindful of potential risks. For even the most experienced practitioners of embedded counselling in educational or health and social care settings, there will always be some clients who are better referred to a specialist counsellor, psychologist or psychotherapist, because they need very clear-cut boundaries. But for the many others, there are advantages in being able to engage in counselling conversations with helpers who are close at hand. For the most part, practitioners of embedded counselling are experienced professionals who are deeply socialized into codes of conduct that strongly emphasize the rights of clients or patients, and the establishment of clear professional boundaries. Similarly, most clients are well able to make a distinction between a 'personal' or counselling conversation, and other types of interaction. Dual relationships in embedded counselling are different from dual relationships in specialist counselling or psychotherapy. In embedded counselling situations, the client will usually have known their prospective counsellor for some time in another role. The client in embedded counselling makes a definite choice regarding who they are willing to talk to based on this previous contact. The client is also usually in contact with other professionals to whom they can complain, or to whom they can turn for alternative help, if things go wrong with the person providing embedded counselling.

Exercise 7.5: *Responding to the challenge of dual relationships*

Within the setting where you practise counselling, what are the different types of dual relationship that can occur? How are these dual relationships negotiated and handled, by other colleagues and by you? What are the warning signs or risk factors that suggest to you that it may not be wise to offer a counselling relationship to a particular client (or group of clients)?

Sensitivity to cultural differences in moral standpoint

The types of ethical issue that arise in counselling situations can often be associated with distinctive ideas about right and wrong that are based in cultural beliefs and attitudes. It is important, therefore, for practitioners to be sensitive to the ways that cultural difference can lead to ethical dilemmas. One of the most important dimensions of cultural difference that can often have an impact on ethical practice concerns the individualism–collectivism dimension. Western cultures, and in particular the more middle-class segments of such cultures, tend to view life from the perspective of the individual. The rightness of a decision or course of action, therefore, is based on whether the consequences are beneficial for the individual. In most other cultures, people view the world from a more collectivist point of view, and a decision is evaluated in terms of what 'we' should do, or whether it benefits 'all of us'. These and other cultural factors are discussed in a classic paper by Paul Pedersen (1997), which criticized the degree of cultural 'encapsulation' (i.e. Western bias) in the ethical guidelines published by the American Counseling Association. Further evidence of cultural differences in the ways in which ethical values are understood in different cultures comes from an analysis by Qian *et al.* (2009) of the recent development of counselling in China. These authors point out, for example, that cultural norms in China mean that it would be unacceptable for counsellors not to accept gifts from their clients, or to refuse referrals of clients from friends, close colleagues and family members.

Exercise 7.6: *Encompassing a diversity of ethical viewpoints in counselling*

What are some of the different ethical and moral values expressed by clients in the counselling setting in which you work? Identify two cases where you have had a sense that your client's ideas of what is 'right' or 'wrong' did not correspond to your own values assumptions. How did you respond to these situations? What strategies or policies has your agency or organization developed in order to respect cultural differences in values and ethical principles? How helpful or effective are these strategies and policies?

Dealing with risk and self-harm

One of the most challenging situations for a counsellor is when people seeking help talk or act in a way that suggests that they may be at risk of harming themselves or harming another person. There are several different forms that risk may take in counselling. The person may:

- plan to take their own life
- be engaged in self-harming behaviour such as cutting, purging, starving, alcohol or drug abuse, unsafe sex, and so on
- be engaged in, or planning to inflict, harm on another person (which may include the counsellor), through physical, verbal or sexual violence, harassment or stalking, criminal activity or unprotected sex (i.e. in cases of HIV/AIDS infection).

While it is necessary to acknowledge that people may have the right to kill themselves, if they have arrived at a position where life is unliveable, or possibly even to threaten other people who they perceive to have wronged them, it is also necessary to take into account that when people refer to risky behaviour *to a counsellor* or other practitioner, they are almost certainly asking for help to avoid doing anything harmful. It is therefore essential for anyone acting in a counselling role to be prepared to respond constructively and actively to such situations. The times when a person seeking counselling talks about risk to self or others can be very difficult for a counsellor to deal with – there is a sense of a great pressure of responsibility, and typically there may be little or no opportunity to consult colleagues – the counsellor needs to respond somehow in the moment.

In any of the types of harm listed above, a counsellor needs to arrive at a position on whether it is helpful to proceed with counselling, or whether the situation requires some other kind of intervention. In order to make this kind of decision, a counsellor should be able to (a) listen out for indications from the person that some kind of harm may take place; (b) engage the person in conversation around their intentions, and the meaning that the harm event holds for them; (c) estimate the level of risk; and (d) implement strategies for avoiding harm.

On many occasions where harm is an issue, the person seeking help may be quite open and explicit about what is in their mind. At other times, however, the person may convey their intentions in a disguised, vague or metaphorical way of talking. There is some evidence that counsellors are not particularly sensitive at picking up subtle clues about harmful behaviour. In a study carried out by Reeves *et al.* (2004), a group of highly trained specialist counsellors were recorded in sessions with 'standardized clients', who had been instructed by the researcher to talk vaguely about suicidal intentions. Very few of the counsellors followed up the implicit cues the clients were expressing around suicidality within the sessions. One explanation for this finding could be that these counsellors were more tuned into the positive aspects of what their clients were saying, and less focused on negatives. Another explanation was that they lacked skill and confidence in initiating conversations around risk.

The key point here is that potentially risky behaviour may be exhibited in a variety of ways. For example, a person who has intentionally cut their arms may not say anything to a helper or counsellor about this, but may have bandaged arms or wear a long-sleeved pullover on a warm day. A person may talk about someone to whom they bear a grudge with clenched fists and angry gestures. A person may share fantasies or images of death or destruction. In any of these cases, it is important for a counsellor to be willing to pause the ongoing counselling conversation, share their concern with the person, and ask the person what they specifically have in mind.

Serious suicidal behaviour is relatively rare, and it is unlikely that a practitioner involved in offering counselling would personally come across more than two or three cases over the course of their career, unless they were working in a specific area such as psychiatry or a suicide helpline. It is important for counsellors to prepare for the possibility of working with suicidal people through training, reading and study, rather than relying on first-hand experience. Excellent accounts of theory, research and personal experience around suicide can be found in Jamison (1999) and Williams (1997). The writings of Firestone (1997a, b) are particularly useful in relation to understanding the ways that different levels of suicidal intern are expressed in the language and imagery that a person might use. Firestone suggests that there exists a suicidal or self-destructive 'voice' to which practitioners can learn to be sensitive.

Assessing the severity of suicidal risk is far from being a precise science. Guidelines for sifting evidence of suicidal thoughts and intentions can be found in Hall and Platt (1999), Joseph (2000), Neimeyer *et al.* (2001) and Palmer (2002). The key indicators of high risk are:

- evidence of previous attempts
- current suicidal thoughts and plans
- access to means and opportunity
- attitude towards help
- current or past mental health problems
- current circumstances and quality of support available from professional and informal supporters
- current alcohol and drug use
- recent life events or anniversaries
- hopelessness and negative attitude towards the future
- male age 16–30.

In general, counselling may be relevant for a person when their expression of suicide is vague, when the person and their circumstances are known to the counsellor, and when the person is actively engaged in help-seeking. Otherwise, it is essential to give serious consideration, in collaboration with the person if at all possible, to organize some form of ongoing, continuing support in which the person's safety can be ensured while they find a way through their current life difficulties.

Other forms of risk, such as deliberate self-harm and violence to others, need to be approached in a similar fashion. Violent behaviour carries with it the additional challenge that the person may become violent towards the counsellor. It is necessary for counsellors to be prepared to deal with the rare occasions when people seeking help become violent or abusive. Strategies for dealing with this kind of eventuality include having colleagues available who can offer assistance, an alarm system, and an ability to use techniques of de-escalation, in which the person is responded to in a calm, accepting manner.

Exercise 7.7: *Ethical issues in counselling a client who cuts herself*

Melissa is 20 years old, and has recently started to cut herself when she feels depressed or unhappy. She has no history of mental illness and no previous involvement with mental health services or with any form of counselling. She lives in a rural community, and access to the nearest counselling or clinical psychology services requires a long journey on public transport. Melissa visits her local GP practice as part of a routine health screening initiative, and is seen by Ruth, one of the practice nurses, who notices the scars on Melissa's arms. She asks Melissa if she would like to talk, and gets the whole story. One week after this meeting, Melissa phones the centre and asks if she can see Ruth again. At this second meeting, she asks for help with the cutting behaviour. Ruth experiences a dilemma: she has completed a counselling skills training course, and she feels as though she has a good relationship with Melissa. On the other hand, she has never worked with a self-harming client before, and she is worried that she is out of her depth. Melissa is clear that she is neither willing nor able to travel to the city for therapy, and direct mental health services in their rural community have been suspended because of spending cuts. What are the ethical issues in this case, and how might they be resolved? Further discussion of this case, and of broader ethical issues in working with clients who self-harm, can be found in White *et al.* (2003).

Using touch

The use of touch represents a sensitive and problematic issue for many practitioners of embedded counselling. Some practitioners, such as nurses and other health professionals, routinely engage in physical contact with patients. By contrast, some teachers and social workers function in occupational environments characterized by fears that touch may be interpreted as sexual or disciplinary. In addition, some people who seek counselling may crave touch and can feel rejected if their counsellor refuses to hold their hand or hug them. Other clients, who may have been exposed to exploitative or sexualized touching or torture during their lives, may be terrified at the possibility that their counsellor might move into their physical space. A further aspect of the role of touching in counselling concerns the attitude of the counsellor, who may have anxieties in this area.

Hunter and Struve (1998) offer some valuable recommendations around the use of touch in counselling:

Touch is appropriate in counselling situations when:

- the client wants to touch or be touched
- the purpose of touch is clear
- the touch is clearly intended for the client's benefit
- the therapist has a solid knowledge base about the clinical impact of using touch
- the boundaries governing the use of touch are clearly understood by both client and therapist
- enough time remains in the therapy session to process the touch interaction
- the therapist–client relationship has developed sufficiently
- touch can be offered to all types of clients
- consultation/supervision is available and used
- the therapist is comfortable with the touch.

It is advisable *not* to use touch when:

- the focus of therapy involves sexual content prior to touch
- a risk of violence exists
- the touch occurs in secret
- the therapist doubts the client's ability to say no
- the therapist has been manipulated or coerced into the touch
- the use of touch is clinically inappropriate
- the touch is used to replace verbal therapy
- the client does not want to touch or be touched
- the therapist is not comfortable using touch.

An underlying concern that is present for many counselling supervisors, trainers and managers, is the fear that touch may be taking place to fulfil the needs of the counsellor, not those of the client. A further worry is that in the (rare) cases where counsellors engage in sexual exploitation of their clients, the early steps of the seduction always involve secretive touching. As a result, there has been a tendency in recent years for the counselling profession to err on the side of safety, and to seek at all costs to avoid counsellor–client physical contact. This is unfortunate and unhelpful, because appropriate touch has a demonstrable healing potential (Hunter and Struve, 1998).

Exercise 7.8: *Your experience of touch in a counselling situation*

Take a few moments to reflect on your personal experience as a recipient of counselling – either formal counselling/psychotherapy or informal/embedded counselling. To what extent, and in what ways, was physical contact involved in this relationship (or in each relationship)? (Include all forms of touch, from a welcoming handshake to a full hug.) What was the impact on you of the touch that took place (or the *absence* of touch)? What are the implications of these experiences for your own practice as a counsellor?

Ethical decision-making

Deciding what to do in a counselling situation when an ethical dilemma comes up is not at all easy. The websites of counselling organizations such as the British Association for Counselling and Psychotherapy also carry detailed codes of ethical practice. However, the ethical dilemmas that confront practitioners are so obvious that they do not require consultation of published sources, or they are so complex and sensitive that the written guidelines do not provide a straightforward guide to action. When trying to arrive at a solution to an ethical dilemma, it can be useful to apply a step-by-step decision-making framework:

1 Collect all relevant information about the situation, the preferences and resources of the person seeking help and yourself as the counsellor, and the possible views of other people who might be affected by the outcome.

2 Consider who benefits from different courses of action. Identify the benefits of what could be done from the point of view of the person, the counsellor and others.

3 Consider the consequences. Identify the consequences of any action from the point of view of the person, the counsellor and others.

4 Identify duties. To whom does a duty exist in the case being examined? For example, does the counsellor have a primary duty or responsibility to the person, or to a wider group, such as the person's family or society as a whole? To whom does the organization within which the counsellor is employed have a duty or responsibility? What is the counsellor's duty to themself?

5 Consult. Use consultation with others; for example, a counselling supervisor or mentor, or published sources, to develop a more complete understanding of duties, benefits and consequences, and to check out your own assumptions in these areas.

6 Decide. Bring together these various factors into a preliminary plan of action.

7 Test the plan. Consult again to check how the plan appears to other people (including the person being helped). Evaluate your plan from the perspective of Stadler's (1986) tests of 'universality', 'publicity' and 'justice' by reflecting on the following questions:

- Would I recommend this course of action to anyone else in similar circumstances? Would I condone my behaviour in anyone else? (Universality)
- Would I tell other counsellors what I intend to do? Would I be willing to have the actions and the rationale for them published on the front page of the local newspaper or reported on the evening news? (Publicity)
- Would I treat another client in the same situation differently? If this person was a well-known political leader, would I treat them differently? (Justice).

In practice, there are occasions when a counsellor may feel that a decision needs to be made immediately, and there is not enough time to work through the steps outlined above. However, even when this happens, it can be valuable afterwards to sit down and work out the intricacies of duty, benefit and consequence that were at stake, and to use consultation – ethical dilemmas are an important topic in consultation and supervision.

The concept of boundary

One of the concepts that has been mentioned several times in this chapter is the idea of *boundaries*. Counselling can be understood as giving a person a safe space, outside of the demands and pressures of everyday life, within which they can choose to talk about a problem in living. This counselling space is like a social or cultural 'bubble' within which the person feels free to say whatever they want, without fear of consequences. In helping to create such a space, a counsellor is in effect building a barrier or *boundary* between the counselling conversation, and the rest of the person's life: what is said during the counselling session stays there. Different rules apply within the counselling space; for instance, it is acceptable to say the unthinkable, or express feelings or wishes that would be unacceptable to others. Most of the time counselling conversations and relationships can be contained within this space or boundary without too much difficulty. On the whole, a counsellor and a person seeking counselling possess a shared understanding of what they are doing together, and the limits of their relationship. Sometimes, however, threats to the integrity of the space, or the clarity of the boundary between counselling and everyday life, can emerge. Examples of such situations include:

- Either the person, or the counsellor, wishes to extend the relationship into friendship, and may suggest meeting on a social basis.
- There may be other types of pre-existing link between the person and the counsellor (they may have a 'dual relationship') and these different roles

become muddled. For instance, a university tutor offers to meet with a student to provide supportive counselling on a regular basis. The student goes along with this, because they do not want to offend the tutor and risk getting a poor essay mark; the tutor realizes the student's essay is a fail, but does not want to add to their troubles by giving a poor mark. This situation soon begins to intrude on the counselling relationship as a hidden agenda that cannot be talked about.

- Other people may be clamouring to be informed about what is being said in counselling sessions.
- The person may express needs that cannot be effectively resolved through counselling, and require urgent action. For example, the person may disclose an intention to harm self or others, or may exhibit high levels of emotion that lead them to be unable to look after themself at the end of a counselling session.

Each of these scenarios can represent a different type of boundary issue that is associated with the possibility of violating core ethical principles such as autonomy, confidentiality and avoidance of harm.

It is essential for anyone involved in offering counselling relationships to have a clear understanding of the boundaries that are appropriate to the work that they are doing. In any counselling situation, there are usually boundaries in operation around:

- Time – when does counselling happen, how long does it go on for, how are the start and finish points signalled?
- Space – where does counselling take place, how private is this space (is there anyone else there?), how are the edges of the space marked off?
- Information – who gets to hear about what has been said in the counselling session (confidentiality)? How is information recorded, what information is held?
- Intimacy – how close is the relationship? How willing is the counsellor to be known? Is touch permissible?
- Access – what kind of contact is possible between counselling sessions? What happens if the person feels a need to talk with their counsellor between sessions?
- Safety – the safety of the person and/or the counsellor both within and outside of formal meetings; for example, what happens if the person becomes violent, or threatens suicide?

For each of these boundary dimensions it can be helpful to map out: (a) what the boundary is; (b) who decides on the boundary, and how it is decided or negotiated; (c) how the person seeking help learns about the existence of the boundary or is invited to negotiate it; and (d) what happens if the boundary is violated.

Exercise 7.9: *Mapping your counselling boundaries*

Take a large piece of paper and some coloured pens, and draw a map of the different boundary dimensions that operate in your counselling practice depicting how these boundaries are created and maintained, and how boundary threats are dealt with. It can be useful to carry out this activity in a group to allow sharing and discussion of how boundary mechanisms function in different counselling settings.

Careful attention to boundaries is particularly important when the counselling is embedded in another helping role, such as that of nurse, teacher or social worker. In stand-alone specialist counselling, many of the boundaries listed above are 'built in' to the basic procedures of the counselling agency – weekly one-hour sessions (time boundary), leaflets to clients explaining confidentiality (information boundary), the counsellor never having any other relationship or contact with the client outside of sessions (intimacy boundary), and so on. In embedded counselling, by contrast, there is always some level of dual relationship between counsellor and person seeking help, and some degree of improvization required in relation to time, space and access issues. It is therefore absolutely essential for anyone engaged in embedded counselling to do as much *preparation* as possible in advance of offering a counselling relationship in terms of thinking through boundary issues and defining personal and organizational limits. It is also crucial for anyone engaged in embedded counselling to use supervision and support on a regular basis as a means of keeping boundary issues under review.

Conclusions

In counselling, ethical issues are not separate from practice – they are part of practice. A counsellor who feels morally secure in what they are doing tends to be more relaxed, and convey a sense of confidence to the client. Similarly, a client who has a fundamental trust in the integrity of their counsellor is more likely to talk about important stuff, and embrace the possibility of change. Each of the ethical domains that have been discussed in this chapter can also be regarded as an aspect of the counselling process. For example, talking about the limits of confidentiality is a necessary step in ethical good practice *and* a means of strengthening the counsellor–client relationship. Asking the client if they wish to proceed with counselling is similarly an element of ethical practice *and* a means of positioning themself as person with strengths and a capacity to decide what is best. While it is important for anyone in a counselling role to be as prepared as they can be to deal with ethical dilemmas through reading, discussion and role-play, the key strategy that needs to be employed in all ethical scenarios is a willingness to proceed on a collaborative basis. Resolving ethical dilemmas is not a matter of applying an algorithm or set of rules in one's head, but instead consists of engaging in a process of consultation and collaborative decision-making with the client, colleagues, and one's supervisor.

Suggested further reading

Further discussion of the issues raised in this chapter in relation to theory and research on counselling ethics can be found in:

McLeod, J. (2009) *An Introduction to Counselling*, 4th edn. Maldenhead: Open University Press (chapter 17).

There are two excellent introductory textbooks on ethical issues in counselling:

Bond, T. (2000) *Standards and Ethics for Counselling in Action*, 2nd edn. London: Sage Publications.

Corey, G., Corey, M. and Callanan, P. (2007) *Issues and Ethics in the Helping Professions*, 7th edn. Pacific Grove, CA: Brooks/Cole.

A key paper, which has served as a cornerstone for discussions of counselling ethics for almost 30 years is:

Kitchener, K.S. (1984) Intuition, critical evaluation and ethical principles: the foundation for ethical decisions in counseling psychology, *Counseling Psychologist*, 12: 43–55.

An invaluable source of information on legal aspects of counselling is:

Jenkins, P. (2007) *Counselling, Psychotherapy and the Law*, 2nd edn. London: Sage Publications.

Working collaboratively: building a counselling relationship

It's good of you to see me
Regular like this.
You know
I remember
You said at the first time I saw you
That sometimes there are things you can't
Speak
To your family
About.
But I know you will listen.
Its funny, but I can't get it out of my mind.
I don't think there's anyone else knows this.
My grand-dad.
Died the week of his 60th birthday.
The same thing.
They were planning a party.
He was laid out.
In my nan's dining room.

Introduction

Problems in living that lead people to seek counselling can usually be resolved in other ways. For example, if a person is experiencing work stress and over-load, they can sit down with a piece of paper and make a plan of action, take up yoga and meditation as a means of relaxation, or read a self-help manual. Each of these methods of stress management can be effective. The distinctive feature of counselling, in comparison with these other coping or change strategies is that counselling primarily operates through the formation of a *relationship*. But what does this mean? What kind of relationship can exist between a person and their counsellor? And how and why does this relationship necessarily have a positive impact? After all, if we look at our lives, we can all identify relationships that are at times destructive or limiting, and may even have difficulty in identifying relationships that have unequivocally been good for us. What is it about a counselling relationship that is different?

At one level, the relationship in counselling is straightforward – it is someone to talk to. If you need to talk something through, then it is essential to have someone who will listen. Beyond this, the relationship in counselling is a relationship with a person who stands outside of the problem, who is independent of one's family, friendship network or work group, and who can respond to the problem in a fresh and unbiased fashion. Beyond this, there is a deeper meaning to the idea of a relationship. A relationship implies an encounter with an *other*, a person who is separate from oneself. At some level, the challenge of making contact with this *other* evokes a long list of questions that a person may have about how they connect with other people in general. For example: Can another person be trustworthy? Can I be understood (do I make sense or do I come across as crazy?) and accepted? Can I be really honest with another person? Can I allow someone else to care for me?

When counselling is embedded in other roles and relationships, for example when it takes place in the context of a nurse–patient relationship, or a teacher–pupil relationship, the significance of the relationship for the person seeking help will mainly be at a practical level – someone to talk to who is reasonably detached from the problem, who is accessible, someone that you know and trust. Nevertheless, even in these situations, there is always a deeper resonance to the relationship. In counselling, a person is not seeking help for an 'objective' problem, such as 'how do I fix my washing machine?' Rather, the person is seeking help for a problem in *living:* 'why did I get into an argument with the man who came to fix my washing machine?' Counselling always comes back to questions around 'who am I and how do I relate to other people?' In talking about these questions, a person expresses their subjectivity (this is who I am) in relation to the 'you' or 'other' represented by the counsellor. In turn, the counsellor is trying to find a way to work together ('how can *we* tackle this . . .?'). This core issue of aloneness and separateness in life runs through all counselling conversations, sometimes in the background, at other times up front.

The aims of this chapter are to suggest some strategies that can be employed in building relationships that are empowering and helpful, and explore some of the ideas that have been proposed

Box 8.1: *Facilitative relationships in your own life*

Take a few moments to think about the people in your life with whom you have had relationships that allow you to express yourself most fully. Describe the qualities of these people. In what ways can your internal image of these relationships be valuable for your role as a counsellor?

Box 8.2: *When professional relationships go wrong*

A piece of research carried out by Dianna Kenny (2004) provides a salutary lesson regarding the importance of relationships in health care. Kenny (2004) interviewed 20 patients whose treatment for chronic pain had not been successful, and 22 doctors who were chronic pain specialists. Participants were invited to give accounts of their experiences of coping or working with chronic pain. Interviews ranged between 45 minutes and 2 hours in length. Analysis of the transcripts revealed a fundamental breakdown in relationships between these people and their doctors. A key theme was what the researcher categorized as 'a struggle . . . to determine who would assume the role of speaker and who would listen' (p. 300). A typical patient statement in respect of this theme was 'they (the doctors) don't even listen to what you have to say . . . you can tell they are not listening at all – they just write up a script and say see you next month. You have to jump up and down or scream at them to be heard'. A typical doctor statement within this theme was: 'people seem to be very hard to educate. They don't understand. They get fixed ideas about where the pain is coming from. It is hard to change their focus'. Another key theme lay in the different beliefs held by patients and doctors regarding the cause and meaning of the pain. All of the patients made statements along the lines of: 'they (the doctors) don't seem to think that you might really be in pain. They think that it is all in your mind . . . They all say "take an antidepressant and go home". You start to think – am I mad or stupid?' By contrast doctors were asserting that: 'It stands to reason. If you have done all the tests possible, and you get nothing, not a hint of a physical problem, what else can you conclude?' These patients wanted, but did not receive, emotional and psychological care from their doctors: 'Doctor can't handle the emotions we present with . . . You try to talk to them, but you see them watching the clock for the next patient'. Rather than being treated as individuals, patients experienced themselves as being typecast as 'just another chronic pain patient'. The results of this study demonstrate very vividly the chasm that can open up between practitioners and their clients when relational factors are neglected. For Kenny (2004), the implications of her findings were clear: it is essential that doctors should learn how to treat patients as co-equals, and engage in shared decision-making.

The idea of building a relationship

In most professional situations, in teaching, social work, and health, the relationship between the person seeking help and the practitioner forms the backdrop to their work together. The focus is largely on what needs to be done, the practical task in hand. The relationship is taken for granted. In counselling situations, the relationship needs to take centre stage, because meaningful counselling depends on the establishment of a bond or alliance that is strong enough for the person to be able to tolerate talking about issues that are emotionally painful, embarrassing and shameful, out of control or confusing. Sometimes, a person who is seeking help, and the practitioner who is in the role of counsellor to that person, may just hit it off from the start, and be able to understand, appreciate and trust each other without difficulty. More usually, however, a relationship needs to be *built*. This is why counselling can take time – the person seeking help may need to test out the relationship before they can come to rely on it. Good counsellors pay attention not only to the problems and dilemmas presented by the person seeking help, but also continually monitor the quality of the relationship or contact they have with the person, and look for ways to strengthen it.

Building a caring relationship is facilitated by two forms of activity. First, the counsellor can invite the person to talk about what matters most to them in terms of how they feel that the counsellor needs to be to allow them to make use of the situation. What matters most might include being honest ('don't lie to me'), discussing things in a particular way (e.g. by *not* asking questions – 'it's like being interrogated' – or by asking questions – 'your questions help me to talk'), or being open about their own experience of the problem ('do you know what it's like to have a habit you can't break?'). Some people in counselling relationships want to know in detail about who will hear about what they say to the counsellor (the limits of confidentiality). Others will want to be reassured about the constancy and availability of the counsellor ('I was just gutted when that other nurse was transferred to a different unit'). Once the person has identified some of their relationship needs, it is important to explore what these needs mean in practice ('what does "not lying" mean to you – what do I have to do to let you know that I'm not lying to you?'). It is not realistic to expect a person to be able to specify all of their desired relationship qualities first time of asking. On the whole, people are not very aware of what they want or need in relationships, and it may be necessary to return to this issue at regular intervals to check whether other elements of 'what you need from me in this relationship' might have come to the attention of the person.

A second activity that promotes relationship-building is to reflect on the impact of what is actually happening when the person and counsellor attempt to work together. A counsellor might achieve this by saying something along the lines of 'would it be OK to pause for a minute to look at what happened there when I asked you that question? I might be wrong, but I just had a sense that you felt angry with me for asking you about that. Is that right?' Alternatively, the counsellor can open up this topic by disclosing their own intentions; for example, 'I'm wondering what might be the best way to take this forward . . . I'm aware that there are lots of questions that I have about what you are talking about, but I don't know whether it would be a distraction to you for me to ask them, or whether it would be useful for you . . . or whether you might have some other ideas about what would be best'.

The aim is to work together to build a relationship that makes it possible for the person to use counselling to move forward in their life. If one of the limiting factors in a person's life lies in the area of having difficulties in making relationships, then the very act of being able to experience a caring relationship with a counsellor may allow them to begin to develop a better capability for developing friendships, work relationships and intimate partnership in everyday real-life situations. Some counsellors worry about the danger of their 'clients' becoming over-involved, and too dependent on them. This danger exists, but is often overstated. If a person is at a point in their life where they are isolated and distanced from others, then it seems inevitable that once they begin to experience a close relationship (e.g. with a counsellor) many previously suppressed aspects of what is involved in relating to another person, such as depending on them, begin to be expressed. The vast majority of people who use counselling have little interest in being locked into a permanent dependent relationship with their counsellor – they want to get on with their lives, and to use the relationship with the counsellor to that end.

When building a relationship, like building a house or anything else, it is always important to be prepared for things to go wrong. Part of the art of counselling is to be aware of, and be skilled in repairing, ruptures in the relationship between the counsellor and the person seeking help. A breakdown of relationship can occur either because it may simply be hard for the person seeking help to trust anyone, or to believe that anyone might care about them. Such a person is likely to dip constantly in and out of being able to collaborate with their counsellor. Alternatively, a rupture can happen when a previously secure relationship between person and counsellor is threatened in some way. In either case, the underlying question that is conveyed by the person to the counsellor is 'can I trust you?', 'is it safe to talk to you?' or 'is it worth speaking to you?'. The task of repairing a caring relationship involves suspending any other tasks that might be in progress, and using some time to talk about how both participants experience the relationship. It is futile and can even be destructively manipulative to attempt to carry out a one-sided analysis of only difficulties that the help-seeker or client might be experiencing in the relationship: relationship breakdown is always a two-way process. If the counsellor does not acknowledge their feelings and uncertainty about what is happening, the message to the person is that they must have a terrible deficit in respect of forming relationships. If, on the other hand, the counsellor is able to refer to their own worries, strategies, needs and blind spots, then the task of repairing a relationship can be carried out as a genuinely collaborative endeavour.

A final point concerning the building of a relationship is that it is a mistake to view this process as solely focused on what takes place in the counselling conversation. As a counsellor, it is useful to think about other good relationships that you might have, and what makes them work well. People with strong relationships remember the facts and stories of each other's lives, celebrate birthdays and achievements, give and receive gifts, anticipate sources of stress and pressure, and much else. Depending on the duration and circumstances of a counselling relationship, some of these behaviours may be relevant. A counselling relationship is different from friendship or a family connection, because it is more circumscribed or boundaried, exists for a purpose, and is usually fairly temporary. Nevertheless, it is a relationship that builds and is strengthened when each of the participants thinks about the other between meetings, and remembers information about the other. In any strong relationship, each person is alive in the life of the other.

The major feature that distinguishes a counselling relationship from most other types of relationship is that a counsellor *listens*. An emphasis on listening is one of the main building blocks of a counselling relationship. There are many other situations in life where a person can tell someone else about a problem that they have been experiencing. However, rarely does the person on the receiving end really listen. For example, telling a friend about a problem will usually elicit reciprocal disclosure from the friend – they will move into describing a similar problem that they have encountered themselves. This is a useful response within a friendship because it demonstrates solidarity and sharing, and may lead to learning something about the coping and problem-solving strategies that are used by the other person. Telling a professional person, such as a doctor, nurse or social worker about a problem, is likely to lead to an advice-giving response, rather than listening. This is because the professional helper may not have time to listen, and also because they will probably believe that it is their job to sort out the problem by offering a concrete, immediate solution.

In counselling, listening is understood as an *active* process. Listening is not a matter of being a passive recipient or recorder of information. In listening, a counsellor is expressing curiosity and interest. It is a form of listening that comes from a position of wanting to know more. There are two senses of wanting to know more. One sense reflects a desire to learn about what happened next, or what the context was within which an event took place. The other sense of knowing more is a curiosity about gaps, pauses and significant moments within the person's telling of their story. A counsellor wants to know more about what is being held back in these moments, what is not being said, and what is perhaps difficult to say. The psychologist Eugene Gendlin (1984b) has described this kind of a listening as a curiosity or sensitivity around the *edge* of the person's awareness of what they are talking about. This curiosity, sensitivity and interest marks out the kind of listening that a counsellor does as not merely listening for information (who did what, what their names were, when it happened?), but listening for *meaning*. A counsellor is listening for clues about what makes this set of events significant for a person, and why they wish to talk about it *now*.

A further aspect of listening within counselling relationships is that a counsellor is characteristically *patient* in their listening. A good counsellor will allow a person to feel as though they have all the time in the world. As an audience, a counsellor rarely interrupts, is willing to allow the person to get to the end of what they want to say, and is curious about how the story ends. A counsellor operates on the basis that there are some things that are very hard to say, and require time to emerge, and that eventually the person will find their own way to say what needs to be said.

Finally, counsellors tack back and forward between listening, and checking out that what they have heard is accurate. Checking out conveys to a person that they are valued, and that understanding what they mean is of paramount importance to the counsellor. Checking out is also a constant reminder to the person that however they might feel at that moment, there is another person who is doing their best to be 'with' them in their struggle.

A counsellor is always doing their utmost to listen with care and attention to what the person is trying to say, no matter what other counselling tasks they might be working on at the time. The message is: 'this is a relationship within which you are listened to, where you are heard, where what you have to say is important'. This dimension of the relationship can be extremely useful for some people. Even if the counsellor is someone with whom they may only meet infrequently, they carry around with them the knowledge that in this part of their life space there is a place where they will be heard.

In recent years, some writers have used the word *presence* to describe the quality of relationship that can exist when a person in a counselling role is willing to be fully 'there' for someone who is seeking to talk through an issue (see Greenberg and Geller, 2001 for a useful introduction to this topic). The notion of 'presence' implies that the counsellor's attention is focused entirely on the person and what they are saying, rather than on any other matters. The idea also implies that the counsellor is doing more than listening to the person – they are also physically and sensually centred, and responding to the whole way of being of the person. There is a co-presence, a being present to each other, that can occur in silence, in the space between words. The idea of presence refers to a kind of deep listening that goes beyond attending merely to the words that the person uses. The concept of presence, or being 'fully present' also acts as a reminder to anyone in the role of counsellor of how important it is to be able to leave aside their own personal 'business' or busyness, if they are to be able to be there, in the present moment, with the person they are seeking to help.

Box 8.3: *Nursing Mrs Q: caring presence in action*

A case study published by Joan Engebretson (2000), a nurse tutor and supervisor, illustrates some of the ways in which 'presence' may be expressed within a caring relationship. The paper focuses on the role of a student nurse, Brenda, in relation to a patient, Mrs Q, who had just given birth to a premature baby the previous day, a boy, who was in intensive care. Mrs Q, we learn, had a history of six previous pregnancy losses – the current baby was the first live birth. Her husband was 'out of town'. Brenda arrived at the post-partum unit at 6.45 am, and was assigned to look after Mrs Q for the day. Within an hour, they were called to the intensive care unit, because the condition of the baby was unstable. Brenda moved Mrs Q's wheelchair close to the isolation unit where her baby had been placed, and after a few minutes drew up a chair and sat beside her. Engebretson (2000) described what happened in the following terms:

> The two sat side by side in relative silence against a backdrop of the continual cacophony of human and mechanical noises. In addition to multiple conversations of doctors, nurses and other providers, there was the ceaseless hum of machinery punctuated by the beeps of monitors going off . . . As the morning advanced, the baby's condition became less stable and increasingly critical. The nurses invited Mrs Q to touch her infant very gently. Brenda sat with her occasionally touching her shoulder . . . it began to be apparent that as the doctors, nurses and various other providers approached Mrs Q and Brenda, there was a noticeable change in their manner. They moved a lot slower and spoke more quietly . . . After some time, one of the nurses placed the infant in Mrs Q's arms. She gently cradled her newborn, softly caressing his head and stroking his back. Brenda lightly placed her hand on Mrs Q's shoulder, arm, or back. Brenda seemed to sense that appropriate touch in this case needed to be very gentle, stable and unobtrusive, almost mirroring the touch Mrs Q used with her infant . . . it felt like time was suspended . . .

In a discussion with her tutor immediately after her work with Mrs Q:

> Brenda related being really scared at first, but she knew she had to be there for this patient. In order to make this connection to her patient she had first to make a connection with something within herself. The only way she could do that was to sit quietly with Mrs Q to help and heal. She discovered that she could reach an 'internal knowing of what to do' . . . going through that experience was one of the most profound experiences of her life, and although it was sad, it was also extraordinarily rewarding.

Engebretson (2000) comments that caring presence of this kind involves connectedness, sharing, loving and 'action beyond the ordinary' in ways that can have an impact not only on the individual recipient of care, but, as in this example, on the whole environment of a clinical unit.

A safe relationship: being trustworthy, reliable and dependable

Another critical characteristic of a counselling relationship is that it is *safe*. A counsellor is someone who is unequivocally on the side of the person, whose aim and purpose is to be helpful. By contrast, a counsellor is not someone who has any intention of using, abusing, harming or exploiting the person who comes for help. The counsellor has no axe to grind, no stake in whether the person decides to do one thing, or the opposite. The counsellor is a person who can be *trusted*.

Trust has a number of different facets. One aspect of trust centres around dependability. Does the counsellor do what they say that they will do? Do they turn up on time? Do they remember key information? For this aspect of trust to develop, there needs to be consistency between what a counsellor promises, and what they deliver. It is for this reason that many people involved in offering counselling roles are careful about checking out expectations with people who come for help, and being clear about what it is that they can and cannot provide. For example, if a person wants or feels they need a counsellor who will be available at the end of a phone in a crisis, it is essential that a counsellor is explicit about whether this level of responsiveness is possible or not. If a counsellor is unable to respond to crisis situations, it is better to say so, and explore the alternative sources of help that might be accessible during these times. A vague offer to a person to 'phone me if you really need to' runs the risk, if the phone is not answered or the counsellor comes across as irritated at being contacted in the middle of the night, of undermining trust.

Another facet of trust is concerned with how a counsellor responds to a person on a moment-by-moment basis. If there are too many discrepancies between what the counsellor says, and how they appear, the person on the receiving end will quickly being to wonder about what is going on. For example, if people who are gay, lesbian or bisexual are told by a counsellor that their sexual orientation is something to be valued and celebrated, but the counsellor looks uncomfortable when they say it, then the person may feel that the counsellor may not be allowing themself to be totally honest and transparent. In such a situation, the person seeking help would be likely to become very cautious about talking about their sexuality or lifestyle to this particular counsellor. Carl Rogers (1961) used the term *congruence* to describe this aspect of the counselling relationship, as a means of drawing attention to the importance for a counsellor of maintaining consistency between what they subjectively thought or felt, and what they said to their clients. Research carried out by Rogers and his colleagues showed that counsellor *incongruence* or falseness or inauthenticity would usually bring any meaningful conversation to a halt. People do not want to talk about their personal issues to someone who is pretending to listen, or pretending to accept their experience, or who seems to be just playing a professional role. What people want is someone who is genuine. For the counsellor, this will involve sometimes being really affected by what a person is saying, and being willing to show the sadness, anger or pleasure that is being felt.

The safety that is associated with a counselling relationship is not only the safety of reassurance, of feeling taken care of and protected, of being held within the hope conveyed by the other that everything will be all right. While this kind of parental caretaking or soothing forms an essential part of any counselling relationship, there is a further form of safety that also forms a necessary aspect of counselling: the sense of feeling safe enough to enter dangerous territory. This is similar to the trust that a person might have in a guide. To build the possibility for that kind of relationship, a counsellor needs to convey to the person an appreciation that they are aware that dangerous territory does exist, that they have the confidence and competence to survive a journey into such territory, and that they believe that the person can survive it too. A counsellor can signal that they feel able to move into painful areas of experience with the person by acknowledging what is at stake ('it's as if you want to let these feelings out but you fear that if you did, the tears would go on for ever . . .'), and talking through what could be done to make the risk bearable; for example, taking the issue piece by piece, or agreeing to meet for a longer session.

For a counsellor, entering a relationship of trust can represent a challenge on two fronts. It is hard for a person to be trusted if they do not feel worthy of trust. From the counsellor's side, being willing to be available to another person in a counselling role implies believing in one's own capacity to deserve trust. Acceptance of this can be difficult for some counsellors. The quality of the relationships between a counsellor and their colleagues can play a key factor around the building of trust. If someone who is engaged in counselling work feels that their supervisor, or immediate colleagues, do not support them in this activity, their capacity to offer secure relationships to those seeking help can be seriously undermined.

At the same time, it is important for a counsellor to recognize that most of the time the people who come to them for help will not trust them unconditionally, and will continue to test them out as a means of guarding against betrayal or disappointment. The issues that people bring to counselling are often topics or events that are hard for them to talk about, because of guilt, shame or embarrassment: it may require a high level of trust before the person feels safe enough to talk openly about what really matters.

Being genuine

From the perspective of the counselling skill model, people are driven to seek counselling because they have been silenced by the absence of other people in their lives who will listen, or the unwillingness or inability of people to engage in meaningful conversation around personal issues. The impact of either of these sets of circumstances is to leave the person with a sense of being invalidated – they are left feeling as though their experience, and their status as a person, does not count for anything and is worthless. To be more specific about the experience of invalidation, there are two broad types of relationship that can result in a person having a sense of not mattering. The first is where other people engage in pretence and dishonesty. The second is where others act in an impersonal and 'professional' manner. (See examples below.)

Joe is 15 years of age and has a learning disability that makes him depend on others to remind and assist him in fulfilling everyday tasks. He has lived with his mother, who has now become ill. Joe has moved in with his aunt and uncle. Although they are caring people, they seem unwilling to answer his questions about when his mother will come out of hospital, and when he can see her. They just tell him that she is 'doing well' and that he will be seeing her 'soon'. However, they are unable to hide their tension and anxiety. Joe becomes more afraid and angry.

Mathilde is 15. In her school, she is a member of an ethnic minority group. She is bullied by one of the older children in the dominant group. Asked by her class teacher one day why she is withdrawn and upset, Mathilde begins to talk about the racial violence and harassment that she has experienced. When asked afterwards by a friend how the conversation with the teacher went, Mathilde replies, 'She asked all the right questions and said all the right things. She even wrote some notes and said she would follow it up. But I could see that she didn't care. She was just going through the motions. I think she was worried about being late for lunch. Don't worry – I won't speak to her again'.

In each of these examples, the person in the helping role has made an effort to respond constructively, but has hidden their own feelings behind a mask. In the case of Joe, his aunt and uncle were worried about their sister's illness, and were trying to shield Joe from the reality of what was happening. In the case of Mathilde, her teacher felt furious but impotent, but had been trained to respond to pupils in a neutral, unemotional manner. Both Joe and Mathilde were *mystified* by what was happening – they had no reliable data on which to judge how the other person felt about the issues that they were bringing up. Their responses – anger from Joe and avoidance from Mathilde – are inevitable in the circumstances.

One of the main things that a person is looking for when they seek counselling is for their experience to be *authenticated* by another person. Authentication can only take place when the listener responds in a human and personal manner, which conveys fellow feeling. If a counsellor comes across as too detached, impersonal and 'professional' or as perpetually nice and agreeable, the person seeking counselling is always left wondering whether they are getting a 'real' response, or whether the counsellor's apparent empathy and concern is all just an act. By contrast, the more that a counsellor is willing to state their true position on things, to disagree or challenge, to acknowledge uncertainty and confusion, express feelings, and set limits on what they are able to give or do, the more confidence the person will have that the counsellor has a genuine interest in them.

One of the most important qualities of a helpful counselling relationship is emotional honesty. When someone is emotionally honest, they tend to be experienced as transparent, as not hiding anything. If, on the other hand, a counsellor is experienced as emotionally elusive or false, then the relationship tends to be undermined, because the person is thrown into a state of doubt through beginning to wonder about what may be being left unsaid by the counsellor.

Exercise 8.1: *The impact of being genuine*

In terms of the people to whom you offer a service, how often are you able to be congruent, authentic or fully 'present' with them? What is the effect on your relationship with your clients when you are able to be genuine with them? What are the organizational factors that facilitate or inhibit the expression of genuineness?

Caring

In deciding to enter a counselling relationship, a person is looking for someone who will *care* about them. The concept of 'care' has been largely ignored or devalued within the counselling literature, probably because it might be taken to imply a lack of professional expertise and detachment. This is a pity because, as the philosopher Heidegger has pointed out, *caring* represents a fundamental aspect of involvement in the world: the experience of caring discloses what is important and has meaning for us.

In a counselling relationship, caring can be expressed by:

- paying attention to the person
- anticipating the other person's needs
- small acts of kindness
- remembering information about the person's life
- thinking about the person when they are not there
- proceeding gently and slowly, and with patience – checking things out
- putting one's own needs aside in the interest of the other
- genuine curiosity about the experience and views of the person
- celebrating the person's achievements.

A further sense of the importance of care in counselling situations can be reinforced by considering that, in seeking counselling, people are allowing themselves to be people who are fragile, vulnerable, in pain or lost.

Exercise 8.2: *Putting caring into action*

How much do you care about the people who you meet in a professional role? How do you express your caring?

Working collaboratively

One of the most important aspects of a counselling relationship is the extent to which the person and the counsellor are able to work together to tackle problems. A useful image of the counselling relationship is that of an *alliance*: the person and the counsellor are allies in the struggle to deal with difficult issues.

On the whole, during counselling, the person and counsellor proceed as if they were 'on the same wavelength' and working effectively together – the issue of the strength of the 'alliance' is rarely raised as a specific topic for discussion. Nevertheless, there are many points within a counselling conversation where the question of working collaboratively is highly relevant:

- At the start – does the person wish to begin a counselling conversation right *now*?
- During a session – are we in agreement around what we are trying to achieve in the long run (goals)?
- Are we in agreement over what we are trying to do right at this minute (tasks)?
- Is this the best way to work through this particular issue (methods)?
- Whose turn is to it talk?
- Is this the time to stop?
- Do we need to talk about this again? When?
- What could we each have done to make that discussion more helpful?

Each of these moments represents an opportunity to stand back from the immediate flow of conversation and interaction between the person and the counsellor and reflect on what is happening. This activity can be understood as *metacommunication* – communicating and reflecting on the process of communication and the state of the relationship. A capacity to engage in metacommunication is a crucial aspect of collaborative working. An invaluable discussion of the nature of metacommunication in counselling can be found in Rennie (1998).

The nature of metacommunication can be illustrated by considering the usual shape and content of a conversation between a person and their counsellor. Most of the time in a counselling situation, both the person seeking help and the counsellor talk about the person's 'problem'. For example, a woman talking about her relationship with her teenage daughter might say: 'We just argue all the time. There doesn't seem to be anything we can do together that doesn't end up in a battle'. The person offering counselling – who could be a teacher, nurse or social worker – might reply by saying: 'that sounds really frustrating . . . it's as though there is a real barrier between you'. And the person seeking help might then go on to say more about other aspects of this issue. In this example, the focus of the conversation is on the problem that has been identified by the person. This is probably the kind of conversation that happens most frequently in counselling encounters – the counsellor acts as a kind of sounding board, and reflects back to the person the main threads of what they have been exploring in a way that helps them to expand on the issue and gain some perspective on it.

In addition to this kind of reflective response, it can be useful for a counsellor to build into their conversational repertoire the careful and consistent use of a slightly different way of responding to the person – *checking out*. The process of checking out introduces important possibilities for conveying value and affirmation to the person, and building the kind of relationship within which difficult issues can be explored safely. It can also have the effect of slowing down the interaction in a way that allows the person some opportunities to reflect on the feelings and thoughts that they are experiencing at that moment.

Checking out basically involves pausing within the flow of the conversation to test out assumptions about what is happening, or to inquire about the assumptions or the experience at that moment of the person who is seeking help. Rennie (1998) describes this activity as 'talking about the process of talking'. There are many different ways in which checking out or metacommunication can be helpful within a counselling session. Some of the most widely used forms of checking out are listed below along with examples of how they might be used to enhance the inter-action around 'my teenage daughter and I argue all the time' that was introduced earlier in this section:

A woman talking about her relationship with her teenage daughter states that 'we just argue all the time. There doesn't seem to be anything we can do together that doesn't end up in a battle'. Her counsellor, a worker in a family support centre, responds using these words: 'that sounds really frustrating . . . it's as though there is a real barrier between you . . .'. The counsellor's response is a fairly standard empathic reflection that picks up on the main feeling that she senses (the client's frustration) and seeks to find an image to capture the key relationship difficulty that is causing the problem (described by the counsellor as a 'barrier'). However, there are a number of ways in which the counsellor might choose to use metacommuni-cation to use her response to the client as an opportunity to reinforce the collabora-tive nature of their relationship. There are at least four metacommunicative strategies that the counsellor could employ at this moment:

1 *Check out the person's reaction to what the counsellor has just said*. The coun-sellor might wonder whether she had accurately understood the meaning for

the person of the situation that was being described, and could check this out by saying: 'that sounds really frustrating . . . it's as though there is a real barrier between you . . . Although, as I hear myself saying that, I'm not sure whether I've got it quite right. I'm aware that there's a lot about your situation that I don't know about . . . Is frustration the right term, or would you use another word . . . and maybe "barrier" is too strong. . .?'

2 *The counsellor being open about her strategies and intentions at that point.* The counsellor may be mindful of the fact that, although the person has mentioned a number of issues that are bothering her, she has a gut feeling that the situation with her daughter is probably the most important or urgent of these. This could be expressed by saying: 'I realize that in the last couple of minutes you've told me about lots of things that are hard for you at the moment. But it's what you said about your daughter that really struck home for me, because it seemed very painful for you, and I have a sense that it might be the link between all these other things you mentioned. What's happening with your daughter sounds really frustrating . . . it's as though there is a real barrier between you . . . My sense is that it might be useful to stay with this for a bit. What do you think? Does that feel right for you?'

3 *Invite the client to focus on her own plans, strategies and assumptions.* The counsellor may not be sure about the agenda or goals of the person at this point in the conversation, so might say: 'the situation with your daughter sounds really frustrating . . . it's as though there is a real barrier between you . . . But I'm not sure whether that's the thing you want to look at more closely now. Is it? Or is there something else that's more pressing?'

4 *Check out her assumptions about what the person might be thinking or intending.* Sometimes a counsellor may come up with a theory, or a guess, about what might lie behind the thoughts or feelings that the person may be experiencing, but without having any real evidence to indicate whether these ideas are valid or not. Often, this kind of counsellor intuition can be sensitive and accurate, and provide a good guide for moving forward. On some occasions, however, the counsellor may have misunderstood the person. It is therefore important to check out any such hunches or theories. In this case, the counsellor may have a sense that the person blames herself in relation to her problem with her daughter. One way of acknowledging this might be to say: 'that sounds really frustrating . . . it's as though there is a real barrier between you . . . As you were speaking about your daughter, I just had a strong feeling that you were blaming yourself for what was happening. Have I got that right, or is it something else?' The person might reply that 'I wouldn't call it blaming myself, it's more that I just don't feel adequate – I don't know what to do'. In this instance, the process of checking out has allowed the counsellor to see that her assumption was only partially correct: the person was being self-critical, but not to the extent of actually *blaming* herself.

Each of these metacommunicative strategies has the effect of standing aside from the immediate content of what is being said to allow a few moments of sharing, discussion and reflection around aspects of the relationship between the counsellor and the person seeking help. In effect, these metacommunicative moves are offering openings to a question that could be summarized as: are we on the same wavelength – do we each understand and agree with what the other is trying to achieve right now? These moves are also consistently emphasizing the affirming and empowering stance of the counsellor in relation to the person. In effect, they are conveying ideas such as 'you are in charge', 'I believe that you are the person who knows what is helpful for you', 'I can only help you if you let me know if what I am doing is working for you'.

Regularly checking out with the person what they think, feel and want, and what you as a counsellor think, feel and want, has the possibility for achieving a wide range of positive outcomes in relation to talking through an issue or problem. It implies to the person that they have choices, and that these choices are important to the counsellor and worthy of being taken seriously. It implies that the counsellor is doing their best to be sensitive and responsive to what the person needs at that moment, and might therefore be a person who can be trusted in the future. It suggests that the counsellor is someone who is genuinely curious and interested in the person, and in the totality of what the person might be thinking and feeling – the counsellor is not pursuing a fixed pathway or agenda. Checking out introduces slight pauses within the conversation, moments within which the person might shift slightly away from the problem, and engage in a bit of reflection around what the problem means to them ('is this about blaming myself?'), or what they can do to change ('am I willing to look closely at this issue, right now?'). It also opens up an awareness that it may be OK to be wrong about some things, and that there are ways of surviving being wrong – a particularly helpful insight for people whose lives may be dominated by perfectionism.

The role of checking out or metacommunication can be important at points in counselling where the relationship, or topic being talked about, shifts in some way. For example, if a person talking about a practical issue, such as a patient talking to a nurse about treatment choices, or a student talking to a teacher about course options, conveys in some way that there is an emotional or personal dimension to the issue that they might wish to explore, then it is good practice to check out with the person whether they would at that moment like to explore their feelings in more depth; '. . you seemed to me to have a lot of feelings around as you were talking . . . there seemed to be tears in your eyes . . . I was wondering if you wanted to take a few minutes with me to look at how these feelings might be a factor in the choices you need to make . . .?' Depending on the circumstances, it may also be important to check out with the person how long they have to talk (or you have to listen to them) and any confidentiality limits that may apply. Similarly, it would often be appropriate to check out with the person that they have reached the end of a counselling episode. For example: '. . . from what you have told me, I think we can both understand why it is so essential for you to make the right decision at this point in your life . . . is there more you wanted to say about that side of things? Would it be OK to go back to thinking about the type of treatment/course that would be best for you . . .?'

Metacommunication is an essential strategy in situations where the relationship between a person and a counsellor may have broken down, or reached a point of impasse. It is not realistic to expect the counselling relationship to proceed smoothly at all times – there will inevitably be points at which a person feels that they are not getting what they need from the counsellor, or the counsellor misunderstands them. At these moments, it is valuable for the counsellor to be able to 'hit the pause button', and invite reflection from both participants around what has been happening. It is particularly important for the counsellor to be willing and able to acknowledge their role in the difficulties that have arisen – a counsellor who insists on attributing the sole cause of any problems to inadequacies on the part of the person or client is not really demonstrating a collaborative style of working, and may come across as blaming and persecutory. A great deal of research into the topic of 'ruptures in the therapeutic alliance' has been carried out by the psychologist, Jeremy Safran, whose writings includes a wealth of practical suggestions on how to resolve relationship breakdown between counsellors and those receiving help from them (see, for example, Safran, 1993; Safran and Muran, 2000).

At a deeper philosophical level, metacommunication is a good way of expressing some of the core values of counselling. Rather than viewing the counsellor and person seeking help as very separate entities, the process of checking out suggests a sense of two people being in a relationship with each other, and requiring to take account of each other's position to be able to work effectively together. The idea of being a 'relational self' rather than an isolated, completely separate 'autonomous self' can be helpful to people who have difficulty in getting and giving support, and this simple conversational strategy can represent a useful and unthreatening way of introducing the possibility of relatedness into someone's awareness. The use of metacommunication emphasizes the worth of the person – their intentions, preferences and experience are being taken seriously.

Box 8.4: *The relationship matters more than counselling techniques*

In research carried out in Australia by Terry MacCormack and his colleagues, counselling was offered to people who were receiving treatment for cancer. The counselling was fairly short term (maximum eight sessions) and was highly structured around specific therapeutic tasks that the patient was taken through by their counsellor. In the study, the effectiveness of two different types of therapy was compared. One form of therapy that was offered was cognitive-behavioural therapy (CBT); the other approach consisted of relaxation and visualization exercises. Interviews were carried out with patients after they had received counselling. The results of the study were striking. Although the people who had received counselling praised the professionalism of their therapists, and reported that the techniques that they had employed had been useful, all of them stated that what had been most important was to be able to spend time with someone who listened and cared. Some of the statements made by participants were:

'I was able to talk and relate to her and trust her, and to talk about things . . . she helped me to keep going'.

'It was like I had another friend to talk to'.

'It was good to have someone objective to talk to, to get things off your chest'.

'He was safe and easy to talk to. So I could say anything and be honest about how I felt'.

'It was nice to have someone coming and talking to me . . . The doctors are hopeless, and they're the ones you have the main contact with . . . I asked for empathy [from my doctor] and he gave me none. . .'.

The authors of this report concluded that participants in the study seemed to be saying that their counselling was 'primarily a "being with" or relational experience (that) . . . provided a unique conversational space to explore/discuss thoughts/feelings, and . . . occurred with an experienced and understanding professional who cared' (MacCormack *et al.*, 2001: 58). The implications of this study are that 'being with' a person, being willing to listen, and being able to express genuine caring, are what matter most to people who are receiving counselling.

Theoretical frameworks for making sense of counselling relationships

The critical importance of the relationship has been widely accepted within the counselling literature. Within this body of theory and research, there have been a number of frameworks suggested that can be applied in making sense of what happens between a person and a counsellor. The most relevant theoretical models for practitioners engaged in 'embedded' counselling are the person-centred, psychodynamic, transactional analysis (TA) and multidimensional approaches. These sets of ideas can be regarded as comprising *tools for reflection* – concepts that can be used in training and supervision, and within the flow of everyday practice, as ways of making sense of what is happening in relationships with people seeking help.

The person-centred counselling relationship

The person-centred approach to counselling, originally developed by Carl Rogers in the USA in the 1940s, and more recently associated with the writings of Dave Mearns, Brian Thorne, Tony Merry, Germain Lietaer and others, has been a major influence on the thinking and practice of many counsellors and people who use counselling skills in their work.

The key idea around which person-centred counselling is organized is that people develop personal and emotional problems because of a lack of relationships within which they can be themselves. Instead, the person may have been exposed to relationships in which they have felt judged and not valued. The remedy for this, according to person-centred theorists, is to provide the person with a relationship within which they can grow and develop. Forming a relationship with the person is therefore an essential aspect of any counselling that is based in the person-centred tradition.

What makes a good relationship? Rogers and his colleagues suggested a set of necessary and sufficient conditions (also known as 'core conditions') that characterized a good relationship between a therapist and a person seeking counselling (the 'client'):

1 Two persons are in psychological contact.
2 The therapist experiences unconditional positive regard for the client.
3 The therapist is congruent or integrated in the relationship.
4 The therapist experiences an empathic understanding of the client's internal frame of reference, and endeavours to communicate this to the client.
5 The communication to the client of the therapist's empathic understanding and unconditional positive regard is to a minimal extent achieved.

Each of these factors is important in the counselling relationship, and the absence of any one of them will undermine the bond between the counsellor and the person seeking help. For example, unconditional positive regard (which can also be understood as acceptance, or a sense of being valued) is essential because a judgemental attitude on the part of the counsellor would merely replicate the key relationship factor that had brought about the person's difficulties in the first place. A positively 'prizing' or acceptant response from the counsellor, by contrast, clearly signals to the person that they are entering a different kind of relationship, one in which they are free to express their true feelings and preferences. Empathic understanding, which refers to a sense of being understood, with the counsellor being seen as able to view the situation from the perspective of the client, is important because it conveys to the person that the counsellor is interested in them, wants to understand, and is not seeking to impose their own ideas or advice on to the person – all of this encourages the person to keep talking, and to give voice to all aspects of their problem.

However, from a person-centred perspective, the single most important quality is *congruence* (also described as authenticity, genuineness or 'realness'). Congruence refers to the capacity of the counsellor to make use of their own experience within the relationship. This involves paying attention to one's feelings (and thoughts, images and fantasies) that come up when the person is talking, and using these to inform one's response to the person. Sometimes, this will mean the counsellor sharing with the person what they are feeling at that moment. At other times, the counsellor will internally take note of what they are feeling, but not say anything about it at that moment. For example, if a person is in the process of talking about an issue, it may be unhelpful to interrupt them to tell them how you are feeling at that moment.

Another key principle of the person-centred helping relationship is *non-directiveness*. This is an attitude or philosophy that the person-centred counsellor adopts. Rather than trying to guide or advise the person, the counsellor adopts a strategy of following them, paying very close attention and showing great interest while letting the person take the lead. The idea here is that the person is the expert on their own life, and that the counsellor is like a companion on their journey.

If a counsellor is in touch with their own feelings and reactions, and relatively open in sharing these with the person, and is consistently following the person in an interested, warm, accepting and curious way, then they will come across to the person as having *presence*, or being present for them. Presence can be seen as a midpoint between being *over-involved* (intrusively over-interested and identifying with the client) and being *under-involved* (cold, distant, detached and 'professional'). A counsellor who displays presence is, as Mearns puts it, in a good position to work at *relational depth*, and form a relationship with the person that will enable them to explore difficult issues.

Carl Rogers (1961: ch. 3) summed all this up in the form of a list of characteristics of a helping relationship:

> Can I be in some way which will be perceived by the other person as trustworthy, as dependable or consistent in some deep sense?
> Can I be expressive enough as a person that what I am will be communicated unambiguously?
> Can I let myself experience positive attitudes towards this other person – attitudes of warmth, caring, liking, interest, respect?
> Can I be strong enough as a person to be separate from the other?
> Am I secure enough within myself to permit his or her separateness?
> Can I let myself enter fully into the world of his or her feelings and personal meanings and see these as he or she does?
> Can I accept each facet of this other person when he or she presents it to me?
> Can I act with sufficient sensitivity in the relationship that my behaviour will not be perceived as a threat?
> Can I free the other from the threat of external evaluation?
> Can I meet this other individual as a person who is in the process of becoming, or will I be bound by his past and by my past?

The image of the counselling relationship that has been developed within the person-centred approach has proved useful for practitioners working in a wide variety of settings. The key ideas within the model – acceptance, congruence/genuineness and empathy – embody a type of relationship which users experience as empowering and affirming.

Box 8.5: *The counselling relationship from the perspective of the client*

Ideas developed within psychotherapy approaches such as person-centred, psychodynamic and TA provide a valuable set of ways of making sense of the counselling relationship. However, these models are primarily formulated from the point of view of the counsellor, and are limited in the extent to which they capture how the relationship is perceived by the person seeking help. In an intriguing study, Bedi *et al.* (2005) interviewed 40 clients who had received counselling for a variety of problems about their perceptions of their relationship with their counsellor. Specifically, participants were asked to describe 'the things that helped form and strengthen the counselling relationship'. What they said in these interviews offers a view of the counselling relationship that differs in significant ways from the image provided by therapy theory. The single most important thing that counsellors did, according to these informants, was to use counselling strategies that were helpful. For example, one person said that the relationship was strengthened when his counsellor 'got me to make a list of my goals'. Although the research participants did mention a number of relationship-building aspects that would be predicted by existing theories of counselling skill – for instance, active listening and attentive body language – they also described a large number of other processes that were unexpected. Near the top of the list of relationship-building activities identified by these service users was the counselling setting ('the counsellor decorated her office with little objects') and accentuating choice ('the counsellor allowed me to choose which chair I would sit in'). Also important for these people was a category of activity that Bedi *et al.* (2005) labelled as 'service beyond normative expectation', or which might be otherwise characterized as 'deep caring', such as 'the counsellor saying to me, "call anytime, or just come in anytime, and there will be someone here, even if I'm not here"'. On the whole, the people who took part in this study did not regard themselves as having much responsibility for building a good relationship. Nor did they describe relationship-building in terms of collaborative working together with their counselling – the majority of those who were interviewed very clearly placed the responsibility for relationship-building in the hands of their counsellors.

The psychodynamic perspective on the counselling relationship

Although psychodynamic theories of counselling have their origins in the writings of Sigmund Freud, contemporary psychodynamic thinking incorporates the ideas of many other figures, such as Erik Erikson, Donald Winnicott and others.

The key idea in any psychodynamically informed counselling is that a person's behaviour is driven or guided by *unconscious* factors: we are not aware of many of the reasons for our actions, or causes of our feelings. From a psychodynamic perspective, throughout their life a human being is exposed to situations of loss, attack, love and hate that evoke very strong, primitive or child-like reactions. These reactions are highly threatening, because: (1) a lot of the time they are not socially acceptable, and (2) if we allow ourselves to consciously acknowledge these reactions we feel overwhelmed, ashamed or guilty. As a result, we use *defence mechanisms* (such as repression, denial and projection) to keep these troublesome wishes, emotions and images out of our minds, and to create an impression of being rational beings.

Within a psychodynamically informed approach to counselling, the counsellor makes use of the concept of defence in the following way: the relationship style of the counsellor is warm and accepting but fairly neutral. It can therefore be assumed that any feelings or fantasies (positive or negative) that the person has towards the counsellor are not triggered by the actual behaviour of the practitioner, but are evidence of *projection* on the part of the person or client. In a counselling situation, this kind of projection is defined as *transference*. The theory is that:

- being in a close relationship (with a counsellor) is threatening or anxiety-provoking in some way
- because it stirs up feelings about other close relationships the person has had in the past
- but it is hard to consciously acknowledge or 'own' these feelings
- so they are projected on to the counsellor in some way.

For example:

Olaf is very sensitive to any hint of criticism from his counsellor. From the outset, he described his counsellor 'really down on me' and 'harsh'. Later in counselling, Olaf starts to talk about how his father always set high standards for him and never gave him praise.

In turn, the counsellor may have feelings about the person/client that are based in their own unconscious projections – these are described as *counter-transference*. For example:

Agnes is an occupational health nurse working with the Fire Brigade. She has a great admiration for firefighters, who she regards as brave and manly. In health counselling situations where it may be appropriate for Agnes to challenge her fire-fighter clients (i.e. when they do not follow agreed rehabilitation programmes) she avoids challenging them, and finds excuses for their behaviour.

At the heart of psychodynamically informed counselling, therefore, is an expectation that the relationship between the person and the counsellor is unlikely to be 'nice'. The task of the counsellor is to provide a secure enough 'holding' environment or 'container' so that the person can feel safe enough to express the positive ('you are wonderful') and negative ('you are cruel and I hate you') feelings that might come up in relation to the counsellor. It is through working together with the counsellor to understand these reactions that the person can get to the point of making sense of the difficulties they have been experiencing in the relationships in their life (it is assumed that all emotional problems ultimately come down to relationships).

It is important to be aware that the theory of transference is controversial, basically because it undermines the idea that the person can be responsible for what they do, and that there can be genuine closeness or a real partnership between the counsellor and person seeking help. The concept of transference can also be difficult to apply in practice, because it requires a great deal of self-awareness on the part of the practitioner to be able to identify when transference or counter-transference reactions are taking place. Specialist counsellors or psychotherapists who use a psychodynamic approach typically undergo lengthy training and personal therapy in order to develop their capacity to work constructively with these processes. Finally, in terms of thinking about whether the concepts of transference and counter-transference are relevant in situations where counselling is embedded in other professional roles, it is helpful to take account of the intensity of the relationship that is likely to develop between the counsellor and the person seeking help. For example, in a one-off 10-minute conversation between a doctor and patient, it is more likely that the discussion will be task-oriented. By contrast, a residential social worker spending many hours each week with a group of adolescents in care is much more likely to be drawn into areas of relationship difficulty and projection.

Exercise 8.3: *Thinking about transference*

How helpful are the Freudian concepts of *transference* and *countertransference* for you in making sense of interactions with people who come to you for help? Identify one client who appeared to have a transference-based way of relating to you. How did you react (counter-transference) to the assumptions that they seemed to be making about you, and their relationship with you? In what ways could or does the theory of transference enable you to develop a more productive cousnelling relationship with this kind of client?

The transactional analysis (TA) approach to making sense of relationships

Transactional analysis (TA) is an approach to psychotherapy that was developed by Eric Berne, Claude Steiner and others in the 1960s. For practitioners whose counselling role is embedded within other professional duties, TA provides a uniquely rich and comprehensive theoretical language for describing and analysing the moment-by-moment interaction between the counsellor and the person seeking help, as well as a framework for understanding the troubled relationships that the person might be experiencing within their everyday life. The basic idea around which all TA theory is built is the notion that the personality of any individual is organized around three distinct 'ego states' – the Parent ego state, Adult ego state and Child ego state (Stewart and Joines, 1987). The Parent aspect of the person consists of parental functions that have been internalized from one's own mother, father and other caretakers. The two key dimensions of the Parent are critical standard-setting, and nurturing. The Adult ego state is the part of the person that responds to the world in a logical, rational, information-processing manner. Finally, the Child in the person can be viewed as the remaining traces of how the individual experienced the world when they were very young. There are two dimensions to the Child – a fun-loving side, and a hurt side. From a TA perspective, a psychologically healthy person will be able to have access to, and express, all of these ego states in appropriate situations. However, many people have developed in ways that make them more likely to rely on certain states rather than others, so that, for example, they may be critical and distant (in Parent ego state) at a celebratory event that calls for a playful Child response.

The application of the ego state model to interactions between two people allows patterns of unsatisfactory or dysfunctional relating to be revealed and understood. For instance, if a person speaks from their Adult, and attempts to engage the Adult of the other person (perhaps through a request for information), but the other person replies in a whiny, hurt child kind of manner ('why are you always bothering me?') the interaction is experienced by the first person as not quite 'right' in some way. Such a response is unlikely to lead to effective collaboration. In TA terms, such an interaction would be described as a *crossed transaction*. Other parts of TA theory develop these ideas in terms of understanding sequences of interactions (games) and patterns of relating that occur across a whole life (scripts). One of the advantages of TA theory, in contrast to some other models of therapy and human interaction, is that much of it is written using colloquial, vivid language, which is accessible and memorable for people who are seeking help – it is not just a theory for insiders. Although there are relatively few specialist TA counsellors and psychotherapists, many practitioners in areas such as health and education study TA at an introductory level and find it to be an invaluable tool for making sense of relationships and interactions that are frustrating or 'stuck'. Another useful facet of TA theory is that it is very clear about its values, and offers some fairly clear-cut ideas about the goals of counselling.

Conclusions

This chapter has explored some of the activities and qualities through which a counselling relationship may be built, and some of the ways in which it might be understood. Many of the issues discussed in this chapter – listening, trust, caring – may appear obvious, or come across as truisms. Surely it hardly needs to be said that a counsellor should be someone who is trustworthy? However, it cannot be emphasized often enough that a good relationship is ultimately what counselling is about. No matter how skilled a practitioner might be at exploring painful emotional issues, and facilitating change, if the person does not trust them, and does not feel a bond and connection, then they will not open up enough to allow the knowledge, experience and competences of the counsellor to have much of an impact on them.

The following chapters explore things that are *done* in counselling – talking through a problem, making a decision, planning behaviour change, and so on. All of this material needs to be read in the light of what has been discussed in the present chapter: what can be done in counselling always depends on the potential of the relationship to allow it to be done. There is a reciprocal connection between the tasks of counselling – the action that is undertaken to make a difference to the problems in living of the person – and the quality of the relationship between counsellor and person. There needs to be at least the beginnings of a strong enough relationship, if the person is to feel safe and supported enough to embark on exploring difficult issues in their life. Then, the process of exploring the issue has the potential to bring both participants together, and cement their relationship, around a shared task. And, finally, the successful completion of that task creates a relationship with a history of shared achievement. In practice, the task dimension of counselling and the relationship dimension are always inextricably linked together – it is only in textbooks such as this that they are separated out at a theoretical or conceptual level.

Suggested further reading

Feltham, C. (ed.) (1999) *The Counselling Relationship*. London: Sage Publications.

Jacobs, M. (2005) *The Presenting Past*, 3rd edn. Maidenhead: Open University Press.

Leiper, R. (2004) *The Psychodynamic Approach to Therapeutic Change*. London: Sage Publications.

McLeod, J. (2009) *An Introduction to Counselling*, 4th edn. Maidenhead: Open University Press (ch. 14).

Mearns, D. and Thorne, B. (2007) *Person-centred Counselling in Action*, 2nd edn. London: Sage Publications.

Merry, T. (2002) *Learning and Being in Person-centred Counselling*, 2nd edn. Hay-on-Wye: PCCS Books.

Rogers, C.R. (1961) *On Becoming a Person*. London: Constable.

Stewart, I. and Joines, V. (1987) *TA today: A New Introduction to Transactional Analysis*. Nottingham: Lifespace Publishing.

Tolan, J. (2003) *Skills in Person-centred Counselling and Therapy*. London: Sage Publications.

9

Exploring issues to make meaning and develop understanding

'It sounds like this keeps going round and round in your head. This picture of your grandfather being laid out. And you can't sort of share it with anyone. Is that right?'

'Aye, I've never told anyone about it. But I keep thinking about it all the time now.'

'I'm wondering if you'd like to talk a bit more about it now, with me? I'd like to hear more, if this would be a good time for you to talk about it. I know from what you've said to me before that you've been trying to be very positive about your treatment. But from where I'm sitting, this image of your grand-dad just seems . . . I don't know . . . frightening?'

'Naw, not frightening. It's more . . . I just keep wondering about him. He looked alone, even though he was in the middle of a room full of people.'

'He was alone?'

'Yes. It's funny. Just when he needed other people, he was alone.'

Introduction

The general task of counselling is that of enabling a therapeutic conversation to take place. Although a number of specific tasks, such as problem-solving and behaviour change, may from time to time emerge from within the conversation, the baseline or 'default setting' for any counselling encounter is that of allowing the person to talk in a way that allows them to find meaning and possibility within the area of their life space that is troubling them. The aim of this chapter is to consider some of the strategies and methods that a counsellor can use to facilitate a meaningful or therapeutic conversation. It is essential to approach these suggestions from a starting point of awareness of personal experience. What are your own experiences of having been involved in meaningful conversation? What made these conversations memorable and full of meaning? Counselling ideas and methods are not a substitute for whatever it is a person has learned to do, but are better viewed as possibilities for adding to, or refining, existing strategies.

A counselling relationship provides space for a particular *type* of conversation which is a bit different from other conversations that a person may have experienced in their everyday life. A person is likely to want to seek out such a conversation because some kind of dilemma, conflict, issue or bad feeling has been present in their life for some time, and they have not been able to resolve it. The experience of the person may include a sense of being burdened, of carrying alone a weight that is crushing. This experience is often accompanied by a sense that it would be helpful to talk about the issue or problem with another person, but without necessarily possessing much of a clear idea of how that conversation might proceed, or what might come out of it. Quite possibly, the person may already have attempted to talk about their issue or problem with a friend or family member, or even with someone in a professional helping role, but without achieving very much.

Coming into the counselling encounter a person will probably have quite vague expectations about what they are looking for, other than to somehow feel better. It is important for anyone who is offering a counselling relationship to reflect on the implications of this kind of starting point. People rarely enter counselling with a specific idea in mind about what will happen. Nevertheless, reflection on the factors that lead people to want to enter a counselling relationship suggests that there are two main expectations that people have in this situation. The first is that the conversation will be meaningful. The second is that the person they are talking to will offer something back – there will be a dialogue.

The wish to engage in a conversation that is full of meaning reflects a desire to make sense, to gain perspective on a problem or issue, to make connections between something specific that may be happening now, and the bigger picture of one's life. A meaningful conversation creates a more complete understanding of the issues that were discussed. Such a conversation is memorable, it lives on in the imagination of the person, and can act as a point of reference. What makes a meaningful conversation possible is the simple fact that once a person starts to talk – about anything – what they say contains a vast amount of *implicit* meaning, which potentially can be brought into attention and awareness. The majority of ordinary, everyday conversation can be thought of as being like verbal table tennis – statements are rapidly batted back and forward between the protagonists without much pause for reflection. In a more meaningful conversation, such as a counselling session, the interplay between speakers is slowed down or even stopped, so that the meaningfulness of statements can be explored. For this to happen, the counsellor needs to be able to initiate a different way of talking. One of the core competences in counselling is to be able to subvert everyday ways of talking, so that the person can engage in what is for them a new form of discourse that creates new meaning. A simple example of how counsellors subvert everyday ways of talking is that in normal conversations, a disclosure by one speaker ('We spent Christmas at home') is usually followed by a matching disclosure by their conversational partner ('We went to my husband's family for Christmas'). In contrast, a counsellor would never automatically engage in matching disclosure, but would tend to say something in reply that would encourage the person to say more about the personal significance of the topic.

The wish to engage in a conversation in which the other person will offer something back reflects a desire to make contact, to share the burden, to enlist the fresh perspective of seeing an issue from a different vantage point. There is a special kind of emotional pain that is associated with being out of contact with other people; a fundamental difference between an issue which a group of people are tackling together, and the same issue being dealt with alone. We live in a predominantly individualist culture where the basic virtue of mutuality is losing ground. A counselling relationship seeks to introduce some mutuality into an issue by providing a space in which *we* (the person and the counsellor together) can talk something through. A dialogical counselling conversation can have additional significance because, on the whole, professional helpers such as nurses, doctors and teachers do not engage much in mutual dialogue, but instead listen, diagnose/assess and then tell the person what to do. There are many situations where this kind of 'prescriptive' approach is both necessary and effective, but in relation to personal troubles it tends not to be experienced as 'being offered something back'. All too often, the recipient of a prescriptive approach to helping has a sense of being categorized, slotted into a pre-existing system. A dialogical conversation, by contrast, is a two-sided, open-ended process.

The remaining sections of this chapter describe a range of strategies for conducting meaningful, dialogical conversations in counselling contexts. This type of conversation can be regarded as the grounding for any form of effective counselling. Occasionally, more specific counselling tasks may emerge from this groundwork. Some of these are discussed in later chapters. But it is important to appreciate that a meaningful conversation can in itself be experienced as very helpful. There are many counselling sessions or episodes where the counsellor may think that nothing much happened, because their impression was that the person was 'just talking', but which the service user may have evaluated as extremely useful. Making meaning and making contact are simple principles, but can make a big difference to people. The following sections explore some of the ways that these ideas can be implemented within counselling conversations.

Exercise 9.1: *The experience of being in a meaningful conversation*

What are your own experiences of having been involved in meaningful conversation? Identify one or two such occasions in your life. What made these conversations memorable and full of meaning? What can you learn from these experiences that you can apply in counselling situations?

Empathic engagement

Empathy is a core building block of any meaningful counselling conversation. The concept of empathy has been central to the practice of counselling and psychotherapy ever since the pioneering research of the American psychologist, Carl Rogers, in the 1950s, which showed that the ability of a counsellor to empathize sensitively and accurately with the experience of their client was a major component in therapeutic effectiveness. Empathy refers to the capacity of one person to 'tune in' to the reality of another person, to 'walk in their shoes', to see the world from that other person's perspective. In counselling, this quality is most valuable in the context of an empathic *engagement* with the person. In other words, it is not enough merely to empathize silently – a good counsellor *communicates* their empathic understanding in a form that the person can receive. Empathy is in fact a subtle and elusive quality. It differs, for example, from sympathy or compassion. These are both valuable human qualities in their own right, but imply a rather narrower response, which expresses fellow-feeling or solidarity for the suffering that a person is experiencing. Empathy, by contrast, embraces a rather wider attempt to take in all, or as much as possible, of the experiential world of the other person, not just the vulnerable or painful aspects. Empathy can also be confused with identification in the sense that a counsellor might respond to a person by saying 'I feel, or have felt, that too' or 'that happened to me, therefore I know what you are talking about'. While empathy always encompasses some degree of willingness to identify with the person, perhaps by imaging what it would be like to be them, true empathic engagement seeks to go beyond those aspects of the other's experience that are familiar, and find some means of connecting to aspects that are unfamiliar or different. An additional challenge in relation to empathic engagement is that it calls for a holistic response to the other, including cognitive, feeling and moral dimensions of the way the person experiences the world, and also an appreciation of the direction in which the person is moving.

In counselling, genuine empathic engagement *makes a difference* to the person who receives it. A useful way of understanding the importance of empathic engagement is through the idea of the person's 'track', as defined by Rennie (1998). When a person starts talking about an issue, it is as though they are on a 'track' – their account has direction and momentum. Non-empathic responses by a counsellor can throw the person off their track, because they indicate to the person that the counsellor has not understood them. At such a moment, the person finds that they wonder whether they need to stop and explain things to the counsellor, or perhaps even think that there may be little point in talking to someone who does not latch on to what they are trying to say. Using an analogy from driving, consistent empathic engagement is about keeping the car on the road – a basic requirement for any kind of journey to take place.

Empathic engagement can have an impact on the person that goes beyond merely keeping the conversation on track. Vanaerschot (1993) has analysed the impact of accurate, sensitive empathic engagement in terms of a number of significant 'microprocesses' in the person:

- feeling valued and accepted as a person. Feeling confirmed in one's own identity as an autonomous, valuable person
- learning to accept feelings by hearing another person put one's own personal feelings into words without shame or embarrassment
- alienation is dissolved: 'am not abnormal, different and strange – there is someone else who can understand me'
- learning to trust one's own experience through the affirmation of that experience by the counsellor
- focusing the person's attention on the core aspects of their issue or problem
- facilitating recall of information – previously 'forgotten' or 'repressed' aspects of the issue may surface
- organizing information – the empathic statement may put things in order.

All of these processes have the effect of encouraging the person to deepen or thicken the story they are telling by incorporating other aspects of their experience. The story that they tell, and the conversation they have with the counsellor therefore more fully represents their possibilities as a person, including their strengths as well as their problems. The opposite process occurs when the counsellor offers a response which is *not* empathic. When a counsellor responds in a way that is 'off the track', the person may 'defer' to the counsellor (Rennie, 1994) and behave as if what the counsellor said was sensible or useful. If this happens consistently, then the conversation can quite rapidly begin to lose any relevance for the person at all.

A counselling conversation can be significantly undermined by the expression of *false* empathy in the form of statements such as 'I understand how you feel'. This kind of statement is an assertion of empathic engagement by the counsellor, rather than an actual demonstration. It does not provide the person with any actual evidence of the counsellor's understanding. When a counsellor makes an attempt to articulate what they understand, as in a statement such as 'you have been talking about the stress of your job, and I just have a sense that you are so tired', then the person has something to work with. It may be, in this example, that the counsellor has picked up the wrong feeling, and that in reality the person feels angry, resigned or sad. But at least the person has received evidence that the counsellor has understood something ('I have bad feelings arising from job stress'), and has an opportunity to put the counsellor right. A danger of false empathy is that it puts the counsellor in the position of an all-knowing expert, which can then inhibit the development of a collaborative mutual exploration of issues. By contrast, real empathic engagement can quite often miss the mark. If a counsellor conveys a sense of tentativeness and genuine curiosity in their attempts to be engaged, and a willingness to be corrected, statements that miss the mark demonstrate the openness of the counsellor to a process of working together.

Empathic engagement is not something that can ever be finally and completely achieved – who can ever fully understand the experience of another person? It is more useful to view empathic engagement as a way of talking, a style of conversation. Empathic statements position the counsellor as interested and willing to learn, but not yet fully knowing. They position the person as interesting and worth knowing, and as having a rich and fascinating story to tell.

The following sections examine some of the practical methods through which empathic engagement can be facilitated in a counselling conversation.

Exercise 9.2: *Being really understood*

Reflect on the feeling of being really understood. Identify one recent occasion when you felt that another person really understood what you were experiencing. How did they express their empathic engagement with you – how did you know that they understood? What was the effect of their empathic sensitivity on your relationship?

Empathic engagement as a process: the Barrett-Lennard model

Godfrey (Goff) Barrett-Lennard is an Australian psychologist who worked with Carl Rogers in the 1960s on some of the landmark research into the role of empathy in counselling (Barrett-Lennard, 1998). During that time, Barrett-Lennard had the opportunity to study in depth what happened when a counsellor was able to engage empathically with a person seeking help. He came to the view that the best way to understand what was happening was to regard empathy as a cyclical process, comprising a series of moment-by-moment interactions between person and helper. His model (Barrett-Lennard, 1981, 1993) can be described in terms of a series of five steps (see Table 9.1).

This simple model has a great deal of practical significance in relation to what a counsellor actually does during the process of empathic engagement. The model suggests that there are four key competences that the counsellor is required to deliver. These are:

1 A readiness to hear the person – this requires being able to set aside any other distracting thoughts.
2 An ability to 'resonate' – to allow the emotional meaning of what the person is saying to be felt at a gut level.

Table 9.1 The Barrett-Lennard model

	The person seeking help	The counsellor
Step 1	Is aware of an issue that he or she wishes to explore	Open and attentive – signalling a readiness to hear what the person has to say
Step 2	Talks about the issue or concern	Actively listens, and allows the emotional meaning of what the person is talking about to physically 'resonate' in them
Step 3	Pauses to hear what the counsellor has to say	Expresses their understanding of what the client has said, usually in the form of a summary
Step 4	Receives what the counsellor has said and conveys their sense of the extent to which the counsellor's summary was accurate and helpful	Observes the person's response to their attempt to summarize and convey understanding
Step 5	Resumes talking . . . the cycle continues	Resumes attentive listening . . . the cycle continues

3 A capacity to use language, to summarize accurately, sensitively, tentatively and succinctly their sense of what the person is trying to communicate.

4 Observational skill – watching and listening to how the client receives what has been offered. If the counsellor's response has been accurate, then there is often a visible sign of relief on the part of the client, as if they are saying 'yes, that's it'. If, on the other hand, the counsellor's response is not quite right, the client may look away, reply with a 'yes, but' statement, or look confused.

This cycle of empathic engagement typically occurs several times within a counselling session. On each occasion, if the counsellor is successful in capturing enough of the essence of what the person is trying to say, then the person will gradually move into a deeper and more personal exploration of the topic. If, on the other hand, the counsellor continues to get it wrong, or not quite right, the client may lose the thread of what they are talking about, may stop trying to communicate by moving on to more superficial topics, or may resort to more vivid and forceful language (e.g. metaphors) to try to get their point across. In such a situation, a good counsellor will try to find some way to repair the situation and get the conversation back 'on track'.

The empathy cycle model not only provides a valuable set of guidelines for competences that counsellors can reflect on in supervision and practice in training, but also makes it clear why the concept of empathy is complex and hard to understand. The model suggests that there are three quite different vantage points in relation to estimating the level of empathic engagement in a counselling conversation. First, there is the counsellor's sense of how open and empathic they are being (Steps 1 and 2). Second, there is the quality of empathy exhibited in what the counsellor says to the person (Step 3) – this is what an external observer would mainly pick up on. Finally, there is the person or client's sense of whether they themselves felt that what the counsellor has said did indeed 'hit the mark' for them (Step 4).

Summing up empathic engagement

The previous sections have explored some of the ways in which meaningful conversation is based on a consistent willingness to engage empathically with the reality or 'world' of the person seeking help. In practice, empathic engagement is expressed through statements that a counsellor makes, in which they strive to summarize what they have understood from what the client has been saying. It is not useful to try to learn a standard 'formula' for responding to clients, because this strategy is quickly perceived as false and lacking in genuineness. There are many different ways of being empathic. It is essential that each counsellor develops a style of 'being with' or 'tuning in' to the person they are helping that is consistent with their personality, role and cultural identity. However, it is important, when making an empathic reflection (or any other kind of statement) that there are two key questions that need to be kept in mind.

1 *What effect does what I am saying have on the therapeutic relationship*? Does the statement convey a sense of working collaboratively? Does it build the client's belief that I am someone who accepts and respects them, and will be open with them?

2 *How does the statement impact on the client's attention*? What does the statement draw attention to (e.g. am I influencing the person to focus on certain themes and drop others)? Do my words invite the person to reflect more deeply on their feelings and sense of self? Or does it draw their attention to external factors (e.g. how other people have behaved to cause their problems)? Does the statement facilitate the person telling their own story, or does it distract them and put them 'off the track'?

Moment-by-moment empathic engagement, when done well, should have the effect of gradually building a net of shared understanding that allows the person to explore personal issues more and more deeply and extensively, and thereby generate connections between events, ideas and experiences in such a way that makes meaning and achieves understanding.

So far in this chapter, considerable attention has been given to the idea of empathic engagement. This is because it represents what is probably the single most important aspect of a counselling conversation. When a person has a problem in living that they wish to talk about, then what they want is someone who will really listen to them, and will do their best to understand the problem from the person's perspective. People want to be heard and understood. When this happens, a basic human connection takes place that is intrinsically supportive and healing. When this does not happen in a counselling conversation then little else will happen, because the person will have a sense of remaining isolated and silenced (whether they admit this or not) and the counsellor's response to the person will be based on an incomplete appreciation of their situation. We now turn to other strategies for facilitating meaningful conversation.

Telling the story

Probably the most basic counselling task is that of giving the person an opportunity to tell their story. When a person experiences a stressful or difficult situation in their life, there seems to be a natural tendency to want to tell the story of these events to at least one other person. Telling the story has a number of positive effects. Organizing a set of memories, images and feelings into a story enables the person to sort out a mass of information that might have previously been whirling around in their mind. The structure of a story allows the person to put these events into a cause and effect sequence ('he said this, and then I did that') which links together action (what happened), intention (goals and plans) and emotion (what was felt). A story also usually includes an evaluative or 'moral' aspect, which weaves in how the person stands in relation to the events that are being recounted – whether they were pleasurable, disgusting, and so on. Quite often a person will seek a counselling relationship within which to tell their story because they do not have anywhere else to tell it. The story that the person wishes to tell may be threatening or embarrassing to other people in their life, or it may be that they are isolated and do not have access to other people who are willing to listen to what they have to say. The need to tell the story can also arise in situations where the person has only been allowed to tell a 'thin' or selective version of their story, and has not had the chance to give voice to a 'thick' version that expresses more fully what they thought, felt and did. One of the important outcomes of telling the story of what has happened, therefore, is that it allows the person to begin to make sense of something that has happened by organizing and ordering feelings and events into some kind of sequence.

Another essential aspect of telling the story concerns the opportunity it affords for enlisting support and feedback from another person. It is possible to imagine that there were significant evolutionary advantages for the human race in sharing stories of threatening (and other) events – the storyteller might be both asking for help and alerting other members of the group to potential danger. In a counselling situation, when a person tells a rich and vivid story of something that has happened in their life, it has the effect of allowing the counsellor to know them much better. A good story is like a snippet of a film that takes the counsellor (or any other listener) right inside the world of the teller. The sharing of a story therefore provides the counsellor with invaluable information about the person, which allows any subsequent response to be better grounded in the reality of the person's experience. If the story is really heard and received, it also helps the person to know that someone else understands them and cares enough about them to be interested in what they have been through. The telling of the story therefore combats isolation and hopelessness.

Box 9.1: *The importance of tentativeness*

Often, the helpfulness of a counsellor statement may depend not so much on *what* was said as on *how* it was said. In a research study that investigated the verbal styles of counsellors, Kimberley Gordon and Shake Toukmanian (2002) analysed the degree of *tentativeness* in counsellor statements. Tentativeness was defined as a response that had 'an element of openness and uncertainty and is delivered in a manner that invites the client to elaborate and expand on what is being communicated' (p. 92). Typically, tentative statements would include a phrase such as 'I get a sense that . . .', 'I wonder if . . .' or 'I'm not sure, but . . .'. Gordon and Toukmanian (2002) found that counsellor statements that were rated high on tentativeness helped the client to explore an issue in more depth, compared to statements that were coded low on this quality. They argued that tentativeness on the part of the counsellor introduced 'beneficial uncertainty' into the awareness of the person seeking help, which encouraged curiosity and a search for additional information. A similar finding emerged from a study by Tarja Kettunen and her colleagues (2003) into the speech patterns of hospital nurses who were offering health counselling to patients. In this research, tentativeness was characterized by 'word repetition, incomplete sentences, stammering, pauses and even hesitation' (p. 333). These researchers reported that tentative speech patterns left room for the patient's ideas, invited exploration, and softened the intrusiveness of some of the lines of questioning that the nurse was following. The results of these research studies suggest that tentativeness can enhance the extent to which a counselling conversation functions to facilitate exploration of issues. It is essential to keep in mind, however, that there can also be occasions when tentativeness may not be the most effective strategy for a counsellor to adopt. For example, if a person has reached a new understanding, and the counsellor wishes to help them to hang on to it and remember it, it may be best to make a clear, unhesitating, confident, non-tentative assertion of what has been understood or agreed. The reason for this is that while tentativeness may enable thoughtfulness, directness may enable memorability.

The skill of facilitating the telling of the story has a number of different elements. In a counselling relationship, the marker for the telling of the story may simply be that the person signals that an issue is concerning them, but then talks about that issue in a general way that does not give the listener much of a sense of what actually happened. This kind of process typically implies that a very thin version of a story is being offered, but there is a thicker and more meaningful version ready to come out. Usually, all that is required is an invitation, such as 'I'm wondering if it might be helpful if you could tell me more about what happened that led to the worries and concerns that you now have about this. Could you take me back to the beginning when it all started?' A key factor at this point is to avoid any suggestion of asking the person to give an explanation, or to 'account for' what they did in any judgemental sense. The aim is, instead, to convey a genuine curiosity about what actually happened, and what the person felt and did at each point. As the person begins to tell their story, it is usually helpful to indicate empathic interest by occasionally summarizing, reflecting back or giving a personal reaction response ('how awful', 'I can just feel how difficult that was'). It is important for the listener, as far as possible, to be able to follow and stay with the story. If there are gaps in the story, or the teller appears to head off at a tangent, it may be useful to intervene with a statement along the lines of 'I seem to have missed something there, you were talking about what he said to you and then you seemed to skip to what happened the next day – I'm not quite sure what the connection was . . .'. However, it is also important to keep in mind that people have different ways of telling their stories, and that by just continuing to listen, everything will become clear in the end. There are finely balanced judgements to be made, between interrupting and seeking clarification on the one hand, and giving the person space on the other. On the whole, professional helpers, such as teachers and nurses, tend to control and constrain the opportunities that their clients have to tell their stories, because they are keen for the person to 'get to the point'. Being patient, and allowing the person to tell their story in their own way, can therefore have the effect of reinforcing the idea that this is a relationship in which they are being offered more freedom to talk things through.

The end point of a telling the story task will often take the form of a 'coda', which brings the conversation back to the present moment, such as '. . . and that's why I told you that I kept feeling so frustrated last week'. There may often be a pause in the conversation at the end of the story as though the teller can stop for breath, or look around, having finished something that needed to be done. This moment is highly significant in terms of what the counsellor does next. During the telling of the story, the teller has 'held the stage', and in all likelihood the counsellor has said little. At the completion of the story, it is the counsellor's turn to say something. There are basically two broad types of response that a counsellor can make at the end of the person's story. First, the counsellor needs to acknowledge the story, and also to respond to the implications of the content of the story. In most circumstances it is crucial to acknowledge the story before attempting any kind of discussion of what it might mean. The medical researcher, Arthur Kleinman (1988), has written very sensitively about a process that he describes as *empathic witnessing* – one human being responding to the troubles, pain and suffering of another human being. This kind of fundamental affirmation of the experience of the teller, and of their courage in telling the story, can be tremendously meaningful for a person. The counsellor can convey this sense of basic acceptance by staying for a few moments with their feeling of the story as a whole, and how it has affected them, and by putting some of this into words. It can be useful to try to find some kind of name or phrase that sums up the story as a whole (e.g. 'the battle you have had to be your own person in the face of everyone else's expectations') because this creates a shared reference point that both person and counsellor can employ if they want to return to the events and feelings of that story at a future date. The second task for the counsellor is to work with the person to explore the meaning and implications of the story. Following the telling of a story, there is often much for the person and counsellor to reflect on: a story will often encompass many significant threads of insight into a person's life, and how they cope with events. A story can be viewed as an opening, or invitation into the person's subjective world. It can therefore lead on to other counselling tasks, such as making sense, making a decision, and so on.

An example of telling the story as a task within a counselling relationship is the time when James, a 14-year-old school student, talked about his problems to his form teacher, Stan. At that stage in his life, James was a boy who had a reputation in the school for being 'difficult' – he would sometimes defy teachers, either by ignoring what they asked him to do, or replying in a sarcastic or joking manner. This behaviour had resulted in most of his teachers becoming more strict with him, regularly checking his work, which in turn triggered further 'difficult' responses. One afternoon, Stan was supervising James during a period of after-school detention. The two of them were alone in a classroom, so Stan took the initiative in asking James if he would be willing to tell him his side of the story. After a bit of coaxing, James began to open up, and told his story. He talked about himself as a person who believed in fairness, and in doing his best. He recalled the first time he had experienced trouble with a teacher. It had been a year ago. James had worked hard on a project, and had felt that his teacher had singled him out for attention by asking him questions about it in front of the whole class. He remembered being so afraid that he was quite unable to say anything in reply to the questions that the teacher had asked him. He then worried about the situation the whole weekend, hardly sleeping or eating. The following week, when another teacher had asked him a question in class, 'I just snapped, and said something stupid'. He talked about how he now felt trapped in a situation that was getting worse with every day. It took about 20 minutes for this story to come out. Stan responded by acknowledging how painful and worrying it must be for someone with the high standards of James to be 'stuck in a trap' of this kind. He added that he appreciated the fact that James had felt able to let him have such a clear picture of what had been happening. Once he had said these things, they were both ready to look at possible strategies for changing the way that James viewed teachers, and they viewed him.

Questioning

In the context of counselling, the use of questioning raises a number of difficult and complex issues. Questions are an integral part of everyday conversation, and can be used for a range of very different purposes: to obtain information ('what time does our train arrive in London?'), to get people to explain or justify their actions ('why on earth did you buy that sofa?') and to reflect on abstract philosophical issues ('what is the meaning of love?').

One of the leading figures in counsellor education and training, Allen Ivey, emphasizes that effective counselling depends on the *intentional* use of language (Ivey and Ivey, 1999). What Ivey is getting at is that skilful counselling requires that the counsellor is sensitively aware of the impact that their communication might have on a person, and as far as possible choose ways of speaking that are facilitative rather than otherwise. Nowhere is this more true that in relation to the use of questioning.

There are times when the use of questions can be perceived by a person seeking help as valuable. For example, questions can convey the genuine curiosity of the counsellor. Sometimes, people want to talk, and find it hard to get started, and appreciate questions that help them to open up. However, too much questioning, or the wrong type of questioning, can have the effect of closing the conversation down. The reason why questioning can be problematic in counselling is that any question constructs a relationship of control: the questioner is in control, because they are directing the attention and awareness of the other person towards coming up with an answer. Being asked a question momentarily overrides the agency and 'track' of the person answering, and forces them to think about what the questioner has asked. Even rejecting the question ('sorry, I don't want to think about that right now') diverts the person from the ongoing flow of their thinking and feeling for the time it takes to ponder on the question and formulate the response of saying that you do not want to respond. Questioning therefore does not fit well within a way of talking that seeks to demonstrate empathic engagement. The essence of being empathic lies in actively checking out with the person that you understand what they are trying to express in a way that encourages a deepening of the conversation.

A question such as 'when did the problem start . . .?' may be heard by the client as a gentle invitation to keep talking. On the other hand, it may be heard in a more confrontational or even authoritarian manner, as: 'I am interviewing you . . . give me the facts'. One of the difficulties with questioning is that there is a (usually hidden) statement behind every question. So, a question such as 'when did the problem start?' will almost always arise from the counsellor's assumption or hypothesis that the start of the problem was significant. Rather than put this as a question (which hides the hypothesis), it is usually better to use a form of words that allows the counsellor's meaning and intention to be more transparent, such as 'from what you are saying, I keep thinking that I don't really have a clear idea of when the problem started in the first place. It would help me to get a feel for how this whole difficulty hangs together if you could say a bit more about that'. Turning a question into a statement does two things: (1) emphasizes that the person seeking help is the expert on their own life, and is in control, and (2) builds a collaborative relationship by sharing aims and assumptions whenever possible.

It is important to recognize that there are different types of question that can be used in counselling including:

- *Closed questions*: intended to elicit specific information. Examples: 'have you reported this incident to the police?', 'how often has this happened in the past?'

- *Open questions*: intended to encourage the person to expand on a theme or topic. For example: 'what other feelings did you have when all that was happening?', 'how have you learned to deal with this when it has happened in the past?', 'what led up to this . . . how did the situation develop?', 'what happened next?'
- *Hypothetical questions*: intended to encourage the person to consider new possibilities (Newman, 2000). Examples: 'hypothetically, if you were able to deal with this situation, what would you do?', 'if we were having this conversation in five years time, what would your life be like?'

Questions have an important role to play in counselling. The key point to keep in mind is that questions are powerful interventions, which can have a strong impact on the helper–helpee relationship and also on the inner process and focus of attention of the person seeking help.

Exercise 9.3: *Using questions in practice*

What kinds of questioning strategies do you employ in your work with people who come to you for help? Over the course of a day, make a note of the types of questions you ask. Can you identify statements behind these questions? To what extent are these questioning strategies effective and 'intentional' – are there alternative ways that you could use to achieve your conversational goals?

Box 9.2: *The health benefits of talking about a problem*

Some intriguing and important research carried out by the American psychologist, James Pennebaker (1997), has established that talking about a problem, or even merely writing about it, can produce significant health benefits. In a classic series of studies, Pennebaker and his team divided volunteers into two groups. One group were asked to write about an issue that was stressful for them, for ten minutes on four consecutive days. The other group were instructed to write about superficial topics. In neither case was anyone else (including the researcher) to read what had been written. A range of health measures were taken before the writing task, at the end, and after a follow-up period. It was found that members of the group who had written about a stressful topic, even for this very limited amount of time, reported fewer health centre visits and better immune functioning at follow-up, compared to those who had written about unimportant topics. In further research, the Pennebaker clinic investigated the impact of different ways of disclosing stressful events (e.g. spoken rather than written). What they found across their extensive programme of research was that the impact of even quite minimal disclosure was quite significant: at the time of writing or talking about the problem, participants felt worse, but afterwards they were happier and healthier. How can this happen? Pennebaker argues that human beings have developed, through evolution, to tell other people about their troubles, as a way of eliciting support and also to disseminate information about potential threat across their social group. However, in the modern world there are many factors that inhibit people from telling others about their troubles and fears (e.g. other people are too busy to listen). This inhibition results in autonomic nervous system activity that becomes stressful if allowed to continue. In addition, active inhibition interferes with information processing – the person does not process the event properly, and is left with ruminations, dreams and other intrusive cognitive symptoms. In contrast, confronting the traumatic or stressful memory, by telling the story of what happened, reduces the physiological work put into inhibition, and enables the person to better understand and assimilate the event.

Opening the door: using vivid language, imagery and metaphor

Being willing to listen very closely to another person is an essential aspect of any counselling role. However, as well as being open to hearing the *whole* of what a person is expressing about the issues or problems in their life that have led them to seek help, it is useful to be ready to tune into the *way* that a person talks about their problem. There are many aspects of a person's way of expressing themselves that can be informative about the person's emotional state; for example, their tone of voice, posture, and the pace and volume of their talk. One of the most useful dimensions of communication, from a counselling perspective, is the occurrence of vivid imagery and metaphor within the person's description of their troubles. It is always worthwhile to make a mental note of the type of images a person uses. Sometimes an image can be so striking that it is worth inviting the person to elaborate on it. In these situations, if a word or phrase almost seems to stand out from what the person is saying, as if it had neon lights around it, then it is almost certain that it conveys a lot of meaning for the person. The image or metaphor on these occasions almost operates as shorthand for a longer story that the person could tell. Inviting them to describe the actual concrete reality of the image of metaphor can be an effective way to allow the story to be told.

A teacher who is experiencing a high degree of work stress, and has a variety of physical ailments, including chronic back pain, has visited his GP three times in the past month for prescriptions for painkillers, none of which have made much difference. On this occasion, the GP suggests that it might be helpful to look at whether similar problems had happened before in the patient's life, and how he had coped in the past, and moves temporarily into a counselling mode:

Person: I had a really bad time a few years ago, and my back was playing up then too. It was really difficult to get through that, and it's always in the back of my mind. Sometimes now I just feel as though I'm skating on thin ice – it would not take much and I would fall back into all that awful stuff I was feeling then. I wouldn't call it depression, but . . .

Counsellor: Would it be OK if we just looked a bit more at what you just said there? My attention was really drawn to that phrase you used – 'skating on thin ice'. It just seems such a vivid image, it really hit me, because it seems to really catch what that situation means to you. I remember you have used an image like that before, when you came to see me last week, to describe your situation. Would it be OK with you to stay with that image for a few moments? I'd be interested to learn more about what that means to you – 'skating on thin ice' . . .

(The counsellor is here expressing curiosity and interest, and using metacommunication/checking out in negotiating agreement over staying with the metaphor.)

Person: That's OK. When you mention it, I realize that it's something I say a lot.

Counsellor: Right, well maybe you could begin by telling me where you are skating – on a rink, a river. . .?

(The counsellor encourages the person to 'dwell in' the metaphor, to explore its sensory qualities, to begin to let the story unfold: what went before . . . what is happening now – who, where, how, why . . . how will it end?)

Person: That's funny, its definitely a frozen lake, with mountains on either side.

Counsellor: Are you going fast, slow . . .?

Person: I'm skating very deliberately. Not fast or slow. I mustn't stop.

Counsellor: You mustn't stop? What would happen if you stopped?

Person: If I stopped I would be more likely to fall through the ice. I must keep going.

Counsellor: So, if you stopped there would be the risk of . . . what?

Person: It would just give way.

Counsellor: And then?

Person:	I would freeze. I would be pulled down. I just wouldn't last for 10 minutes. It would be the end.
Counsellor:	So you must keep going. Are you OK if you keep going? How do you keep going?
Person:	If I can get to the other side I'll be fine. I'm not sure how I keep going. I grit my teeth and tense my muscles. If I relaxed for even a moment I'd be gone.
Counsellor:	So you keep going, trying to get to the other side. And is that far away – the other side . . .? What's it like over there?
Person:	Quite far, but I can see the people there.
Counsellor:	The people . . .?
Person:	Yes, there are people there who are trying to help me to get to the other side. Giving me advice. I know I'll be all right if I can make it over to where they are, so they can take care of me.
Counsellor:	So these people are really rooting for you?
Person:	Yes, definitely.
Counsellor:	Thanks for that. I know it may seem silly to be talking about skating and so on, but it did seem to me that what you were saying there was somehow important. What came over to me was that you have to keep moving, very carefully and deliberately, or you will disappear into a depression like you had before, but there are people who can help, if you can get to them. Is that right?
Person:	Yeah, that's it in a nutshell.
Counsellor:	It's making me think that maybe the pills I've been prescribing you are only part of the answer. Could we look at what would be involved in actually getting this support that's on offer from these people?

In the remaining time in the consultation, the conversation between the stressed teacher and his doctor centres around the possibility of taking some time off work, and how this time might be used to make contact with people who would be sources of support. The GP suggests that an appointment could be made with the cognitive-behaviour therapist who visits the practice, who could be another source of support, and who might have further ideas about dealing with work pressure. Throughout their conversation, they never make use of the word 'depression', both of them choosing to use the person's own terminology of 'the ice' to refer to the problem.

This example illustrates some basic features of the use of metaphor and imagery within counselling conversations. The metaphor that was generated by this person – skating on thin ice – could easily have been ignored by the helper. It is a fairly commonplace image, which can be taken for granted. However, it can be seen that for this person, in the context of what he had said before (mainly describing lists of symptoms), this image was vivid and conveyed new meaning. The metaphor functioned something like a door into the individual world of the person seeking help. The counsellor can choose to open this door, or not.

The majority of powerful, evocative metaphors refer to physical, bodily qualities (Lakoff and Johnson, 1999), and as a result an invitation to the person to put these concrete aspects of the metaphor into words ('describe where are you skating . . . how far away is the other side?') is likely to allow the person to become more aware of their own bodily sensations (emotions and feelings) that are bound up in the imagery.

Metaphors also provide opportunities to develop the relationship between the person and the counsellor through working together to explore the meaning of the metaphor. The image can then become a shared language between them – on any future occasion they would both understand what was at stake if they used the term. Research by Angus and Rennie (1988, 1989) into the use of metaphors in counselling sessions showed that what people found helpful was when their counsellor collaborated with them around a joint discussion of the meaning of the image or metaphor.

Because they are vivid and out of the ordinary, metaphors are highly memorable. A person is more likely to remember a vivid metaphor following a counselling session than they are to remember other topics and ideas that have been discussed. Metaphor can therefore help to link together counselling and everyday life.

The writings of George Lakoff and Mark Johnson have made a very significant contribution to the understanding of metaphor (Lakoff and Johnson, 1980, 1999). They have suggested that each metaphor both highlights and hides meaning. In other words, a metaphor draws attention to particular aspects of an experience, while pushing other aspects into the background. So, for example, the image of 'skating on thin ice' that was used earlier highlights the ideas that the person is busy and active, and is visible to other people. It is a metaphor that perhaps makes it harder to see and appreciate a side of this person's stress and depression that is reflected in being alone, hidden and safe. From a counselling perspective, it can be useful therefore to listen out for counter-metaphors, or examples of images that describe a very different set of experiences. It can also be helpful to invite such images by using such prompts as: 'if you weren't on that frozen lake, where would you like to be?'. However, rushing prematurely into the elicitation of alternative or counter-metaphors, before an initial metaphor has been fully explored, runs the risk of not being respectful of the person by not being willing to join them where they are now, and instead rushing them in the direction of where the counsellor thinks they *should* be headed.

The use of metaphor in counselling allows the possibility for making use of important human resources, such as imagination, creativity and the capacity for play. 'Metaphor talk' in counselling can often be energizing and connecting, and can lead to new discoveries. Further ideas around working with client metaphors can be found in Kopp and Craw (1998).

Exercise 9.4: *Using metaphors in practice*

What metaphors do you use most often in your conversations at work? What metaphors do your colleagues and clients use? What meanings are highlighted and hidden by these metaphors? Are there occasions when you deliberately extend the use of a metaphor over a number of conversational turns? How helpful has this been?

Conclusions: how and why 'just talking' can make a difference

This chapter has explored the idea of using a counselling space for 'just talking' – helping the person to put their problem in living into words. Different sections of the chapter have examined various ways that a counsellor can try to engage in conversation that is as meaningful and productive as it can be. But, in the end, this is all about 'just talking'. While the following chapters introduce and discuss some of the *specific* tasks that may emerge from a process of talking, it is essential for anyone engaged in offering counselling relationships to realize that most of the time for most people 'just talking' is a hugely valuable activity. Having a meaningful conversation about a topic of personal significance can be regarded as the basic *general* task of counselling. Why is this? How can it be that 'just talking' can make a difference? As a means of drawing this chapter to a conclusion, it is relevant to review the reasons why talk in itself may be therapeutic or healing, or may lead to learning and change. Some of the key factors are summarized below.

- *The counsellor as someone to talk to*. Probably the most valued testimony that a client can pay to a counsellor is to regard them as a person who is always worth talking to, who they will seek out when they need to talk something through. Knowing that there is a person within one's social network who can function in this way is a source of great strength.

- *An opportunity for reflection*. A person who chooses to talk about a problem is already actively engaged in trying to make sense of their situation, and find solutions. The act of talking creates many opportunities for further, deeper and different reflection. As the person talks, they are mapping out their story, and describing their experience. As they do this, they are listening to their own words, and reflecting on the meaning and implications of what they have said. A speaker listens to what they are saying in a way that is fundamentally different from merely thinking about things (i.e. having a dialogue 'in your own head'). The person also has an opportunity to reflect on how the listener responds to what they say, both in terms of their moment-by-moment interest and reactions, and their verbal replies.

- *Discovery of implicit meaning*. What a person says almost always carries more meaning than they are aware of at the time. This phenomenon can be demonstrated by recording and transcribing any interview or counselling conversation, and analysing all the possible meanings that are expressed in each utterance. A counsellor who is closely listening to what a person is saying will usually be able to pick up, and feed back, meanings that go slightly beyond what the person assumed that they were saying. For example: 'you talk about feeling sad, and at the same time I'm wondering if you are also perhaps angry or resentful'. Alternatively, a person may become aware of implicit meanings by reflecting on what they have said: 'it was only when I really started to talk about it that I realized that I am actually really annoyed about what happened'. The consequence of this kind of process is that as a person talks the problem may become more 'meaning-full', and they develop a 'thicker' story that allows them to connect current troubles to other themes, events and resources in their life.

The following chapters introduce a range of counselling tasks arising from specific issues around maintaining or repairing a personal niche within a culture and society. However, *just talking* can be regarded as a general task, which is always being carried out during a counselling session, whatever else might be happening. A useful or *therapeutic* conversation occurs when a person is able to talk about a problem or issue in a way that allows them to express what they think and feel in ways that allow new possibilities to come into view. This kind of conversation can be regarded as healing or therapeutic in nature because it contributes to a sense of resolution or closure of a wound, a source of pain. A therapeutic conversation goes beyond a mere reporting or cataloguing of troubles, and involves using the presence of, and connectedness with, another person in a supportive and life-enhancing dialogue.

This chapter has described a number of ways of deepening conversation: empathy, sensitivity to stories, attention to positioning, metaphor and rhythm. However, the single most important aspect of a therapeutic conversation is the experience of having someone *listen:* good counsellors are good listeners. The reason that listening is so powerful is that it creates an experience for the person seeking help, of being with another person in relation to their problem in living. For the person seeking help, there are always significant parts of their experience, or their story, that they have had to carry alone. The more that the helper listens, the more the problem emerges as something that they both know. It is almost as though the problem, and the pain, fear, shame and confusion that accompanies it, begins to be brought into being in the room between them. Once this happens, they can begin to 'walk around' the problem together, examining it from different angles, and deciding what to do with it. To some extent, listening is about information-gathering, about learning the facts of what happened in the person's life, who was involved and how the problem grew. But, more than that, it is about being willing to enter the life of the other by being a companion and a witness. Listening in the fullest sense is always personal; it always involves an emotional and a moral commitment from one person to another. The person seeking counselling is making a commitment to being known, and the counsellor is investing themself in a willingness to know.

The importance of 'just talking' cannot be overemphasized. Over and over again, people who have used counselling report that what was helpful was the chance to talk, to have someone listen, to be heard, and to share embarrassing secrets. However, within the flow of conversation, there are sometimes specific tasks that may come into focus. The reason why these tasks emerge is that a counselling conversation always takes place in relation to some kind of life goal, and always has the purpose of advancing that goal. It is as though, when engaged in 'just talking' about a problem, the person is looking out for ideas about what to do about the problem. Often, the answer to what to do about a problem emerges from talking, or even arrives fully formed. Sometimes, though, there may be a sense that an answer or solution is possible, but that it needs to be worked out in a more structured or planned manner. It is to an examination of these occasions, when counselling is oriented towards a clear-cut issue, that we turn in the following chapters.

Suggested further reading

Rennie, D.L. (1998) *Person-centred Counselling: An Experiential Approach*. London: Sage Publications.

CHAPTER 10

Making sense of a specific problematic reaction

'I seem to be getting more tired than I was a few weeks ago. I don't understand why this is happening'.

'Is this something you'd like to talk about?'

'It is, I'm worried that I might be slipping back'.

'Can I ask you, is this happening every day, or all day, or are there particular times that you can identify when it happens?'

'It's not all the time — it comes and goes'.

'There's different ways we could look at this. But I'm thinking — what about talking me through the most recent time this has happened. Like a moment-by-moment account. Would it be OK to do that?'

Introduction

The previous chapter introduced some ideas about how to help clients talk about their problem in order to gain a perspective on what is happening in their lives and make meaning out of what may appear to them to be worryingly senseless and chaotic experiences. When a person talks in an open-ended way about their problems, it is probable that at regular intervals they will make a reference to specific events that exemplify the troubles they are experiencing. Alternatively, if the person is talking in a general way about issues, the counsellor may invite them to describe a specific instance that illustrates how the issue plays out in everyday life. These occurrences in counselling represent valuable opportunities for counsellors, because they allow the counsellor to learn more about what the person thinks, feels and does on a moment-by-moment basis. As a result, the activity of focusing on the meaning and significance of a *specific problematic reaction* comprises a core task in most counselling relationships. No matter what other types of tasks are being pursued, at some point it is inevitable that a counsellor will need to work with the client around making sense of, and learning from, puzzling things that the client has done. The aim of the present

chapter is to consider how to approach this kind of task in terms of using counselling methods to make sense of what has happened, and to explore implications for
future action.

Examples of problematic reactions

There are two types of problematic or puzzling reaction events that arise in counselling. The first type consists of statements by clients that something has happened
in their lives that does not make sense to them. Examples include:

'Why do I let him treat me like a doormat? He visited yesterday and I ended up
giving him money. Why did I do that?' (Woman speaking to a worker at a domestic
abuse project).

'I don't seem to be able to organize myself. I gave myself yesterday morning to sort
out my filing system, but I spent the whole time following up a non-urgent housing
needs case instead. I seem to be trying to make my life harder' (Social worker,
during a meeting of a peer support group).

'No matter how much I tell myself it's stupid, and no matter how much I want
to stop, every time I see a sharp object, I immediately start to think about how
I could use it to cut myself. I just wish I could stop doing that – one day it will
go too far. For example, yesterday I found a nail in the workshop and brought it
back to my cell' (Prison inmate talking to a member of a suicide and self-harm
helpline).

'I was in a meeting with colleagues and I started to feel really depressed and
hopeless about everything. Where did that come from?' (Businessman consulting
his GP for help with sleep problems).

Making sense of a puzzling personal reaction to a situation is a counselling task
that is generally marked by a self-questioning statement along the lines of 'why am
I doing this, and how can I do something different?' It is often enough for the
practitioner-counsellor to reply to such a statement by saying something along
the lines of 'is this something we could look at together?' or 'do you think it might
be helpful to take a few minutes to talk about that a bit more?'

A second means through which puzzling or problematic events or reactions are
mentioned in counselling is in response to a counsellor's question. In the example
below, a client has been talking about a general problem, and the counsellor
invites them to share a specific example:

Client: I keep having these arguments with my mother. She is trying to help, I know she is. But she does it in a way that is very controlling and manipulative. I find myself going along with what she is saying, and agreeing to her suggestions. But then later, when I am on my own I burst into tears because I realize that what I have agreed to is just not the right thing for me.

Counsellor: I get a sense that this is a big problem for you. You have mentioned it before, and I can see how upset you are when you're talking about it now. It's like you really need your mother to help you at the moment, but in fact what she does just makes you feel worse, because somehow you are not able to stand up for yourself when you are with her. I was wondering, to help me to understand in more detail what is happening if you could describe a particular occasion when this has happened? Would that be OK?

In this instance, the counsellor has gained a feel for the overall pattern of the client's difficulty, and now wishes to anchor that understanding in a concrete example.

This kind of counselling episode can be viewed in the context of two contrasting types of client goals. The client is seeking to *understand* why they act in the way that they do. They also want to *change* what they do. Spending some time looking at the meaning of a puzzling or problematic event represents one step that can be taken towards these goals. Usually other steps will be necessary as well. For example, realizing the significance of a puzzling event may lead into a focus on behaviour change (Chapter 12), negotiating a life transition (Chapter 16), or in fact any other counselling task.

Exercise 10.1: *Making sense of a problematic reaction in your own life*

When was the last time that you exhibited a puzzling reaction to a situation? Take a few minutes to write a description of the situation, how you reacted, and how you felt afterwards. What was strange or puzzling about the way you responded in this situation? Are you now able to make sense of your reaction? Who or what helped you to develop an understanding of what happened? What have you learned from this whole event that might help you to work with a client wishing to make sense of a problematic personal reaction?

Making sense of problematic events: theoretical perspectives

As a counsellor, it is important to understand why it is that clients' accounts of specific concrete events are so valuable. There are basically four theoretical perspectives that are relevant to an understanding of this aspect of the counselling process, derived from *narrative theory, experiential psychotherapy, personality theory* and *cognitive-behavioural therapy (CBT)*.

- *A narrative perspective on problematic reaction events.* A narrative approach to counselling emphasizes the ways in which the client uses language and conversation in order to be known to the counsellor. When a client talks in general terms about their problems; for example, describing what 'usually' happens, or lumping specific events into broad categories (e.g. 'I worry a lot', 'we argue'), then the counsellor is allowed to know the client at a relatively superficial level. The counsellor can appreciate what is bothering the client, and what they want from counselling, but is not close to the lived moment-by-moment experience of the client. By contrast, when the client describes a specific example, it is as though the counsellor is able to be there in that event with the client. A detailed concrete description includes information about what the client thought and felt at different points in the event, how they made decisions, and how they evaluated different aspects of what happened. In other words, a narrative perspective suggests that detailed stories of specific events allow the counsellor to get closer to the client. It is as though such stories open a door into the personal world of the client. Further elaboration of this perspective can be found in McLeod (1997b, 1999, 2004a, b, 2005).

- *An experiential therapy perspective.* Experiential therapy is a therapy approach that shares many of the assumptions of client- and person-centred therapy. The most influential version of experiential therapy is associated with the work of Les Greenberg and Robert Elliott. This approach was initially described as process-experiential therapy (Greenberg *et al.*, 1993) but has more recently been renamed as *emotion focused therapy* (EFT) (Greenberg, 2001). A useful way of thinking about problematic reaction events was developed by Greenberg *et al.* (1993) and has remained a cornerstone of this approach to therapy. These theorists suggest in the task of *making sense of a problematic reaction*, the issue that the person is describing is essentially one that is based on what can be described as a *self-split*. In effect, the person is saying that part of them does something, while another part of them is critical of that activity. This duality or tension in the person's experience of self is central to understanding the problem. It is as though the person is arguing with themselves. If the task of *making sense* is to be successfully completed, at some stage it will almost certainly be necessary to invite the person to consider the issue in these terms. It is therefore helpful for a counsellor to be on the alert for clues concerning the nature of this underlying conflict from the outset of the work on the task. If the person is intending to move on to engage in the further task of changing their behaviour, it will undermine their ability to achieve change if, in effect, they are still arguing with themselves.

● *The perspective of personality theory.* A key figure in the field of contemporary personality psychology is Jefferson Singer, who argues that the sense of identity of an individual, and the image that they present to others, is largely organized around *autobiographical memories* (Singer and Blagov, 2004). The idea here is that each of us engages in many activities each day, with the result that over the course of a life there are thousands of memories that we can potentially draw on when describing who we are. However, typically, each of us has a stock of a few vivid personal memories to which we continually turn when thinking about our lives, or telling other people about the events in our lives. These self-defining memories, or autobiographical memories, are therefore of great signif-icance when working with clients in counselling. It is as if the core emotional and interpersonal issues with which a client struggles over the course of their life are encapsulated in a small number of vivid 'scenes'. In some ways this can be viewed as a perspective that makes sense of life patterns in terms of a drama, such as a play or film that consists of a series of scenes in which core issues are enacted. The implication of this theory to the task of using counselling to make sense of problematic reactions is that a problematic reaction event is probably a recent 'scene' that repeats or reinforces a pattern that is exhibited in the person's earliest autobiographical memories. For example, the client described above, who allows her mother to control her, can probably generate descrip-tions of childhood events or scenes in which her mother did not allow her the freedom to play, or to make her own decisions. The current problematic reac-tion is therefore possibly an expression of a much wider pattern in the client's life. As a result, it may be that successfully exploring the significance of a recent or current event may at some stage lead the client to make this wider connec-tion: 'oh, now I understand, this is how its always been with my mother'. However, each current (or future) replaying of this scene gives the client an opportunity to play it differently. Talking about niggling odd reactions that happened a couple of day ago may lead to talking about major stuff.

● *Why specific events are important from a CBT perspective.* Cognitive-behavioural therapy (CBT) adopts a structured approach to behaviour change that seeks to identify sequences of behaviour, cognition and emotion that contribute to dysfunctional states, and then to look for an intervention that will disrupt these sequences and instead allow the person to construct new patterns of coping (Westbrook *et al.*, 2007). From a CBT perspective, broad-brush descriptions of 'what usually happens' are of little value. In order to use CBT methods to help a client to change, what is necessary is to generate fine-grained descriptions of how the person thinks and feels in specific situations. Client accounts of specific problematic reactions are therefore the kind of information that is required in order to make it possible to use CBT techniques, if this is what the client believes will be valuable for them.

Taken together, these theoretical perspectives underscore the importance in counselling of *concreteness* – the skill of keeping the client grounded in the specifics of what is actually happening in their life. Problematic reaction events are of particular relevance, in this context, because they represent concrete instances that the client feels are worth talking about.

Box 10.1: *The importance of respectful curiosity*

Successfully enabling a client to make sense of a problematic reaction is very much a matter of creating a structure or scaffolding in which they are able to describe what they experienced, and reflect on what it might mean, and draw conclusions. Although there are powerful theories and methods that can be applied to this task, it is essential for counsellors to use these ideas to *sensitize* them to possibilities, rather than as fixed protocols to which they must adhere. An attitude of *respectful curiosity* is a sound foundation for this kind of work (Morgan, 2001). The client is after all talking about things that are hard for them to say. If these things weren't hard to say, they would have been able to sort them out for themselves.

Counselling methods for working on problematic reactions

There are various methods that a counsellor can employ when working with a person on the task of making sense of a problematic experience, such as a puzzling reaction to a situation. As with any counselling task, 'just talking' can be helpful. The longer that a client talks about what has happened, the more opportunity they have to reflect on the meaning of their actions and reaction, and to make connections between this particular event and other events that come to mind as they are speaking. It can therefore be very useful to use basic counselling skills to facilitate a discussion of a problematic reaction, using the person-centred counselling principle of following the client and trusting in the client's ability to find their own resolution to the issue. This kind of process can be augmented by inviting the client to create a diagram or image of what happened, or to act out the event through role-play. These techniques may be useful for some clients as a means of allowing them to externalize their feelings.

A particularly effective means of working on this type of task has been developed by Greenberg *et al.* (1993). They suggest that what seems to work best is to invite the person to talk about their puzzling or problematic reaction in a way that highlights the feelings and emotions associated with that event. The method essentially consists of three stages. First, the person is invited to recount in the first person an example of one time when the problematic reaction occurred. By telling the story of a specific event in detail, from an 'I' position ('I did this, and felt that . . .') the person is drawn into vividly re-experiencing what happened on a moment-by-moment basis. This way of talking yields a rich description of how the person thought and felt at each point, and particularly highlights the intentions of the person, making it possible to identify the competing intentions that were in play ('I wanted to run away, but at the same time I was telling myself that I needed to face up to the challenge'). It is helpful to use counselling skills in a sensitive manner to facilitate the telling of the story, for example, through summarizing and non-verbal signs of attending. Once the client has completed their description of the problematic event, it is valuable to offer an overall narrative summary that encompasses your understanding of what led up to the event, the unfolding of the event itself, and the later consequences of that experience. A useful set of ideas for this kind of lengthy summary or checking out can be found in Omer (1997). A key aspect of the counsellor's response to the telling of the client's story is the extent to which it captures and feeds back the feelings and emotional themes in the client's experiencing of the event.

The second stage of the task involves making sense of the event in terms of the conflict between these competing intentions, or parts of the self, and finding a way of making a *meaning bridge* between them, so that these different and contrasting personal impulses or beliefs can work together and be in dialogue rather than in conflict. Greenberg *et al.* (1993) advocate the use of two-chair work (see pp. 251–5) to facilitate this process. However, it is possible to use more conventional conversational means to achieve this segment of the task, or to invite the client to make a drawing of the conflicting parts of self that were activated by the situation that they were in.

The closing stage of this process involves examining the implications of what the client has learned in the previous stages. Ideally, the client should develop a sense of 'yes, that's what its all about', and then be in a position to discuss the implications of this realization for how they handle such situations in the future.

A case example

The use of the Greenberg *et al.* (1993) approach to *making sense of problematic reaction* task can be seen in the following case example.

Melissa, a business adviser, was consulted by Kamaljit, a businessman, who was seeking advice around the process of transferring control of his manufacturing company to his son Kenny. During a point in the consultation where Melissa and Kamaljit were reviewing the timetable for the hand-over, Kamaljit mentioned that he was worried about some of his recent tendency to 'fly off the handle' with his son over 'really trivial incidents'. He stated that: 'I just cannot understand what is happening. We have been working together perfectly well. He knows more about the business than I do. Why have I suddenly started to lose my temper like this? Do you think that I should go on one of these anger management courses?' Melissa wondered whether this statement might be a marker for an underlying issue that could be crucial to the successful management of the business plan, and decided that it might be useful to spend some time exploring the topic in more depth. She asked Kamaljit whether he thought that it might be worth taking a few minutes looking at these occasions where 'your temper enters the equation', with the aim of 'maybe getting to the bottom of what is happening here'. He agreed. Melissa then invited him to select one incident where he had 'flown off the handle', and to describe to her in detail what had happened, as if it was happening in the moment. With some difficulty, and frequent prompting to remain 'in the moment', he began to re-enter his experience of an angry moment a few days previously:

Kamaljit: I am sitting at my desk. Kenny comes in with a copy of a contract he has been working on, with a new supplier, for me to sign. I read through it. Just a few pages. It's fine. I look up. He is checking his email on his mobile phone screen. I get really angry with him and tell him that he should pay more attention, and that this is no way to behave in a business meeting.
Melissa: How did he react to that?
Kamaljit: He apologized and put the phone away.
Melissa: I'm wondering what was happening for you at that moment you got angry? What were you thinking and feeling?
Kamaljit: Oh, the usual. I don't matter any more. They don't need me.

Melissa then invited Kamaljit to explore the meaning, for him, of the sense that 'they don't need me' at this stage of his life. Quite quickly, he was able to identify ways in which he continued to be needed, and might be needed more in his post-retirement future, as well as aspects of his work role that were being lost. By expressing both sides of this tension within his sense of his own core self or identity (i.e. 'I am someone of value, who looks after everyone in the family' vs. 'I am over the hill and they don't need me'), he arrived at a more balanced understanding that helped him to make sense of not only these specific incidents with his son, but also more broadly of his feelings about the changes that were taking place in his life as a whole.

In this example, Melissa possessed sufficient counselling skill to be aware that Kamaljit's mention of 'flying off the handle' with his son might be a marker for an aspect of his life that might repay further exploration. The manner in which Kamaljit referred to the events that had taken place with his son conveyed that these occurrences were puzzling for him, in being out of character (i.e. not the result of a general behaviour pattern or trait) and inappropriate (i.e. not a rational response to the immediate situation). The events were therefore difficult to reconcile or integrate with his usual story of who he was and how his life was lived. The implication was that his response to his son meant something significant, and that this meaning would be worth knowing about. In her response to Kamaljit, Melissa needed to check out that he acknowledged that his reaction to his son was problematic, and that he was willing to look at it further with her at that moment. After all, he may not have felt safe enough with Melissa to allow their conversation to go down that path at that stage in their relationship. When he confirmed that he would wish to look at the matter further, she then made a tentative suggestion concerning a *method* by which he might do this (by telling the story in detail of an actual incidence of the problematic response).

The end point of effective completion of this particular counselling task occurs when the person arrives at a new or enriched appreciation of what it was about them that made the situation such a problem. In the case of Kamaljit, by understanding the factors behind his problematic anger reaction, he was able to change the way he responded to his son, Kenny, without difficulty – simply by reminding himself, and inviting Kenny to remind him, of the meaning that these situations held for him. If he had attempted to develop ways of managing and controlling his anger (i.e. moved straight into planning behavioural changes), in the absence of this stage of making sense of his problematic actions, he would probably have continued to suppress his painful feelings of 'not being useful and more'. The chances are in such a scenario that the part of him that did feel hurt and unheard would have undermined his efforts to change with the result that any anger management programme would have been ineffective.

This case example also illustrates the relevance of other theoretical perspectives. By asking him to recount the story of a specific instance of 'flying off the handle', Melissa was able to get closer to the actual lived experience of Kamaljit, as predicted by narrative theory, in a way that allowed her to understand him better and be more facilitative around possibilities for change. The detailed description generated by Kamaljit provided a platform for behaviour change even though CBT methods were not used at this point in the counselling. Kamaljit's story was connected to an important dimension of his autobiographical memory store – images of being a provider and being in charge – that stretched back to childhood.

Box 10.2: *Paying attention to what is not being said*

When a client is telling the story of a problematic reaction, it is obviously important to listen to what they are saying. It is just as important to pay attention to what is *not* being said in terms of gaps in their account. The psychoanalytic researcher, Lester Luborsky, has established that in terms of emotional and relational content there are three key elements in a personal story: the wishes of the protagonist, the response of other people to what the protagonist or storyteller wants, and the response of self to these reactions (Luborsky *et al.*, 1992, 1994). If any one of these elements is missing from a story, from the point of view of the listener/counsellor, the result is a sense that the account is incomplete. In such circumstances, it can be useful as a counsellor to inquire in a gentle way about the missing element by saying something along the lines of 'that was such a powerful experience, but I was just wondering – when your mother reacted to you like that, what was your own response to her?' A further perspective on what might be missing comes from a paper by Jodie Wigrem (1994) who observed in her practice that clients who were describing an emotionally painful or threatening event tended to skip over the bits of the story that were too difficult to tell. Like Luborsky, she found that it could be helpful to be tentatively curious about what was missing, and invite the client to fill in the gaps. For many clients, it is only when they have been able to tell the *whole* story that a problematic reaction can begin to make sense.

Conclusions

Talking in a concrete, specific way about problematic events and actual experiences is a thread that can be traced through all effective counselling. If there is a good relationship between a client and their counsellor, the former will tack back and forwards between general descriptions of their troubles, and specific detailed examples. If the client does not generate specific examples, there is something wrong – either they do not feel safe enough with the counsellor to get to the reality of what they are experiencing, or the reality is too painful or shameful to describe to anyone. This task area is unusual in that there exists a research-based approach, developed by Les Greenberg and his colleagues, that is available as a guide. However, it is important to apply their model with sensitivity, and to be willing to follow the lead of the client if it does not seem to them to be helpful.

Suggested further reading

The key source of guidance on how to accomplish this type of counselling task:

Greenberg, L.S., Rice, L.N. and Elliott, R. (1993) *Facilitating Emotional Change: The Moment-by-moment Process*. New York: Guilford Press. (Chapter 8.)

Resolving difficult feelings and emotions

Yes, you're right
Like my granddad
I'm alone at the same time as being surrounded
By people
Who love me.
Sometimes it's unbearable.
Sorry.
It's like
A different kind of pain
That I carry around.
Some really bad feelings.
Right here.
It's different from the cancer pain.
Sometimes I almost
Want
To go away and cry
Sorry.

Introduction

When someone wants to talk to a counsellor, at some level it is because they 'feel bad' about something. No matter how much the counselling process focuses on cognitive and rational decision-making and action-planning, there is always an emotional dimension to the work. As a result, for the majority of clients who enter into ongoing counselling, there will be a need at some point to look at feelings and emotions with the goal of resolving them, changing them or making sense of them. This chapter provides an introductory guide to the topic of working with emotions in counselling. Some theoretical perspectives are offered as a means of developing an understanding of the significance of emotions. A number of counselling strategies or methods that have been developed for emotion-oriented work are also described.

Exercise 11.1: *Your personal emotional profile*

How comfortable are you with the expression of emotions? Are there emotions with which you feel relatively comfortable, and other emotions that are hard for you to express or hear? What are the implications of your personal emotional profile for your work as a counsellor?

Making sense of emotion

On the whole, we live in a world in which rationality is valued and emphasized over emotion. There are a number of reasons for this. Emotion is an immediate, bodily response to a situation, which has direct and clear implications for action. For example, fear triggers flight. Most of us live in complex, crowded urban environments in which we are constantly faced with multiple competing stimuli and rules, where a thoughtful, considered response is usually most effective. In this environment, a spontaneous emotional response is likely to lead to trouble. We therefore learn early on to suppress our emotions in the interest of getting along with people. In the past, individuals tended to learn about people and relationships through face-to-face contact, such as listening to another person telling a story, or viewing a drama being enacted on stage. In these situations, the bodily emotion of one person can be directly communicated to others. In contrast, in contemporary societies, we largely learn about people and relationships through watching TV or reading novels. Both of these are emotionally 'cool' and disembodied media. When watching a TV programme, we are placed in the position of a very distant observer, rarely able to connect with the subjective physical emotion and feeling of any individual actor or character. We are also in a position of being able to switch off at any moment, and make the character disappear.

Despite the uneasiness and ambivalence about emotion that permeates much of our culture, it is essential to recognize that feelings and emotions are an essential part of life. One of the most important functions of a counselling relationship is that it provides a space in which there is permission to feel, and to express emotions. It may be useful to regard emotion and feeling as sources of meaning, or as signal systems. An inherent aspect of being human is the capacity to perceive, think and reason, to use concepts and ideas to guide action. In parallel to this system of cognitive information-processing and decision-making, there is an emotion-based system, which operates directly on various bodily functions such as heart rate and respiration. While cognitive processing sorts information in terms of possibly thousands of concepts and categories available in language, the emotion system sorts information in terms of a smaller set of categories that have been biologically wired in through evolution: anger, fear, joy, loss, pleasure and disgust. From a counselling perspective, therefore, feeling and emotion always have some *meaning* in relation to what is happening in a person's life space or personal niche. Feeling and emotion are bodily signals that provide information about the basic attitude or action tendency of the person towards an event, other person or situation. For example, certain emotional responses are part of a basic biological 'fight–flight' response, indicating that there is something in the environment that is threatening and which evokes either anger (destroying the threat or making it go away) or fear (escaping from the threat). The emotional reactions that people tend to want to explore in counselling are those where the meaning of the emotion is not clear to the individual, either because the emotion state is fleeting and vague, consisting of a general sense of emotional pain, or is confused/confusing (why do I keep feeling angry and losing my temper?). When a person really knows and accepts what they feel about something, then they usually do not seek counselling.

The reason why feelings and emotions are often vague and confused is that people may have grown up in a family or wider cultural environment in which particular emotions were unacceptable. For instance, many men have learned that it is not 'manly' to feel sadness and loss, or even fear. Many women have been socialized into believing that is not appropriate for them to feel angry. As a result, men may feel afraid or ashamed about any possibility of personally feeling or expressing sadness. Women may feel fear and self-disgust about any possibility of feeling or expressing anger. Instead of sadness, men may get angry. Instead of anger, women may get anxious or fearful. While these are very broad generalizations, which should never be simplistically applied to individual lives, they do illustrate a basic truth about emotion, which is that *the emotions or feelings that a person exhibits may hide or protect other emotions or feelings that are harder to acknowledge*. It can be useful to take account of the concept of *authenticity* with respect to feeling and emotion. When a person is expressing genuine feelings, what they say has a sense of being authentic, and will have a direct emotional impact on anyone in contact with them. For example, even listening to a radio interview with a grieving disaster victim, whom one has never met, is many thousands of miles away, and speaking in another language, can be a profoundly moving experience. By contrast, attending a family funeral accompanied by weeping relatives can evoke a sense of detachment. When a person expresses a genuine or authentic feeling or emotion, there is typically a physical sense of relief or release, and a sense of resolution in relation to the issue or problem that is associated with that emotion. These are valuable indicators of whether a feeling or emotion is primary, or may be a secondary emotion that may mask a more basic one. It is rarely helpful to challenge a person seeking help on the grounds that they are expressing false or pretend emotions. The emotions they are expressing are real enough to them, at that moment, and worthy of consideration and respect.

The point here for a counsellor is to be willing to listen to their own gut sense that there *may be more to come*.

The Canadian psychologist, Les Greenberg, has made a major contribution towards developing an understanding of the role of feelings and emotions in counselling (Greenberg, 2001; Greenberg *et al.*, 1993). He uses the term 'emotion processing' to convey the idea that what a counsellor should be trying to do is to collaborate with the person seeking help to allow the meaning of an emotion to unfold, bit by bit. This is achieved essentially by staying with the emotion and looking at all its different aspects. Any counselling method that is used in work around emotions is trying to do just this – to help the person to reflect on what the emotion is, where and when it happens, what it leads to, and what it means.

It is valuable to make a distinction in counselling between *feeling* and *emotion*. Both are part of the same embodied, internally sensed way of responding to the world. Both are sources of meaning and information. However, feeling can be regarded as an ever-present inner sensing that can be referred to at any moment. Feelings are typically multifaceted – there are many sides to what one feels in a situation, or many threads of feeling of which a person may be aware. Emotion, by contrast, is more specific. It takes over the body, and can usually be identified as one thing; for example, anger. In counselling, feelings are always part of the equation. For a counsellor, understanding what a person is talking about is hugely influenced by the feelings they convey, and by what is felt by the counsellor when they are listening. In counselling, strong emotion occurs less often. When it does occur, though, it demands attention. Effective counselling skill requires the courage to be willing to be with another person when they are expressing strong emotion, as well as the sensitivity to be able to enter the person's everyday feeling-world.

Exercise 11.2: *The impact of the organizational context*

What is the emotional profile of your workplace? Which emotions are allowed, and in what circumstances? Which emotions are suppressed? What happens to people who express taboo emotions in your office or clinic? What are the implications of your organizational emotion profile for you as a practitioner, and for the people who use your service?

Types of emotion tasks in counselling

There are three broad categories of counselling task that involve working with feeling and emotion. These are:

1 *Exploring feelings that are elusive, vague or hidden*. The marker for this task arises when the person may have a vague sense of how they feel about an

issue, but be unable to put this into words, or to be able to stay with the feeling long enough to really know what it is about. Sometimes a person may claim that they do not feel anything at all. The counselling task here is to bring what is felt sufficiently into awareness for it to become a source of meaning and information that can be useful to the person. For example, Gina, a supervisor in a medical laboratory, consulted her human resources (HR) manager about how best to handle one of the technicians who was persistently late in arriving for work. Following Gina's account of the issue, the HR manager asked her 'I can see that the facts here are fairly straight-forward. But there seems to be something else around too. Maybe this isn't relevant, but as you were talking I found myself wondering how you felt about this person'. This question threw Gina off balance. She replied that she was not aware of having any particular feelings about this colleague. The HR manager asked her whether she would be willing to just pause for a second or two and reflect on any feelings that she might be aware of at that moment. After a brief silence, Gina laughed and said that, yes, she real-ized that she was very fond of this technician: 'she reminds me of my own daughter, she is very warm and affectionate, and makes a big difference to the team – she is the one all the others will turn to if they need to talk about something'. In discussing the situation further, Gina became able to recog-nize the ways that her unwillingness to admit her liking for her colleague had resulted in her taking too formal and rigid an approach to the lateness problem, which in turn prevented her from holding the type of 'friendly' conversation with her that might have resolved the problem in a creative fashion. For Gina, becoming more aware of how she felt was the vital clue to the solution of her difficulty.

2 *Giving expression to emotions that are being held back*. If a strong emotion is stimulated by an event, it seems that there is a basic human need to express that emotion in some way. If the emotion is not expressed or released, the person may have a sense of incompleteness, or 'unfinished business' which can interfere with normal functioning. The idea that emotions demand expression, and that it can be psychologically and physically damaging to hold back emotion, can be traced to the ancient Greek theory of *catharsis*. The marker for this kind of task may simply be that the person recognizes in themselves that there are emotions near the surface: 'I just need a good cry' or 'I feel so angry inside but I just can't do anything with it'. The counselling task involves creating the conditions for, and facilitating, the safe release of the emotion. Ali was a refugee, who had fled with his family from an oppres-sive regime. Safe in Britain, and waiting for his work permit to be finalized, Ali began to visit his GP every two weeks with a series of ailments – back pain, stomach spasms, headaches. On one of these visits, the GP asked Ali if he thought that it might be helpful to book a longer consultation to give them more time to talk about Ali's situation in more detail, and whether

these different illnesses might be linked in some way. Ali readily agreed, and on his way out of the room, joked that 'you'd better watch out doctor. Have some tissues ready for our next meeting. Once I start to talk, I have five years of tears waiting to come out'. At the beginning of their next consultation, the GP invited Ali to tell him the whole story of what had happened to him in leaving his country and travelling to Britain. Within a few moments, Ali was in tears, as he described scenes of fear, torture and loss. The doctor moved his chair alongside Ali, and placed his hand over Ali's hand. He encouraged Ali to keep talking, to continue with his story, and occasionally reassured him that 'you are all right now, you are safe here'. At a follow-up consultation, one week later, Ali reported that 'it was the first time I have felt well in years. I have been busy with voluntary work and looking after the children, and haven't been thinking about headaches and backaches at all'.

3   *Limiting or managing the expression of emotions that are experienced as being out of control.* The emotion-focused tasks that have been described above share an aim of learning how to bring buried or suppressed feelings into awareness, and accepting what they may contribute to a person's participation in life. By contrast, another type of emotion-centred task in counselling can comprise the effort to control the experiencing, expression and enactment of emotions that are regarded by the person as being unwelcome, or out of proportion to the situations in which they find themself. Alistair was a policeman who had worked on a motorway patrol for several years, witnessing on a routine basis a large number of fatal road traffic accidents. His colleagues and his wife had noticed that he seemed to be 'on a hair trigger', and likely to become verbally, and occasionally even physically, angry at the slightest provocation. Persuaded to consult the force occupational health physician, Alistair could not be convinced to accept a referral to a psychologist: 'I'm not mental, I just need to sort this out'. The occupational health doctor decided to invite Alistair to return for a longer consultation to explore the issue further. At this meeting, he asked Alistair if he would be willing to look at whether there was a pattern to his anger episodes. Alistair agreed, and, after describing three recent incidents in which he had 'lost his head', began to see that he needed further help in order to regain his self-control in work situations. He said: 'there are times when I need to take command of people and speak in a clear loud voice to give them directions for their own safety, but I can see now that I am going much too far'. The remainder of the session was spent discussing what he could expect from a clinical psychologist, and the process of the referral.

These three forms of 'emotion work' can be the main focus of counselling in some instances, or may be subsidiary to other tasks. For example, helping a person to deal with a relationship problem may often involve feelings of anger or loss with reference to a troublesome 'significant other'. The third emotional processing task described above – limiting the expression of emotions that are experienced as being out of control – can usefully be considered as a type of behaviour change task (see Chapter 12). The remainder of the present chapter will discuss some of the methods that can be used in counselling when a person is seeking help to make sense of feelings and emotions that are vague and elusive, or are being held back.

Exercise 11.3: *Being aware of emotions in everyday life*

Over the course of a convenient period of time (an hour, a day), keep a note of the emotion and feeling terms that people use in their conversations with you (and you use in your conversations with them). Are there any patterns that you can identify? For example, do men and women, and people from different ethnic or social class groups seem to talk in different ways about feelings? What has been the effect on you, and your interactions with others, of specifically listening for emotions?

Methods for working with emotions in counselling

A variety of methods can be used to facilitate the awareness and expression of feelings and emotions, and exploration of their meaning. The following sections briefly describe some of the strategies that may be helpful in this kind of work.

Developing a sensitivity to feeling and emotion

Some counsellors seem to operate as if the emotional life of the people they are trying to help was irrelevant. These are counsellors whose responses predominantly lead the person in the direction of talking about what they *do* and what they *think*, rather than what they *feel*. They do not pay attention to emotion cues, or invite the person to explore feelings. This is a very limited approach to counselling, which is missing out on important information about the significance of events in the person's life. Some other counsellors seem to operate as though emotional expression and catharsis were their primary goal. This is not effective either as a general rule. Both research and practical experience suggest that feelings are always linked to situations, relationships and events, and that what is helpful is not just to express the 'raw' emotion, but to learn more about what the emotion *means*, what it says about the situation, relationship or event in question. There may be some occasions when a person really needs just to express and 'let go' of a strong buried emotion, but this is a relatively rare event in counselling. Usually, what is more helpful is to enable the person to make use of their emotions as a guide to action. In a sense, a lot of counselling is about the development of what Daniel Goleman (2005) has called 'emotional intelligence', which involves making it possible for the person to be more aware of their emotions and what they mean. To be able to offer this to people seeking help, anyone in a counselling role needs to be aware and sensitive around the dynamic flow of feeling and emotion within their relationship with the person with whom they are working.

Counsellor competence around the awareness of feeling and emotion is based on a willingness to *listen for feelings* at all times during a counselling encounter. Primarily, listening for feelings means being sensitive to the feeling words that a person uses, and weaving these into the conversation. However, it can also involve being on the alert for the *absence* of feeling words. Some people have difficulties in dealing with problems in living because they are unable to refer to their feelings and consciously acknowledge how they feel. The classic example of this is the person who may be very attached to people in their life, but never tells them how much they love them or care about them, or enjoy their company. A state of lacking feeling words has been labelled 'alexithymia', and people with psychosomatic complaints are often alexithymic. A sensitive counsellor may find that a person's body language, tone of voice, or even the events they are describing, hint at a feeling that they seem to be unable to put into words. In these circumstances, it can be helpful for the counsellor very tentatively to offer feeling words for the person to 'try out for size'.

In a counselling situation where it is possible to maintain a relationship with a person over an extended period of time, as a counsellor you may find that the person keeps coming back to the same feeling state again and again. They may consistently get angry, feel tired, get depressed, or whatever, no matter what trigger situation they are in. Recurrent feelings that appear to be not quite appropriate to the situation can often be a sign that there are buried feelings in the background. What seems to happen is that a person can 'specialize' in emotion states that they are familiar with, rather than entering other emotion states that may seem to them to be scary and out of control. As a counsellor, it is valuable at these times to be as sensitive as possible to the presence of possible hidden feeling states; for example, by catching the flash of anger that accompanies an expression of repetitive sadness.

Box 11.1: *Making sense of recurring patterns of feeling: the concept of 'rackets'*

Transactional analysis (TA) is a good source of ways of describing the kinds of psychological and interpersonal processes that trouble people in their lives. In TA theory, it is assumed that people who live productive and healthy lives will have access to, and appropriately express, a wide range of emotions – anger, fear, sadness, happiness – in response to different situations that they encounter. Many of us, however, tend to return to the same feeling state, no matter what the situation. In TA language, such recurrent patterns of feelings are described as *racket feelings*, which are defined as: 'a familiar emotion, learned and encouraged in childhood, experienced in many different stress situations, and maladaptive as an adult means of problem-solving' (Stewart and Joines, 1987: 209). This phenomenon is explained in terms of a process of *rubberbanding* – the assumption is that when under stress, a person is swiftly and unconsciously catapulted back into what they learned to do as a child, as a way of coping with scary situations. The emotional state that then emerges is the one that was functional, as a child, in gaining parental support and care. There is another aspect of racket theory that is also significant as a means of understanding apparently inappropriate or self-defeating emotional responses, which is the idea of *stamps*. The concept of 'psychological trading stamps' is now somewhat dated. It refers to the practice of supermarkets in the 1960s of encouraging trade by giving customers stamps which were pasted in books and cashed at a later date. (Now this is done through loyalty cards.) The point about stamps is that they are saved up and traded in at a later date. The application to emotional life is that some people may feel racket feelings but do not express them at the time, while storing them up for an emotional outpouring in the future. The person or people who are the recipients of the eventual emotional cashing-in are typically surprised by the intensity of feelings which may be unleashed – they do not realize how much patient collecting lies behind the emotion event that they are witnessing. These ideas from TA theory undoubtedly are not the final word in relation to the question of recurring patterns of feeling and emotion. But they are stimulating and thought-provoking, and show how ordinary language can be employed vividly to express quite sophisticated ideas about emotional dynamics in a way that can communicate with many people who are seeking help around such issues.

Finally, one of the best ways for any counsellor to heighten their awareness to feelings and emotions in a counselling session is to *listen to your own feelings*. There are at least three ways in which the counsellor's own feelings comprise a vital source of information about what is happening in the counselling relationship. First, a counsellor who listens to their feelings may become aware that what they are feeling consists of a feeling that they brought into the counselling session, and which has nothing to do with what the person seeking help is talking about. For example, a person in an embedded counselling role may be feeling frustrated and angry because of some work hassles. There is a danger that these feelings may get in the way of tuning into the emotional world of the person seeking help. Part of sound preparation for a counselling session involves setting aside personal emotional processing in order to be able to concentrate on what the other person is feeling. Second, what a counsellor feels when with a person seeking help can often take the form of a kind of emotional *resonance*: it is as though the counsellor is resonating like a tuning fork to the feelings being emitted by the other person. Therefore, a lot of the time in counselling, how *you* are feeling may be a good clue to how the person is feeling at that moment (although this always needs to be checked out). Third, what the counsellor feels in response to a person may be *how other people also feel in relation to that person.* For example, if you feel angry or annoyed with a person to whom you are offering counselling, it may be that other people (their friends, family, work colleagues) may sometimes feel the same way too. This awareness can be used carefully to explore questions such as: What is this person doing to make me feel angry? Do I respond in the same way that others do (which others, and in what circumstances?) and what does this response do in terms of the kinds of relationships this person has with these people?

Emotional sensitivity in counselling is a matter of mastering a kind of dual attention: listening to oneself at the same time as listening to the person seeking help. This is why training in counselling places such an emphasis on what is sometimes called 'personal development' work. A huge part of this personal development consists of learning about one's own emotional life as a means of being better able to tune into the emotional worlds of others.

Creating an environment that is conducive to the expression of emotion

If a person is using counselling to work on an emotion or feeling, it is probably because they are to some extent embarrassed, ashamed or inhibited about acknowledging or expressing that area of emotional life. If the person was *not* embarrassed or ashamed, the chances would be that they would be able openly to display that emotion in everyday circumstances. It is therefore helpful to make sure that the person feels safe enough to express emotion. For instance, the person may be reassured to be told that the counsellor is comfortable with the expression of feelings, or that they can go at their own pace, or have plenty of time for this task. The person may be worried about whether anyone outside the room will hear them, or see them when they leave, or whether there are facilities (tissues, a washbasin, mirror) for putting on a 'face' for the outside world. It is probably easier to express feelings in a soft environment; for example, a cushioned armchair that can be hit or stroked, rather than in an office furnished with hard upright chairs. The counsellor too may have concerns in these areas – 'what if my colleagues hear shouting coming from my office?', 'if this person breaks down, I'm sure I will start to cry too, and how will I be able to be ready for my next patient?'

Using the person's 'feeling language'

Sensitivity to the language with which the person talks about their experience can provide a number of possibilities for facilitating feeling and emotion. One of the ways that people avoid getting in touch with their feelings is to talk quickly, or shift topics frequently. People sometimes do these things because they may be aware at some level that talking slowly, or staying with a topic, would mean that the feeling or emotion associated with that topic, or that was being felt at that moment, might become overwhelming. Many 'standard' counselling responses, such as reflecting back what the person has said, allowing silences, and talking in a gentle, measured voice, can have the effect of slowing the person down, and helping them to keep in touch with what they are feeling in that moment. There may be specific words, phrases or images that are particularly evocative for the person. Often, these phrases and images will be embedded in the person's speech, produced by the person as they are talking about an issue. From the counsellor's perspective, these words can almost jump out of the conversation and very obviously possess a great deal of meaning. The counsellor can reflect these words or images back to the person, or may even invite the person to repeat them, and report on what happens when they try this.

Paying attention to what the person's body is saying and doing

Because feeling and emotion are bodily phenomena, there are several ways that careful attention to what is happening at a physical level can be used in emotion work. When a person uses an emotion word, it can be helpful to invite them to indicate where that feeling is located in their body, and then to focus their awareness on that part of the body and what they feel right there. Bodily movement is an important means of expressing emotion – when we are happy we dance, and when we are angry we hit things. When a person refers to a feeling or emotion, or seems to be feeling something, it can be valuable to draw their attention to any gestures or movements that seem to accompany the feeling, and either to give words to that movement ('what is your clenched fist saying?', 'if the fingers that are stroking your other arm had a voice, what would they say?') or perhaps repeat and exaggerate the movement ('clench the fist more, and hold it there for a few moments – what happens when you do that?'). Breathing is closely linked to the expression of feeling and emotion. A highly effective way of controlling or choking off an emotion is to hold one's breath or breathe as shallowly as possible; the release of emotion is typically accompanied by long, deep breaths, sighs and yawning. There may be times when a counsellor can become aware that a person is holding their breath, or is breathing as little as possible. At these moments, it can be useful to point this out to the person, and invite them to breathe deeply and regularly, perhaps also breathing along with them for a few seconds. Another bodily indicator of emotion is tummy rumbling. Some counsellors believe that tummy rumbling, in the absence of overt hunger, is a signal that there is a deeply held, buried feeling struggling to be expressed. If asked, and if they are not too embarrassed, a person will often be able to report on the feeling or desire that lies behind the rumbling.

Using enactment

When a person wishes to express strong feelings, but finds it hard to 'let go', it may be helpful to use *enactment*. Usually, a strong emotion is felt *in relation to* another person. For instance, someone may feel angry with a colleague, or feel the loss of a parent. In these circumstances, it can be difficult to enter the emotion fully when merely talking to a counsellor – there can be a tendency for the person to talk *about* their feelings, rather than entering directly into them. A face-to-face counselling conversation is also a situation in which a person will probably be exerting a certain amount of self-control, and will be monitoring what they say rather than allowing themselves to be lost in or taken over by feelings. Inviting the person to perform their feelings through dramatically enacting their interaction with the object of their emotions can be a very effective strategy for facilitating emotional expression. The person can be asked to imagine that they are talking directly to the imagined other person: 'what do you want to say to them – just talk to them as if they were here'. There are several variants of this method, such as imagining the other were sitting on a chair, allowing the other to answer back, and encouraging repetition of key statements ('say it again – she's not listening to you') (this counselling strategy is often described as 'two-chair work' – see Greenberg *et al.*, 1993). During this kind of enactment, it can be helpful if the counsellor sits alongside the person, rather than opposite them. This has two effects. First, it reinforces the enactment, and makes it possible for both the person and the counsellor to speak to the other. Second, it creates a situation where the person is not expressing strong feelings directly at or towards the counsellor – it may be embarrassing to express anger directly to a counsellor, when the person knows that the true target of their anger is someone else. A further variant on the method of enactment can involve expressing feelings through a letter written to the other person. This letter may be brought into a later meeting with the counsellor, may be kept, or may be ritually destroyed, to represent the act of moving beyond the feelings that it carries. People may find it useful to write letters on consecutive days as a way of allowing all of their feelings to emerge, bit by bit.

Experiential focusing

The psychologist, philosopher and psychotherapist, Eugene Gendlin, has developed a method of *experiential focusing*, which is widely applicable in situations where a person is struggling to make sense of, or give expression to, a feeling or emotion (see Cornell, 1996; Gendlin, 2003; Purton, 2005). Gendlin argues that the meaning of any situation, relationship or event in which a person is involved is captured in a bodily 'felt sense' to which the person can refer. The felt sense includes a wealth of *implicit* meaning, not all of which is explicitly known or understood by the person at any particular point. If a person can be enabled to stay with (or *focus* on) their felt sense of a situation, then the layers of meaning that are bodily present can begin to be symbolized and consciously known. Usually, symbolization occurs in the form of language – the person finds words and phrases that emerge from the felt sense and seem to capture threads of its meaning. However, symbolization can also take the form of an image, pictorial representation, sound or bodily movement. For Gendlin, the activity of helping a client to focus on an unclear felt sense comprises a basic therapeutic process that occurs in virtually all forms of effective counselling. This is because a central problem that many people have in their lives is that of not allowing themselves to stay close enough to what they are feeling for long enough to allow the broader personal meaning of what is happening in their life to emerge. Gendlin would argue that people avoid focusing on their felt sense of a problem by blocking their internal awareness by incessantly talking, being 'busy' or not paying attention to bodily feelings and sensations. The group of practitioners associated with this approach have developed a set of simple procedures for helping people to access their felt sense and make use of what they find there. They have encouraged the use of these focusing instructions in peer self-help communities worldwide (see Boukydis, 1984), and with clients experiencing a variety of health problems. Experiential focusing is a method that is readily incorporated into counselling that takes place embedded within other professional roles. Gendlin's (2003) book, *Focusing*, provides clear guidelines on how to use this method. These guidelines are also available on the *Focusing Institute* webite: www.focusing.org/.

Personal and family rituals

A ritual is an activity or routine that is invested with special significance by a person or group of people. Human beings have always used rituals as ways of dealing with conflict, and marking life transitions. For people seeking to resolve emotional difficulties, ritual may represent a valuable means of expressing troublesome feelings in a controlled setting. For example, a person who is troubled by feelings of depression and hopelessness may counter these emotions by starting each day with a set of yoga exercises which symbolize hope and renewal. In Talmon (1990: ch. 3) the story of a client, Mary, is described. Mary was angry with her father for a variety of reasons, and wished to exclude him from her life. Together, she and her husband, along with the counsellor, devised a ritual in which Mary read out with powerful emotion a 'decree of divorce' from her father, while the counsellor set on fire a photograph of her father, accompanied by music played by her husband. This ritual carried out during a counselling session had an enormous impact on Mary in signalling a transition between a self that had been dominated by her father to a new self that was free and ready to enter a different phase of her life. Within the counselling and psychotherapy literature there are many examples of rituals that have been devised for different therapeutic purposes (Imber-Black and Roberts, 1992; McMillan, 2006) and which can be adapted for use in micro-counselling situations. Ultimately, in a counselling setting, the rituals that will make most sense for a person are those that are co-constructed, that take shape from the ideas of the counsellor and person seeking help working together, rather than anything that is 'off the shelf'.

Using cognitive-behavioural therapy (CBT) techniques to control emotions

If a person seeks help around the goal of controlling emotions, it may be valuable to consider the use of CBT techniques. Cognitive-behavioural therapy (CBT) encompasses a range of methods that have been designed for, or can be adapted to, the task of emotional self-control. Some of the CBT techniques that can be applied in this situation include:

- Keeping a diary of when and how 'emotion events' occur – with the aim of identifying what triggers them off and what seems to prevent them.
- Exploring an emotional event in detail, and working backwards from the event to the step-by-step sequence of events that preceded it. This can then lead to working together to find ways of interrupting the emotion-inducing sequence (e.g. by saying to oneself to 'keep calm', or by thinking about a pleasant image).
- Finding alternatives to the emotion. For example: 'if you did not get angry/ burst into tears/freeze with fear, what else could you do?'.
- Learning relaxation skills – in many situations, being able to move into a previously learned relaxation or breathing routine can give the person a few moments to pause and reflect on their choices (e.g. whether to express the troublesome emotion or do something else).
- Identifying the thoughts and processes of 'self-talk' that trigger emotions. For example, someone may make themself angry because they may tell themself that other people are looking down on them – this is an irrational or dysfunctional thought that can be challenged by the counsellor.

The particular usefulness of CBT techniques lies in its applicability in working with people who do not particularly want to understand their emotion, but are just interested in controlling it, and people who prefer a more structured, rather than exploratory, approach to counselling. People who are scared or embarrassed about expressing their feelings in the presence of the counsellor may also prefer a CBT approach, which on the whole does not require any kind of 'here-and-now' emotional expression. There are many self-help books and websites that provide CBT-based information on how to control emotions such as anger and fear. The movie *Anger Management*, starring Jack Nicholson and Adam Sandler, depicts in a somewhat extreme way how some of these techniques can work in practice.

Expressive arts as tools for working with feelings and emotions: dance, movement, drama, drawing and sculpture

Issues around emotions often centre around the fact that feelings and emotions are processes that take place in a reality that is largely outside of the verbal. Once emotion-oriented counselling gets to the stage where the person can clearly talk about their feelings, either most of the work has been done or the person has switched into intellectualizing about their feelings, and the opportunity has been lost. The expressive arts comprise a mode of engaging with emotional experience that can powerfully tap into non-verbal ways of knowing and communicating. For example, the availability of a lump of plasticine or similar material can give a person an opportunity to allow their hands to express their feelings in the moulding of a shape. The availability of paper and crayons can allow image and colour to be utilized. These are arts tools that are readily accessible, and which will be non-threatening to most people who are seeking counselling. In some situations, more complex forms of expressive activity, such as drama or dance, may also be possibilities.

Cultural resources

The task of working on feelings and emotions may take place solely within a counselling session, or may include activities that the person decides to pursue elsewhere within their life space. The direct work of the counsellor, in relation to feeling and emotion, can therefore in some cases be restricted to planning and rehearsing where and how the person might feel safe to express strong emotion. There exists a broad range of cultural resources and settings that can be facilitative for someone struggling to resolve an emotional issue. As mentioned earlier, letter-writing can represent a powerful means of channelling feelings. Other forms of writing, such as poetry, can also be used. Other people may opt to express rage and anger by shouting at a football match, or in the privacy of their car, or allow tears to come by visiting a graveside or spending some time looking at photographs of loved ones. A hugely valuable source of emotional healing for many people is music – listening to, or playing, a piece that evokes a certain emotional state may allow a person to stay with that state long enough for its personal meaning and significance to emerge and be worked through. Films, which can be purchased or borrowed on video or DVD, can allow a person seeking to come to terms with an emotional issue to enter imaginatively into the world of a character who is also experiencing such an issue, and vicariously to participate in the process of resolution as experienced by that figure. Novels can supply a similar sort of learning – the key here is not to suggest to the person seeking help that they should copy the way that a character in a film or novel has dealt with their emotional difficulties, but that the story can represent one *possible* way of coping. For people who are stuck in an emotional impasse, the idea that there are different possibilities can be liberating. Another important cultural resource is self-help and self-improvement books; for instance, around such themes as coping with grief, being more assertive and willing to express anger, or dealing with fears.

Box 11.2: *Cultural differences in emotional expressiveness*

In a study by Kamer Shoaib and Jennifer Peel, a number of Kashmiri women living in Oldham, England, were interviewed about their views of counselling. Some of these women were users of counselling or mental health services, while other were not. Interviews were conducted in the language preferred by the participant. One of the main themes to emerge from this study was the difficulty that many of these women had in translating statements about their emotional life into English. Some Kashmiri emotional terms did not have any meaningful English-language equivalent. The authors noted that 'many poignant phrases for emotions made use of the head and the heart, for example . . . "emptying the heart", "in my head the weight will lighten" and "my heart's pain will reduce"' (p. 92). These findings confirm the results of other studies of emotional expressiveness in members of Asian and other non-Western cultural groups. In these cultures and languages, emotions are not denoted by psychological terms such as 'anger' or 'anxiety', but tend largely to be indicated by reference to parts of the body such as the head, heart and stomach. Moreover, some forms of feeling appear to be culture-specific, and may be extremely difficult to understand or appreciate from a different cultural standpoint. The result of these differences in emotional expressiveness has meant that within health care systems dominated by practitioners from majority Western cultural groups, 'minority' clients have often been offered interventions that are not appropriate. When working with a person from another cultural group, it is therefore important for a counsellor to be curious and open in relation to how feelings and emotions are described. These are also opportunities to learn new ways of thinking about feelings. After all, 'emptying the heart' is a phrase that, as Shoaib and Peel (2003) suggest, is indeed poignant, and which for many people who are not Kashmiri may capture a vital truth about the experience of sadness and loss.

Using silence

The end point of a 'working with emotion' task will normally be when the person decides to stop. This may occur when there are no more feelings to come out, or when the person has just done as much as they can on that occasion. Following an 'emotion event', it is probable that a person will view the world in a different light, and have some new insight into their problem. However, they may not want to talk much at that moment – if counselling is taking place in a situation where a series of meetings is possible, it is usually best that any kind of extended reflection around the meaning of any emotions and feelings should be saved by the counsellor for another day, rather than forcing reflection and analysis that could interfere with the emotional learning that has taken place.

Making use of supervision

It is important to be aware that a counsellor working in this territory is likely to be affected by the expression of strong emotions and painful feelings. Human beings have a capacity to 'resonate' to the feeling states of others. A counsellor who is accompanying a person in a counselling task that involves an opening-up of emotion is inevitably affected by this process, and needs to be ready to deal with it, through such means as doing their own 'talking it through' by consulting colleagues or a supervisor. It can be particularly useful for the supervisor to be sensitive to the feelings that a counsellor expresses when describing their work with a client. Often, the feelings that the counsellor brings to a supervision consultation can be understood as the client's emotions that they are 'carrying' or have 'picked up'. It may need another person, such as a colleague or supervisor, to point this out, to enable the counsellor to become aware of what has happened.

For those whose counselling is embedded in another professional role, working with a person around emotion-focused goals and tasks may be the hardest aspect of their counselling role. This is because most professional roles, such as that of teacher, nurse or social worker, require the performance of rationality and control, whatever the circumstances. Much professional training involves socialization into subtle (or not so subtle) methods of 'cooling out' clients or colleagues who might be becoming too 'heated' that are characteristic of life in large bureaucratic organizations (Fineman, 1993; Hochschild, 1983). The emphasis in counselling, of being willing to move into the 'danger zone' of emotion and trouble, can represent one of the most challenging areas of interface between the values and practices of counselling, and those that exist within day-to-day organizational life. Supervision and consultation are invaluable as ways of resolving the issues that arise around this interface.

Exercise 11.4: *Reflecting on what you have learned*

One of the important psychological theories of emotion, touched on at various points throughout this chapter, is that individual people tend to have emotions in which they 'specialize' and feel or express a great deal, but that these 'preferred' or familiar emotions conceal deeper emotions that may be experienced as shameful or threatening. To what extent would you say that this theory holds true for you personally, or for other people that you know well? If this theory is valid, what are its implications for your work with people who seek counsel from you?

Conclusions

Difficulties with emotions lie behind many, or even all, of the main categories of psychological problems for which a person might seek help from a counsellor or psychotherapist. Depression can be understood as a sadness/anger problem. Anxiety is about fear. Relationship problems stem from anger. Low self-esteem can be understood as feeling ashamed to share what you really feel. Being willing and able to move beyond vague diagnostic categories such as depression or anxiety, and get closer to what is really bothering a person, is a major counselling competence. Working with emotions can be likened to stepping out of 'talking about' problems in living, and stepping into the danger zone where these problems are actually *felt*. This step also takes the person and the counsellor closer to the lived reality of the person's life space or personal niche. This is because emotions are always, ultimately, linked to people, events and objects within that niche. Being sensitive to the person's feelings and emotions allows the counsellor to get beyond general statements such as 'I feel anxious a lot of the time', to more specific statements such as 'I am afraid of my boss, he is a bully'. It is through talking about these specifics that the person and the counsellor can find some leverage in relation to ways of changing what is happening.

It is possible to see that there are many strategies that can be employed in counselling situations in order to help a person who is experiencing difficulty around acknowledging or expressing feelings and emotions. When the task faced by the person seeking help is that of expressing and exploring emotions, the skill of counselling lies in being willing to talk, to create a space in which feelings and emotions can be allowed a voice in the conversation: the range of methods described in this chapter are merely ways of facilitating such a conversation. As always, the potential impact of any method depends on the strength of the relationship between the counsellor and the person seeking help.

Suggested further reading

Gendlin, E.T. (2003) *Focusing: How to Open up your Deeper Feelings and Intuition*. New York: Rider.

Greenberg, L.S. (2001) *Emotion-focused Therapy: Coaching Clients to Work Through their Feelings*. Washington, DC: American Psychological Association.

Oatley, K. and Jenkins, J.M. (1996) *Understanding Emotions*. Oxford: Blackwell.

Working together to change behaviour

12

'I've been thinking about what you said — about being alone and at the same time surrounded by people'.

'I know, that's a big thing for me'.

'I was wondering — do these people know how you feel about what's happening for you? Who have you told? Who have you *really* told?'

'Not any of them, not really. I see what you're getting at — how can they help if they don't know what I need. It's what you keep saying to me: 'asking for what I want . . . taking care of myself . . . not being the strong man all the time'. All that stuff.'

'Exactly. Would it be useful to take a few minutes to look at how you could start to tell them? For example, what's stopping you, and what could you do differently?'

Introduction

It has been emphasized throughout this book that a counselling relationship is based on listening, following, being receptive, and giving the person a space in which they can begin to develop their own solutions to problems. It is essential to remember when in the role of counselling that 'just talking' can make a real difference to a person. Often the primary counselling task that a person is seeking help to fulfil is simply that of *talking*, of putting feelings, concerns and hopes into words. However, there are other occasions within a counselling relationship when the person may have a very specific idea of what they want to work on, or work out, in terms of a habit or pattern of behaviour that is troubling to them. This chapter focuses on the counselling goal of *behaviour change*. The topic of behaviour change includes a wide range of issues that people may present in counselling, encompassing quite specific, self-contained habits such as 'keeping my paperwork up to date', through more far-reaching behavioural patterns such as weight loss or smoking cessation, changes in interpersonal relating ('how do I stop getting into arguments with my co-workers?'), and changes that embrace many aspects of a person's life ('how do I live now that my spouse has died?'). We live in a society in which the pace of change appears to be ever increasing. Indeed, the rise of psychology as a discipline within the twentieth century can be viewed as a cultural response to the need of ordinary people to get a handle on the challenge of how to change and adapt in the face of new work patterns and social norms. As a result, the counselling and psychotherapy literature contains a proliferation of ideas about how to facilitate change. Some of these ideas are presented in this chapter. Emphasis is placed on the importance of breaking the change process into achievable step-by-step progress towards an ulti-mate goal. But first, we consider the key question: why is it so difficult to change behaviour?

Exercise 12.1: *Your personal experience of behaviour change*

Identify one occasion when you attempted to change your own behaviour in some way. What strategies did you use? What worked and what did not work for you? What have you learned from this experience that you can use in your work with clients?

Why behaviour change is hard to achieve

One of the major differences between counselling, understood as a skilled and intentional activity, and the type of everyday help-giving that takes place between people who are friends or family members, lies in the way that behaviour change is understood. From a common-sense perspective, if someone has a problem, then the obvious response is to suggest or advise that the person should do something different. This advice is often backed up by personal experience, of the type 'when that happened to me, what I did was . . .'. From a counselling perspective, this kind of advice can be seen as almost always being a complete waste of time. The reason why behavioural advice is usually futile is that, as anyone who works as a practi-tioner in a helping role can testify, it is clear that for most people changing a pattern of behaviour that has perhaps been established over several years is a very difficult thing to achieve.

From a counselling perspective, while simple advice on behaviour change may indicate that the listener cares enough to try to find a solution to the complainant's problem, and is doing their best to help, it will rarely lead to a significant or sustained shift in what the person actually does. But why is this? Why is behaviour change so hard?

There are at least three reasons why changing behaviour is difficult. First, a person's behaviour tends to develop in balance with their social environment. In other words, the significant people in an individual's life have come to expect that the person will behave in certain ways, and the subtle 'reward system' that takes place in interactions between people (in the form of approval, affirmation and avoidance of criticism) consistently maintains or reinforces established patterns of behaviour. Our behaviour is shaped to a large extent by the situation that we are in, and self-initiated change (such as one person saying to another 'I wish I could take more exercise') will normally run against the grain of situational forces, such as the cost, time and effort of joining a fitness club. The second reason why it is hard to respond effectively to a request from someone to help them with a behaviour change issue is that *if it was easy for them to change, they would have done it already*. For example, on the whole people do not feel that it is necessary to talk it through with anyone else when they want to change the kind of soap they use in their bathroom. That is because it is easy to choose another brand of soap at the supermarket, try it out, and decide whether you like it. A student asking for help to change their study skills behaviour, by contrast, is a markedly different scenario – here, the person seeking help would be motivated by a fear of failure (or actual failure), and would usually have tried out various different new approaches to setting up a study regime without success. Asking for counselling help from a professional person around a behaviour change issue is therefore normally preceded by a history of unsuccessful attempts to change – the person has already tried all the obvious solutions. A third reason why behaviour change is difficult is that the person may well have a personal investment in staying the way they are. No matter how much a person may protest that they really want to change, there will be some part of their sense of who they are that identifies with their present pattern of behaviour. Doing something radically different can be scary – it is a step into the unknown. So, no matter how much a student may want to become better organized and get good grades, if they have a sense of themselves as 'someone who just passes and is one of the crowd', then attaining 'A' grades and being noticed by tutors may be quite threatening.

Box 12.1: *The limited value of making helpful suggestions as a means of enabling behaviour change*

Transactional analysis (TA) theory includes an elegant analysis of the limitations of advice-giving as a strategy for facilitating behaviour change. Berne (1964) suggested that it made sense to regard sequences of apparently self-defeating interactions between people as psychological 'games'. Within his model, a 'game' is a series of interactions between two or more people that leads to a well-defined, predictable outcome in the form of an experience of frustration or some other form of negative emotion. Berne regarded games as a substitute for genuine relating between individuals. He believed that although people often are afraid to engage in honest and intimate interaction with others, we all nevertheless have a basic need for social contact – a game provides a structure for such contact without running the risk of too much closeness. In his book *Games People Play*, Berne identifies a large number of psychological games, ranging from all-encompassing long-term life games ('Alcoholic', 'Now I've Got You, You Son of a Bitch'), to more benign or briefer interaction sequences such as 'Ain't It Awful'. One of the games that can occur frequently in counselling situations is 'Why Don't You – Yes But' (YDYB). In this game, a person asks for help or advice, and the other players make suggestions. For example:

Person: My life is so stressful, I feel tired all the time and my social life is suffering. What can I do?
Counsellor: Why don't you keep a diary and look at how you could cut down on your work commitments?
Person: I've tried that – there's nothing I can change.
Counsellor: So what about looking for another job?
Person: I can't afford to take a drop in salary, so that's not realistic.
Counsellor: What about trying some relaxation tapes or meditation?
Person: I've tried them too – finding the time to do them just makes me more stressed.

This kind of interaction is clearly futile as a piece of counselling. But what makes this kind of suggestion-giving so hopeless? Berne (1964) argues that the apparently rational, Adult-to-Adult request made by the person seeking help in fact conceals a different kind of transaction – between a needy Child and someone (the counsellor) who is unwittingly pushed into the position of all-knowing Parent. The pay-off for the person initiating the game is that the helper will always prove to be inadequate (none of their suggestions will be worth following up), which then leaves the instigator reinforced in a basic sense of being someone who cannot be helped, or who is beyond help. In other words, the game allows the person to maintain a superficial contact with another person without being called upon to explore what is really true for them – in this case a deep feeling of hopelessness and despair about their life.

It can be seen that in this case almost any kind of counselling response – empathic reflection, open and curious questioning, encouragement to say more – would be more useful than giving suggestions. It does not matter how sensible and valid the suggestions might be – because they have not arisen out of a shared process of problem-solving based on mutual understanding, they will almost certainly be met with a polite and appreciative response of 'yes . . . but . . .'.

It should be emphasized that although behaviour change is an important goal for many people who seek counselling, it is a big mistake to assume that change is necessarily what someone wants from this kind of help. As well as change, the goals of counselling include acceptance, understanding and meaning-making. Indeed, in many cases it is impossible to bring about change in the absence of these less tangible outcomes.

This chapter provides an overview of the tasks and methods that are associated with the crucial counselling goal of helping someone to change a troubling or self-defeating pattern of behaviour. The aim of the chapter is to provide tools and strategies that make it possible to move beyond just contemplating change, and arrive at the point where actually doing something different can become a reality.

Doing something different: step-by-step progress

Looking at the process of behaviour change as a kind of journey serves as a reminder that this activity necessarily consists of several steps. An essential weakness of advice-giving is that it offers the person seeking help a one-step solution. In effect, advice is saying to a person 'just do *this*, and you will be alright'. A counselling approach, by contrast, is based on an appreciation of the complexity of change. Competence as a counsellor involves recognizing that the goal of behaviour change can only be achieved through the completion of a number of sub-tasks. One implication of this perspective is that it makes it possible to see more clearly the contribution that can be made by micro-counselling conversations, where counselling is embedded in another practitioner role, and time may be short. Sometimes, a practitioner-counsellor may not be able to see a behaviour change goal through to completion, but may nevertheless be able to assist the person to fulfil one or more tasks that are necessary elements of the whole sequence. Because behaviour change is often difficult, a person may choose to tackle it by attempting one step or task at a time.

The necessity of tackling behaviour change in a step-by-step manner is illustrated in the experience of Gavin, who had suffered heart failure, and had been told that his future survival depended on his ability radically to alter his lifestyle by cutting out smoking, alcohol and fatty foods, and introducing a diet regime. In hospital, Gavin received health advice from the nurses, physiotherapist and nutritionist attached to his ward, and seemed highly motivated to put his new programme into action. However, on his first check-up visit with his GP, it became apparent that he was not keeping to the recommended diet and exercise schedule. He agreed to have brief fortnightly meetings with the practice nurse to support him in bringing about these vital health-related changes to his behaviour. The nurse asked him to keep a food and exercise diary, which they discussed at each visit. However, she also checked out the barriers to change in Gavin's life. It emerged that he saw himself as an 'action man' who 'worked hard and played hard'. Asked what this meant in practice, he admitted that it meant working long hours at the office, and drinking on Friday and Saturday with his friends at the pub. The nurse invited Gavin to talk about how he felt about this. He spoke of being 'trapped' between two sides of himself – the side that wanted to stay healthy, and the side that thought he 'could survive anything'. The nurse also invited him how his friends would react to him if he stopped drinking and smoking. He replied: 'Well, they would give me a hard time, but in the end they would accept it – one of the others went through something similar – he gets called "the driver" now'. They then discussed how he could overcome these barriers, and the nurse made a point of asking him about these issues at every subsequent appointment. Only then were they able to move to the difficult and demanding task of changing Gavin's diet – giving up foods he liked and through trial and error replacing them with foods that were good for him, and gradually building up his exercise regime. It took him six months. At a later consultation, his GP congratulated him on his progress, and asked him what had made the difference. He replied: 'it was the nurse, I couldn't let her down'.

Just as in the case of Gavin, meaningful behaviour change is hard work – there is no magic wand that can be waved that will instantly make everything different. The counselling tasks that are described in the following sections represent a number of ways of breaking down an overall goal of behaviour change into a set of constituent sub-tasks. In effect, all of these sub-tasks can be seen as ways of slowing down the process of behaviour change, so that the person ends up with an approach to their problem that takes into account as many factors as possible, rather than consisting of the kind of headlong rush to 'do something different' that often leads to disappointment and a sense of defeat. Although the tasks described below are in a 'logical' order, starting with tasks that address barriers to change, then moving to implementing and finally maintaining change, it is not helpful to assume that for any individual person these steps are necessarily worked through in this kind of logical sequence. Some people will only want help with one or maybe two of these tasks – they will be well able to do the rest of it themselves. Other people will shuttle back and forward between tasks, as they slowly find their own way forward.

How does the problematic behaviour fit into your life as it is?

Another approach to helping a person to make sense of a pattern of behaviour that they wish to change is to invite them to suspend their opposition to the problem, and reflect instead on what the presence of the problem does for them. The underlying assumption here is that anything a person does must have some kind of function in their life. In order to pursue such a conversation, it can be helpful to employ the language of *externalization* of problems (Morgan, 2001). For instance, to return to the case of someone who wishes to control his anger, it might be useful to ask him about when 'the anger' visits him, and how it influences his life and his relationships with others. He might reply that the effect of the anger is to 'keep my colleagues in their place'. Another way of talking about this kind of process is to invite the person to think about what the problem does for them, or what the payoffs are for them, of having had this problem over a period of time. It would be unusual for anyone consciously to develop a problematic pattern of behaviour as a means of achieving payoff or rewards, and a person seeking help would most likely reject any such suggestion on the part of their counsellor. It is therefore important to engage in this kind of conversation with sensitivity. The idea is not to interrogate the person in an accusatory fashion, but to gently open up a topic for reflection and consideration.

There are several reasons why this counselling task can represent an important step in successful behaviour change. First, it allows the person to begin to map out what they may *lose* by changing how they act in some situations. This can be a catalyst for starting to think about how these needs might be taken care of in alternative ways. Second, if the person can look closely and honestly at what their problem does for them, they may well come across some surprises – payoffs that they had not previously thought about. Such discoveries can be very helpful in promoting hope, since the person may be enthused and energized by the idea that they are now doing something different, rather than merely repeating what happened during previous attempts to change. Finally, the question 'how does the problem influence you?' prepares the ground for the reverse question: 'how do you influence the problem?' This line of conversation, which is discussed more fully below, brings into focus the active capacity of the person to do different things in certain situations, rather than being always dominated by 'the problem', and can represent a very fertile means of enabling the person to accept that they may indeed have the power within them to be able to do something different.

Imagining how things could be different

When a person is seeking help to change their behaviour, an important counselling task centres on the exploration of what it is that the person actually wants to achieve. At the moment of seeking help, the person may be so burdened by the existence in their life of a troublesome pattern of behaviour that all they can think about is – somehow – getting rid of it. Their approach to change is dominated by a sense of what they do *not* want to do – *not* eat as much, *not* be a doormat passive, *not* get angry, and so on. Any behaviour change plan based on 'not doing' is doomed to failure, because the only way that real change will happen is if the person is able to replace the unwanted behaviour with a new pattern of behaviour. The trick in the end is always to acquire, practise and master the new behaviour, rather than just suppressing the old pattern. It may be useful to think in terms of training for a sporting activity. If a person is trying to become better at playing tennis they may go through a phase of being dominated by what *not* to do – do not hit the ball in the net, do not hit it beyond the baseline, and so on. This kind of learning strategy tends to have very limited success. Someone can only become a competent tennis player by having a positive image of what it is they want to achieve. This positive image can come from watching a top tennis player, such as Roger Federer, or, even better, through coaching that gives the person a feel for what it is like, for them, to hit a good shot. The key is that the person gains a vision of what it is they are striving for, and can assess their performance against that ultimate end point, thereby making adjustments to what they do in order to get closer to the ideal. All effective sports coaching involves this kind of cognitive rehearsal of good performance. For the majority of tennis players, there is a limit to what can be gained by using Roger Federer as a model, because he is capable of strokes that are physically impossible for ordinary human beings – a less perfect 'ideal' works better for most people.

In a counselling context, therefore, if a person has identified a personal goal of changing their behaviour in some way, it is useful to listen for an opportunity to invite the person to talk about what it is that they actually want. This task can be entered by questions such as 'how would you like it to be?' or 'what would your life be like (or what would you be doing differently) if you changed this pattern of behaviour?' The *Skilled Helper* counselling skills model developed by Gerard Egan (2004) includes a valuable analysis of the process of working with the person seeking help in order to identify their 'desired scenario'. The solution-focused approach to therapy (see O'Connell, 1998) employs the 'miracle question' for this purpose. The client is asked to imagine that a miracle has taken place overnight, and their problem has been completely eradicated. They are then invited to describe what their life is like. (Before using the miracle question, it is important to study, or, even better, receive training in how it is used by solution-focused therapists – it is a powerful method but needs to be applied at the right time and the right way, otherwise the client may become confused about what is being suggested.) Other ways of enabling the person to identify their preferred behaviour are to ask if there are any individuals who they would take as models ('who would you like to be like?') or whether there have been times in their life when they exhibited the behaviour that they are now seeking to acquire (or reacquire).

There are several ways in which holding a conversation about the detailed specification of a new or amended pattern of behaviour can be helpful. It allows the person to be clear about what they are trying to achieve, and at the same time to share this vision with their counsellor. Usually, it leads to the construction of a more detailed description of the preferred behaviour, in place of a general or global description, which outlines specific small changes that can be accomplished one at a time. It can instil hope in a person, and be motivating for a person to disclose to someone else what it is that they *really* want, and to have this desire taken seriously. Finally, this kind of conversation opens up the possibility of using imagination in a creative and positive way. Rather than imagining terrible things that may happen ('I will be stuck like this for ever'), the person can playfully imagine good outcomes and a better life.

Are you ready?

A great deal of research and clinical experience in counselling and psychotherapy has shown that the issue of *readiness to change* represents a key factor in any work around behavioural change. The exploration of the person's views around their readiness to do things differently is therefore an important counselling task. Many practitioners have found that it has been useful to employ the *stages of change* model developed by James Prochaska and Carlo DiClemente. From their experience in working in a health arena in which many patients were resistant to changing illness-promoting behaviours such as smoking and drinking, these psychologists developed the idea that there are major differences between people in relation to their readiness to change. They formulated a five-stage model of the change process to account for these differences. Their model is known as a 'transtheoretical' theory because it intentionally integrates ideas from various schools of therapy into an overarching framework. The stages of change observed by Prochaska and DiClemente (2005) are:

1 *Precontemplation*. The person has no immediate intention to make changes in relation to the behaviour that is problematic. For example, someone who is a heavy smoker may be aware that their behaviour is a health risk, but is not yet willing to face up to the possibility of quitting.

2 *Contemplation*. At this stage the person has decided to change their behaviour, but at some point in the future; for example, at some point within the next six months.

3 *Preparation*. Has taken some initial steps in the direction of behaviour change. For example, a person seeking to stop smoking may have collected information about the availability of cessation clinics, nicotine patches, and so on.

4 *Action*. The person has changed their problematic behaviour for less than six months, and is still in a position of consolidating their new patterns of behaviour, and avoiding temptation.

5 *Maintenance*. Avoiding relapse or coping with episodes of relapse over a longer period of time.

As further time elapses, and the previously problematic behaviour or habit is defeated, the person can be viewed as entering a final *termination* stage – the problem is no longer relevant to them, and they do not need to give it any attention.

The value of the stages of change model in relation to working together to do something different is that it suggests that quite different counselling tasks may be required at different stages of the change process. For example, the tasks for the person at the precontemplation phase may include consciousness-raising, involving collecting information, and validating and accepting their point of view and state of readiness (rather than establishing a critical or coercive relationship). The tasks at the contemplation stage may include decision-making, and exploring the meaning of the person's ambivalence.

David is a retired engineer who is a volunteer member of a Circle of Support and Accountability that was set up to enable the reintegration into society of high-risk sex offenders. For more than two years, David has been a member of a small group of volunteers, drawn from all walks of life, who have met on a weekly basis with Simon, a 30 year-old man who had received two jail sentences for sexual offences with young boys. David learned about the stages of change model during the training course he attended, and has found that it helped him to make sense of what he calls the 'learning curve' that has taken place between Simon and his team of supporters: 'at the start, it was very much a matter of talking about the consequences of what he was doing, and making sure that he knew that we would be using our contacts in the neighbourhood to check that he was meeting the conditions of his probation contract. As time went on, though, what we talked about started to shift quite dramatically. There were some really emotional times when he was looking at himself really deeply. More recently, it has been mainly a matter of providing support for what he calls his "new life".'

Further information about the stages of change model, and its application in counselling can be found in Prochaska and DiClemente (2005). These authors have also published a self-help guide, *Changing for Good*, based on the principles of the model (Prochaska *et al.*, 1994). For practitioners whose counselling is embedded in other work roles, the most useful aspect of the stages of change model probably lies in the ways in which it can be applied in understanding the difference between the point at which a person is actively committed to changing their behaviour, and the prior stages where they may be vaguely aware of a need to change, but are not yet ready to commit themselves. There are many micro-counselling situations in health and social care settings in which practitioners routinely work with people who are 'precontemplative'; for example, in relation to smoking cessation, weight loss, domestic violence, and alcohol or drug abuse. Practitioners operating in these settings may find it helpful to consult the literature on *motivational interviewing* (Miller and Rollnick, 2002), which offers a set of strategies and methods intended to facilitate/motivate the individual to move beyond precontemplation and contemplation and to engage with the tasks associated with preparation for change and then action. Further information on motivational interviewing in Chapter 13.

Do you have the right kind of support?

It is very difficult to make significant behavioural changes on one's own through planning and 'will-power'. Lack of support from other people constitutes an important barrier to change, and ensuring that adequate social support is available represents an important counselling task for many people seeking help around a behaviour change goal. The role of the counsellor in relation to this task can involve checking out with the person the amount of support that is available, and how accessible it is. It may be valuable in some instances to rehearse or run through strategies for enlisting support. Part of this task may involve discussion about the ways in which the counsellor can offer support. In some counselling situations it may be possible to meet with key supporters to explore their perceptions of how they can help. Support may come from individuals already within the person's social network, such as family, friends and work colleagues, or may encompass new people, such as members of self-help groups. Support may be dispersed over a number of people, or be concentrated on one main 'ally'. Support may be provided face to face, by telephone, or by email. If the person seeking help has difficulty in identifying potential supporters, it may be useful to invite the person seeking help to think about 'who would be least surprised to hear about your success in changing this behaviour?' There is no special counselling method that is associated with the task of ensuring support – this is a task that relies on the person and the counsellor being willing to spend some time on it, and pooling their ideas.

Implementing changes

At the point when the person begins to make actual changes in their life, it is important that everything possible has been put in place to ensure success. It is usually a good idea for a counsellor to run through some typical situations that may occur for the person as a means of refining the person's strategy for change, and also as a way of checking that the person's expectations are realistic (e.g. that it is not a 'complete disaster' if it goes wrong the first time), including their plans for accessing support (to celebrate success, or to talk through what happened if they were not successful). It can be useful for the person and the counsellor almost to enact likely scenarios, or at least talk through them as a form of rehearsal. It can also be valuable sometimes for the person to write down their plan, or a checklist. This talk can be initiated by the counsellor with a question such as 'would it be useful to go through what will happen tomorrow when you . . .?'. It is important for the counsellor to keep the focus on concrete behaviour (what the person will actually do), rather than allowing the conversation to slide into statements of motivation, will and intention ('I'm really up for it this time'; 'I know I'm ready').

Anticipating and preventing relapse

The *stages of change* model developed by Prochaska and DiClemente (2005), introduced earlier in this chapter, suggests that relapse is an almost inevitable consequence of most attempts to change behaviour – it is very difficult indeed to continue to do something different without ever slipping back into old ways. An essential counselling task, therefore, when a person is on the point of implementing change, is to consider the issue of relapse. It is usually helpful to explain the concept, and to be candid about the likelihood that some relapse will occur at some point down the line. The questions that may need to be discussed include: How will you know if relapse has happened? What are the factors that might make you vulnerable to relapse? What will you do if you have a relapse? How will you use support at these times? How can you learn from a relapse episode about your change strategy? One of the biggest dangers associated with relapse is that the person will 'catastrophize' the situation, and jump to an extreme conclusion such as 'I'm no good' or 'it's a waste of time, this isn't going to work', and abandon all the good work that they have done up to that stage. The more that the counsellor has been able to introduce the idea that relapse is normal, routine, predictable and surmountable, the less likely it is that the person will jump to a catastrophic interpretation of what has happened. It is always important to keep in mind that a person engaging in behaviour change that they consider to be significant enough to merit the help of a counsellor will in all probability be in a state of high emotional vulnerability when they begin to try out new ways of doing things, and will as a result perceive a relapse as a major setback.

Planned follow-up sessions where possible relapse incidents can be explored can be a valuable source of support for the person if the counsellor is in a position to offer ongoing contact over a period of time.

The aim of the preceding sections of this chapter has been to introduce some of the tasks that are most frequently involved in counselling where behaviour change is a goal. The underlying theme of the section is that of the counsellor building a relationship with the person characterized by a willingness to be close to them in every step of the behaviour change journey, and being curious and questioning about every aspect of the process. The next section of the chapter looks at some well-established behaviour change methods.

Counselling methods for facilitating behaviour change

At the point when a person seeking help is clear that their goal is to change an aspect of their behaviour, and has identified at least some of the component step-by-step tasks that are necessary to move towards that goal, it is helpful to invite the person to think about *how* they believe would be the best way for them to accomplish their objectives. There are four main strategies that have been used by counsellors to facilitate behaviour change: *dissolving the barriers to change, planning and setting targets, activating resources,* and *setting up a project.* These strategies are discussed in the following sections.

Exploring and dissolving barriers to change

One method of bringing about change that has been advocated by many counsellors and psychotherapists is based on the idea that if a person has enough insight and understanding in relation to whatever it is that is motivating or causing them to act in a dysfunctional manner, they will be free to behave in ways that are more life-enhancing and productive. This approach is associated with long-established forms of counselling and psychotherapy, such as psychodynamic psychotherapy, and person-centred counselling. The key idea is to focus not on the problem behaviour, but on the person who is engaging in that behaviour. For example, someone who abuses alcohol may have a history of emotional neglect and abuse, and may have low self-esteem. From this perspective, binge drinking may be viewed as almost emotionally and interpersonally necessary for the person as a means of assuaging emotional pain, and living up to other people's views that one is 'no good'. In this approach, counselling that concentrates on plans and programmes that aim to encourage 'alternatives to drinking' are missing the point: it is the sense that the person has of who they are that needs to change. There is no doubt that this approach can be effective. However, it can take a long time, and requires the establishment of a strong, ongoing relationship with a counsellor. It therefore may not be a realistic option in many embedded counselling settings where there may be a great deal of pressure on time, and other professional tasks to fulfil. Nevertheless, in these settings, dissolving barriers to change may be an important method in relation to sub-tasks (described earlier in this chapter) such as *making sense of problematic behaviour* and *imagining how things could be different*.

Cognitive-behavioural methods: setting targets and implementing a programme

The behaviour change methodology that is believed by many specialist counsellors and psychotherapists to be maximally effective in facilitating behaviour change, and is backed up by a substantial amount of research, is *cognitive-behavioural therapy* (CBT). Attractive features of this approach for many practitioners and clients are that it is businesslike and down to earth. The key idea in CBT is to analyse the behavioural patterns of the person (the problem behaviour and the new preferred behaviour) in terms of an A–B–C formula: *antecedents, behaviour* and *consequences*. Anything that a person does on a regular basis is regarded as being elicited or triggered by a stimulus or situation (antecedent) and reinforced or rewarded by its consequences. This formula is the basis for a simple, yet effective behaviour change method. The first step is to collect information over a period of time concerning the exact, detailed problem behaviour that is exhibited by the person, the situations in which this behaviour occurs, and the consequences that follow from it. The next step is to devise a plan or programme in which the problem behaviour is gradually eliminated or extinguished, while at the same time the desired behaviour is gradually introduced. The third step is to ensure that the new behaviour is maintained in different situations over a period of time, rather than abandoned when the going gets tough.

The A–B–C formula encourages the person seeking help and their counsellor to devote their attention, initially, to two areas: antecedents and consequences. These are the crucial points of leverage in relation to the problem behaviour. For example:

Trudy was a school support worker who was called in to work with Andy and his family on account of Andy's problem with school attendance. Trudy spent a long time listening to the family, asking them to describe exactly what it was that happened on school days, and showing a lively non-judgemental curiosity in everything that they had to say. At the end of this phase, she brought out a sheet of flip chart paper and some pens, and started to map out what she thought was going on, while inviting the family members to add details or make corrections. She made a list down the centre of the page of all the activities that Andy engaged in on a typical day when he did not go to school – his reason for not wanting to go, the argument with his parents, the parents going to work, Andy having the house to himself, watching TV, and so on. In a different colour, she made a list on the left-hand side of the page of the possible triggers for these events. For example, non-school days were more likely to happen when Andy had not done his home-work, or there was a test, and unresolved arguments were more likely if both parents needed to be at work earlier than usual. On the right-hand side of the page, in a third colour, Trudy listed some of the consequences of Andy's behaviour – falling behind with his work and feeling panicky, enjoying daytime TV, being on the receiving end of sarcastic comments from teachers, assembling an impressive collection of music downloads, missing out on lunch and games with his friends, and so on. As she was doing this, all of the members of the family started to make connections, and imagine alternatives. For instance, a parent staying at home for two days would have the time to be able to make sure that Andy did his homework in the evening, and to help him with it, as well as making staying at home seem less attractive for Andy, since he would not be able to watch TV and download music from the PC. It also became apparent how stressful, demanding and challenging some aspects of Andy's school life were, and how important it would be to make sure that he received regular rewards in recognition of his efforts. At the end of one meeting, all of the members of the family came away with new behaviours that they agreed to initiate, which were listed on a page pinned to the kitchen noticeboard. Trudy agreed to meet with them two weeks later to check on their progress.

The CBT literature contains a wealth of ideas for behaviour change techniques, and workbooks that can be used by counsellors and clients in relation to specific behaviour change problems. However, at its heart, CBT is a common-sense approach that relies on the application of some simple, yet powerful, ideas, in a systematic manner. Like any other method, it works better when there is a good relationship between the person seeking help and the counsellor – notice how respectful and accepting Trudy was in a counselling situation where it would have been all too easy to be drawn into taking sides and condemning Andy's 'laziness' or inadequacy.

Activating resources

A quite different method of working with a behaviour change task is to pay attention to occasions when the problem behaviour does *not* occur, rather than the occasions when it *does*, or episodes when the person has dealt with the problem behaviour successfully, rather than when they have failed to deal with it. The underlying assumption behind this strategy is to activate the person's existing resources and strengths, rather than focusing on their weaknesses. This general approach is associated with solution-focused therapy (O'Connell, 1998) and narrative therapy (Morgan, 2001). The key idea is that there will almost always be times when the person has in fact been able to behave differently (narrative therapists describe such events as 'unique outcomes' or 'glittering moments'), and that the widespread human tendency to become preoccupied with problems (and how awful things are) will have obscured these achievements from view. The job of the counsellor, therefore, is to assist the person to identify the moments of success in relation to the problem behaviour, and then to build on the personal resources that are behind these 'glittering achievements'. This method can be difficult to implement if the person seeking help is so gripped by a sense of the total control exerted by the problem that they just cannot (or will not) allow even the slightest possibility that good moments might occur. On the other hand, it has the potential to be highly energizing and liberating because (a) the solutions that are generated are wholly the product of the person, rather than being suggested or 'set up' by the counsellor, and (b) it wholly ignores the failures and deficits of the person and celebrates their achievements.

Further ideas about how to activate a client's personal strengths and resources can be found in Flückiger *et al.* (2010).

Behaviour change as a project

A lot of the time people struggle to change their behaviour because the things they are trying to alter have become ingrained habits that have over a long period of time become 'second nature' – the person is hardly aware that they are doing the action that they wish to modify or eradicate from their life. One of the ways of organizing the series of tasks that may need to be carried out for behaviour change to occur is to regard the whole enterprise as a 'project'. Viewing the change process as a project can help the person to distance themselves from an undermining sense of failure when their change efforts do not immediately work out for the best. Talking about the work as a project can also help the person and the counsellor to work together – each of them is making suggestions in relation to a shared endeavour. The image of a project also brings to mind the metaphor of building something new, which may involve dismantling previous structures, making plans, reviewing progress, celebrating achievements, and so on. Using 'project' language can have the effect of externalizing the problem, and providing a channel for the person's creativity and imagination.

Box 12.2: *The role of homework assignments in behaviour change*

Having a really good discussion within a counselling session of how and what to do differently, and how to change problematic behaviour, is of little value if the person then does not implement any changes in their everyday life. One of the useful strategies for bridging the gap between the counselling room and real life is the practice of agreeing on *homework* tasks. Homework tasks in counselling can be suggested by the person or by the counsellor, and can range from quite structured and formal tasks, such as writing a journal or completing worksheets, to more informal or flexible tasks such as 'listening to other people more', 'practising slow and deep breathing as a way of coping with my anxiety' or 'visiting my grandmother's grave'. There has been a substantial amount of research carried out into the process of agreeing homework tasks in counselling (see, for example, Mahrer *et al.*, 1994; Scheel *et al.*, 1999, 2004). Although homework is often considered as a method that is primarily employed by cognitive-behavioural therapists, there is plentiful evidence that counsellors using a wide variety of approaches are all likely to use homework with at least 50 per cent of their cases (Ronan and Kazantzis, 2006). Based on a review of the research evidence, Scheel *et al.* (2004) have developed some useful guidelines for using homework in counselling. These include: the homework assignment to be based on collaboration between counsellor and client; describing the task in detail; providing a rationale for why the task is of benefit to the person; matching the task to the person's ability; writing down the task; asking how confident the person is about fulfilling the task and if necessary modifying the task accordingly; trying out the task during the session; asking about how the person got on with the task at the next meeting; and celebrating or praising the person's achievement of the task. In some counselling situations, it is also possible to use reminders to maximize the chances that the task is carried out. For example, a number of smoking cessation projects phone up patients between sessions to check on their progress. Also, counsellors who use email contact with clients as an adjunct to face-to-face contact can quite easily send a brief email message between meetings.

A narrative perspective on behaviour change

As a counsellor, it is a mistake to become so preoccupied with the task of behaviour change that one forgets or neglects the more fundamental task of giving the person a chance to tell their story and be heard. There are many ways in which behaviour change can be understood as a particular form of storytelling. The founders of narrative therapy, Michael White and David Epston (1990), have always talked about behaviour change in terms of a process of *re-authoring*. For them, the identity or sense of self of a person is constituted by the stories that the person tells about themselves, or are told about them by other people. From this point of view, what happens when the person is seeking to change their behaviour is that they are developing a new story to tell about who they are (e.g. the previous story may have been 'I am someone who struggles to pass exams' and the new story might be organized around a narrative of 'I am someone who has learned how to manage the stress of exams'). Once the new story has been created by the person, perhaps through working together with a counsellor, the next step is to try it out on audiences. After all, other people need to know that 'I do well in exams' – if they are still telling the old story of the person as an exam-flunker, this will undermine the person's efforts to do something different.

The implications for counselling of adopting a 're-authoring' perspective are that it becomes important for the counsellor to listen carefully to the stories that a person tells about themselves. Are they success stories or are they failure stories? If they are failure stories, what new material can be introduced into the storyline that will allow the person to tell it as a success story? The principal method that narratively oriented counsellors use to assist people to construct success or solution stories is to encourage them to identify their own strengths and resources. For example, the counsellor may ask the person with an exam-taking issue if there were ever occasions when they had done well in an exam, or even had coped with an anxiety-provoking situation. The person's answers to these questions are clues to resources and strengths, which can then become the building blocks for a new story. However, even CBT methods can be understood in narrative terms. The careful analysis of the problem behaviour, agreement around behavioural targets, and plans for how to meet these targets, all are designed to produce a success experience for the person. This success experience is then woven into their story of who they are and what they can do – it is re-authoring by another route.

There is another very significant dimension to the concept of re-authoring. It is a concept that has a political side to it. In a lot of cases, the problems that people have, and the behaviour that they want to change, are the result of stories that *other people* have told about them. Frequently, these other people are authority figures such as parents, teachers, social workers and psychiatrists. The stories may be reinforced by being framed in bureaucratic or medical language, and enshrined in massive case files. For example, someone with a problem around exams may turn out to have based their self-story as a learner around the fact that 'my Dad told me I was stupid – he told the teachers too, and they believed him'. For such a person, arriving at the point of being able to tell their story in terms of statements such as 'I am intelligent, I am a competent learner' is a matter of personally authoring their own story, rather than having it authored by someone else. The person becomes the *authority* on their own life.

Exercise 12.2: *Reviewing the behaviour change strategies that you use in your work*

What are the types of behaviour change issues that arise in the people with whom you work as a practitioner? What are the methods that you have found to be most and least effective in facilitating change with these individuals? On the basis of what you have read in this chapter, what other methods might be valuable?

Conclusions

It is impossible in a chapter of this length to do justice to the huge topic of facilitating behaviour change. The aim has been to provide an outline of some ideas and methods that may be used in embedded counselling relationships. The key themes that have been emphasized within the chapter are:

- Behaviour change is difficult to achieve, and there are many barriers to achieving this type of goal.
- Effective and lasting change requires a step-by-step approach with the ultimate goal of behaviour change broken down into a number of constituent tasks.
- There is no one 'right' method to facilitate change – people differ a great deal in terms of the change processes that are meaningful to them. A good starting point is usually to inquire about what the person has done to initiate and implement changes in their life in the past.
- It is seldom effective to try merely to eradicate or extinguish unwanted habits – what works better is to replace these behaviours with alternative activities.
- Each of the various change methods that are written about by professional psychologists and psychotherapists can ultimately be reduced to a set of common-sense strategies, which can readily be applied by practitioners whose counselling role is embedded in other work functions.
- The single most important thing that a person as a counsellor can do for anyone who is seeking to change their behaviour is to function as a supporter and ally in their journey – the quality of the relationship is crucial in helping the person to persevere with their change objectives.

The example of bereavement (see Chapter 18) can be used as a framework for understanding the process of behaviour change. In bereavement, as in all forms of behaviour change, there are basically three things that need to be done. First, it is necessary to let go of the past. This may involve making sense of what has happened, and grieving for the person who has gone. The second task is to deal with what is happening now, the chaos of a life that may be missing one of its foundation stones. Third, it is necessary to plan for the future, to build a new repertoire of behaviours and relationships. The example of bereavement is particularly important and evoc- ative for a number of reasons. It evokes the image of people grieving differently – there are huge individual and cultural differences in the way that people respond to death. It evokes an appreciation of the cultural, social, family and interpersonal networks of meaning, relationship, belief and ritual that help people to make the necessary changes to their lives following a bereavement. Coping with loss is always done together as well as done alone. The meaning of bereavement, and the potential avenues for dealing with it, depend on the personal niche within which an individual lives their life. All of these aspects are true of any kind of behaviour change.

Suggested further reading

Egan, G. (2004) *The Skilled Helper: A Problem Management and Opportunity Development Approach to Helping*. Belmont, CA: Wadsworth.

Grant, A., Mills, J., Mulhern, R. and Short, N. (2004) *Cognitive Behavioural Therapy in Mental Health Care*. London: Sage Publications.

Morgan, A. (2001) *What is Narrative Therapy? An Easy-to-read Introduction*. Adelaide: Dulwich Centre.

Westbrook, D., Kennerley, H. and Kirk, J. (2007) *An Introduction to Cognitive Behaviour Therapy: Skills and Applications*. London: Sage Publications.

Problem-solving, planning and decision-making

I need to decide whether I can go to our grandson's graduation ceremony. It's too far to drive to London. I don't know if I could cope with the stress of flying. I'm a bit worried about going by train, because I just don't know what would happen if I was taken ill on the train. My wife is assuming we will go. I've been avoiding talking about it. I just don't know what to do.

Introduction

An important set of counselling tasks centres on the process of making *choices*. There are many situations in which people seek help, and want to talk things through with someone who is independent of their immediate situation, because they cannot decide what to do. Depending on the circumstances, clients may view this kind of task in a variety of different terms: choosing, solving a problem, reviewing options, devising a plan, or making a decision. Each of these tasks involves a process of collecting, appraising, organizing and analysing information, leading to a conclusion to which the person makes an emotional and behavioural commitment. The aim of this chapter is to explore some methods for facilitating client completion of problem-solving, planning and decision-making tasks.

Examples of problem-solving and decision-making tasks in counselling

In some professional roles that involve a counselling element, problem-solving and decision-making issues may arise on a regular basis. In other counselling roles, such tasks may occur less frequently. Examples of such tasks include:

- Health professionals working in the fields of HIV testing, genetic screening and pregnancy testing routinely engage in conversation with clients around whether to proceed with testing, whether to start a family, and whether to go through with a termination of pregnancy. These conversations may encompass planning and problem-solving dimensions; for example, around how to tell family members about the decision that has been made.

- Social workers working with older clients find that their clients, and other family members, wish to talk with them around such issues as making plans for ongoing care, developing strategies for reducing risks of accidents in the client's home, and deciding on when or whether residential care or respite care is necessary.

- Teachers and tutors explore career and education options with their students in order to help them to decide on which course of study to follow, or whether to remain in education or to seek employment.

These are just some of the instances in which the focus of the counselling process is on this kind of task. Typically, decision-making takes place alongside other counselling tasks that may also need to be addressed. For example, a family struggling to support a parent with Alzheimer's disease may need to make some decisions, but there may be relationship issues, life transition themes, and painful emotions that require attention at the same time.

Exercise 13.1: *Reflecting on your personal experience of decision-making*

What was the last significant life decision that you made? What was the process that you went through in making this decision? Were there distinct stages in the process? Who or what helped you to arrive at a decision? What was unhelpful? What ideas can you take from this personal experience that you can apply in helping your counselling clients to make decisions? It can be useful to carry out this exercise in a group in which each person's decision-making story is shared as a means of developing an awareness of the different decision-making styles and strategies that exist.

Problem-solving and decision-making skills and strategies

There are many techniques that have been developed by counsellors, psychotherapists, psychologists, management consultants and others to facilitate and support processes of problem-solving, planning and decision-making. The single most useful method that can be employed in relation to decision-making is probably 'just talking'. Making it possible for a person to look at a choice from all angles, and explore how they feel about all the options, in a situation where the listener has no preconceived ideas about which course of action is right or wrong, is enormously helpful. However, it can also be that sometimes the person circles endlessly around a problem or decision without arriving at any conclusions. It is therefore valuable to be able to offer clients some kind of structure through which they can organize the activity of decision-making. An initial period of exploratory discussion can be useful, even if the counsellor feels sure that sooner or later some structuring devices will need to be introduced.

There are many common-sense cultural resources that can be used to structure conversations around decision-making and problem-solving. Some people find it helpful to construct some kind of 'balance sheet' – a piece of paper where the factors for and against each choice are listed and may then be weighted in terms of which is the most important. A slightly more elaborate version of a balance sheet is a force-field analysis, where the forces pressing in different directions can be mapped on a piece of paper. This technique can be helpful in identifying the sources of different forces ('it's my mother who wants me to follow option A, while its my boyfriend who is pressing me to take option B'). In some situations; for example, when a person is thinking about a career choice, a SWOT (strengths, weaknesses, opportunities and threats) analysis may be valuable. An important part of the value of any of these 'mapping' techniques is that they slow down the decision-making process, thus allowing more time for reflection. They also allow the person to generate a comprehensive analysis of the factors involved. Written maps 'externalize' the task, enabling the person and counsellor to work side by side to come up with ideas and move them around on the page.

Another useful strategy in relation to decision-making is to introduce the concept of *implications*. Using a brainstorming approach ('let's just imagine – without censoring any ideas that come up – what might happen if you decided to . . .') or a mapping technique, the person can be encouraged to look beyond the immediate consequences of a decision, and consider the long-term consequences. Alternatively, it may be that some imagined catastrophic long-term consequences ('if I quit this job I'll never find another one') can be seen as being not too awful once they are openly discussed with a counsellor. A further widely used strategy is to *prioritize* aspects of the issue; for example, how satisfactory is each of the possible solutions that have been generated in respect of a problem?

Systematic approaches to problem-solving and decision-making

A lot of the time, the kind of everyday techniques that were outlined in the previous section are sufficient to allow a client and counsellor to work through a problem-solving or decision-making task. There are some situations; for example, if a counsellor has a high proportion of clients who present this kind of issue where it can be sensible to consider making use of more formal counselling protocols that have been developed in this area. There are two counselling models that are particularly relevant: *problem-solving therapy*, and *motivational interviewing*.

Problem-solving therapy

Problem-solving therapy is an approach that has been developed by Arthur and Christine Nezu and Thomas D'Zurilla in the USA, Dennis Gath in the UK, and others. The basic assumption in this approach is that poor problem-solving skills will result in demoralization, lack of hope, anxiety and depression. Counselling therefore has two parallel goals: to help the person to resolve specific current problems, and to develop skills and confidence around their general problem-solving ability. The problem-solving process consists of seven steps:

1 clarify and define the problem
2 set a realistic goal
3 generate multiple solutions
4 evaluate and compare solutions
5 select a feasible solution
6 implement the solution
7 evaluate the outcome.

In advance of working through these stages of problem-solving, the counsellor explains the model to the client, and makes sure that they understand the rationale for the approach being taken. Throughout the counselling, this understanding is reinforced through regular reviews of progress, and the use of handouts and worksheets. If the client has more than one problem, it is important to decide on which problem to address first, and complete the sequence in relation to that issue before moving on to the next. The counselling process also includes identifying rewards that the client can claim on the successful completion of each problem-solving task.

The literature on problem-solving therapy represents a valuable resource for counsellors because it encompasses extensive discussion of theory and research, and a wealth of practical examples of problem-solving in relation to a wide range of client issues (D'Zurilla and Nezu, 1982; Nezu *et al.*, 1989, 1998). A useful summary of how problem-solving therapy works in practice can be found in Mynors-Wallis (2001). The integration of problem-solving therapy into routine health care practice conducted by GPs is discussed by Pierce and Gunn (2007).

Motivational interviewing

Motivational interviewing is an approach to facilitating decision-making that was developed by Stephen Rollnick and William R. Miller in the 1980s (Miller and Rollnick, 2002). The main area of application for motivational interviewing has been in the area of addictions in working with people with drug and alcohol problems around making a decision or commitment to change their behaviour. However, the principles of motivational interviewing can be employed in any situation in which a person is struggling to make a major life decision.

The theoretical roots of motivational interviewing are in Rogerian or client-centred/person-centred therapy. However, in classic client-centred therapy the counsellor adopts a rigorously non-directive stance in the sense of following the client's 'track' in respect of whatever topic the client wishes to explore. By contrast, in motivational interviewing the counsellor negotiates with the client that they will specifically focus on a decision that the client needs to make

In practice, motivational interviewing relies on four basic principles:

1 *Empathy*: the counsellor seeks to view the issue from the frame of reference of the client.

2 *Developing discrepancy*: the counsellor explores with the client tensions between how clients wants their life to be (the ideal) and their current behaviour (the actual).

3 *Acceptance* or 'rolling with resistance': the counsellor does not try to pressure the client to make a decision, but instead accepts that a reluctance to change is natural, and invites exploration of this resistance.

4 *Client autonomy*: the counsellor respects the client as someone who has the capacity to arrive at the right decision for them in the present circumstances.

When these principles are implemented, a counselling space is constructed in which the client feels that they are in a relationship in which it is possible to talk honestly about all aspects of a decision, and as a result to be able eventually to make a genuine commitment to a new course of action that is grounded in a comprehensive exploration of all possible aspects of the issue.

An example of motivational interviewing in action

Eleanor is a young woman who is a single parent with a two-year old son. She has had involvement with social workers for many years around a range of issues. Her current dilemma is whether to place her son (Stephen) in a nursery so she can restart her own career. Her mother strongly believes that Eleanor should make use of the nursery place that is on offer, and will not listen to any other point of view. On the other hand, Eleanor's neighbour strongly believes that the children can be emotionally damaged by nursery education. As part of the process of making a decision on this issue, Eleanor decides to speak to her social worker:

Eleanor:	I'm really desperate. I need to decide by next week whether or not to take the place at the nursery, and I don't know what to do.
Social worker:	It's such a big decision for you to make. I get the sense that you're feeling under a lot of pressure and that this stress isn't helping you to get to the point that you are comfortable about what is best (*an empathic response that reflects an appreciation of the client's situation, and is not trying to persuade her what to do*).
Eleanor:	Absolutely – I feel completely at the end of my rope.
Social worker:	From what you have said to me before about this, my understanding is that ideally you think that it would be good for Stephen to mix more with other children, and good for you to meet people in a job situation and have more money, but that you are not sure whether he is ready for nursery yet (*acknowledging discrepancy*). Is that the way it seems to you, or are there other aspects of the situation that are important too? (*acknowledging the client as the 'expert' – reinforcing client autonomy*).
Eleanor:	Yes, that's the main things.
Social worker:	That suggests that there are other aspects of it too . . .? (*affirming client autonomy*).
Eleanor:	Yes, maybe. I just don't know if I could cope with him being upset. You know, like leaving him there if he was crying or having a tantrum.
Social worker:	Because that would upset you . . . and maybe also make you worried that he was being traumatized? *(empathy)*
Eleanor:	Exactly.
Social worker:	Can I say how it seems to me? (*personal feedback*). I'm wondering whether there are two parts to this. At one level you know that nursery is the right thing for you and for Stephen. But at another level it's scary to think about what will be involved at a practical level around things like 'can I cope with him being upset'? (*reframing*)
Eleanor:	You're right: deep down I *do* know what I want (*example of 'commitment talk'*).

One of the advantages of motivational interviewing is that it has generated a great deal of support materials and activities in the form of books, websites and training courses. There is substantial research evidence that motivational interviewing is effective with a range of different client groups. Motivational interviewing is a good example of a counselling protocol that consists of a set of basic counselling skills that have been packaged together in a particular way in order to enable a particular type of therapeutic task to be completed. When using motivational interviewing, it is essential to keep two things in mind. The first is that motivational interviewing strikes a subtle balance between facilitation and persuasion. In some of the motivational interviewing literature, it can come across as though the role of the counsellor is to lead the client in the direction of what is self-evidently the 'right' answer (e.g. losing weight, stopping drinking, etc.) because that option corresponds to prevailing societal values. However, the power of motivational interviewing is based on counsellor openness to whatever is right for the client at that point in their life, and genuine acceptance of the client's right to choose. The case of Eleanor illustrates this point: it could have been a good decision for her to stay at home with her child, and it could equally have been a good decision for her to use the nursery place that was on offer; her social worker favouring one choice rather than the other would probably have resulted in a continuation of the decisional impasse. The second critical aspect of motivational interviewing is that strictly speaking it is a method for making a commitment around a decision, and not an all-purpose counselling approach. For example, Eleanor might have arrived at a point where she made a definite decision to send her son to nursery, but still might need some further support from her social worker around dealing with her strong emotions around 'abandoning' him, or being assertive with the nursery staff around how she wanted them to respond to her son.

Box 13.1: *Using supportive challenging to facilitate problem-solving*

During the process of working through a decision-making or problem-solving task, one of the responses that the person may well appreciate from the counsellor is a certain degree of *supportive challenging*. Most people, when faced with a decision, will recognize the value of a 'critical friend' or 'devil's advocate' role. Of course, the primary task of the counsellor is to maintain a supportive and collaborative relationship, so it is important to make sure that challenging does not become over-adversarial in ways that might undermine or threaten that relationship. The most effective challenging is based on a capacity to gently point out possible inconsistencies or contradictions in what the person has said ('from what you are saying now, the key factor seems to be X . . . but it seemed to me that from what you were saying a few minutes ago, the key factor was Y – I'm not sure how these factors fit together for you'). Another type of facilitative challenging can involve pointing out when the person might be avoiding some aspect of the decision ('you have written down all these "for" and "against" statements on the balance sheet – I'm aware that we have discussed all of them apart from these statements in the corner that you wrote in a red pen').

When decision-making and problem-solving gets stuck

In some counselling situations, a conversation about making a decision may continue for a long time without arriving at any definite decision or action plan. If this happens, it can be worth looking at whether the current decision reflects a more fundamental conflict or tension within the person's life as a whole, or whether there are other ways to facilitate an effective decision-making process. There are many personal characteristics that are associated with difficulties in decision-making and problem-solving. For instance, individuals who have *perfectionist* tendencies may find it hard to be satisfied with anything that is not an 'ideal' solution to a problem, that 'ticks all the boxes': compromise is just not possible and uncertainty is threatening.

An example of problem-solving gone wrong

Steve is a community housing support worker who has spent a lot of time working with Gareth, a retired single man who persistently reports trouble with neighbours who are noisy and inconsiderate. Typically, Gareth tries to ignore the insensitive behaviour of his neighbours, or at best writes them a polite note (which they ignore). In their conversations, Steve encouraged Gareth to express his anger and annoyance to his neighbours as a means of letting them know how he really felt. Gareth could see that this strategy made sense, and agreed with Steve that he would try it, but never carried it through. When asked why, he replied that, 'I know that letting myself get angry with them would be a much better way to get the message across. Every time I talk to Steve, I know that I end up deciding to do this. But I just can't do it. I was always taught that emotions are a waste up time, or even destructive'. What happened with Gareth could be understood in terms of a life-long tension within his sense of who he is: between a current intention to feel and express emotion, and an injunction to be 'good' and not cause trouble. The reason why the problem with his neighbours is so hard for Gareth is that their actions had created a situation in which he was led to make a choice to act in a way that challenged his core sense of self. This example acts as a reminder that arriving at a decision is not merely a matter of logically working through the practical implications of what is the best thing to do right now – sometimes making a decision can require revisiting one's position on core life issues (safety vs. freedom; autonomy vs. relatedness; trust vs. suspicion). In a relationship where counselling sits alongside other professional tasks and roles, there may not be enough time and space to work through these deeper issues. Steve and Gareth came to an understanding that directly expressing his frustration to his neighbours was not a realistic option for Gareth, so they moved on to consider other potential solutions.

In his discussion of how problem-solving and decision-making occur in everyday life, Lawrence Brammer (1990) points out that it is misleading to assume that these activities are necessarily, or wholly, based in logical, cognitive analysis.

In fact, studies of problem-solving in adults have found that many people adopt an *intuitive* approach in which they pay attention to vague feelings as a source of direction, and seek to clarify these 'hunches' as a means of progressing towards solution. The effectiveness of this type of problem-solving is enhanced not by following the kind of logical steps outlined in problem-solving therapy (see above), but by tuning in to elusive feelings and emotional states by using relaxation and meditation techniques, imagery and experiential focusing. The position adopted by Brammer (1990) is consistent with the findings of research by Loewenstein *et al.* (2001) which found that emotions are much more likely to be aroused by personal decisions that the person perceives as risky, in contrast to more everyday or routine forms of problem-solving and decision-making in which rational cognitive processes are predominant. It makes sense to assume that people are better able to deal with low-risk decisions on their own, and seek help from counsellors when faced by high-risk, emotion-laden decisions. A further valuable perspective on non-rational decision-making can be found in a study by White and Taytroe (2003), who found that thinking about a problem immediately before going to sleep contributed to finding a resolution to that problem through the process of dreaming about it. The implication here is that there are some occasions where a common-sense, rational approach to problem-solving may not be sufficient, and that it may be valuable to consider a range of creative or non-linear methods.

Box 13.2: *The significance of decision-making styles*

A massive amount of psychological research has been carried out into the ways in which people solve problems and make decisions. One of the issues that has been examined in this research concerns the ways that individuals exhibit different decision-making styles. In one study, Scott and Bruce (1995) identified five types of decision-making style:

- *Rational:* logical and systematic appraisal of all relevant information.
- *Intuitive:* guided by what 'feels right'.
- *Dependent:* consults other people and follows their advice.
- *Avoidant*: leaves things to the last minute.
- *Spontaneous*: makes decisions on the spur of the moment.

In some cases, the difficulties that clients have in making decisions and solving problems may be linked to an overreliance on one style of decision-making, and a lack of flexibility in situations where other styles would be more appropriate. For example, a rational decision-making style is desirable when making a major financial decision, but may not be much help when friends phone up with an invitation to meet them in the pub.

Exercise 13.2: *Reviewing your repertoire of methods for facilitating client problem-solving and decision-making tasks*

Divide a piece of paper into two columns. In one column, make a list of methods or strategies you already possess that you can draw on when a client identifies a problem-solving or decision-making task. In the other column, make a list of problem-solving and decision-making methods or strategies that you have read about in this chapter, or in other sources, that you would like to learn more about.

Conclusions

This chapter has offered an overview of some of the issues and strategies that are associated with counselling tasks in the domain of problem-solving and decision-making. As with other counselling tasks, it is clear that most counsellors and clients have access to a wide range of ideas about how to carry out this kind of work by virtue of their everyday life experience. Beyond the common-sense application of basic counselling skills, there are also a number of specific therapy approaches that have been developed in this area. What is important in working with clients around problem-solving and decision-making is to be sensitive to what the client thinks that they need to do in order to arrive at a solution, and to engage in metacommunication (checking out) to establish a shared agreement around the path or procedures that will be followed. It is also valuable for the counsellor to be actively involved in the process; for example, by writing down suggestions, supportively challenging ideas that are proposed, and reviewing progress. Finally, it is sensible to keep an eye open for wider personal issues. For example: why does this person need my help to make this decision, rather than being able to make it on their own, or by talking to their spouse? Why is it that we have carefully analysed all the options in great detail and yet no acceptable solution or decision has emerged?

Suggested further reading

A counselling skills approach that highlights processes of decision-making and problem-solving, and which has been widely adopted by practitioners in a range of occupational settings, is the *Skilled Helper* model:

Egan, G. (2004) *The Skilled Helper: A Problem Management and Opportunity Development Approach to Helping*, 8th edn. Belmont, CA: Wadsworth.

Wosket, V. (2006) *Egan's Skilled Helper Model*. London: Routledge.

Finding, analysing and acting on information

14

> Look at this stuff that I got from the doctor when I saw him today. Claiming benefits, how to change my diet and lifestyle, how to not worry and have a good sex life with a heart condition, what to do in an emergency, a form to join the local cardiac survivors club. Lots of stuff. There's a DVD in there somewhere too. What am I expected to do with all of it? At least he gave me a nice folder to keep it in.

Introduction

Counselling can be viewed as comprising the completion of a series of tasks or sub-goals that take the client step by step towards the achievement of their goal (whatever it is that they want to get from counselling). This perspective brings into focus some aspects of counselling that are often ignored in mainstream theories of therapy. The aim of this chapter is to examine the ways in which counsellors can work with clients to carry out a task that has traditionally not been given much emphasis in the literature – that of *finding, analysing and acting on information*. In the past, information-giving was regarded by many counsellors as something that was done by teachers and health educators, not by psychotherapists and counsellors. There are perhaps two reasons why the role of information in counselling has received increasing attention in recent years. First, if clients are understood to be actively involved in dealing with their problems in living, it is obvious that one of the things they will be doing is to search for information, from wherever they can find it, that helps them to make sense of the issue with which they are struggling. Second, in contrast to the era in which pioneers of therapy such as Carl Rogers developed their approaches, we are now living in an information age in which huge amounts of material are available on the internet and TV, and in widely distributed, affordable and accessible magazines and books.

This chapter explores some of the situations in which using information can emerge as a specific counselling task, and at some of the methods and strategies that counsellors can use in facilitating the effective use of information by their clients. The chapter then reviews the role of self-help reading materials as a valuable source of information for clients.

Examples of collecting and using information in embedded counselling

Sarah knows that both her mother and grandmother suffered from a genetically transmitted condition. On the recommendation of their GP, Sarah and her partner, Mike, attend genetic counselling, where they learn that there is a small but significant chance that if they have children together the condition might be passed on to them. They ask for more time with the counsellor to work through the implications of this information for their life together.

Shulamit is coming to terms with the death of her spouse in a road traffic accident, and has had some meetings with a community nurse who works with the intensive care unit at the hospital that looked after her husband in his final days. It becomes clear that in order to make sense of what happened Shulamit wants to have as much information as possible about how and why the accident occurred, and that to do this she will have to arrange to read the police report on the incident. She knows that she wants to do this, but is very fearful about what she might learn.

Stan has a long history of misuse of drugs and alcohol. The social worker who has responsibility for monitoring the safety and well-being of Stan's children also tries to find time to encourage Stan in his efforts to deal with his addictions. Stan learns about a religious community that runs an intensive residential programme for addicts, and compiles a folder of articles and website printoffs about what it has to offer. He asks his social worker if he could discuss this information with him to help him decide whether the programme might be relevant for him, and how he might get a place on it.

Alec has had a serious accident at work in which he was trapped for several minutes under some heavy machinery and nearly lost his life. Afterwards, he feels as though he is 'going to pieces' – he can't sleep, and feels afraid in many situations. He consults his GP, who explains that Alec is showing symptoms of post-traumatic stress disorder (PTSD) and provides him with further information about this condition. At the end of this consultation, Alec still feels vulnerable and 'not himself', but also reassured that his problem has a name, and can be treated.

Exercise 14.1: *Your experience of collecting and using information in relation to a personal issue*

Identify a recent occasion when you collected information in order to help you to deal with a personal issue. Examples might include: understanding an illness, disability or source of stress; finding out how to help someone in your family with a particular problem; and facilitating your own personal development, such as being more assertive or being better organized. What did you do to collect and analyse this information? What helped or hindered you in this process? What roles did other people play; for instance, at what points did you talk to others about what you were doing? In the end, in what ways did you make use of this information you collected in order to accomplish your underlying goals? Finally – what have you learned from this experience that might be relevant to how you assist clients to collect, analyse and use information?

When the counsellor-practitioner is the source of information

There are some occasions when a practitioner; for example, a health care professional, is in a position of providing information to a client, and also supporting the client as they work through the implications of the information and its emotional meaning. Examples of this kind of situation include breaking bad news; for instance, a diagnosis of serious illness, or explaining the treatment regime in a condition such as diabetes. An excellent discussion of the issues involved in this type of information-using scenario can be found in Nichols (2003: ch. 4).

Methods for making effective use of information in counselling

The process of working with clients to make use of information depends on the goals of the client, and the type of information that is involved. Information can represent a source of immediately applicable practical knowledge; for instance, instruction in how to carry out a breathing exercise, or it can comprise background understanding, such as learning about how sexual abuse or trauma affects people. An information 'episode' in counselling can take the form of a brief conversation, or can consist of a process of inquiry over several months. The impetus to see information can come from the client, or from the counsellor. The complexity of these factors makes it impossible to be prescriptive about how to tackle information-using tasks in counselling. It is important to use basic counselling skills in a flexible way to work alongside the client so that they can make use of information in ways that are useful for them. There are some basic principles that are also relevant:

- *Respect the client's wish to be better informed*. A search for information reflects the client's willingness to use multiple sources of help in resolving their problem in living. As a counsellor, you put a lot of effort into being well informed – your clients are motivated by similar intentions.

● *Integrate information into the counselling process and relationship.* If the client is scouring the internet and library catalogues to acquire information, but this material is not acknowledged or discussed in counselling sessions, the client may think that the counsellor is not interested in these efforts, or may even develop a sense that the counsellor believes that this work is foolish or misguided. These risks can be countered by building time into counselling sessions to review the value of information sources.

● *Engage directly with the information that the client is collecting.* If the client is accessing information sources with which the counsellor is not familiar, it can be hard to pursue a meaningful discussion about how that material might be used. There are times when a counsellor may need to borrow a book from a client, or visit a website, to see for themselves what the client is learning. It may be necessary to be clear with the client that the counsellor would only be able to do this on a limited basis, because of the time involved.

● *Be willing to challenge the client's interpretation of information.* There are many ways in which people can be taken in the wrong direction by information they have come across. This is perhaps particularly likely to occur when the information user is in a state of emotional crisis, and as a result is drawn to information that assuages painful emotions and avoiding information that might exacerbate these feelings. Clients may reject valuable information that is written in a style that is not congenial to them; they may be selective in what they take from a source, or they may misunderstand some ideas. In challenging a client around these situations, it is counterproductive for any counsellor to end up re-enacting anything that resembles the client's memory of being told off or corrected by a critical parent or teacher. The ultimate value of any information lies in the meaning that it has for the client. If the client has interpreted information in a way that differs from the counsellor's interpretation, it is not that one is right and the other is wrong, but that consideration of both perspectives may lead to an even better appreciation of the material.

● *Give some consideration to the role of information in the client's life as a whole.* Reading self-help books will have a different meaning for someone who is academic and socially withdrawn, compared to someone who is barely literate and highly sociable. Various forms of information-using in counselling may represent a continuation of coping skills that the person already uses, or a willingness to take a risk and try something new. These are factors that may require to be taken into account in thinking about how much support a client may need around the basic mechanics of information-using.

● *Keep a focus on the practical outcomes of any information that is collected.* The ultimate purpose of collecting and analysing information in the context of a counselling relationship is to contribute to the accomplishment of the client's goals. It is essential to invite the client to talk about how they are making use of any information that is collected, review the implications of the information, and to construct plans for putting these implications into action.

These principles provide a framework for thinking about how information can be creatively used in counselling, and a basis for developing a personal style as a counsellor in relation to this task area.

Box 14.1: *Toxic information*

Not all information is helpful. There are some websites that actively promote suicidal or violent behaviour or that idealize anorexic body size. There are many pornography sites that undermine respectful and loving sexual relationships. Beyond these examples of information sources that are clearly emotionally and personally destructive, there are other websites and books that present a one-sided or biased understanding of issues.

Conceptualizing information-gathering as a 'personal research project'

A good way to help a client think about how to collect and use information effectively is to draw on the cultural resource of the concept of 'research'. Most people have had experience of carrying out research projects at school or college, and have an appreciation that a 'research project' involves identifying a clear research goal or hypothesis, deciding on the type of information that would be appropriate to the aim of the study, systematically collecting and filing information, evaluating the validity of data, arriving at a conclusion, and then constructing and disseminating some kind of report. Each of these stages in a research project is relevant to the way that information is collected and used in counselling. The image of a personal research project not only provides an overall framework for an information task, but also invites the client to think about how long the whole process might take. It also positions the counsellor as a consultant to the research process, or as a research supervisor, and perhaps also as a research audience.

In a case study of his work with a man who had become severely depressed on retiring from his job, the client, Tom, felt utterly worthless and had received many different kinds of psychiatric treatment, which had only made him worse. Madigan (1999) describes how he suggested that Tom and his wife might conduct a research project in which they wrote to people they knew, and ask them to 'describe an experience that you have had with Tom that you see as neither boring or unaccomplished, and indicate what kind of future you would like to enjoy alongside Tom' (Madigan, 1999: 148). This letter was co-written by Tom, his wife and the counsellor. They received 41 replies, which they then analysed in terms of possibilities in Tom's life, and presented the results to the counsellor, who helped them to decide on how they might put these possibilities into action. They then held a party to celebrate the achievement of completing the project successfully. The case of Tom represents one example of how information-collecting can usefully be conceptualized in terms of a research project. Although the precise way in which this concept might be applied will necessarily be different for each client, the general idea has a great deal of applicability. It is intrinsically a collaborative way of working, which acknowledges and brings forward the strengths and resources of the client.

Box 14.2: *The information needs of clients may not match the way that information is organized by experts*

Genetic counselling is a particularly fruitful area for research into the role of information in counselling, because it has such a strong focus on the provision of information, and the links between information-giving and the eventual decisions made by clients. In one study, Shiloh *et al.* (2006) interviewed clients before they entered their first genetic counselling session about the questions they wished to ask the counsellor. They also looked at what happened during the counselling session. The key findings from this study were that clients exhibited distinctive informational preferences. They wanted to ask questions in a specific order that reflected their personal situation. They wanted information on the outcomes of different courses of action, and they wanted information stated with certainty, rather than in probabilistic terms. By contrast, the counsellors preferred to follow a predetermined sequence of issues, tried to provide information about the general background of the patient's problem rather than focus on outcomes, and had a tendency to describe outcomes in probabilistic language. This study illustrates the extent to which effective use of information is not merely a matter of locating a source of expert knowledge: knowledge needs to be delivered in a form that corresponds to the priorities of the information-seeker.

Using self-help literature

The use of self-help reading for psychological problems (sometimes described as 'bibliotherapy') has become very popular in recent years. There are a number of reasons for the expansion of this mode of help. Many people prefer the convenience, privacy and cost-effectiveness of working through problems on their own, rather than consulting a counsellor or psychotherapist. Many health care systems around the world have responded to the combination of high demand for mental health services and limited funding, but using self-help reading as a 'front-line' form of help. This in turn has led to a great deal of research being carried out into the effectiveness of self-help reading. On the whole, this research has shown that for some clients using a self-help book, manual or website can produce well-being outcomes that are equivalent to those obtained in face-to-face therapy (Bower *et al.*, 2001). Finally, commercial publishing houses have actively promoted the virtues of self-help books, and public libraries have stocked them, thereby making such resources easily accessible.

One of the issues that arises in relation to the use of self-help books is the question of the quality and reliability of the information that is provided. On the whole, professional practitioners tend to feel more secure in recommending self-help books that are grounded in evidence-based models of therapy. Reviews of the quality of popular self-help books have been compiled by Norcross *et al.* (2003) and Redding *et al.* (2008). Reviews of new self-help books are routinely published in professional journals such as *Therapy Today* in the UK.

There are several distinctively different styles of self-help book. For example, *Mind Over Mood: Change How you Feel by Changing the Way you Think* (Greenberger and Padesky, 1995) is organized as a practical manual with several activities and worksheets for the reader to complete. By contrast, *Depression: The Way Out of your Prison* (Rowe, 2003) is written as a discussion and overview of ideas and research around depression. Finally, *A Life Less Anxious: Freedom from Panic Attacks and Social Anxiety Without Drugs or Therapy* (Pavilanis, 2010) is written from a first-person autobiographical perspective, and tells the story of someone who has overcome panic and social anxiety. Each of these books includes similar, scientifically informed information, but the information is packaged quite differently in each case. There is some research evidence from Varley *et al.* (2011) that information presented in an 'if–then' format that requires the reader to think about how they can apply what they have learned in specific situations in their life is more effective than information that is not linked to real-life scenarios in this way. On the other hand, the Varley *et al.* (2011) study was conducted with people who were using self-help materials on their own, with no additional assistance from a counsellor. It might be expected that if a counsellor was involved, they would encourage the client to make 'if–then' connections. The advantage of personal accounts of recovery, such as the book by Pavilanis (2010), is that the reader can readily identify with the story being told, and gains hope through learning about the success that the author has achieved. The advantage of more discursive books such as Rowe (2003) is that they challenge the reader to think about issues in a rigorous manner, and do not prescribe one particular kind of solution – the reader is empowered to make their own conclusions and connections. The point here is that there is evidence that all three self-help formats are popular and effective – the key is to help each client to find the type of book that works for them.

There has been a great deal of research into the efficacy of self-help reading. The most comprehensive of these reviews, carried out by Den Boer *et al.* (2005) and Menchola *et al.* (2007) found convincing evidence that self-help reading is particularly effective when the client is also making use of face-to-face contact with a counsellor, and where the client actively chooses to make use of reading resources rather than being 'prescribed' self-help by a practitioner (Mead *et al.*, 2006; Salkovskis *et al.*, 2006). Situations where the client is in control of when and how self-help materials are used appear to be reliably associated with better outcomes. By contrast, poorer outcomes occur when the client feels that they are being sold short by being asked to read a manual rather than speaking to a counsellor.

A further consideration in relation to the use of self-help information sources is that these materials tend to be organized and packaged in terms of psychiatric categories such as depression, anxiety and eating disorders. There are two difficulties that can arise in relation to this practice. First, some clients do not wish to identify themselves as 'mentally ill', and as a result are resistant to even considering such books are relevant to them, even if the actual content of these books may be non-stigmatizing and empowering. Second, the real-life problems that many people experience cut across psychiatric categories. For example, it is quite possible for someone to be depressed *and* anxious *and* trapped in a cycle of self-destructive overeating. In these circumstances, specific self-help books and websites may be too narrowly focused, and the idea of working through three or more self-help manuals may be offputting.

Overall, there is evidence that information from self-help books and websites can be very helpful for people who are facing emotional, behaviour and relationship problems. There are many ways in which counsellors can integrate these information sources into their work with clients.

Exercise 14.2: *Self-help resources that you can recommend to your clients*

In the counselling that you do, what are the client issues that emerge most frequently? What are the specific self-help books or websites that might be most useful for your clients in relation to these issues? Over a period of time, work your way through the books and web pages, and identify a list of sources that you think would complement your own counselling style, and be viewed by your clients as accessible and relevant. Check whether it might be possible to make some of these books available to your clients by lending copies that are purchased by your organization, or whether your local libraries might be willing to stock them.

Box 14.3: *The idea of 'stepped care'*

The increasing use of self-help materials in the NHS and other health care systems reflects the adoption of a strategy of 'stepped care': if a person has a psychological problem, then they are offered the least intrusive and least intensive kind of treatment first (self-help resources) and then only offered more intensive and costly interventions (such as counselling or cognitive-behavioural therapy (CBT)) if the first 'step' is not sufficient. Although this policy makes sense from the perspective of health service managers and administrators, it is less satisfactory from the perspective of clients and counsellors. Many people only seek help as a last resort, and by the time they enter the health care system, they know that what they need and want is to have access to the caring presence of a skilled practitioner. From a counselling perspective, the evidence seems to point to self-help as being particularly effective as an adjunct to face-to-face counselling, or as one task or thread within a broader approach to the client's problems, rather than as a stand-alone treatment.

Conclusions

Working with clients around collecting and analysing information relevant to their problem is potentially enormously valuable but may also be challenging. There is much information that is available that provides conflicting guidance, or is hard to interpret. The process of integrating what can be learned from information sources into one's life requires sifting through complex material, and retaining a healthy scepticism towards the pronouncements of authority figures. It can therefore be very helpful for clients to have someone who can act as a companion on this part of their journey. This is not a role that is necessarily straightforward for counsellors. Counselling skills training tends to focus on what happens between client and counsellor in their moment-by-moment interaction, whereas making sense of information is something that the client mainly does outside of counselling sessions. The skill of facilitating a client to collect, analyse and make use of information involves making a space within counselling for information-related questions and activity to be discussed. It is unusual to change someone's life by reading a book or website. However, reading in the context of a relationship with a practitioner who is interested and supportive around making connections between what has been read and effective action does have the capacity to change lives. What seems to be crucial in facilitating this process is to invite the client to envisage it as a personal research project, and to approach relevant sources of information in an active and purposeful manner.

Suggested further reading

The use of self-help information in counselling is discussed in further detail in two valuable papers:

Norcross, J.C. (2006) Integrating self-help into psychotherapy: 16 practical suggestions, *Professional Psychology: Research and Practice*, 37: 683–93.

Zuckerman, E. (2003) Finding, evaluating, and incorporating internet self-help resources into psychotherapy practice, *Journal of Clinical Psychology*, 59: 217–25.

A valuable guide to the issues involved in making sure that clients arrive at a valid understanding of information that is provided to them can be found in:

Nichols, K. (2003) *Psychological Care for Ill and Injured People: A Clinical Guide*. Maidenhead: Open University Press (ch. 4).

CHAPTER

15

Undoing self-criticism and enhancing self-care

'How have things been this week?'
'OK. I had a bad day on Tuesday'
'What happened?'
'I tried to paint the back bedroom. Got terrible pains in my chest. Its so stupid. I feel pathetic. I *should* be able to do that kind of stuff'.

Introduction

One of the underlying themes of almost all counselling is the issue of *self-care*. The other side of self-care is its absence, which is generally expressed through *self-criticism* or self-undermining, or even in more extreme cases by self-destructive behaviour such as risk-taking, self-neglect, self-harm and suicide. Self-criticism and lack of a capacity for self-care is found in people who seek help because they feel anxious in social situations, because there is a voice in their head telling them they are not as interesting as the other people in the room, and in people who are destroying themselves and their families through patterns of abuse of alcohol and drugs, compulsive gambling, or use of pornography. We live in a culture in which rejection and social exclusion, stereotyping, and interpersonal harsh criticism are part of everyday life. A central component in many of the problems that people bring to counselling is the internalization within the consciousness of the individual, and assimilation into their core sense of who they are as a person, of these condemnatory attitudes, messages and injunctions.

The aim of this chapter is to reinforce the usefulness of identifying *undoing self-criticism and enhancing self-care* as a key component, or task, within the process of counselling. The chapter discusses ways of making sense of the experience of self-criticism, before moving on to consideration of methods that can be used to bring about change in this area.

The issues that are discussed in this chapter transcend all theories of counselling, and as a result many different terms have been used by different writers to describe what is basically the same set of characteristics. Within the chapter, two main terms are employed. *Self-criticism* is a term that seems useful because it is something that a lot of people do. It refers to words, thoughts, statements and tones of voice. Alternative terminology includes concepts such as automatic thoughts, irrational beliefs, negative self-talk and negative schema. *Self-care* refers to what people do; in particular, the way that people damage themselves through their own actions. Beyond these concepts, some counsellors talk in terms of ideas such as *self-acceptance* and *self-esteem*, or having a sense of *mattering*, being paralysed by *shame*, or engaging in *self-attacking, self-undermining or self-sabotage*. Recently, some therapists have started to use concepts of *self-compassion* and *self-soothing*. Each of these concepts buys into slightly different discourses and sets of assumptions. In working with clients, what is important is to find the words that fit for them.

Exercise 15.1: *Mapping the influence of self-criticism on your own life*

Take a few moments to list the ways in which you can be 'your own harshest critic'. What are some of the ways in which you doubt your own ability, or undermine your chances of success in various ventures? Looking back over your life, to what extent, and in what ways, have you been able to ameliorate this tendency? Who or what has helped you to be less self-critical? In what ways can this personal learning serve you as a source of ideas, methods and examples that you can use with clients who are seeking to take better care of themselves?

Examples of self-criticism and lack of self-care

Tina is married with two teenage children who take up a lot of her time and energy – they need to be driven to various venues for sport, drama and leisure activities. She is also the primary caretaker for her father, who lives with the family and has developed Alzheimer's disease. Tina contacts a voluntary agency that organizes respite care for people with dementia, and is visited by a social worker. Within the first 10 minutes of their discussion, the social worker says to Tina: 'I know that we have just met, but what comes across to me is that you are just trying to do far too much, and that your own health will be at risk if you carry on much longer like this. Yes, we can arrange respite care once a month. But my guess is that you actually need a lot more help than that. Would it be OK to talk for a bit about how things have got to this stage? Is it hard for you to ask for help, or is it something else?'

Chris is a violin teacher in a busy comprehensive school. One of his pupils, Jasmine, is an excellent violinist, one of the best that he has worked with over the course of a long career. However, she performs extremely poorly in music exams and solo performances. They are both frustrated by this situation. After one disastrous exam, she bursts into tears and says to him: 'I am just so useless, I will never be able to play in public, I'm a complete failure'.

Jimmy has a long involvement with the criminal justice system, and has just come out of prison after a one-year sentence for handling drugs. In his first meeting with the police officer who is assigned to him as part of an offender rehabilitation project, Jimmy is asked about whether he has any ideas about further training, or a career pathway that would provide an alternative to crime. 'Yes, sure, definitely', he replies, 'they all ask me that – all the social workers and probation officers I have ever met. And I tell them all the same thing. I'd love to work out of doors, in landscape gardening or horticulture or something like that. But nobody would have me on a course and nobody would give me a job – they just look at who I am, where I come from and what I've done and they'll say – "no way"'.

Lisa has been married three times, and has four children. Pregnant again, she receives a visit from the community midwife, who takes a history of her previous pregnancies and medical conditions. In the course of the conversation, the midwife asks about the level of support that Lisa has now, for example, in respect of someone to look after the other children when she goes into labour. In her reply, Lisa states that her current partner has left her, as did all her other spouses at this stage in her preceding pregnancies.

Exercise 15.2: *Listening for self-criticism*

During a counselling conversation, it is important to be sensitive to manifestations of ways of talking that indicate that a client may be locked into a pattern of destructive or self-limiting self-criticism. There are many clues or 'markers' that can be observed; for example, when a client describes themself in negative terms or in a contemptuous tone of voice, or compares themself negatively to other people. One way to become more sensitive to these processes is to listen to a recording of a counselling or psychotherapy session, focusing solely on what the client is saying. It is best to use a recording of a real session, rather than one that uses an actor as a client. If it is hard to get access to a recording, reading a transcript of a session is also possible. What you are likely to find is that troubled people engage in a lot of self-criticism. You may need to listen to or read the material more than once in order to pick up subtle indicators of self-criticism. If you have time, once you have finished listening to the client, turn your attention to how the counsellor attends to the client: how often does the counsellor acknowledge or otherwise address the client's self-critical behaviour?

Making sense of self-criticism: theoretical perspectives

A lot of the time, people who seek counselling may not be consciously aware that they undermine themselves through self-criticism and self-destructive life choices. Other clients may be aware that they engage in such activity, but feel helpless to do anything about it. In either case, it may be necessary to work with the client to find a way of making sense of why it is useful to spend time on the task of *undoing self-criticism*, and to develop an understanding of how different strategies can be used to address this issue.

Cultural perspective

With some clients, it can be meaningful to describe criticism, hostility and rejection as a pervasive element of contemporary culture, which shapes the way that all of us think about ourselves and live our lives. Among the many ways in which modern culture perpetuates such attitudes are *racism* and *colonialism* (some people are regarded as genetically inferior to others), *social class divisions* (some people are born to rule, and others are born to do what they are told), *militarism* (conflict is resolved through destroying other people), *sexism, homophobia* and *exclusion* of disabled people, and so on. Each of these social structures is organized around a belief that some people are no good, or less good, or will never be any good. The link between these cultural realities and the lives of individuals is a process of internalization – if we are exposed to such beliefs often enough, there is a risk that we 'swallow' them, or 'buy into' them. The value in counselling of evoking a cultural perspective is that it normalizes or universalizes the problem. In effect, the counsellor is saying that 'this is something we all have to deal with at some time in our lives'. A cultural perspective also allows the client to think about the ultimate origins of their self-critical statements.

Box 15.1: *An epidemic of perfectionism*

Perfectionism is a way of thinking that appears to have become a widespread problem in contemporary society. We live in a consumer society in which the demands of economic growth mean that an ever-increasing array of images of perfection are displayed in advertising and product placement in regular TV programmes and magazine articles (the perfect body, the perfect home, the perfect marriage). We also live in a society in which there is 24/7 access to these media. On top of these factors, there are increasing standards being expected from young people in the educational system (e.g. pressure to get into good universities) and in the job market. This epidemic filters down to individuals in the form of self-criticism based on perfectionist external standards. One of the most frightening manifestations of perfectionism is in the area of eating disorders, where people suffering from anorexia ('I can never be thin enough') starve themselves to death. A particularly valuable account of how a combination of therapy, self-help and social action can be used to combat the perfectionist search for ultimate thinness can be found in Maisel *et al.* (2004). A useful cognitive-behavioural therapy (CBT)-oriented self-help book on combating perfectionism is available in *Overcoming Perfectionism: A Self-help Guide Using Cognitive-behavioural Techniques* (Shafran *et al.*, 2010).

Stress and coping theory

The concept of 'stress' refers to the experience of being subjected to an accumulation of external demands, pressures and daily hassles. Stressors can be understood as challenges or demands that cannot be immediately dealt with, but which add up over time into a catalogue of worries – a burden. From the perspective of stress theory, the way that people deal with stress is through *coping strategies*. The absence of stress represents a situation in which a person's coping strategies are not being tested. By contrast, high levels of stress push the coping capacity of the individual to breaking point. Concepts of stress and coping are widely accepted within contemporary society, as well as being the topic for a great deal of research. It makes sense for many clients, therefore, to view their difficulties as resulting from high levels of externally induced stress. In counselling, it can then be possible to invite the client to consider the difference between constructive and maladaptive coping strategies. The former arise from the person's strengths and connectedness with others, and involve such strategies as planning, learning, expressing feelings, and asking other people for help. By contrast, maladaptive coping strategies encompass types of behaviour that are obviously self-destructive, such as eating and drinking too much, procrastination, and withdrawing from other people.

Person-centred theory

The theory of person-centred counselling and psychotherapy developed by Carl Rogers and others (Rogers, 1961; Mearns and Thorne, 2007) positions lack of self-acceptance as the root cause of personal problems. From a person-centred perspective, we are all born with the potential to express our feelings and emotions, to develop close relationships with others, and to be productive and intelligent. During childhood, however, we are exposed to *conditions of worth*: our parents only accept certain aspects of our capacity to be a person and reject other aspects. For example, parents or other authority figures may say things like 'don't try to be clever' (suppress your intelligence), or 'big boys don't cry' (suppress your vulnerability and hurt). As a result, we develop a definition of ourselves, or self-concept, that allows us to express particular parts of who we are, but not others. These denied parts of the person may come to be viewed as threatening, and subject to self-criticism if they are revealed ('there I go again, being big-headed'; 'it's pathetic how I just want to cry when these things happen'). On a moment-by-moment basis, the effort that the person is putting into preventing themself from giving expression to what they are actually experiencing is termed *incongruence*. The theory of person-centred counselling suggests that exposure to a climate of acceptance in a relationship with a counsellor who is genuine and empathic will over time allow a person to accept the hitherto denied or suppressed parts of their own self. A person-centred perspective offers an explanatory framework that makes a lot of sense to people as an account of how and why they engage in destructive self-denial and self-criticism. It also provides a means of understanding what a person needs to do in order to overcome self-criticism: learn to accept oneself.

Self-multiplicity theory

An important theoretical approach that has meaning for many people is the notion that the self, or the person, is a dynamic system that comprises different parts, and these parts can be in conflict with each other. The idea that human personality or identity is not necessarily experienced as an indivisible or unified whole, but that there exist splits in the self, reflects powerful themes in western culture. The publication in 1886 of the short novel *Dr Jeckyll and Mr Hyde* by Robert Louis Stevenson, appeared to act as a cultural marker for an acknowledgement of the experience of 'divided self'. The idea of self-multiplicity has been incorporated in counselling and psychotherapy theory and practice by a wide range of writers (see, for example, Mair, 1977; Mearns and Thorne, 2007; Rowan and Cooper, 1998). Probably the most accessible version of this way of thinking about self and relationships can be found within the literature on transactional analysis (TA) (Stewart and Joines, 1987). Here, the source of self-criticism is characterized as the *critical parent* ego state, which consists of critical injunctions and labels that typically live on in the mind of the person as a memory of actual statements made by authority figures. The idea of the critical parent and its counterpart, an inner *nurturing parent* that functions as a source of encouragement and self-soothing, makes intuitive sense to many people. They also open up a potentially very productive line of questioning for a counsellor. When a client makes a negative self-statement (e.g. 'I'll never be any be any good'), it can be helpful for the counsellor to inquire 'who said that to you?' Being able to identify sources of negative self-talk back *then* can create a space in which the person can decide that these ideas may no longer be valid *now*. A further way of looking at self-multiplicity, which is consistent with TA and other psychological models, is to think in terms of *voices* (Penn and Frankfurt, 1994; Stiles, 1999). There are two advantages to using the idea of 'voice' to refer to parts of the self. First, it does not make any assumptions about personality structure or self-organization. Second, it invites attention to the immediate physical reality of what is happening: people move in and out of different voices as they speak. For example, a person may talk at one moment in a soft and faltering voice, which may be an expression of a suppressed and vulnerable aspect of their experiencing, and then at the following moment in a louder, sarcastic voice that belittles or contradicts what they have just said.

These are some of the theoretical perspectives that can function as ways of making sense of the operation of self-criticism in the life of a client, and the goal of attaining a more satisfactory level of self-care. A key assumption that informs all of these theoretical perspectives is that punitive self-criticism is highly prevalent in people who seek counselling. There do exist, of course, other patterns – individuals who appear to have little or no capacity to critically regulate their behaviour in a socially acceptable manner, and individuals who exhibit uncommon amounts of self-regard. These people, sometimes labelled as impulsive/psychopathic or as narcissistic, may well lead troubled lives, but are relatively unlikely to seek front-line counselling – they regard the problem as being caused by other people, not by anything they could change in themselves. They may end up being referred to specialist secondary care psychotherapy or mental health services. A further related assumption in respect of these theories is that they certainly do not advocate entirely eliminating self-criticism from a person's way of being. It is certainly valuable to be able to observe oneself and to set appropriate standards for one's behaviour. The aim of counselling is to enable the person to attain a satisfactory (as defined by them) balance between a capacity to celebrate personal achievements and a capacity to question them.

Box 15.2: *The difference between counselling and advice-giving*

The notion of self-care reinforces the distinction between counselling, on the one hand, and advice-giving on the other. In advice-giving, a problem is 'fixed' or 'sorted' – a solution is found and that is the end of the matter. Counselling, by contrast, is always *person*-centred as well as *problem*-centred. In counselling, the aim is not merely to resolve a specific issue now, but to enable the person to learn enough to be able to cope with similar problems in future. Effective counselling therefore involves paying attention to the person's repertoire of self-care strategies, and finding ways to support and extend them.

Methods for undoing self-criticism and enhancing self-care

Because self-criticism is such a pervasive issue in counselling, there are many methods that have been developed for addressing it. There are many ideas in other chapters that are also relevant to facilitating *undoing self-criticism* tasks. In this section, three specific techniques are introduced that are of particular relevance in this area of work: *cognitive restructuring, identifying and decontaminating parts of the self*, and *using a strengths perspective*.

Cognitive restructuring

The revolution in counselling and psychotherapy that is associated with the emergence of cognitive therapy in the 1960s was based on the development of methods for helping people to *think* about their problems in different ways. The key idea in cognitive therapy is that 'automatic' negative thoughts or self-statements exist that are on the edge of a person's awareness, and are activated when the person is in situations that they have learned to define as risky, threatening or difficult. These thoughts can then guide the person in one of two directions. The person may try to escape or avoid the difficult situation. Alternatively, they may find that they have become more fearful, perhaps to the extent of entering into a state of panic. The emotional significance of either of these patterns is reinforced if the person then engages in *rumination* in the form of a lengthy internal rehearsal of their inadequacies. There are many strategies that can be used to reduce the force of these cognitive patterns:

- Keeping a systematic record of these thoughts in the form of a diary: where and when they occur and what emotional states they lead to.
- Socratic dialogue: questioning and gently challenging the assumptions that underpin exaggerated or irrational beliefs. For example, if the client states that 'I am not as good as everyone else', the counsellor might respond by asking: 'do you mean *every* one in the world . . . what about Hitler, aren't you as good as him?'). The aim of this technique is to assist the client to break out of a fixed way of thinking.
- Thought stopping: the client practises saying 'stop' out loud when they engage in rumination, and then does something different.
- Rehearsing positive self-talk, such as 'I know that this is a scary situation for me, but I have several ways of coping with it and I know that I will come out all right in the end'.
- Directly testing assumptions through behavioural experiments (in a group, a person who thinks that 'no one will find me interesting' can go round the group asking other members whether they agree with this self-appraisal).
- Reframing: defining a difficult situation in positive terms (e.g. 'presenting a seminar paper is an opportunity to show the other members of the class how much hard work I have done, and to test out some of my new theories about the topic we are discussing').

More detailed discussion and description of how to use these cognitive methods can be found in Greenberger and Padesky (1995) and Leahy (2003), and many other sources. Fascinating accounts of behavioural experiments are included in Bennett-Levy *et al.* (2004).

Identifying and decontaminating parts of the self

The notion of self-multiplicity is associated with a number of counselling methods. The first step in this way of working is to invite the client to describe and name different parts of the self, either using concepts from a pre-existing theoretical framework such as TA or using their own terminology. It can be helpful to use visual techniques to assist in this process; for example, by the client or counsellor making a diagram of how different parts of the self fit together. It may be that making a picture or a sculpture can be more effective than just talking in enabling the client to express and clarify the different parts. The value of naming and/or visually depicting these entities is that it allows both client and counsellor then to talk about what these parts or voices mean in terms of the way that they influence the person's life. A useful idea in relation to pursuing this kind of discussion is the TA concept of *decontamination* (Stewart and Joines, 1987), which refers to the way that the meaning or functioning on one part of the person is controlled or suppressed by another part. For example, a person may potentially be aware of a playful and creative part of who they might be, but as soon as this potential becomes suppressed it is submerged and silenced by a critical voice saying 'don't be so stupid'. This overlap between two valuable parts of the self (a playful part and a careful part) inhibits the capacity of the person to enjoy themself, and so is not functional. It is clearly more satisfactory for the person to be able to have fun, and to be safe, rather than having to sacrifice one for the other. Two-chair work is a specific technique that can be useful in allowing different voices or parts to first of all be separate from each other, then to find a means of working together constructively. In the brief example of two-chair work displayed in Box 15.3, it is possible to see how a harsh inner critic becomes personalized and softened, and a point of contact or a 'meaning bridge' is established between the two voices or parts around 'caring', a value to which they both can subscribe. Some clients find two-chair work to be too embarrassing and exposing, but the same process can be followed within a normal client–counsellor conversation or through art-making; the advantage of two-chair work is that it highlights and dramatizes the dialogue. Although two-chair work was first devised by Fritz Perls, the founder of Gestalt therapy, the best present-day descriptions of this method can be found in the writings of Les Greenberg and his colleagues (Greenberg *et al.*, 1993; Greenberg, 2001).

Box 15.3: *An example of two-chair dialogue*

Counsellor:	We keep coming back to this tension between the bit of you that is desperate to have fun and dance, and that Calvinist voice that sternly commands you to 'be serious'.
Client:	Yes, that's the way it is, the dancing only ever gets a chance if the John Knox is obliterated with beer, which is not the way I want to be.
Counsellor:	I'm wondering, would it be OK to stay with this for a few minutes. I'd like to set up a conversation between these two bits. Would you be willing to try that?

Client:	Like with the chairs?
Counsellor:	Yes. Why don't you just be the side of you that wants to dance, and put the John Knox side on that chair there. What do you want to say to him?
Client (looking at other chair):	I like dancing. There's nothing wrong with dancing. I resent the way you make me hang back and not join in. (*changes to other chair*)
Client (*looking at first chair*):	I'm just trying to protect you. You could get yourself in a lot of trouble if you make an exhibition of yourself. (*moves back to first chair*)
Client (*looking at other chair*):	What are you talking about? I want to make an exhibition of myself!
Counsellor:	Who is that in the other chair?
Client:	(*laughs*) It's my grandmother. I can hear her saying that. She used to get so wound up when I went out clubbing when I was a student. She was so worried about guys spiking drinks, or assaulting me, and so on.
Counsellor:	Because she cared?
Client:	Sure, definitely (*tears*).

Using a strengths perspective

Historically, counselling and psychotherapy theory and practice have paid a lot of attention to the problems and difficulties being experienced by the client, and less attention to the client's resources and strengths. This imbalance has shifted in recent years in recognition of the vital role that strengths and resources play in enabling people to deal with challenging and threatening experiences in their lives. A strengths perspective underpins important contemporary approaches to counselling and psychotherapy such as narrative therapy and solution-focused therapy, and has been highly influential in social work practice (Saleebey, 2002). All of the examples of narrative therapy theory and practice discussed in other chapters of this book can be read as instances of strengths-oriented counselling. There are two principal moves that constitute a strengths-based approach to working on *undoing self-criticism* tasks. The first is to adopt a stance of curiosity and interest around the strengths, resources, gifts, competences and resources that are available to the client. In taking this step, it is important to keep in mind that many of these strengths may be implicit, or may not have been used for some time. The client may be enjoined to remember times in the past when they had overcome difficulties, or had accomplished worthwhile objectives, as well as to identify current strengths. Some of the questions that can be employed in facilitating such exploration are listed in Table 15.1. The second move is to invite the client to activate these strengths and resources in the service of coping with current difficulties. This stage would usually involve making contact with people who have been supportive and helpful in the past – a process that narrative therapists describe as re-membering (Morgan, 2001). In this way of working, the counsellor is not seeking to develop a deep person-to-person relationship, but instead is seeking to act as a catalyst for the person to move from a sense of self as deficient to a sense of self as resourceful. Once this step is taken, quite often the client is off and running – able to find what they need within their own resources rather than requiring ongoing support from a counsellor. Case examples of how a strengths-based approach can be used in a social work context, with clients with quite severe self-undermining tendencies, can be found in Yip (2005, 2006). What can be seen in these cases is that apparently quite simple strengths-based interventions can have a significant impact on people's lives.

TABLE 15.1 Questions to elicit acknowledgement and discussion of a client's strengths

- How have you managed to survive (or thrive) thus far, given all the challenges you have had to contend with?
- What have you learned about yourself and your world during your struggles?
- Which of these difficulties have given you special strength, insight, or skill?
- What are the special qualities on which you can rely?
- What people have given you special understanding, support, and guidance?
- When things were going well in life, what was different?
- What now do you want out of life?
- What are your hopes, visions, and aspirations?
- How far along are you toward achieving these?
- When people say good things about you, what are they likely to say?
- What is it about your life, yourself, and your accomplishments that give you real pride?

Source: Saleebey (2002)

Exercise 15.3: *Focusing on a person's strengths, gifts and assets*

Identify one client with whom you have a counselling relationship. If you are not currently working with clients, identify someone from your training course or place of employment. Sit quietly in a relaxed posture for 10 minutes, and reflect on what you know of this person, and what you regard as their personal strengths, gifts and assets. Towards the end of the time you have devoted to this activity, make a list of these positive attributes and take a little more time to consider how these qualities might be more fully harnessed by the person to help them to lead a more satisfying and productive life.

Conclusions

This chapter has attempted to demonstrate the extent to which the task of undoing self-criticism and enhancing self-care weaves through many of the issues that people bring to counselling, and the completion of this kind of task can be accomplished in many different ways. The methods for undoing self-criticism that have been introduced in the chapter have highlighted ideas and strategies that provide ways of introducing new perspectives and possibilities into clients' lives. However, as with any counselling method, the ultimate success of the approach depends on the quality of the relationship between counsellor and client. In order to combat their harsh self-critic, what clients want and need is to work with someone who is affirming and encouraging around their potential to achieve their goals and be the person they want to be. Although there may be times when it is helpful for a counsellor to challenge or confront a client around the way that they do not look after themself, this strategy is only facilitative if the client continues to believe that the counsellor is resolutely on their side.

Suggested further reading

Albert Ellis was one of the founders of cognitive therapy. His ideas are still widely used today in the form of rational-emotive behaviour therapy (REBT), and as part of the repertoire of many front-line counsellors who practise in a pluralistic or integrative manner. The most influential of the many books published by Ellis, in which he introduces the idea of 'irrational beliefs' is:

Ellis, A. (1962) *Reason and Emotion in Psychotherapy*. New York: Lyle Stuart.

A widely-used self-help book that addresses self-criticism from a cognitive perspective is:

Fennell, M. (1999) *Overcoming Low Self-esteem: A Self-help Guide Using Cognitive-behavioural Techniques*. London: Constable & Robinson.

For several decades the work of Paul Gilbert has represented an invaluable resource for all those seeking to undo the damage caused by self-limiting thinking in lives and relationships. An excellent introduction to his current ideas can be found in:

Gilbert, P. and Irons, C. (2005) Focused therapies and compassionate mind training for shame and self-attacking. In P. Gilbert (ed.) *Compassion: Conceptualisations, Research and Use in Psychotherapy*. London: Routledge.

The writings of Barry Duncan and Scott D. Miller, particularly their concept of the 'heroic client', are hugely valuable in creating a mind-set for counselling that seeks to identify, celebrate and apply the client's strengths:

Duncan, B.L., Miller, S.D. and Sparks, J. (2004) *The Heroic Client: A Revolutionary Way to Improve Effectiveness through Client-directed, Outcome-Informed Therapy*, 2nd edn. San Francisco, CA: Jossey-Bass.

A self-help book that includes a wealth of ideas about how to work creatively with parts of the self is:

Stone, H. and Stone, S. (1993) *Embracing Your Inner Critic: Turning Self-criticism into a Creative Asset*. New York: Harper.

Negotiating life transitions

That nurse said to me today that she thought that maybe I needed to face the fact that I have moved to a different stage of my life. I'm not superman any more who works all the overtime that's going, goes to the pub with my mates and builds an extension to the kitchen at the weekend. She said 'you're in a new phase, that has its own satisfactions'. That'll be the day — over the hill at 59. I don't think so.

Introduction

The previous chapter discussed the examples where a person made a decision to change a fairly specific and well-defined set of behaviours, such as losing weight, getting more exercise and becoming more sociable. However, there are other behaviour change issues that are on a different kind of scale. People tend to have periods in their life when relatively little change takes place, and then other periods that are characterized by fairly dramatic shifts from one status or way of living to another when their personal world is significantly disrupted in a major way. The idea of *transition* is a valuable concept in counselling, because it provides a way of thinking about large-scale personal change events. Transitions can be unexpected and unplanned, or relatively predictable. Examples of sudden transitions are:

- losing a job
- winning the lottery
- becoming ill
- divorce
- the loss of a loved one
- termination of pregnancy
- moving to another area or country.

In addition, there are predictable or 'normative' changes built into the life-course that inevitably affect all (or most) of us, such as:

- leaving home
- becoming a parent
- retirement from work.

An understanding of the process of transition is valuable for anyone in a counselling role, because it is at such moments of transition that people feel the need to talk to someone (e.g. a counsellor or helper) outside of their immediate situation, who can help them to gain some perspective on what is happening. Negotiating a difficult life transition represents an important counselling task. While there are a number of specialist counselling agencies that offer help to people undergoing specific transitions, such as marital separation and divorce, or bereavement, relatively few people make use of them (compared to the overall number of potentially eligible individuals). There are also many transitions that do not fall readily into the terms of reference of these agencies. For these reasons, many people experiencing transition look for counselling help from whatever professional source is available to them, such as a nurse, doctor or other worker.

This chapter explores some possible ways to work with clients in order to enable them to negotiate different types of life transition. The chapter considers ways of making sense of the transition process, and methods of facilitating productive conversation and action around transition issues.

Examples of episodes of embedded counselling around transition issues

The following examples illustrate some of the counselling goals, tasks and methods that can be associated with working together around life transitions:

Margaret and her three children had lived on a Caribbean island that was largely destroyed by a volcanic eruption. Evacuated by the Navy, they ended up in Britain being taken care of by a Church group who provided housing and other support for refugees. Although Margaret and her children spoke English, they had great difficulty in understanding the accents of the people in the neighbourhood within which they had been located, or of being understood by them. The country seemed dark, damp and unwelcoming. Over the space of two years, a small team of support workers helped Margaret and her children to reconstruct their lives, using a combination of assistance in practical issues around work, health and education alongside a willingness to take time to listen and talk.

Judith is several weeks into the first year of senior school. She enjoyed the junior school where she knew everyone and had a good relationship with her class teacher. However, the transition to senior school has been very difficult.

She feels as though she has been separated from her friends, is unable to make new friends, and has not come to terms with the demands of the timetable and homework. The teacher responsible for support and guidance notices Judith's isolation and distress, and asks if she would be willing to meet during the lunch hour. When invited to talk, Judith bursts into tears and describes a long list of problems. With Judith's permission, the teacher makes a list of these problems and suggests that they might look at how they can deal with them one at a time. Over the next three weeks, they come up with a set of coping strategies that Judith can employ, and keep monitoring how they can be applied within the different difficult situations that Judith encounters during her school day. By the Christmas break, Judith has settled in, and at their final lunchtime meeting her teacher brings in a special cake to celebrate her achievements.

Agnes and Simon are going through the whole process of applying to adopt a child. The social worker carrying out their assessment tells them that they have the potential to be excellent parents – they have a strong relationship, they are financially secure, and have good support from their own families. She adds: 'but over the meetings I have had with the two of you, the same question arises in my mind: are you *ready* to make this huge change in your lives? You seem to really enjoy the life you have. I get a sense that you both feel you are going to lose all of that if a child moves into the spare bedroom upstairs. Is this something we could talk about?'

Andy works in a shelter for homeless young people. The main part of his job consists of making sure that food and bedding is available, and that his clients have access to health care. When he can, he tries to listen to their stories and help them to make sense of their lives. When interviewed by a journalist about his work, he says that: 'the largest group we get here are kids from families where their mum and dad have been alcoholics or drug users, or have been abusive to them in some other way. They get to a stage when they just can't take it any more so they move out. It's just like any of us – there comes a point where you have to leave home and try to make it on your own. But for them, there's no support, no preparation, no fall-back, nothing. So they crash'.

These brief examples show how transition issues can emerge as a central focus in embedded counselling work. Judith's teacher uses her own adaptation of cognitive-behavioural therapy (CBT) methods, culminating in the use of a ritual (eating together) to mark the completion of the change in personal status that had taken place. With Margaret and her family, a team of support workers developed relationships that were supportive and resourceful. With Agnes and Simon, a social worker skilfully used supportive challenge to invite further exploration of a contradiction in her clients' feelings and attitudes.

> ## Exercise 16.1: *Reflecting on your own experience of transition*
>
> Choose a recent significant experience of transition in your own life. In thinking about how that process unfolded, can you identify stages that you passed through in terms of your feelings, attitudes to what was happening and your behaviour? What helped you to get through this shift in your life? What was hindering or unhelpful? Finally – what can you take from your own personal experience of transition that can inform the way that you work with clients around similar issues?

Making sense of transition: theoretical perspectives

One of the most useful things that a counsellor can do for clients who are experiencing transition issues is to suggest that what is happening can be understood as involving a life transition of some kind. Usually, clients are caught up in coping with immediate pressures and difficulties, and do not necessarily think about their stress in terms of a bigger picture. The invitation to consider day-to-day difficulties in terms of a transition from one stage of life to the next immediately allows the client to adopt a broader perspective. There are several theoretical frameworks that have been developed by psychologists and other social scientists that can be offered to clients as a means of making sense of the transition through which they are passing. Four of these frameworks are described below: *psychodynamic life-course theory*; the *transition curve model*; *narrative disruption theory*; and the *ecological perspective*.

Psychodynamic life-course theory

Psychodynamic theory is an approach to counselling and psychology that has evolved from the psychoanalytic ideas of Sigmund Freud. One of the cornerstones of psychodynamic thinking is the assumption that someone's personality or sense of identity evolves and develops over the course of their life. From a psychodynamic perspective, therefore, it is always useful to think about the problems being presented by a client in *developmental* terms: what are the developmental processes that have occurred in the past that have resulted in the person possessing certain strengths and problems, and what is the developmental challenge that the person is facing right now? The psychodynamic model of stages in the life course that was devised by Erik Erikson is widely used by counsellors and other practitioners as a means of making sense of transition issues (see Table 16.1). Further explanation of the content of this model is available in McAdams (2000), Sugarman (2003, 2009) and innumerable introductory and developmental psychology textbooks and websites.

There are several aspects of the Erikson model that can be applied to counselling and discussed with clients. In using these ideas with clients, it is of course

TABLE 16.1 Erikson's model of psychosocial stages

Psychosocial issue/stage of development	Age
Trust–mistrust	Birth to 18 months
Autonomy–shame	18 months to 3 years
Initiative–guilt	3–5 years
Industry–inferiority	6–12 years
Identity–role confusion	12–18 years
Intimacy–isolation	18–35 years
Generativity–self-absorption	35–60 years
Integrity–despair	60–death

essential to use language that makes sense to the client. For example, the concept of 'autonomy' may come across to some people as abstract and academic – 'being able to stand up for yourself' could be an alternative and more acceptable way of talking about this idea. One of the ways in which the model can be used in counselling is that it suggests that people need to work out different kinds of personal and emotional issues at different points in their life. For example, teenage years are often characterized by a struggle to define 'who am I?', reflected in rebellion against parental values, and trying out different roles and lifestyles. However, the model suggests that there is a shift in early adulthood to a new question: 'how can I form a close and loving relationship?' and then later in adulthood to 'how can I be a parent and offer something to the next generation?' The stages identified by Erikson therefore allow clients to get some kind of handle on the broad emotional and interpersonal agenda that they are facing at any particular point in their lives. This can be particularly relevant at the point of entering or leaving a new stage.

A further aspect of Erikson's model is that it suggests that the success that the person has had in negotiating previous stages will have an influence on how well-prepared they are in respect of handling the next stage that they enter. For example, a person who has learned to trust other people, and to have a balanced sense of their own autonomy as a human being, is in a good position to develop intimacy in a close relationship. By contrast, someone who has never been able to trust will possibly find it quite hard to manage intimacy in a relationship. In counselling, this perspective allows the person to begin to make links between the current issues around which they are struggling, and the kind of love and support (or lack of these equalities) that was available to them at earlier times in their life.

Erikson's theory is in fact very hopeful and optimistic about these matters. He argued that each developmental stage allows the person to revisit, and relearn interpersonal skills that were not fully developed in the past. So, for instance, a person who experienced inconsistent or negligent parenting in the early years of their life may have an underlying distrust of other people and the world in general, but then finds new opportunities to learn about trust at school, in peer relationships in adolescence, in partner relationships in young adulthood, and so on.

The final facet of this model that is relevant for counselling is that it suggests that most of the time we are not consciously aware that these processes are occurring.

If we do become aware of these issues, we are able to do something about them – we become able to learn and to change. One of the counselling skills that is highly relevant here is that of *making meaning* – the counsellor is able to offer the client in a collaborative and open way the possibility that some of Erikson's ideas (or the ideas of similar theorists) might help them to be aware of what is happening for them, and to make sense of what they are experiencing.

The transition curve model

There are several useful models of transition and crisis that have been developed (see Hopson and Adams, 1976; Hopson, 1989; McAdams, 2000; Sugarman, 2004, 2009). These provide a useful framework for making sense of the experience of the person seeking help. All of these models suggest that a person in transition goes through a series of stages of readjustment such as:

1 Shock – exhibited either as excitement ('this is great') or numbness ('it's not really happening').
2 Provisional adjustment – the 'honeymoon period'.
3 Gradual loss of confidence. Increase in depression ('I can't cope').
4 Crisis point – despair and hopelessness.
5 Reconstruction/rebuilding a new life: *either* accepting the new situation and reconstructing self/identity (leading to a higher level of confidence/competence than at the start), *or* quitting and giving up.

When using a transition model, it is essential to be flexible – in any individual case the progression from one stage to another may occur quickly, or take a long time, and the individual may 'skip' stages or repeat them.

The implications of this kind of transition model for the work of the counsellor are that it:

● Draws attention to the fact that transition involves ups and downs – it is not a smooth process.
● Suggests that it may not be of any use to attempt any kind of counselling during the 'shock' phase – the person is dealing with an overload of new information and will not be able to process it – at this stage basic safety and care are crucial, and forming a relationship that the person may be able to use for counselling purposes at a later date.
● Implies that helping a person through a transition involves paying attention to (1) letting go of previous attitudes, relationships and behaviours, (2) changing behaviour (e.g. learning new skills, making new friends) and (3) cognitive restructuring (learning to see yourself in a different light).

For any counsellor working with a particular group of people seeking help, it is important to become attuned to the specific ways that the transition cycle plays out in the lives of that set of people. For instance, in bereavement it may take many months or even years before a person is ready to reflect on the implications of their loss, whereas in students beginning studies in another country the pressure to read-just, and to deal with the experience of transition, is immediate.

The narrative disruption model of transition

From a narrative perspective, we create and maintain our personal identity, and are known to other people, through the stories that we tell about ourselves. Underpinning the day-to-day stories of what we do, there is a basic life story, an overall life narrative or script that sums up who we are. For example, maybe people live their lives in accordance with a storyline that is along the lines of 'I will work hard, look after my family and children and make a contribution to society, then I will be able to enjoy the fruits of my labours in my later years'. When a person experiences a serious illness, this life story is shattered – it cannot be told; it no longer fits the reality of life on an everyday level. For example, a person who is crippled by multiple sclerosis or coronary heart disease may not be able to work, and may find that instead of caring for others, they have become an object of care. This kind of narrative disruption has been studied by many health psychologists and sociologists (Frank, 1995, 1998, 2000; Williams, 1984), who argue that many of the emotional and relationship problems experienced by people who are suffering from chronic health conditions can be understood as arising from the challenge of reshaping and realigning their life story. One of the most influential models of this process has been developed by the American sociologist, Arthur Frank (1995), who argues that a health crisis triggers a period of narrative *chaos* for the individual – they no longer know how to talk about who they are, and other people in their life are similarly constrained. For many people, there is a strong pull to develop a *restitution* narrative: 'things are bad but I will do everything possible to get back to the way I was before I got ill'. Other people develop a *quest* narra-tive: 'I have to learn to move on in my life and find meaning and connection with people in different ways'. An appreciation of the significance of these contrasting ways of talking about a transition is potentially valuable for counsellors; for example, in reflecting back to the person the alternative ways of making sense of their situation, and the implications of these stories for them as individuals as well as for the other people in their lives. Although the research in this area has focused on the experiences of people undergoing health crises and transitions, it seems clear that these ideas are also highly relevant for those whose transitions are in other areas of their life, such as employment, marital status, housing, being subject to natural disasters, being a victim of crime, and so on.

An ecological perspective on transitions

A recurring image throughout this book is that of a person as existing within a social and cultural *ecological* system – engaged in making a space, niche or home for themself within the social and cultural world within which they live. The global culture within which all of us live our lives is immensely complicated and presents us with multiple possibilities and choices. In the distant past, human society was organized around relatively small, highly structured groups, such as clans or tribes, that lived close to nature. In the absence of a written language, knowledge and information were conveyed in the form of songs and stories. Many of the characteristics of that earlier way of life still remain with us; for example, in the importance that most people place on loyalty, and in the power of narrative. But the development of written language, mechanized transport, an economic system based on money and capital, and the information technology revolution, have contributed to the existence of a culture of cities. In a city, many separate and different cultural worlds can coexist within the same geographical area.

Building a *personal niche* involves at least three types of interlocking activity. First, there is the task of connecting to other people by maintaining a network of personal relationships. These relationships usually include some mix of family and kinship ties, intimate or partner relationships, friendships, work colleagues and casual acquaintances. Second, a person lives within a set of stories that they tell about themself, and which are told about them. These stories reflect, and draw upon, the stock of stories that are available within a culture; for example, in myths, novels and movies. Third, a personal niche comprises objects, spaces and territories that have meaning for a person; for example, the musical instrument that they play, the food they eat, their bedroom, their garden, and the view from the top of a particular hill. A highly significant object and space is always the physical body of the person, and how they create a home for their self in their body and express their identity through their body.

A sense of well-being, or satisfaction with life, depends on the extent to which the personal niche reflects a sufficient degree of coherence or integration between the story that a person lives within, and the relationships and objects through which their story is played out. For example, if someone has constructed their personal world around a story of being 'happily married', and their partner wants to leaves them, then they have a problem. If someone has created a world around 'being a student', and has constructed a niche that is based on access to a university campus and involvement in student activities, then undergoes a transition to 'being a civil servant', a new personal niche may need to be created.

An ecological perspective provides a useful set of ideas for counsellors working with people undergoing life transitions. The task of negotiating a transition can be viewed as involving building a new niche. This encompasses deciding on what relationships, places and activities need to be in the niche, and how to identify and engage with these elements. It requires deciding on which parts of the old niche can be retained, and which need to be left behind. This way of thinking highlights the purposefulness, resourcefulness and creativity of the client.

Box 16.1: *Transition counselling by nurses in an infertility clinic*

Research carried out by Helen Allan has explored the experience of transition in women undergoing treatment in a fertility clinic to enable them to have a child (Allan, 2001, 2007). This research is unusual in using in-depth interviews and participant observation to capture what goes on during an extended and highly stressful (and often unsuccessful) transition process. What emerged from this study was that many of the women using the clinic had few other outlets for expressing their hopes, fears and disappointments, but that is was also very hard for the nurses and medical staff to engage with what their patients were feeling, due to lack of training, time and organizational support. Allan (2001: 53) described how the nurses conveyed 'emotional awareness' to their patients through 'hovering' and 'focused support':

Hovering described the physical presence of the nurse during a doctor–patient consultation where she might be listening or focusing on the consultation while carrying out another activity. At any time she might become involved through the invitation of the doctor or patient or intervene on her own initiative. Focused support was an action which usually took a very short time when there was a need or an opportunity because of the public nature of nursing and the constraints imposed by the presence of other staff. Focused support might be a touch, an explanation, a question, a joke or acting on the patient's behalf as an advocate to question a doctor's order.

However, even these fairly minimal forms of empathic engagement in the emotional pain being felt by women receiving infertility treatment was enough to create some sense of the clinic as a supportive environment.

Box 16.2: *Trauma as an extreme form of transition*

In recent years, post-traumatic stress disorder (PTSD) has been identified as a distinct psychiatric condition, and various treatment approaches have been developed to address this condition (Meichenbaum, 1994; Scott and Stradling, 2006). Post-traumatic stress disorder (PTSD) occurs when the person has been exposed to a highly traumatic and threatening event. The typical signs of PTSD are intrusive memories of the events, such as flashbacks, alongside attempts to avoid thinking about what had happened. Avoidance can sometimes only be achieved by self-medication through alcohol and drugs. The person suffering PTSD tends to experience a loss of trust in the world, and experiences even minor setbacks and stresses as highly threatening. This set of symptoms can lead to sleep loss and fatigue, secondary relationship problems, difficulties at work and depression. Although the literature on PTSD tends to be dominated by high-profile trauma-inducing events, such as involvement in warfare, or being the victim of terrorism or natural disaster, there is in fact a surprising amount of 'everyday' traumatic stress around. Events such as car accidents, domestic violence, bullying, sexual violence, robbery and childbirth can lead to PTSD reactions, so it is not unusual to come across people who are suffering from undiagnosed, or mild, traumatic stress. Part of the preparation for a counselling role requires being informed about the specialist services that are available locally for people experiencing PTSD. Usually, clinical psychologists provide a good source of expertise in this condition. However, it is also worth reflecting on the meaning of traumatic stress disorders, and what they can tell us about other, less dramatic forms of transition. At the heart of the PTSD response is the need to cognitively process information that is not readily assimilated into the person's previous way of making sense of the world. When we encounter a routine life difficulty or irritation (the car won't start), we can usually make sense of it quite readily (the battery is flat). By contrast, when something traumatic and completely unexpected happens (I was waiting in the queue at the bank and a masked man with a gun rushed in), then it is very hard to make sense of what all this might have meant (Could I have died? What would have happened to my children? Why me? Could I have done anything different?). What is required is to find some way to construct a coherent story or narrative around what happened. This can be achieved by slowly remembering and piecing together an account of the event, but reliving the event may be very hard because each strand of memory may be associated with fear and terror.

Methods for working with clients around negotiating a life transition

There are no specific methods or therapy protocols that have been developed for working with people around negotiating their way through life transitions. Usually, working on this kind of task involves using counselling skills to help the person to talk, make sense of their situation, develop some ideas about what they can do, and out these ideas into action. There are some counselling activities that can be introduced into this process:

- *Constructing a timeline*: a timeline is a graph made by the client, usually with time (years or months) along a horizontal axis drawn across the centre of the page, and well-being or sense of security or some other valued state plotted on the horizontal axis, with positive times indicated above the horizontal axis and negative times below it. The person might also annotate the graph with images or phrases that function as labels for specific events (e.g. 'when my mother died', 'when I met George'). A timeline is a useful means for enabling a client to reflect on processes in their life that have occurred over a period of time. Typically, a timeline is drawn during a counselling session, and then forms the basis for a discussion between the counsellor and client. The client may add elements to the graph during the course of the conversation to record memories or understandings that have emerged. It is important that the client retains ownership and control over the timeline, rather than the counsellor writing on it. Towards the end of the discussion, in some circumstances it can be useful for the counsellor to invite the client to think about the future: 'ideally, what would you like to happen next – fill in the graph for the next 12 months or so?'.

● *Writing an autobiography*: an autobiography is the equivalent of a narrative version of a timeline, stretching over the whole of a person's life. Clearly, writing an autobiography is time-consuming, and the client would need to be willing to devote time to this activity outside of counselling sessions. The counsellor also needs to be willing to spend time reading the client's autobiography. This kind of writing is quite demanding, and it can be valuable to offer the client some guidelines, such as those developed by McAdams (1993), which include ideas such as starting off by identifying the different 'chapters' in one's life, and giving each chapter a title. Another useful strategy for constructing an autobiography is to think about the key 'scenes' in one's life (as if writing a film script). The value of an autobiography is that it allows all kinds of transition shifts over the course of a life to be identified, and also allows the writer plenty of opportunity for reflection on the meaning of past events. Once completed, an autobiography becomes a document that can be shared with others, and an accomplishment that represents a source of pride, and satisfaction for the writer.

● *The choice map*: a valuable means of reframing stressful life transitions is to view them as creating opportunities to make new choices around the direction of one's life. The *choice map* technique developed by Lewchanin and Zubrod (2001; see also McLeod, 2009) represents a powerful visual tool for clients to plot the choices they have made at previous transition points in their life and thus be able to view their current choice-point in the context of fulfilling or self-denying decisions that they have made in the past.

● *Working with photographs*: some people build up large collections of photographs of family events. It can be useful to invite the client to bring in a selection of pictures that reflect stages or themes in their life. A photograph functions as an external object whose meaning can be discussed by the client and counsellor together. Photographs are emotionally evocative, and close examination of each picture will typically allow nuances in relationships and emotional states to emerge. A further means of using photographs is to invite the client to take pictures of their current personal niche, and if relevant a recent past niche, as a way of opening up discussion and reflection around what is important in the person's life, and also what might be missing.

● *Asking about the cultural meaning of transition*: there is a sense in which all major world cultures are organized around beliefs and rituals to mark the significance of normative life-course transitions such as birth, marriage and death. Particular sub-cultures may also develop rituals around transition events such as leaving school, graduating from university, leaving home, coming out as gay, moving into a new neighbourhood, divorce, retiring from paid employment, and so on. There are several ways in which the cultural meaning of transition may be relevant for counselling. It may be that the person is troubled by a transition because they have somehow missed out on a valued cultural ritual ('I left that firm after 20 years of hard work, and nobody seemed to care'). It may be that there are support groups, internet communities or self-help books available for people undergoing particular transitions (cultural resources). It may also be that the person is troubled by cultural meanings or messages around their transition. These meanings may not even be fully in awareness, but all the same are shaping the person's attitudes and feelings. For instance, in some middle-class communities, young people take a 'gap year' between school and university. An individual who did not follow that path might be haunted by a sense that they are therefore 'boring' or 'unadventurous'. In counselling, the use of the word 'should' can be a clue to this kind of issue: 'I *should* have taken more opportunity to travel when I was younger'.

● *Creating rituals*: a ritual is an event that brings people together to share a meaningful and memorable experience that embodies certain core values and beliefs about the world. World cultures have developed innumerable rituals to facilitate passage from one status to another; for example, single to married, life to death. In contemporary society, rituals that are based on organized religion may not be viewed as relevant by many people. However, it is possible to devise personal or family rituals that serve the same function, and which may even have a special meaning for participants by dint of being personalized and unique. A party is a form of transition ritual that is widely used; for example, a family leaving a neighbourhood might hold a leaving party; someone who has been divorced might hold a party to mark their freedom. Other rituals are more idiosyncratic, such as setting fire to lecture notes on completion of a degree, or burying one's favourite running shoes at the top of a hill when illness makes it impossible to continue to run marathons.

When working with a client around life transition issues, it is important to keep in mind what the client actually wants to do at that point. For some clients, it may be enough merely to acknowledge that a transition is taking place. For some clients, it may be useful to hear the suggestion of creating a ritual – maybe they will only be ready to construct and carry through that ritual many years hence. As with all aspects of counselling, the client is the judge of what is enough in terms of being able to use counselling to help them to move towards their goals.

Exercise 16.2: *Your own skills in working with transition*

Based on your personal life experiences, and also your counselling training and reading, what ideas and methods do you feel comfortable and competent in using with clients around transition issues? Are there particular transition events that are frequently reported by the clients in the organization in which you work? What are the cultural resources that are available within the organization, or in the broader community, to support people undergoing such transitions. Taking these questions as a whole, what is the counselling 'menu' that you feel able to offer clients in relation to the task of negotiating life transitions?

Conclusions

The concept of transition, and the notion that an important aspect of counselling can be involved assisting people to make sense of life transitions, represent powerful ideas within counselling theory and practice. The concept of transition bypasses medical or psychiatric definitions of troubles, and instead positions the difficulties that the person is experiencing firmly within a socio-cultural perspective. In addition, the concept of transition invites access to a rich array of cultural resources. The concept of transition also carries a message of hope: yes, the person is deeply troubled and in pieces, but this is a necessary and inevitable step towards a different role or life stage. In many organizational settings, thinking about counselling in terms of transitions can open up possibilities around different forms of preventive work: it is going to be hard for many new students at a university or new mothers in a health centre to negotiate the transition they are facing, so why not offer them information and support ahead of the event to prepare them for what they are facing and to maximize the chances that they will seek help from trained practitioners at an early stage if they need it.

Suggested further reading

One of the classics of twentieth-century social science, *The Wounded Storyteller*, captures the experience of forced transition due to illness in a way that is also applicable to many other types of transition event:

Frank, A. (1995) *The Wounded Storyteller: Body, Illness, and Ethics*. Chicago, IL: The University of Chicago Press.

Goodman, J., Schlossberg, N.K. and Anderson, M. (2006) *Counseling Adults in Transition: Linking Practice with Theory*, 3rd edn. New York: Springer.

Sugarman, L. (2009) Life course as a meta-model for counselling psychology. In R. Woolfe, S. Strawbridge, B. Douglas and W. Dryden (eds) *Handbook of Counselling Psychology*, 3rd edn. London: Sage Publications.

Dealing with difficult relationships

'It's that one doctor. I just don't seem to be able to relate to him. The rest of them are no problem, and the nurses and physios are great'.
'What happens with him? What is it that makes it so bad?'
'I've thought about this. It's the way he makes a joke in the first few seconds of the conversation'.
'What is it about his jokes?'
'They're not funny'.
'Not funny — what's so hard about that?'
'More than not funny. Its like a subtle put-down. Throws me off balance. And by the time I've got over it the consultation is over. I always forget to ask him the questions that Anita has told me I need to ask'.

Introduction

One of the tasks that can sometimes emerge in counselling is that the person wishes to explore difficulties in relating to others; for example, around communication, assertiveness, making friends, intimacy, dealing with interpersonal conflict, and similar problems. These issues can reflect general difficulties occurring in all relationships, rather than a problem within a specific relationship. In addition, there are times when a client needs to understand or resolve a specific relationship with another person. This chapter considers some possible ways of making sense of difficult relationships, and some methods that can be employed in working on this kind of task. In practice, when a client identifies an issue with another person, there will almost certainly be other tasks that arise, such as making sense of what is happening, or negotiating a life transition (i.e. leaving a person, or making a commitment to enter into a different kind of relationship with them). The material in this chapter needs to be read from a standpoint or assumption that these other issues are being dealt with: the aim is to focus solely on the face-to-face discomfort or conflict that is associated with direct contact with a troubling 'other'.

An example of embedded counselling around difficulties in relationships

As a social worker in a busy local authority department, Lisa's job involved liaison with several other organizations to secure services that would meet the care needs of her clients. Her role required her to keep her senior social worker informed about any new initiatives involving other agencies, so that he could make sure that the social work department was adopting a consistent and coherent set of procedures and standards. This time, something had gone badly wrong. Attending a meeting with representatives of another agency, the senior social worker learned about a set of projects that Lisa had developed with them, but had not told him about. Furious, and claiming that 'this isn't the first time this has happened', he insisted that the human resources (HR) department get involved to the extent of issuing a formal warning to Lisa around her work performance. The HR staff member who met with Lisa arranged to have a long session with her. In their conversation, Lisa explained that while she felt that she was a good social worker in terms of her work with clients, she felt 'at a loss' in terms of relating to her colleagues in the department. She had no friends on the team, and so lacked informal support and information networks. She felt highly anxious every time she needed to communicate on any topic to the senior social worker or anyone else in authority. Invited to give some examples of what happened when she tried to communicate with colleagues, Lisa described a series of scenarios characterized by a persistent inability to be heard by others. She said that she had long ago given up trying to do anything about this 'paralysing fear'. She then turned to her HR colleague and said: 'is there anything you can suggest that might help me to break out of this pattern?'

Exercise 17.1: *Responding to Lisa*

Imagine that you are the HR representative working with Lisa on this issue. You have 45 minutes available to you to continue the conversation outlined above. What would you say next in response to Lisa's plea for help? What themes and possibilities might you want to pursue as the conversation continued? Are there any other counselling tasks that might be relevant in this case beyond a focus on dealing with relationship difficulties? (It is advisable to complete this learning task before reading the remainder of the chapter).

Methods for working with relationship issues

There are several methods that can be used by counsellors around tasks of developing interpersonal skills and resolving relationship difficulties. Descriptions of some of these methods are provided below, along with illustrations of how they might be applied in a brief counselling session with Lisa.

Talking it through

The 'default mode' of working with most counselling tasks is 'just talking' – allowing the client an opportunity to explore all aspects of an issue, begin to make sense and find meaning in their experience, and consider possible measures that they could take to make things different. Given the space by her HR colleague to talk, what emerged for Lisa was a story of how enormously stressed and unsupported she felt in her work. She talked about how she went home in the evening and 'just collapsed', and that her health and personal relationships were being increasingly badly affected by her job. When asked how this level of stress influenced her relationship with her senior social work colleague, she replied that 'when I see my clients, they are pretty damaged people, with awful lives, but I get something back from them – in their own way they appreciate what I am doing, and I have a sense of connection with them. But with him, there's no connection. I could be anybody. He's more interested in statistics than people. I know its irrational, but when I have to interact with him it's like all the bad things about the department and the job come together at the one time'. Her counsellor continued the conversation by saying 'What comes across to me is that you have a feeling of being really powerless to influence what happens when you meet this person. Is that the way it is for you? It's just that in other situations you come across as quite bossy and in control. But all that goes out the window when you're in a meeting with *him*'.

Analysing critical incidents

A 'critical incident' is a specific, concrete example or instance of a type of event that a person finds problematic. Talking in general terms about interpersonal situations that are troubling may be useful in enabling the person to begin a process of exploring this topic. General discussion also allows the counsellor to gain a sense of the overall scope of a problem and the person's depth of feeling in relation to it. However, in the long run it is unlikely that anything will change unless the person becomes more specific. Descriptions of critical incidents can be elicited by questions such as 'can you give me an example of one time when that happened?' or 'can we look together at what happened at one of these difficult meetings?' It is helpful if the counsellor can work with the person to tease out their behavioural 'script' for that situation, building up a detailed, moment-by-moment picture of the whole sequence of what happened by collecting information on:

- Who was involved – what was the situation (context)?
- What did the person think and feel and what were their plans and goals before the event?

- What actually happened – what did the person think, feel and do at each moment, and what did other participants appear to be thinking, feeling and doing?

- What happened next, how did the situation or interaction end or resolve itself, what did the person feel about what had happened, and what did they learn?

- How typical was this incident – how did it differ from other similar incidents?

- What did you do well here? Given that this was a difficult situation for you, what did you think, do or say that you feel pleased about?

- Does the person have an idea of a preferred outcome – what would they ideally have liked to have happened?

It is best if this information emerges naturally as the person tells their story of the incident, rather than the counsellor conducting an interview where the person is passively responding to a series of questions. The aim is to instil a spirit of mutual exploration and problem-solving that will carry over into a phase of identifying alternative strategies, and then trying them out. Moving into this phase can be initiated by the counsellor by first summarizing what they have learned (empathically engaging and checking out) and then asking the person whether describing the incident has lead them to be aware of anything they might do differently to achieve a better outcome. After the person has identified some new strategies, the counsellor may wish to make some additional suggestions. Once an agreement has been reached about some different behaviours and strategies that might be tried out, the conversation can move on to a discussion of where and how they might be applied in practice. In the context of working with Lisa, her HR adviser invited her to give a detailed account of a recent meeting with her senior social worker colleague. She described a sequence in which she felt very anxious about before going in to meet him, and at various points in the conversation deliberately decided not to pass on crucial information to him, because she assumed that he would not like to hear it, and might become angry. She also recounted that by the end of the meeting she felt exhausted and 'wrung out'. The HR adviser-counsellor drew a diagram on a piece of paper to depict her understanding of what she had heard, and asked Lisa if she had any idea about what she might be able to do differently at various key points in the meeting scenario that might make things easier for her. Lisa was able to identify two possibilities. First, she could ask someone else to attend the meeting with her, because this would prevent her colleague from losing his temper. Second, she could prepare a written report in advance, and hand it to her colleague, so that she would not be tempted to avoid passing on the 'bad news'.

Box 17.1: *Couple counselling and mediation work*

The counselling methods described in this chapter are based on an assumption that the counsellor is working with the client as an individual. However, there are many situations in which it can be helpful to meet together with both participants in a dispute. The most common examples of conjoint counselling are couple counselling (Payne, 2010), where both spouses attend, and mediation work, where two or more work colleagues attend counselling together (Doherty *et al.*, 2008). Although these forms of counselling draw on basic counselling skills and ideas, they are also informed by bodies of specialist skills and knowledge – it is important for anyone thinking about working with more than one client at a time to gain some training that will prepare them for the unique challenges and opportunities associated with this area. The key strategy in couples and mediation counselling involves the practitioner structuring the meeting so that each person gets a chance to talk, and is also encouraged to listen.

Identifying unique outcomes

An alternative method for working with interpersonal and social skills difficulties is not to focus on an instance of the problem (critical incident analysis) but to take the opposite approach and find some examples of occasions where the person coped well. Narrative therapists, such as Michael White and David Epston, use the terms 'unique outcomes' and 'glittering moments' to refer to episodes that stand out for the person as being times when they were not defeated by a problem, but managed to resist it. Identifying unique outcomes is made easier if the person and counsellor have together been able to come up with a phrase they can use to refer to the 'problem'. For example, in the case introduced above, the social worker, Lisa, talked about being overcome by 'paralysing fear'. Her counsellor might invite her then to find examples of times when she had managed to resist the fear in some way, or when it had perhaps not been present at all. For people who are locked into a self-defeating pattern such as 'paralysing fear', it may take some time to think of examples of counter-instances or 'glittering moments'. However, because of the inherent resourcefulness and creativity of individuals, such instances always exist. Once the person has identified a glittering moment, the counsellor can invite them to describe what happened, perhaps using some of the questions from the critical incident method outlined earlier. This can lead to a discussion around such themes as 'what do you do to invite paralysing fear into your life?', 'what do you do that keeps paralysing fear at bay?', and 'who would not be surprised to hear about your success in overcoming paralysing fear?' These questions introduce various possibilities for the person taking charge of the situation by recognizing how they allow the problem into their life, what is involved in living a life in which the problem does not play a role, and what sources of support exist to help them to maintain a problem-free life. Further details on this method of working with interpersonal (and other) difficulties can be found in Morgan (2001). In Lisa's case, she was able to identify two occasions when she did not experience paralysing fear when speaking to senior colleagues. In reflecting on what it was that had made it possible for her to be free of fear at these times, she came up with a number of ideas: these were occasions when she had just come back from holiday, and felt less stressed, they were times when she believed passionately that what she had to say was vital for the well-being of her clients, and the meetings were held in the staff coffee area rather than round a table.

Social skills training

The social skills training approach was developed in the 1960s, mainly through collaboration in Britain between social psychologists (notably Michael Argyle) and clinical psychologists such as Peter Trower. The key idea in social skills training is that individuals possess a number of micro-skills that are required for effective interpersonal communication with others, and that the absence of these skills is associated with failure to interact with other people in particular situations. Examples of social skills include:

- observation and interpretation of facial emotional cues
- eye contact, voice quality and volume, interpersonal distance (how close you sit or stand next to someone)
- leaving conversational openings (rather than just droning on and not allowing the other person a chance to say anything)
- taking advantage of conversational openings (being a listener and knowing when it is your turn to talk, rather than rudely interrupting the speaker).

The strategy of social skills training is first to help the person to be aware of their social skills deficits, then to observe how other people successfully deploy particular skills, then practising new skills through rehearsal with a counsellor (or with members of a social skills group) and finally applying the skills in real-life situations. Video recordings can be used to allow the person to observe how they interact with others. Further information about the social skills approach can be found in Hollin and Trower (1986), Trower et al. (1978), Trower (1979) and Twentyman and McFall (1975). In the counselling session between Lisa and the HR adviser, it became apparent to both of them that Lisa had a strange unwillingness to look at other people when she was talking to them. She admitted that she preferred to deal with people over the telephone, so she would not need to look at them. The HR adviser, in her counselling role, pointed out that 'not looking' could have the result of cutting Lisa off from important information around how people were reacting to what she was saying. She agreed that this might be true. They acted out a brief scenario of reporting to a manager, once with no one looking, and once with continuous eye contact. Lisa agreed that she 'felt less paranoid' in the second scenario. She agreed to try this out over the next week and then come back and discuss it further. In the second meeting, she reported that 'looking' had made an enormous difference.

Rehearsal and role-play

From a counselling perspective, the issue of interpersonal and social skills is unusual in that it represents an area in which it is possible to enact the problem within the counselling room itself. In Lisa's case the HR adviser-counsellor invited her to try out a brief role-play 'experiment' around holding a conversation with or without eye contact. This kind of technique has the potential to produce detailed information about what a person thinks, does and feels in a particular situation. This material can then be discussed in terms of what might be done differently, and so on. One of the advantages of role-play and rehearsal is that this sort of activity can be both energizing and expressive, and deepen the person's engagement in the counselling process. *Two-chair work*, described on pp. 251–5, is a specific type of method that is used by many counsellors to enact the dynamics of how a person interacts with someone else. In one chair the client speaks as their self, and in the other chair they respond as the 'difficult' person. The client moves back and forward between the chairs as the interaction proceeds. With this method, the counsellor can be the equivalent of a stage director, encouraging each protagonist to intensify and dramatize what they are saying to each other in order to bring hidden attitudes and emotions into the open. An alternative can be that the counsellor plays one of the roles. If counselling is carried out in a group, then there is the possibility that different members of the group can play all the roles, so that the client can have the opportunity of observing what they look like when they are in particular situations. Beyond these relatively limited and straightforward approaches to using live enactment in counselling, there are also more elaborate drama-based models that can be studied and applied, such as *psychodrama* (Karp et al., 1998) and the *theatre of the oppressed* methods devised by Augusto Boal (1979, 1995). These latter techniques are perhaps hard to integrate into embedded counselling, but it can be useful for practitioner-counsellors to try them out during training as a means of learning about the possibilities that live re-enactment has as a means of enabling people to change the way they relate to others.

Self-help manuals

We live in a society characterized by a high degree of social mobility and change. As a result, many people feel uncertain about how to deal with everyday interpersonal and social situations, ranging from telling someone that you are annoyed with them (anger management) to organizing a dinner party. This pervasive uncertainty around social rules and etiquette generated a massive library of self-help books, some of which may have a role to play in counselling. When working with a client around the task of resolving a relationship difficulty, there are therefore many possibilities around referring to such books, or to recommend, lend or give a book to a person. Some clients are happy to work through a self-help text on their own, while others may prefer to use a book as a supplement to face-to-face counselling sessions. Practitioners working in particular areas may find that self-help books on communications and relationship topics are available for their specific client group, and reviewed in their specialist professional journals. Most public libraries carry good stocks of self-help books. Some of this material is also available on the internet. In the case of Lisa, her counsellor suggested that she might find it helpful to have a look at the best-selling assertiveness book, *How to be Assertive in Any Situation* (Hadfield and Hasson, 2010), and also at the popular sociological analysis of work stress written by Madeline Bunting (2004). Lisa bought herself copies of both books, and reported that they each gave her some useful ideas that she was able to apply in her relationship with her colleagues. She also added, however, that reading these books helped her to realize that she was not the only person who experienced this kind of problem – it was reassuring to learn that she was not alone in having this kind of difficulty, and that her relationship issues were definitely not a sign of impending mental breakdown.

Using community mentors, supporters and role models

Typically, a person who is struggling to deal with an interpersonal or relationship issue may find other people within their social world who can help them in a variety of ways. Often, they may have overlooked the potential value of these people, and may need the assistance of a counsellor to activate these resources. The narrative therapy tradition (Morgan, 2001) and the community support approach developed by Milne (1999) represent useful sources of ideas about how to facilitate engagement with mentors, supporters and role models. For example, a counsellor adopting a narrative approach might encourage Lisa to make contact with resourceful individuals within her social network who might be able to tell her their own personal stories of dealing with isolation and stress at work. One method of deepening the significance for Lisa of this strategy might be to ask her to think about the times she had been successful in communicating with her senior colleague, than asking 'who would be least surprised to hear about the success you have had in overcoming this problem?', and urging her to bring her 'supporter' up to date with what she had achieved.

Referral to a counsellor or psychotherapist

The case of Lisa raises the question of the limitations of the use of counselling skills by an embedded practitioner. Lisa's HR adviser asked her if she would be interested in meeting for a couple of brief sessions to talk though the difficulties she was having around communicating with colleagues. However, if Lisa felt that she needed more time, she might wish to look at other possibilities, such as referral to the Employee Assistance Programme (EAP) counselling service provided by the local authority. After a couple of meetings with the adviser, Lisa decided that it 'wouldn't do any harm' to make an appointment with an EAP counsellor, so the adviser initiated a discussion around what to expect, how to make the best use of counselling, and what alternatives were available (e.g. seeing a private practice psychotherapist). She also offered to see Lisa again at any stage to support her through the counselling process. The HR adviser was well prepared to guide Lisa around the issues involved in entering therapy, because she had made it her business to inform herself on the pros and cons of workplace counselling services (Carroll, 1996; Carroll and Walton, 1997; Coles, 2003) in relation to specialist counselling and psychotherapy that might be available from other sources, such as the NHS, third sector agencies or private practice.

Box 17.2: *Using here-and-now immediacy in counselling around relationship issues*

When a client talks to a counsellor about a specific relationship that is troublesome, they are also at that point in a relationship with the counsellor. It is quite possible that some of the issues that are being described as occurring between the client and their troubling 'other' are also being exhibited on a moment-by-moment basis in their way of relating to their counsellor. For example, Lisa complains that her senior social work colleague is unfeeling and does not listen to her, but also at times acts as though her counsellor was adopting a similar attitude to her. At one stage, she breaks off from what she is saying, and asks her counsellor if she really appreciates the seriousness of Lisa's situation, and the depth of her despair. The counsellor is alert enough to wonder what might lie behind this question, and asks Lisa to say more. This line of exploration allows Lisa to acknowledge that she is assuming that the counsellor is similar to her difficult colleague. In turn, the counsellor is then able to initiate further exploration of what this perception might mean in terms of Lisa's general pattern of being with others, and to reassure her that she does care (which strengthens their bond). This counsellor is using the skill of *immediacy* as a means of opening up a deeper exploration of her client's relationship issue, and as a way of deepening their own collaborative relationship. A good source of further information on using immediacy is found in Hill (2004).

In relation to any of these methods, the key challenge when working on an interpersonal skill task lies in not becoming too prescriptive and directive. The counsellor may be able comfortably to perform the skill that is troubling the person, or may possess a clear idea of how the skill *should* be performed, and can fall into the trap of telling the person what to do, rather than working through the issues collaboratively step by step. The counsellor can be a valuable resource ('here's what I might say in that situation') but always needs to be aware that they might not be the best, or only model for the person. If a counsellor becomes too much like a teacher in the process of carrying out this sort of task, it limits the extent to which the person has agency and ownership, or is in control of the process of change.

A useful image for a counsellor in relation to this type of task is that of functioning as a *coach*; a coach preparing their player for other times when they are on their own, and faced with the real business of the game. A coach is encouraging and supportive, and helps the player to build images of effective plays. However, a coach also knows that there are many occasions when the player will lose, and uses the experience of losing as a source of potential learning. The fields of counselling/training around interpersonal skills issues, and sports coaching, have converged in recent years in the form of an area of practice known as *life coaching*. For any counsellor whose work involves regular requests from people to explore interpersonal and social skills issues, the literature, and training courses in the area of life coaching provide an invaluable source of ideas and methods. A good source of further information on life coaching is Skibbins (2007).

Box 17.3: *Working with conflictual relationships: restorative practice in schools*

One of the hardest types of relationship issue to deal with is when one person has acted towards someone else in a violent or bullying manner. Typically in these situations there is a recourse to institutional procedures (e.g. a student may be suspended from school) or the legal system (the police may be brought in). The end result of these actions is to punish the perpetrator, with a failure to achieve any kind of reconciliation or learning. In response to the limitations of these traditional ways of dealing with this type of difficult relationship, several groups in different centres around the world have developed a model of *restorative practice*. The aim of this kind of intervention is to restore the relationship between those who have been in conflict with each other, so that they can both (or all) remain members of their community. Restorative practice is carried out in a small group meeting, attended by the protagonists in the conflict, and one or more facilitators, with the aim of conducting a dialogue based on principles of respect, dignity and care. The meeting usually proceeds through a series of stages:

- Setting the scene: who is here? Why are we here?
- Doing the business: what happened? Who has been hurt? How were they hurt?
- Are we willing to make amends?
- How shall we do that? Restoring the dignity of the persons involved; restoring relationships; doing what it takes.
- Following through: what happens next?

Although this way of working has mainly been used in schools and the youth justice system, it is applicable in many other situations where interpersonal conflict has occurred. The restorative practice model provides a structure in which counselling skills and values can be deployed in a focused manner for a particular purpose. Further information about this approach can be found in Drewery (2007), Jenkins (2006), McCluskey *et al.* (2008) and on a number of websites.

Exercise 17.2: *Your ability to work with clients around relationship difficulties*

Take a few minutes to review the ideas and strategies that are available to you in working with clients around resolving specific relationship difficulties. What are the counselling methods with which you feel comfortable and competent, and that you would be able to use with a client? What is your further learning agenda in this area? What are the theories and techniques about which you would like to learn more?

Conclusions

The task of dealing with a difficult relationship represents a challenging yet potentially highly satisfying area of counselling practice. It can be challenging because the act of facing up to what is going wrong in a relationship may lead the client to confront sensitive personal issues, or make difficult decisions. It can be satisfying because resolving an impasse with another person can be source of great relief for a client, and can unlock energy, creativity and hope. A further facet of the challenge of counselling around relationship problems is that it can touch the counsellor themselves in unexpected ways; for example, by reawakening some of their own relationship struggles. This is therefore an area of counselling where it is essential for counsellors to be willing to make use of supervision and consultative support.

Suggested further reading

A wealth of ideas about understanding different types of relationships, and how they can go wrong:

Josselson, R. (1996) *The Space Between Us: Exploring the Dimensions of Human Relationships*. Thousand Oaks, CA: Sage Publications.

Coming to terms with bereavement and loss

'I feel really down this week'.

'Any idea what that's about?'

'Yes — Danny died. He was one of the guys in the physiotherapy class. I can't believe it. He was the same age as me. Had worked in the same industry. Looked as though he was getting better. Strong as an ox. Then — gone'.

'That's terrible news. You look in a state of shock . . . Can you tell me a bit more about Danny? What kind of contact did you have with him? What was he like?'

Introduction

Loss is an inevitable part of life. It is intrinsic to being human that we form relationships and bonds with other people, and that over the course of our lifetime many of these individuals will move on or die. Issues around coming to terms with loss are present in most counselling work, even when they do not represent the primary presenting problem of the client. The present chapter explores some of the ways in which a collaborative pluralistic approach to embedded counselling can be used in working with clients around grief and loss. The chapter focuses largely on the challenge of working with people who have been bereaved. However, the basic principles of bereavement counselling are also relevant to working with clients around other loss experiences, and in work around transitions (Chapter 16).

Bereavement potentially has an impact on the whole of a person's life, from their innermost feelings and beliefs through to where they live and how much money they have to spend. A key aim of this chapter is to consider how the counselling tasks framework provides a flexible framework for encompassing all aspects of bereavement counselling. It is also clear that people deal with their grief in different ways, and find value in different kinds of counselling intervention. The chapter therefore includes a section that describes some of the methods that can be used in bereavement counselling.

The process of coming to terms with a bereavement can take a considerable amount of time. It is unlikely that any one practitioner will be involved with a client all the way from the stage of anticipating a death, through to the point where they are able to look back on their loss in a reflective manner. It makes sense to think in terms of a *loss journey* (Machin, 2008: 6): different practitioners (doctors, nurses, funeral directors, social workers, police, housing managers and others) interact with the person at different points in the journey, and provide support around specific tasks at each stage. It is certain, therefore, that practitioners working in all human service agencies will come across grieving clients on a regular basis. As a result, this chapter also addresses organizational issues around the provision of bereavement support.

An example of a task-oriented approach to bereavement counselling

Judith is a midwife in a community maternity unit with a particular interest in the emotional needs of parents of stillborn children. She completed a certificate course in counselling skills, and was encouraged by the manager of the unit to develop counselling provision specifically for grieving parents. A purpose-designed coun-selling room was created in the unit, where she could meet with parents, and she is allocated one day each week to visit clients in their homes. One of the patients with whom she worked over a period of more than one year was Sheena, an unmar-ried young woman of 21 whose son died shortly after he was born. Judith's involve-ment with Sheena incorporated a range of counselling tasks:

- *Talking through an issue in order to understand things better.* There were many occasions where Sheena just needed to talk, to 'get this stuff out of my head'. At the beginning, Sheena talked a lot to her partner, mother and friends, but felt as though she needed to protect them from some of the pain she was experi-encing, and saw Judith as a safe place to say anything she needed to say. As time went on, other people became less willing to talk about the baby, so Judith became an even more important outlet.

- *Making sense of an event or experience that is puzzling and problematic.* There were several situations where Sheena was shocked and scared about her own reactions to events: she thought that she saw her baby in the hospital and in prams in supermarkets; she became very angry with one of the doctors and she had powerful dreams. These were embarrassing things for Sheena to discuss with anyone other than Judith, who was able to help her to understand her experiences in terms of processes of grief.

- *Problem-solving, planning and decision-making.* Judith helped Sheena to make plans for a commemoration event for her son, and to create a box with objects and photographs from her time in the maternity unit. She also helped Sheena to make contact with a support group for parents of stillborn babies.

- *Changing behaviour.* Sheena became quite isolated after the bereavement, and did not want to socialize with other people. She realized that this pattern was unhelpful for her, and talked with Judith about strategies for re-entering social life.

- *Dealing with difficult feelings and emotions.* For several months, Sheena described herself as living in a world of emotional pain. Talking with Judith helped her to disentangle the strands of the pain into a sense of loss and a powerful rage. Judith introduced some ways of channelling these emotions, using artwork and two-chair work, and also provided opportunities for Sheena to 'give in to my tears'.

- *Finding, analysing and acting on information.* Soon after the death of her son, Sheena was desperate to understand what had happened. Judith supported her in arranging a meeting with the consultant to get an explanation of how and why her baby had died. Part of the preparation for this meeting involved deciding on which questions to ask, and how to remain rational.

- *Undoing self-criticism and enhancing self-care.* A major theme in Sheena's thinking after the event was that she must be to blame for what had happened. This psycho-logical self-criticism spilled over into lack of self-care around diet. Judith offered support and challenge around these issues during counselling conversations.

- *Negotiating a life transition.* The bereavement was experienced by Sheena as a major turning point in her life. Towards the end of their contact with each other, Judith invited Sheena to spend one of their meetings reflecting on what she had learned from her loss, and how she wanted her life to be different moving into the future.

- *Dealing with difficult or painful relationships.* Sheena had always had a trou-bled relationship with her mother. Through the time of the bereavement, her mother made a great effort to be supportive, but Sheena found it hard to accept her help. At the same time, Sheena's partner became more and more emotion-ally withdrawn, and eventually they separated. These issues were explored in counselling with the result that Sheena became able to differentiate between 'mum then' and 'mum now', and allow her mother to be closer to her.

This case is unusual in the sense that one practitioner-counsellor was able to accompany her client all the way through her grief journey. However, it illustrates the pervasive quality of the impact of loss, and the value of adopting a counselling framework that acknowledges all dimensions of the experience of clients. For Sheena as a counsellor or helper, the idea of a counselling 'menu' provided an invaluable means of separating out the different strands of Sheena's life that needed to be repaired. On most of the times they met, Sheena was 'all over the place', struggling to cope with the messy interconnectedness of various issues. In response, Judith offered a reliable presence, empathic and also business-like: 'what I am picking up for you is that there are these three things that are really bothering you today – X and Y and Z. Does that seem right to you, or have I missed something? OK, what order will we take them in? Let's see if we can make some progress on each of them, one at a time, in the time we have available'.

Exercise 18.1: *Your personal experience of loss*

Construct a loss timeline (there are instructions on how to draw a timeline on pp. 265–6). Use this line to illustrate the losses you have experienced in your life, and how these events have been associated with high and low points across the course of your life as a whole. Once you have created your loss timeline, reflect on the extent to which you have been able to come to terms with various losses, or whether there are some grieving processes that are still ongoing for you. Finally, give some further consideration to the ways in which your experience of loss has left you with knowledge and sensitivity that you can use in your work with grieving clients, or areas of vulnerability that might make you resistant to opening yourself up to the grief of another person. It can be very helpful to carry out this learning activity in the context of a supportive group.

Making sense of the experience of loss and grief

As with any problem that a client brings to counselling, it is helpful for a client experiencing a bereavement to be able to get some kind of handle on what they are feeling in terms of a coherent and convincing explanatory framework. There are four theoretical frameworks that are particularly widely used by bereavement counsellors: *psychodynamic attachment theory, Worden's tasks model*, the *dual process* model and *narrative* theory. Behind these specially loss-focused theories, there are many other ideas within the counselling and psychology literature that can be valuable in relation to specific aspects of bereavement work, for example, ideas around emotions (Chapter 11) and transitions (Chapter 16).

The use of attachment theory in bereavement counselling

The psychoanalytic psychotherapist and researcher, John Bowlby, made a contribution to counselling and psychotherapy theory and practice that had an immense impact over the last 50 years. Bowlby highlighted the significance of *attachment* bonds in human relationships. The basic idea behind Bowlby's work is the notion that the survival of babies and infants is contingent on their capacity to form a secure attachment with a carer or carers. Babies are not able to look after themselves, so need to have someone else who will feed them, keep them warm and dry, and provide stimulation and social contact. This aspect of life is so important for human beings that attachment mechanisms are biologically 'wired in' to the human nervous system. Bowlby was able to show that the availability of an emotional 'secure base' in early childhood was associated with an ability to enjoy successful intimacy relationships, friendships and work collaboration in later life. By contrast, when the mother or other carers behaved in a way that was inconsistent or neglectful, the person was likely to develop a pattern of *insecure attachment* that persisted through the rest of their life. In an extensive programme of research, attachment researchers have been able to identify three distinct patterns of insecure attachment:

- *Preoccupied/ambivalent*: the person has received inconsistent patterns of care in childhood, which has left them wishing to be close to others, but feeling powerless to do anything to make this happen, angry when other people let them down, and not easily comforted.

- *Dismissive*: in childhood the person's physical needs were taken care of, but there was little emotional closeness – as an adult they act as though they do not need to be close to anyone else.

- *Fearful*: the child was exposed to active neglect or abuse, and as a result wants to be close to others but experiences high levels of fear and anxiety when this happens.

These ideas have several implications for bereavement counselling. Attachment patterns are exhibited in the way that an individual copes with loss. On the whole, a person who has a secure attachment style is likely to be able to use anyone else who is available to them (friends, family, professionals) to work through their grief in a straightforward and balanced manner.

People who have emerged from childhood with different types of insecure attachment patterns will respond to loss in ways that are shaped by their attachment style: a person with an ambivalent attachment style will have a strong need to talk, but will quite possibly blame others as a means of deflecting attention from their own vulnerability; a dismissive attachment pattern is associated with appearing to be unaffected by a loss, until feelings are triggered by a later event; fearful attachment is expressed through turmoil – a chaotic response to the loss that shifts unpredictably between emotional states. These attachment styles are reflected not only in the way that the person exhibits grief and loss in their everyday life, but also in the way that they relate to counsellors and other professional practitioners around the issue of their bereavement. From a psychodynamic perspective, attachment patterns can be viewed as a form of transference. In turn, the counsellor's own attachment style shapes their counter-transference response to the client. For example, a practitioner with a dismissive attachment style will tend to minimize the significance of a client's loss. In recent years there has been a vast outpouring of research and clinical writing around the role of attachment in counselling and psychotherapy. The most accessible account of how attachment theory can be applied in counselling practice can be found in the writings of the British psycho-analytic psychotherapist, Jeremy Holmes (1999a, b, 2000, 2001).

Worden's bereavement tasks model

Many widely used bereavement counselling texts, such as Lendrum and Syme (2004) and Mallon (2010) are organized around the idea that the person experiencing loss passed through a transition that comprises a series of stages of learning to cope. However, the recent thinking on this topic has tended to question the notion of fixed stages, which have been replaced by the idea that dealing with bereavement confronts the person with a set of *tasks*, which may differ in salience for each individual, and which may be carried out in no particular order. An influential model of bereavement was formulated by William Worden (2001), who identified four key tasks of mourning:

1 To accept the reality of the loss.
2 To work through the pain of grief.
3 To adjust to an environment in which the deceased is missing.
4 To emotionally relocate the deceased and move on with life.

Worden (2001) argues that the notion of stages or phases of grief implies a certain level of passivity on the part of the grieving person – there is nothing much that they can do other than wait for the effect of 'time as a great healer'. By contrast, his task model opens up an agenda for the client and counsellor to work together on making a difference. The Worden model is consistent with the task model and counsellor's menu outlined in this book. However, the Worden tasks are broader in scope than the task list introduced in Chapter 5. The latter are possibly more useful in specifying micro-steps that can be taken within specific counselling meetings, whereas the Worden tasks model is perhaps particularly useful in exploring with the client the work that may need to be done in more general terms. It is important to note that Worden's (2001) book covers a lot more than just the tasks of mourning model. In it, he discusses the nature of grief in great detail, and the ways in which different psychological and social factors can have an influence on the grieving process. The book also incorporates several vivid case vignettes.

The dual process model of coping with bereavement

A valuable perspective on the experience of coping with loss has been developed by Margaret Stroebe and Henk Schut (1999), who identify two broad types of psychological activity that are involved in grieving: *loss-oriented* and *restoration-oriented*. Loss-oriented tasks include dealing with the intrusion of feelings of loss and despair, and letting go of ties with the deceased person. Restoration tasks include doing new things and developing new relationships. Clearly, in any individual case, the balance between these tasks will be unique. One of the way in which this model is relevant for counselling is that Stroebe and Schut (1999) suggest that the person *oscillates* between these two orientations. For example, a period of time devoted to restoration-oriented activities may be helpful for a person, but will inevitably expose them to many reminders and emotional triggers ('it was great to go to the theatre today with my new friends, but it was also painful that X could not be there'). Similarly, a period of time immersed in feelings and memories will inevitably lead to a sense of wanting to do something different. The dual process model implies that both stages and tasks occur, but in a dynamic back-and-forward manner.

Box 18.1: *Myths of coping with loss*

In a classic paper, Wortman and Silver (1989) reviewed the research literature on loss and grief, and came to the conclusion that there are no fixed and predictable patterns of coping with loss: there are major differences between people in terms of how severely they are affected, how long the grieving process takes, whether they go through stages of anger and depression, and so on. Wortman and Silver (1989) urge caution on the part of those working in the field of bereavement against allowing themselves to be caught up in prevailing 'myths' around the grieving process. The implication is that while theory and research on bereavement may be valuable as a means of sensitizing practitioners to *possible* patterns of coping with loss, in the end the touchstone always needs to be the reality being experienced by the client themself.

A narrative perspective on bereavement

A narrative approach to grief and loss challenges the assumption, implicit in other models of bereavement, that the ultimate goal of grieving is to 'move on' in the sense of putting the loss in the past and constructing a new life. A narrative perspective emphasizes the idea that well-being and meaningful engagement in social life is based on being able to develop a rich and coherent life story or biography, which is connected in myriad ways to the stories and biographies of others, whether alive or dead. From a narrative perspective, therefore, the process of coming to terms with bereavement involves finding an enduring place for the story of the deceased person in the ongoing lives and stories of those who knew them. This idea is summarized very well in a classic paper by the British sociologist and loss theorist Tony Walter (1999a: 7, emphasis in original):

> . . . survivors typically want to talk about the deceased and to talk with others who knew him or her. Together they construct a story that places the dead within their lives, a story capable of enduring through time. The *purpose* of grief is therefore the construction of a durable

biography that enables the living to integrate the memory of the dead into their ongoing lives; the *process* by which this is achieved is principally conversation with others who knew the deceased.

Walter suggests that many people living in modern industrial societies have a great deal to learn in respect of mourning, from the attitudes and practices of people in traditional societies, where the dead are 'placed within life' in many ways on an everyday basis.

There are many strategies for using counselling to accomplish this kind of narrative continuity of the deceased. One example can be found in the 'saying hullo' method devised by Michael White (1998). In one case study White (1998) described a way of working that centred on a process of incorporating the deceased person into the life of a surviving spouse (Mary) who was still deeply affected by the loss of her husband, Ron, five years after his death. White asked questions that invited Mary to 'say hullo' to Ron, such as:

- If you were seeing yourself through Ron's eyes right now, what would you be noticing about yourself that you would appreciate?

- What do you know about yourself that you are awakened to when you bring about the enjoyable things that Ron knew about you?

- How could you let others know that you have reclaimed some of the discoveries about yourself that were clearly visible to Ron?

This kind of conversation positions the deceased person not as a fixed set of memories that exist in the mind of the grieving person, but as an active participant in the life not only of the survivor but also the lives of other people as well.

The underlying philosophy and principles of a narrative approach are explored in more detail by Walter (1999b) and in the writings of the American psychotherapist Robert Neimeyer (2005, 2006; Neimeyer *et al.*, 2006).

The various theoretical perspectives on the grieving process that have been discussed in this section do not need to be viewed as mutually exclusive. It is not necessary to regard some of them as 'right' and others as 'wrong'. Grief and loss is a complex phenomenon, and different people make sense of it in different ways or at different points in their grief journey. For counsellors, these theories can be used as *resources for understanding* or as 'lenses' through which the experience of bereavement can be viewed.

Box 18.2: *Bereavement as a result of suicide: a special case*

A situation in which someone finds themselves bereaved due to the suicide of a friend, family member or close work colleague represents a particular challenge in counselling. The usual process of grief is overlaid with complex layers of confusion, shock, guilt, shame, betrayal and anger, and questions about whether vital clues were missed and opportunities to save the person were lost. There are two books that are particularly valuable (for both practitioners and clients) in relation to bereavement by suicide: Silent Grief: Living in the Wake of Suicide (Lukas and Seiden, 2007) and A Special Scar: The Experiences of People Bereaved by Suicide (Wertheimer, 2001).

Methods for working with bereavement issues

The case of Sheena, introduced earlier in this chapter, illustrates the all-encompassing nature of bereavement, and the way that counselling may involve many different types of counselling task and many different counselling methods. In principle, all of the methods described in previous chapters may be potentially relevant when working with a client around issues of bereavement and loss. As with any issue, the single most helpful method is probably 'just talking'. However, there are some methods that are particularly widely drawn upon by bereavement practitioners:

Using metaphor

People who are struggling with loss may have a sense that what is happening for them is chaotic and out of control, and also that it lacks meaning. Within the person's way of talking, however, they may be using metaphors that can be further developed to create hope and meaning. It may also be useful for the counsellor to offer such metaphors. The kinds of metaphors that can be particularly useful in bereavement counselling include the idea that life is a *journey* and that the loss is a stage in that journey, and that as beings in nature, we all participate in a *cycle* of death and renewal. In some situations, it can be useful to convey a metaphor in the form of a 'healing story' (Burns, 2005, 2007).

Creative arts methods

The use of creative art media such as drawing and painting, sculpting, music, and photography, can play a key role in many aspects of the bereavement counselling process. For example, in a counselling session, the emotional reality of the client's feelings for the lost person may be more readily expressed if the client brings in a photograph of the person, or a piece of music that is associated with the person. Creating a drawing, painting, montage or sculpture may allow the person an outlet for feelings, and also a way of representing and organizing different strands of thought and feeling. Creating a piece of art, such as a picture, can also assist reflection and meaning-making in functioning as an external object that the client and counsellor can discuss together. Such objects also serve as markers of progress: 'I remember the emotional state that led me to make that picture, and I realize that I don't feel like that now'.

Cultural resources

There are many cultural resources that people can use as sources of meaning and guides to action when dealing with loss. These resources include: novels, poems, music, movies and drama; self-help books and websites; support networks and groups for people experiencing different types of loss. In addition to these bereavement-specific cultural resources, there are innumerable generic cultural resources, ranging from tending a garden through to joining an evening class, that may be experienced as healing by particular individuals.

Box 18.3: *Pets and animals as cultural resources*

There is a great deal of evidence that interacting with animals can have a positive impact on health and well-being. For example, having a dog offers companionship, an opportunity to be in a caring role, regular exercise and an unthreatening way to interact with new people. A useful review of the benefits of animals as an adjunct to counselling can be found in Wells (2011).

Spirituality

For many people, spiritual practices and religious observance represent important ways in which they make sense of bereavement and loss, and make a healing connection with other people. In working with clients who are experiencing bereavement, it is always useful to invite them to talk about their religious and spiritual involvement, and the ways in which they are able to draw on these areas in coping with their loss.

Cultural sensitivity

The meaning of death, and the rituals that are associated with it, vary significantly across different cultures. When counselling a client around bereavement issues, it is helpful to ask about any cultural beliefs and expectations that might be relevant to the way they are feeling. Sources of further information on cultural aspects of death and grief can be found in Dickenson and Johnson (1993), Hockey *et al.* (2001) and Walter (1999b).

Exercise 18.2: *Mourning in different cultures*

Write a description of the mourning rituals that are associated with your own cultural group; for example, how funerals are conducted, and what happens at home and within families to commemorate losses. Interview at least two other people from different cultural backgrounds around how these issues are dealt with in their cultures. If you are a member of a learning group that includes representatives from different cultures, you may be able to carry out this activity in your group. The aim of this learning exercise is to develop awareness of the diversity of ways in which grief can be understood and managed.

Box 18.3: *Bereavement counselling with people with learning disabilities*

There are a range of issues that need to be taken into consideration when working on bereavement issues with a person who is living with a learning disability. The client may not readily understand the concept of death, and they may have reduced autonomy in respect of being able to carry out grieving rituals such as visiting a graveside. A valuable source of further information in respect of this area of counselling is *Bereavement Counselling for People with Learning Disabilites* by Sue Read (2007). Among other things, this book includes examples of handouts and visual materials that can be used with clients from this group.

The organizational context of bereavement work

There are a number of specialist bereavement counselling services that have been established, such as CRUSE in the UK, which tend to focus on the needs of people with more severe grief reactions, and usually work with clients some time after the bereavement, rather than in the immediate aftermath of the loss. There are also counselling services, and social workers trained in counselling approaches, within most hospices. Beyond this, the majority of bereaved people who seek help and support from beyond their family network turn to a wide range of practitioners including clergy, other members of faith communities, health care professions, funeral directors, teachers and social workers.

The evidence from research seems to suggest that while formal bereavement counselling is effective in many cases (Schut and Stroebe, 2005; Stroebe *et al.*, 2005), there are many clients who enter counselling but do not seem to be at the right point to make best use of it – it is those people with complicated and severe grief reactions that are helped most by formal, regular scheduled therapy. Formal counselling services that have been organized on an 'outreach' basis, where all people in a community who have been bereaved are routinely invited to receive counselling, do not appear to be particularly helpful (Schut and Stroebe, 2005). The key factors here are that the person has not made a deliberate decision to seek help, may not be motivated or ready to take advantage of counselling, may not need it, or may even be disturbed by the offer of help. These findings make intuitive sense – in the time immediately following a death, a person is to a large extent in a state of shock, and not ready to talk, Also, there are many cultural resources available to people to help them cope with their grief (Hockey *et al.*, 2001; Walter, 1999b). For example, religious rituals and teachings are immensely valuable for many people during their experience of loss. There are also many novels and films that sensitively present healing images of the meanings of death. It is likely that professional nurses, doctors, teachers and others who may be the first line of support for people who have been bereaved, and are sensitive enough to respond to moments when the person wishes to talk, have a particularly important role to play. It is essential for those offering embedded counselling to be aware of situations where the person is undergoing complicated grief, where the loss has perhaps triggered other underlying issues, and be in a position to make a referral to a specialist service.

Within large organizations in fields such as education, health care and social services, responding to the needs of clients and service users who are coping with death and bereavement is a recurring issue. Typically, such organizations tend to provide training for practitioners in how to support clients who have experienced loss, and develop links with representatives of faith communities and counselling services. Large organizations may also develop policies around staff absence, family or colleague bereavement, and methods for conveying accurate information to members of the organization (e.g. when a child has died, everyone in the school needs to be told), and remembrance services or other similar events. It is usually helpful if there is one person who has the responsibility for co-ordinating these functions. At an organizational level, a death can have a 'ripple' effect. For instance, in a busy hospital patients will die every day, but the unexpected death of a well-known member of staff may have an impact on dozens of patients and colleagues. The way that an organization responds to loss is likely to remain in the memory of staff and service users – it represents a key symbolic and practical indicator of the caring ethos of the organization as a whole.

Beyond the organizational level, there are also bereavement counselling services that are organized on a regional or national level to respond to the needs of people at times of natural disaster, accidents, war, terrorist attack and multiple shooting incidents. It is clear that the immediate requirement is for some kind of 'psychological first aid' (see Chapter 19), but there may be demand for bereavement counselling at a later date. In some instances, self-help organizations are set up to support people who have been affected by specific incidents.

Exercise 18.3: *Reviewing your learning requirements around working with loss*

Based on what you have read in this chapter, and other sources you have consulted, make a list of what you *already know* about working with clients around issues of grief and loss. Make another list of areas that you now feel that you want to know more about – theories, interventions, research – in order to be better prepared for working with clients around these issues.

Conclusions

In many ways, the issues associated with bereavement counselling function as a microcosm for the field of counselling as a whole. Coping with bereavement and loss is a universal human experience. Bereavement is not primarily a 'mental health' issue (although it may become one), but instead represents a life event that potentially can challenge all aspects of a person's being and relationships. Counselling can be valuable in coming to terms with bereavement, but so can many other types of activity – the question of the place of counselling alongside other cultural resources arises as a central question in respect of how bereavement support is organized and delivered. Bereavement is an experience that inevitably impacts on the work roles of practitioners in all areas of human service provision, and raises questions around the level of training and preparedness that is provided for those working in such roles.

The main message of this chapter is that there exists a rich literature around the topic of bereavement counselling, and many ideas about how to make sense of grief and loss and how to facilitate a process of personal healing. The multifaceted nature of reactions to loss, and the fact that bereaved individuals may call on others for emotional support at different stages in the grief journey, underscores the value of adopting a flexible approach to counselling that focuses on collaboration around specific tasks that are most salient for the person at particular moments.

Suggested further reading

Two invaluable collections, which place bereavement and loss in a broader cultural and social context through well-chosen excerpts from many key sources, are:

Earle, S., Bartholomew, C. and Komaromy, C. (eds) (2008a) *Making Sense of Death, Dying and Bereavement*: An Anthology. London: Sage Publications.

Earle, S., Komaromy, C. and Bartholomew, C. (eds) (2008b) *Death and Dying: A Reader*. London: Sage Publications.

The issues involved in providing organizational-level emotional support and counselling for bereavement have been the focus of considerable attention within the schools system. Some of the practical ideas and policies that have emerged from these debates can be found in:

Holland, J. (2008) How schools can support children who experience loss and death, *British Journal of Guidance and Counselling*, 36: 411–24.

Katz, J. (2001) Supporting bereaved children at school. In J. Hockey, J. Katz and N. Small (eds) *Grief, Mourning and Death Ritual*. Maidenhead: Open University Press.

Mallon, B. (2010) *Working with Bereaved Children and Young People*. London: Sage Publications.

A comprehensive review of recent developments in theory, research and practice around the topic of bereavement counselling can be found in:

Neimeyer, R.A., Harris, D.L., Winokuer, H.R. and Thornton, G.F. (eds) (2011) *Grief and Bereavement in Contemporary Society: Bridging Research and Practice*. New York: Routledge.

A review and critique of theories of grief can be found in:

Small, N. (2001) Theories of grief: a critical review. In J. Hockey, J. Katz and N. Small (eds) *Grief, Mourning and Death Ritual*. Maidenhead: Open University Press.

In the end, bereavement counselling rests on an openness to talking about the meaning and significance of death. The writings of Irving Yalom represent an invaluable resource for counsellors in respect of facing up to the reality of death as part of life. His recent book on this topic masterfully brings together the fruits of decades of thinking, clinical practice and research on this topic:

Yalom, I. (2008) *Staring at the Sun: Being at Peace with your own Mortality: Overcoming the Terror of Death*. London: Piatkus.

Dealing with difficult situations in counselling

'There is something I am wanting to bring up'.
'OK. This sounds scary'.
'You said that your days of painting and decorating were over. No more climbing up ladders. And now you're telling me that you spent the weekend doing just that. What's going on? I'm feeling a bit annoyed with you. And also worried — this isn't good for you'.
'I know, I know. Anita said the same thing'.

Introduction

A central theme within this book has been the idea of the counselling 'space'. It has been argued that counselling represents a unique and invaluable form of support with respect to life in complex societies, through making available a relationship which offers a blame-free, safe space for reflection on problems in living, and the development of solutions. Earlier chapters have examined what is involved in creating such a space, then using it for different kinds of purposes. The aim of this chapter is to consider some of the issues involved in *maintaining* a counselling space, particularly in relation to threats to its integrity and functionality. This chapter looks at *difficult situations* – moments in counselling where it may become impossible to continue with a counselling or therapeutic conversation.

It is important for a skilled counsellor to be able routinely to monitor what is happening in the counselling relationship, to be aware of any possibility that a threat to the space may be building up. In order to be able to respond to the person in a caring and responsible manner, anyone in a counselling role should have a clear idea of their strategies for dealing with difficult situations. For this reason, *preparation* for offering a counselling relationship should always involve a process of working through 'worst case' scenarios, so that the counsellor is as ready as they can be to cope with any difficult situations that may arise. In these situations, the person seeking help may be at their most vulnerable, so it is especially important for their counsellor to have a clear idea of how they will handle whatever comes up.

In this chapter, a range of difficult situations are described with suggestions offered for ways of responding to them. Within the limits of this chapter, it is not possible to provide an exhaustive coverage of all of the strategies that might be employed in dealing with these scenarios. In many cases, organizations will have their own protocols for handling difficult issues, which will draw on resources that may be available locally; for example, the immediate involvement of a more experienced colleague. Further information and ideas for dealing with difficult situations can be obtained from the list of recommended reading at the end of the chapter.

Losing it

Suicidal and violent behaviour are possibilities that may occur in any kind of helping agency. In situations where suicidal or violent intentions emerge, practitioners whose counselling is embedded within other professional roles should be able to draw upon procedures and protocols that have already been put into place within their place of work. There is another type of crisis, however, that is more specifically associated with counselling, which can be characterized as 'losing it'. This kind of episode occurs when a person is exploring a life problem that has a strong emotional content, and reaches a stage at which they become overwhelmed by fear to the point that they become unable to continue to engage in rational dialogue. It is as though the person's psychological processes close down to keep them safe, and they become out of touch and detached from what other people might consider to be 'reality'. There are three main forms of 'losing it' that can take place in counselling sessions:

- panic attacks
- dissociation
- hallucinatory and delusional behaviour.

Each of these phenomena make it hard, or impossible to continue pursing any of the counselling tasks described in Chapters 5, because effective involvement in such tasks requires a capacity to respond to another person and engage in some kind of collaborative conversation or dialogue. When a person has 'lost it', they have withdrawn from dialogue with external others, and are largely focusing on some aspect of their own inner experiencing.

Panic attacks are associated with a set of reactions that take place when a person experiences high levels of anxiety in a specific situation. Typically, a person will have a panic attack when they feel trapped and enclosed with no possibility of escape. This may happen in a lift, aeroplane, or any other enclosed space. A counselling session, where a person might have a sense of being 'on the spot' or under pressure, can quite easily be experienced in this kind of way. What seems to happen in a panic sequence is that the person begins to have thoughts of being trapped and powerless, which in turn triggers a physical 'flight' response, characterized by fast, shallow breathing. This physiological activity quickly produces a whole set of other physical symptoms, such as a feeling of pins and needles in hands and arms, pressure across the chest, and a sense of faintness. The person then pays attention more and more to these symptoms, which are experienced and highly alarming, and generate an even higher level of thoughts of being out of control, or even of dying. In turn, these thoughts and images of being out of control and dying lead to even faster, shallower breathing, and more physical symptoms. A panic attack is a spiral which can lead to loss of consciousness or actual flight (the person runs away, or tries to). The person will subsequently be motivated to avoid the situation that triggered the attack, and will be even more fearful if required to enter that situation. There are several accessible sources of information on managing panic, which are of value for both counsellors and those seeking help (e.g. Baker, 2003; Ingham, 2000).

Dissociation can be regarded as a cognitive process for dealing with overwhelming threatening thoughts (e.g. memories of highly distressing and traumatic events) and emotions by not allowing these thoughts and emotions into awareness. The person achieves this by focusing their attention on something that is neutral or safe as an alternative to what is threatening and painful. There are usually two processes that enable a person to do this. First, the person may attempt to stop breathing. This cuts off their awareness of what they are feeling, and almost makes time 'stand still'. Second, the person may find an image in their mind to attend to, or may focus their attention on an apparently meaningless object in the room, such as the corner radiator, or a light bulb. From the perspective of the counsellor, the person will be experienced as having 'gone away' – they will act as though they do not hear what the counsellor is saying, and are almost unaware of the counsellor's presence. A less extreme variant of this pattern can occur when a person deals with threatening thoughts and emotions by changing the topic of conversation – from the perspective of the counsellor this activity is experienced as a lack of continuity or coherence in the conversation.

Hallucinations and delusions can be viewed as ways that a person has developed over a period of time for dealing with persistent impossibly difficult and stressful thoughts and emotions. What seems to happen is that these thoughts and emotions become organized into voices that the person hears, imaginary people or objects that they see, or belief systems that they organize their life around.

Box 19.1: *Working with people who are hard to reach*

Sometimes, a person may be looking for help with a problem in living, but experience great difficulty in expressing what they need. Such individuals may have a life that is characterized by general communication problems; for example, people who have learning difficulties or Alzheimer's disease. Other people may be incapacitated by temporary states of fear, anxiety or voice hearing, which may make it hard for them to stay focused on a conversation. The American person-centred therapist, Garry Prouty, has developed some useful methods for making basic emotional and interpersonal contact with people who are hard to reach. He recommends that a counsellor faced by a person who is withdrawn or unable to communicate effectively should concentrate on solely making concrete and literal empathic reflections. Prouty (2000) describes five types of basic contact-making reflections:

1 *Situational reflections*: statements of the counsellor's awareness of the person's situation or environment. For example: 'you are sitting on the sofa'.
2 *Facial reflections*: statements that seek to capture the pre-expressive feelings of the person, as embodied in their face. For example: 'you are smiling'.
3 *Word-for-word reflections*: restatements of single words, sentences and other sounds made by the person.
4 *Body reflections*: the counsellor moves their own body to match the postures or movements made by the person.
5 *Reiterative reflections*: if any of the previous types of statements appear to be effective in establishing contact, they are repeated.

The assumption behind these literal empathic reflective methods is that the person has for the moment lost contact with the external world, and that if re-contact is to occur, it needs to begin with simple moves that are unthreatening under the control of the person, and uncomplex. Of course, it is essential to offer these statements in a gentle and respectful manner. Prouty (2000) offers an example of his work with an older woman, Dorothy, who was an institutionalized resident of a psychiatric facility. She mumbled for about 10 minutes, while Prouty reflected back whatever words he could make out. Then, she made a clear statement, 'come with me', which Prouty again reflected back. She then led him to the corner of the day room, and they stood there silently for some time. She put her hand against the wall and said 'cold'. He put his hand also on the wall, and repeated 'cold'. He noted that 'she had been holding my hand all along; but when I reflected her, she would tighten her grip'. Dorothy's words then gradually began to make more sense: 'I don't like it here. I'm so tired . . . so tired' (*with tears*). (Prouty, 2000: 69)

Further information about this method can be found in Prouty *et al.* (2002) and Peters (1999). What it offers is a disciplined and caring means of patiently staying as close as possible to the experience of someone who is withdrawn, until the point where they feel able to enter into a reciprocal relationship.

There are a set of basic methods for responding to these difficult situations. Essentially, a counsellor confronted with any of these types of 'losing it' response needs to be able to engage constructively at the *cognitive, bodily* and *social-interpersonal* levels. At a cognitive level, the person is likely to be generating a steady stream of 'self-talk' (things they are saying to themselves in their head, or are being said by voices or internalized critical others) that are quite destructive and negative; for example, 'I can't cope', 'I am going to die', 'I am worthless', and so on. It can be helpful for a counsellor to keep talking in a calm and reassuring manner and introduce more positive self-statements into the person's awareness, such 'you will be all right', 'my sense is that you are afraid now, but we can see this through together'. It may be that the counsellor can introduce hopeful images or statements that the person has shared on a previous occasion. It may also be helpful for the counsellor to offer an explanation of what is happening and what can be done, such as 'I think that what you were beginning to talk about was something that is very frightening for you, and now you need to cut yourself off from it by . . . I think what might be helpful now could be if you listen to me and . . .'. Another very important area for a counsellor to attend to is the physical or bodily response of the person, particularly their breathing. People who are in a process of 'losing it' are often breathing fast and shallow, or slow (holding breath). It can be useful for a counsellor to draw the person's attention to their breathing ('I'm aware that you seem to be . . .') and instruct them in breathing regularly and deeply. For example, it may be effective to invite the person to 'breathe with me – in as far as you can – one, two, three, four, five, six, seven – and out again – one, two . . .'). In panic situations, it can be useful for a person to breathe into and out of a bag, or their cupped hands, as a means of reducing their oxygen intake. In some situations, the person's posture may be frozen, or hunched over (which inhibits breathing) and it can be useful to encourage them to begin to move, perhaps to walk. Finally, a common feature of these ways of coping is a withdrawal of contact from the other, and a retreat into a private world. It can be helpful to encourage the person to look at the counsellor, to engage in eye contact, and (if appropriate in the context of the relationship) to touch. Accompanied by calm, confident talking on the part of the counsellor, the re-establishment of interpersonal contact can both enable the person to pay less attention to their own inner processes, and to gain a sense of safety and security ('there is someone here I can trust, and rely on') that can make whatever it was that was scary seem a bit more bearable. These are not methods in themselves that are necessarily going to eliminate panic, dissociation or voice-hearing from a person's life forever – they are strategies for helping someone who is seeking counselling to manage their thoughts and feelings in the moment, so that they may, if they choose, continue to engage in a counselling conversation.

Within Western society, experiences of panic, dissociation and hallucination are often addressed through psychiatric interventions, such as administration of drug treatment, or by specialist psychotherapeutic interventions such as cognitive-behaviour therapy (CBT). Although the methods being described here are consistent with a psychiatric or CBT approach, they are better viewed as a crisis-management strategy, designed to enable the person to make use of a counselling relationship and space to talk. In most cases, it will be helpful to explore with the person the potential value of receiving more specialist help for their panic, voice-hearing or dissociation. It is therefore important for anyone offering a counselling relationship to be informed about the possibilities for such specialist help that is available within their community, and the procedures for making referrals.

Box 19.2: *Mental health first aid*

An important development over the past decade has been the creation of training materials and practical guidelines based on a model of *mental health first aid* devised in Australia by Betty Kitchener and Anthony Jorm. The aim of this initiative is to provide ordinary people with concepts and techniques that they can use to come to the assistance of anyone who is experiencing a mental health crisis. Further information on this approach can be found in Kitchener and Jorm (2009). Similar protocols have been developed for emergency services workers responding to accidents or disasters under the title of *psychological first aid* (Uhernik and Husson, 2009). These programmes are potentially of great value in introducing and disseminating counselling ideas into organizations, because it is possible to teach people about mental health first aid in a brief seminar. Those within organizations who have already completed counselling skills training are in a good position to champion the adoption of mental health aid through being trained as trainers.

Referring on

The final section of this chapter deals with the process of *referring on* a person seeking help to a specialist service or agency. Being willing and able to refer individuals to other sources of help is an essential competence for any practitioner who is offering counselling that is embedded in another professional role, such as that of nurse, doctor or teacher. The kind of factors that can bring the issue of referral into the frame are when the person seeking help:

- needs more time than the counsellor is able to give, or more frequent meetings
- is primarily looking for practical information and advice, rather than an opportunity to 'talk things through'
- describes problems in living that the counsellor believes are beyond their capacity to work with
- might gain a lot from making use of a specialist agency where there are practitioners available who have a wealth of knowledge and experience in relation to the type of problem the person has described (i.e. there is somewhere better for them to go)

- is involved in a prior relationship with the counsellor that would be incompatible with the creation of a secure and confidential counselling space.

It is important to realize that counselling, as envisaged in this book, is a generic form of helping, through which, in principle, many types of problem in living can be addressed by many different types of practitioner. The strength of counselling is that, compared to other forms of help, it is flexible and accessible – a matter of talking to someone who is equipped to listen and engage in a therapeutic conversation. However, it is also necessary to recognize that there exists a huge array of professional and voluntary groups and agencies that have developed knowledge and skill in helping people to deal with specific types of problems. There is little point in any counsellor struggling to help someone with a problem when there are other practitioners available who may have better resources in relation to that problem.

The key steps in the referral process for a counsellor are: (a) knowing about alternative resources that are available; (b) engaging the person in a discussion around the possibility of seeing someone else; and (c) making the referral and managing the 'passing over' stage. These are each quite sensitive tasks.

Part of the work of preparing to offer counselling relationships involves building up a network of agencies to whom people may be referred, and keeping this database updated. It is necessary for any service or agency to know about the type of client they are willing to work with, the kind of service they offer, how a person can access the service, who pays, and the waiting time. It can be extremely useful to make contact, formally or informally, with someone who works in the service, so that any detailed issues can be explored on a personal basis if and when a referral needs to be made. It is also helpful to collect information about the service that could be read by the person seeking help; for example, leaflets and website details. This level of detail is required because the person seeking help may be in a state of urgency and neediness that could make it hard for them to tolerate ambiguity or uncertainty ('I think the CBT service should be able to help you but I'm not sure whether you need to be referred by your GP'), and because there is a tendency for specialist services to be inaccessible due to long waiting times, complex referral routes, cost (e.g. private practice clinics) or location (e.g. only based in big cities and therefore out of reach of people in rural areas or unable to pay travel costs).

Making a suggestion to a person that it might be valuable to consider an alternative source of help represents a sensitive moment in a counselling relationship. Almost certainly, for a counsellor to reach a point where referral might seem useful, they will have learned quite a lot about the person, and begun to form a relationship with them. From the perspective of the person seeking help, having opened up to a counsellor, it can be very hard to hear a referral suggestion as anything else but a form of rejection ('I don't really want to see you again') or as a sign of personal deficiency ('I must be too crazy for her . . .'). To minimize these reactions, it is useful for a counsellor to be as open as possible about their reasons for bringing up the topic of referral, and to allow sufficient time for the issue to be explored collaboratively.

At the point of making a referral, it is important to do everything possible to prepare the person for the new form of help they will receive ('what you will find is that the therapist in the CBT clinic will work in a different way to me . . . for example, they will probably expect you to do "homework" assignments, such as keeping a diary . . .'). It is also essential to be clear to the person about the information that has been transmitted to the new therapist – they may assume that a new helper will know everything about them, or be upset that they know anything at all. It can also be valuable in some circumstances to continue to see a person for a while after they have started to work with a different practitioner, or to arrange to see them at some time in the future to 'catch up' on developments in their life – these practices can also help to soften any sense of rejection that there may be.

It is perhaps easiest to think of referral as involving access to specialist professional services. However, there are many other sorts of community resource that may be just the right environment for a person. These can include self-help groups and networks, Church groups, educational programmes and political action groups. Community resources can also include individual people who have their own personal story to tell around overcoming a problem.

Exercise 19.1: *Evaluating the success of referrals*

What are your procedures for referring people on to specialist services? How do you know whether these procedures are satisfactory for the people who are referred?

When confrontation may be necessary

The fundamental standpoint for any counsellor is that of collaboration – standing alongside the person and being their ally as they seek to resolve problems in living. Sometimes, however, it may be necessary to take a more oppositional stance, and challenge or confront a person. There are a number of situations in which the difficulty that the counsellor is experiencing in remaining an ally of the person seeking help are so distracting to them that some kind of confrontation is inevitable. These situations can include:

- when the person is lying to the counsellor
- when the person continues to engage in self-destructive actions, despite extensive exploration around the underlying issues
- when the person is using the counselling to gain external advantage; for instance, a student who only appears to attend counselling to secure a note that will justify an extension on an essay deadline
- when the person is exploiting or threatening the counsellor; for example, using the counsellor as an object of sexual arousal.

In each of these situations, and in other situations that might be imagined, the integrity of the counselling space is at stake, because if the counsellor does not do something then they would be unable to continue with any degree of authentic self-respect.

When challenging or confronting a person, it is important for a counsellor to make 'I' statements and take responsibility for their own personal judgements and feelings. It is also important to confront only in a context where the person has been otherwise valued or affirmed to prevent the possibility of coming across as persecutory. It is helpful to be specific about which actual behaviour of the person triggered a particular reaction; for instance, using the formula: 'when you said/did . . ., I felt/thought . . .', and to avoid 'totalizing' statements that generalize about the whole of the person: it is best to separate the issue or behaviour from the person as a whole. When confronting someone, check out that the recipient has heard what you are saying, and understands your key points. It is also essential to take care of safety issues – it is very clearly not a good idea to confront someone with a history of violence while alone in a building. The experienced psychotherapist, Irvin Yalom (2002), has written that his rule of thumb is, wherever possible, to 'strike while the iron is cold'. In other words, confronting from a state of anger or frustration, or when the person is themselves angry or upset, may result in a situation where neither side can be heard, with the result that the viability of the relationship may be threatened.

Confronting is generally a scary experience for counsellors, who tend to be people who want to be liked and to be seen as nice and helpful. It can therefore be particularly important for anyone involved in a counselling role to make use of consultation and supervision in respect of this kind of episode. However, explicit confrontation is relatively rare in counselling. Challenge and disagreement can be regarded as intrinsic parts of the process of dialogue that is the bedrock of good counselling. Confrontation, on the other hand, is something stronger. It is not part of routine counselling practice, but is an action that arises from a threatened breakdown of the counselling space.

Exercise 19.2: *Your personal experience of confrontation*

What is your own personal experience of being confronted by someone in a position of authority in a work setting? Did this episode lead to a productive conclusion? What did the person do in confronting you that was constructive, and what did they do that was destructive? What have you learned from this event that can inform your use of confrontation and challenge in counselling?

Conclusions

A central theme that has run through this chapter is the idea of *crisis* – difficult situations in counselling tend to be those in which there is a crisis to be resolved; either a crisis in the life of the person seeking help, or a crisis in the relationship between the person and the counsellor. In responding to crisis, it is important not to assume that the acute difficulty being experienced is necessarily characteristic of the person (or the relationship) as a whole. As James and Gilliland (2001: 19) put it: 'crisis is a perception of an event or situation as an intolerable difficulty that exceeds the person's *immediately available* resources and coping mechanisms'. In other words, the person may be able to draw on resources and coping mechanisms that are not immediately available, but can be brought to bear on the situation.

Crisis episodes in counselling, when the safe space of the relationship is under threat for whatever reason, are likely to elicit a complex mix of emotions, thoughts and action tendencies. At a point of not knowing how to cope, a person may express anger and hostility, anxiety and fear, or sadness/loss, depending on the meaning of the situation in their eyes. Their thinking may be dominated by a sense of being violated, they may be thinking ahead to the possible consequences of what is happening, or their thinking may be oriented towards the past, and fixated on terrible events that have happened previously and which cannot be recovered or fixed. In relation to their behaviour, the person may be actively trying to resolve or sort out the crisis event, they may seek to evade or escape the event, or they may be paralysed and immobilized, perhaps even engaged in behaviour that is unproductive, self-defeating and disorganized. Any of these patterns and reactions can be experienced during difficult situations in counselling by the person and possibly also by the counsellor. In such circumstances, it is particularly important for a counsellor to be able to draw on principles and strategies that they have worked out in advance (preparation and training) and to be able to make use of the support of colleagues.

Another theme that threads through the issues discussed in this chapter is the degree to which difficult situations represent a challenge to the values and collaborative stance of a counsellor. At times when the person seeking help is happy to engage in a two-way conversation about the problems in their life, it is a relatively straightforward task for the counsellor to treat the person as an equal partner, respect their agency, believe in their capacity for growth and development, participate in joint decision-making, and so on. At the crunch points; for example, when the person is suicidal, is fearful and withdrawn to the point of not being able to leave their chair, or furious at what they perceive as a betrayal of a counsellor who has told them they will need to see someone else, the balance changes. At these points, it may be necessary to be quite directive; for example, by questioning the person about their plans for suicide, or being clear about the limits of their caring and commitment ('I'm sorry, but I just am not able to give you the time that you need'). At the same time, in taking control and exerting authority to maintain the safety of the person (or their own safety in their role as counsellor), a counsellor should be mindful of the fact that at some point in the future a more collaborative way of working will need to be recreated.

Difficult situations are not smooth or easy. They are hard work and even scary. However, they provide opportunities for taking the relationship between a person and a counsellor, and the bond of trust between them, much further. None of the difficult situations described in this chapter are trivial. On the contrary, they reflect real challenges to people, sometimes even challenges of life and death. Being able to work through these challenges successfully, even if untidily and with difficulty, can bring people together and can be the source of much learning.

Suggested further reading

Creative ways of thinking about, and responding to, mental health issues are described in:

Barker, P. and Buchanan-Barker, P. (2005) *The Tidal Model: A Guide for Mental Health Professionals*. London: Brunner-Routledge.

Newnes, C., Holmes, G. and Dunn, C. (eds) (1999) *This is Madness: A Critical Look at Psychiatry and the Future of Mental Health Services*. Ross-on-Wye: PCCS Books.

Newnes, C., Holmes, G. and Dunn, C. (eds) (2000) *This is Madness Too: A Further Look at Psychiatry and the Future of Mental Health Services*. Ross-on-Wye: PCCS Books.

Romme, M. and Escher, S. (2000) *Making Sense of Voices: A Guide for Mental Health Professionals Working with Voice Hearers*. London: Mind Publications.

The literature on crisis intervention contains a great deal of wisdom and practical knowledge around how to approach difficult situations in helping relationships:

James, R. (2012) *Crisis Intervention Strategies*, 7th edn. Belmont, CA: Wadsworth.

Taking account of cultural diversity

'Do you think it makes any difference that I'm Scottish?'
'What do you mean?'
'You know, the way I bottle up my feelings'.
'I guess that would be a factor'.
'Are you joking? You know it's a factor'.
'You're right. I was joking. I think it's a huge factor'.

Introduction

The basic content of any kind of counselling consists of conversations around the most *personal* aspects of the client's life: understanding why they feel the way they do, making significant life decisions, and resolving conflicts in close relationships. The way that any person approaches such issues is inevitably framed by the ideas and beliefs that they have acquired from the culture or cultures within which they have grown up. In addition, the ideas that a person holds around what is helpful, or how emotional wounds can be healed, are similarly derived from cultural sources. One of the paradoxes of counselling is that discussions of intimate, personal issues are at the same time explorations of the possibility of cross-cultural communication: to what extent do I *really* understand what being married, or being angry, means for this person?

To be an effective counsellor it is necessary to develop a capacity to relate to people from a wide range of cultural backgrounds. Most counsellors will encounter clients with whom they make an instant and deep connection, as if the person was a member of the same family, or had grown up on the same street. However, the majority of clients will be different from the counsellor in some important respect. The aim of this chapter is to outline some of the ways that counsellors can make connection with, and do useful work with, people from diverse cultural traditions. The chapter considers two main topics: making sense of cultural diversity, and practical strategies for counselling in situations of cultural diversity.

> ## Box 20.1: *Decoding the ways in which cultural diversity is discussed in the counselling literature*
>
> The various terms that are used to discuss the topic of cultural diversity in the counselling literature illustrate different standpoints that can be adopted in relation to this issue. A concept that is rarely explicitly used, but is frequently implied in counselling books and articles, is the notion of cultural *universalism*. This notion refers to an assumption that in terms of psychological processes or counselling interventions all people are basically the same, and that cultural differences can be disregarded. The terms *cross-cultural* and *intercultural* are used to refer to situations in which the counsellor and the client are viewed as representing unitary contrasting cultural backgrounds (e.g. a 'black' counsellor and a 'white' client). The term *transcultural* is used by counsellors who acknowledge cultural differences but seek to find ways to transcend these factors. The idea that corresponds most closely to the approach taken in this chapter is *multicultural*, which adopts a position that in contemporary society personal identity is built up from multiple sources of cultural difference. The concept of multicultural counselling is associated with the work of Paul Pedersen (1991), one of the leading figures in highlighting the key role of cultural factors in counselling practice.

Making sense of cultural diversity

There are two types of cultural diversity that need to be considered by counsellors. First, there is the impact of what might be described as 'world cultures'. This idea refers to broad cultural groupings or traditions, such as Islam, Christianity, Judaism and Buddhism. In practice, these broad categories are typically encountered in the form of more specific ethnic cultures, such as Catholic Hispanic-American, Sunni Muslim, Maori or Scottish Presbyterian. Sometimes, even broader categories are used, such as 'Asian' or 'Western'. The key point about these cultural traditions is that they are all-encompassing and deep-rooted. They have been around for a long time, and shape individual attitudes and behaviour in ways that are taken for granted by members of these traditions to the extent that they may not be consciously aware of them. People are born into one or more of these cultural traditions.

A second source of cultural diversity consists of a multiplicity of sub-cultures that exist within any major culture or society. There are some sub-cultures, such as social class and gender, that are fairly diffuse but nevertheless highly influential. There are other sub-cultures that include substantial numbers of people, but at the same time remain fairly clearly defined. Examples of this kind of sub-culture would include the deaf community, and the lesbian, gay, bisexual and trangender (LGBT) sub-culture. There are local, temporary or small-scale sub-cultures, such as eco-warriors or Manchester United supporters. Finally, powerful cultural worlds can be generated by some occupations or professions. For example, for some people, membership of the police or armed forces or Microsoft may be a defining characteristic of their cultural identity.

The key point here is that the cultural elements that are potentially involved in a counselling interaction are potentially highly complex. As a result, it is rarely satisfactory to seek to understand an individual in terms of their membership of a single cultural group. In a contemporary world in which there are high levels of social and geographical mobility, the majority of people when asked identify with multiple cultural influences. Someone may have grown up in a middle-class, white, Christian culture in Sheffield, but then have moved on in their life to incorporate aspects of gay and Buddhist cultures, and read Japanese comic books. At different points in counselling, any or all of these cultural influences may be relevant.

Exercise 20.1: *Mapping your own cultural identity*

One of the best ways to appreciate the complex nature of cultural identity is to reflect on the cultural influences in your own life. Take a large sheet of paper and some coloured pens, and spend some time drawing or mapping the different elements of your own cultural identity. Some suggestions that may help you to engage with this task are:

● Write as many answers as possible to the question, 'who am!?'
● What does 'home' mean to you? Where and when have you felt most at home?
● What are (or were) the cultural identities or cultural worlds of your parents and grandparents? Which aspects of their cultural realities have you incorporated into your own life?

It can be useful to carry out this exercise in a group: comparing your own cultural identity with that of other people can be a valuable means of highlighting your appreciation of your own unique sense of self.

Once you have constructed and reflected on your cultural identity map, if possible allow yourself some more time to consider the implications of this exercise for your role as a counsellor in relation to how some clients might view you (or pigeonhole you) in cultural terms, and what might be the implications of this kind of labelling (e.g. could it inhibit some clients from talking about certain issues?),

---

Some basic dimensions of cultural diversity

Although there are many different cultural traditions within which clients might place themselves, it is possible to identify a set of basic dimensions that seem to be capable of capturing most cultural variation (Hofstede, 2003). It is important for counsellors to learn to be sensitive to these cultural dimensions as a means of making sense of the cultural assumptions of particular clients, and how these assumptions may either match, or be in tension with, their own beliefs and attitudes.

- *Individualism–collectivism:* cultures vary along a continuum of individualism versus collectivism. Individualist cultures emphasize the rights of the individual, and people in such cultures tend to see themselves as largely autonomous and self-contained. By contrast, people in collectivist cultures identify themselves as part of a family or community. They are likely to talk about 'we' rather than 'I', and assume that many important life decisions will be made for them rather than by them. The individualism–collectivism dimension is highly significant in counselling. Most of the well-established models of counselling, such as person-centred therapy or cognitive-behavioural therapy (CBT) have a strong individualist bias, due to their focus on how the individual client thinks or feels. As a result, some of the ideas and methods from these approaches may need to be adapted or modified when used with clients from collectivist traditions. Conversely, collectivist-oriented forms of counselling, such as family therapy, may be uncomfortable for people with individualist values. As with any cultural factor, it is a mistake to view individualism–collectivism as an either–or position. There may be important individualist themes or possibilities in the lives of people who have grown up in strongly collectivist cultures (and vice versa). Working in a culturally sensitive manner involves being able to map the relative influence of these cultural systems on the specific problem that the client is trying to resolve at that point in time.

- *Egalitarianism:* in some cultures, there is a general acceptance that everyone is more or less equal, and that, in principle, anyone can become the President or Prime Minister. These cultures are characterized by informal styles of dress and speech, and a relatively narrow band of income distribution. Other cultures are characterized by visible and clear-cut differences in power and authority. These differences are observable on a day-to-day basis in the deference that is exhibited by those in 'lower' classes or castes to those in 'higher' groups. A further aspect of this dimension can be seen within religious and spiritual practice. In some religious groups, priests are set apart from other members of society. In other groups, spiritual direction is shared between members of a communion. The cultural dimension of differentiations of power and authority has an impact on counselling through the kinds of counsellor–client relationship with which clients are comfortable, or which they expect. Clients in cultures with low overall power difference tend to be drawn to collaborative ways of working in which the counsellor is a facilitator rather than an 'expert'. By contrast, people from cultures with marked power differences will often expect the counsellor to take the lead, and provide direction.

- *Rationality–spirituality:* historically, human societies have been organized around various forms of belief in the power of gods or spirits to control the fate of individuals and communities. It is only relatively recently, beginning in Arab and European cultures around the Mediterranean, and then spreading throughout Europe and more widely that cultures have emerged that are based on a predominantly rational or scientific worldview. The rationality–spirituality dimension of cultural difference can be relevant in counselling in two ways. First, it is associated with differences in the way that people view events that have occurred in their lives. From a spiritual perspective, an event may be 'fate', or an 'act of God', or the result of 'evil spirits' exerted by others. In any of these cases, the individual is not personally responsible for what has happened. From a scientific or materialist perspective, on the other hand, the individual is regarded as being in control of their own life, and therefore responsible for whatever happens to them. In counselling, a rational-scientific cultural viewpoint is consistent with encouraging the client to take responsibility for change. On the other hand, that same viewpoint may make it hard for people to *accept* the situation they are in. A spiritual perspective on life is more likely to be associated with a wish to make sense of events in holistic terms, and to talk about problems in living in their broadest context, whereas a rational perspective is more likely to lead to a desire to analyse events in minute cause-and-effect detail. The second way in which a rationality–spirituality continuum may have an impact on counselling is in terms of the types of solutions or forms of healing that the client regards as relevant for them. Although a person from a spiritually oriented culture may well want to talk to a counsellor about their problems, they may well also be using prayer, meditation, traditional medicine or other spiritual practices at the same time. A culturally sensitive counsellor will want to acknowledge and encourage these practices, and explore how they can complement whatever it is that the counsellor and client are doing within the counselling relationship.

- *Gender differentiation:* currently, the concept of gender differentiation is possibly the most widely debated dimension of cultural difference. To what extent are men and women equal and similar in respect of tasks such as bringing up children, caring for others, holding down management roles in organizations, and fighting in wars? If there are differences, to what extent do these factors reflect inequality in status and value? At an everyday level, the question of gender differentiation plays out in the way that men and women look and dress, the places that they meet, and in income, health and educational outcomes. Gender differentiation also shapes the way that sexual orientation is understood: is it acceptable for men and women to have same-sex partners? The fundamental question of what it means to be male or female permeates many aspects of counselling. How does the client feel about speaking to someone of the same or opposite gender? How does the client understand their role in life in relation to work and family? How acceptable is it for the client to express certain emotions?

- *Significance of space and place:* a final dimension of cultural difference is reflected in the importance that people attach to the physical environment in which they live. This dimension is largely ignored in mainstream models of counselling, and in most counselling training. On the whole, people in modern industrial cultures live in urban spaces where nature is controlled and 'outside' spaces (rooms, buildings) are largely interchangeable. By contrast, people in traditional cultures have a strong investment in particular places, which have meaning for them in terms of the story of their community and their connection to the rhythms of nature. The significance of particular places may be emphasized through the practices or rituals that are associated with these sites. These factors have an influence on counselling in ways that are only beginning to be understood. For example, some people may find it hard to trust a counsellor until they feel that they have been formally welcomed into the counselling space, perhaps by being offered food or drink, or presenting a gift. Also, people who have been brought up with a reverence for place may be 'unsettled' not because of a dysfunctional way of thinking or relating to others, but simply because they do not have a 'place' where they can have a sense of belonging.

Practical counselling strategies: responding effectively to cultural diversity

In order to work effectively with clients from different cultural traditions, it is necessary to not only be informed about the ways in which cultures are organized, and the role of cultural factors in personal identity, but also to possess practical skills in addressing these issues in relation to actual clients. The list of multicultural counselling skills or competences listed below draw on basic counselling skills that were introduced in Chapter 5.

Active curiosity

Preparation for offering counselling relationships to people who are culturally different involves actively fostering a sense of cultural curiosity – a willingness to acknowledge cultural difference and to ask questions. Taking the step of talking about potential cultural difference and misunderstanding with a person seeking help positions the counsellor as being open to finding ways of overcoming the effects of difference. Keeping quiet about these factors, by contrast, either puts the responsibility for addressing issues of cultural difference onto the person seeking help (at a time when they probably have more pressing matters to talk through) or banishes them to the realm of the unsayable and unsaid (Cardemil and Battle, 2003). Inviting and initiating exploration of cultural and racial issues and differences in a counselling session is a key competence for anyone intending to offer counselling relationships. There are many situations in counselling where both the counsellor and client are aware of cultural difference ('my parents are from India, and she is obviously English middle class – will she really understand my dilemma around leaving home?'; 'I am married with three children, and my new client has just come out as gay – I have no idea what it must be like for him to enter that new world'). At these moments, it is up to the counsellor to invite discussion around the implications of this awareness ('in terms of this problem that you are talking about, I was wondering whether it might be an issue that we come from different backgrounds . . . for example, I don't have any direct experience of . . . I was wondering what it is like for you to talk to me about it . . .'). This kind of statement is a form of *metacommunication*, which invites the client to clarify what would be best for them. Some clients prefer to talk to a counsellor from a different cultural background, because it offers them a contrasting perspective, or because they are worried that someone from their own cultural group might know them, might condemn them, or might not maintain confidentiality. Other clients are happy enough to help their counsellor to gain a satisfactory level of understanding of their cultural beliefs. However, there are some clients who just cannot get beyond the real or actual fear that their counsellor just does not 'get it', or is being patronizing or intrusive in asking questions about their cultural background. These clients may well be best served by seeing a counsellor who shares their cultural identity, or is already knowledgeable about it.

Box 20.2: *The practical consequences of not being willing to talk about cultural difference*

Thompson and Jenal (1994) and Tuckwell (2001) carried out research where counsellors were paired up with clients from a different cultural background. Half of the counsellors were instructed to avoid any mention of client–counsellor cultural or racial differences, while the other half were asked to initiate discussion around these factors. What was found in both of these studies was that avoiding talking about salient cultural differences resulted in counselling sessions that were frustrating for the client, and where the client gradually became more distanced from the counsellor and less involved in the counselling process. By contrast, in the culturally sensitive counselling condition, the client was able to hold a brief conversation with the counsellor about their different backgrounds, and then move on to talk about their actual personal problem.

Self-awareness

One of the basic skills of counselling involves continual *self-monitoring* of thoughts, feelings and action tendencies elicited by the client, or by the issues being explored by the client. Counsellor self-monitoring represents an invaluable source of information about the client's inner world (if the counsellor is able to resonate empathically to the client's emotional state) and to the way that other people might respond to the client ('if I feel detached when this client speaks, then maybe other people in her life have the same reaction to her'). Self-monitoring also enables the counsellor to identify any personal barriers or unresolved issues that may prevent them from being fully present for the client. This final aspect of self-monitoring is particularly important in situations of cultural diversity. In her research into counsellors' experiences of working with clients whose cultural background was different from their own, Tuckwell (2001) found that several counsellors reported a pervasive *fear of the other*. In some cases they had a powerful sense of the troubled history of cultural or racial relations between their two peoples, and feared that this might lead to expressions of anger or rejection. In other cases they were afraid that they would fail to understand their client, or that they would engage in cultural stereotyping. Acknowledging that this type of fear is occurring for them is potentially valuable for counsellors working with clients from different cultural worlds. It is a signal that something important is happening. It may represent a stimulus to personal development work around personal attitudes to race and ethnicity. In the moment, it signifies a call for courage in being willing to overcome personal anxiety and allow a genuine dialogue to take place.

Making use of cultural resources

One of the most effective ways of dealing with cultural diversity is to redefine the client's culture as not being a problem or barrier, but instead as a positive resource. The concept of *cultural resources* was introduced in Chapter 5, to describe the many types of activity that may be available to members of a culture as ways of dealing with personal problems. For example, if someone with a middle-class European cultural background is feeling depressed, going to the gym can be energizing, lead to a sense of personal accomplishment, and function as a means of making contact with new people. For someone on a low income, with a Latin American background, personal fitness trainers and gym memberships may not figure in their cultural landscape. However, going to a café or bar where they can dance the tango may serve a similar function. To make use of cultural resources in counselling, it is necessary to build up an understanding of the client's 'personal niche', the individual cultural world that they have constructed from the wider culture within which they live. It is important to be curious about, and sensitive to, resources that the person may have employed in the past but no longer utilizes. For example, a person may have gone to Church, or had a dog, or cultivated a garden, but for various reasons has let go of this valuable practice. Within narrative therapy, the concept of 'remembering' is used to describe the process where the counsellor encourages their client to reconnect with people, places or activities that had been healing or supportive for them in the past. A basic principle of using cultural resources in counselling is that the counsellor does *not* make suggestions ('I think it would be useful for you to get more exercise by doing some hillwalking'), because the probability is that the client is not in a good state to learn something new – the counsellor's 'prescription' just adds to their stress. Instead, the counsellor is seeking to reactivate activities and relationships that have worked for the client in the past. The kinds of question that can be used to invite the client to engage with cultural resources include: 'is there anything in your life; for example, some activity that you do or have done in the past, that might help you in dealing with the problem we have been discussing?', 'are there people in your life who might be able to support you at this time?', and 'who in your life would not be surprised to learn about your success in overcoming this problem?'

Making counselling accessible to people from different backgrounds

Once the client has engaged with counselling, and a counselling 'space' has been created in which client and counsellor can discuss matters, it is possible for the counsellor to ask the client about the potential influence of cultural differences, and modify the counselling accordingly. However, there are a number of important processes that occur outside the counselling space, which need to be considered from a diversity perspective. One of the most obvious factors is concerned with any written information that is provided for clients; for example, leaflets that explain that counselling is available, or how counselling works, and self-help reading material. This information is only usable by clients who can read the language in which it is written, or in the case of visually impaired persons can access it through other means. Language differences are also a factor that may require interpreters to be available, and for counsellors to know how to make use of interpreters. There are many people who need to have particular kinds of physical environments to be able to make use of counselling; for example, private rooms with wheelchair access. An essential element in preparing to offer counselling, whether in an embedded counselling role or in a specialist service, is to anticipate the ways in which different groups of people will be able to know that counselling is available, and what they might need in order to be able to participate in a counselling process.

These four areas (active curiosity, self-awareness, use of cultural resources and attention to access) represent basic competences for ensuring that counselling is being carried out in a way that is sensitive to cultural diversity. However, these strategies are empty unless they are accompanied by a genuine interest in the different worlds that people create, and a willingness to examine personal stereotypes and assumptions.

Box 20.3: *The concept of microaggression*

One of the leading figures in theory and research on multicultural counselling, Derald Wing Sue, uses the term *microaggression* to refer to 'brief and commonplace daily verbal, behavioral, or environmental indignities, whether intentional or unintentional, that communicate hostile, derogatory, or negative racial slights and insults toward people of color' (Sue *et al.*, 2007: 271). Three forms of microaggression can be identified: *microassault* (use of racist language or active discrimination against members of ethnic minority groups); *microinsult* (e.g. a minority employee is asked 'how did you get that job?'; and *microinvalidation* (nullifying the reality of the target person, for example, by telling them they have overreacted if they comment on having been subjected to negative attitudes). Shelton and Delgado-Romero (2011) have documented numerous examples of microaggression experienced by lesbian, gay, bisexual and queer clients in therapy. These studies suggest that members of low-status cultural groups are exposed to excluding and wounding responses on an everyday basis in ways that are largely outside of conscious awareness. The implication for counselling is that this kind of interaction occurs within the counselling sessions, and that counsellors may not be aware that it is occurring. It seems clear that microaggression undermines the establishment of productive and trusting counselling relationships. To counteract this tendency, counsellors need to examine not only their attitudes and knowledge around cultural issues, but also the subtle ways in which they interact with people from different cultural groups.

Conclusions

The key to taking account of diversity in counselling is *respect*. When a counsellor does not show respect for the way that a client lives their life, and their beliefs, then it is very unlikely that any kind of meaningful counselling process will take place. By contrast, if a counsellor is actively curious about the client's world, as demonstrated by checking out assumptions and requesting information and feedback, the client gets the messages such as: 'you are special', 'I can learn from you', and 'I am interested in the way you see things'. These are messages that support collaboration, and which help clients to develop self-esteem and a sense that they have the capacity to overcome their problems.

It is a good idea as a counsellor to be interested in culture *all the time,* rather than just shifting into 'cross-cultural mode' when a client appears who is visibly different from oneself. Cultural beliefs and assumptions are always relevant to the development of problems in living, and cultural resources always play a part in the resolution of these problems. Initiating discussion of cultural factors as a matter of course means that a counsellor develops confidence and competence in working with such issues, and is less likely to be paralysed by a 'fear of the other'.

Finally, it is necessary to keep in mind that there is a common bond of humanity across all people (we all love and are loved, we all have families, we all get depressed . . .) *and* there are profound differences between people in the way that they understand and make arrangements around these common experiences. As in so many areas of counselling, the trick is to keep sight of both of these apparently incompatible truths. The truth of difference means that, as a counsellor, I will always work hard at making sense of your unique reality. The truth of our shared humanity means that I am confident that at some point we will be able to connect with each other.

Suggested further reading

The key figure in developing an understanding of cultural dimension is the Dutch social scientist Greet Hosftede:

Hofstede, G. (2003) *Culture's Consequences: Comparing Values, Behaviors, Institutions, and Organizations Across Nations*, 2nd edn. Newbury Park, CA: Sage Publications.

Extended discussion of the issues raised in this chapter can be found in:

Lago, C. (2006) *Race, Culture and Counselling: The Ongoing Challenge*, 2nd edn. Maidenhead: Open University Press.

Lago, C. (ed.) (2011) *The Handbook of Transcultural Counselling and Psychotherapy*. Maidenhead: Open University Press.

Lago, C. and Smith, B. (2010) *Anti-Discriminatory Practice in Counselling and Psychotherapy*, 2nd edn. London: Sage Publications.

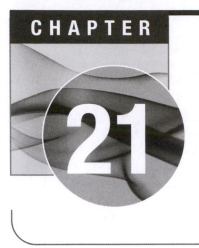
Putting it all together: using supervision and consultation to do good work

Can I have a few minutes to talk about Donald? Older man. Been seeing him every couple of weeks for six months. Usual stuff — medication, dealing with questions, tests. He had never talked about what it all meant to him. Tremendous family support. Last week it all poured out. What? Yes, of course — *what* poured out? I guess the main thing was about dying, which he knows at some level but not at another. But the immediate thing was letting his children know how he felt about them. All the things he wanted to say before it was too late. He's feeling himself getting more tired and not facing up to anything. Never been one to get emotional. Anyway, he came up with the idea of making a speech at his birthday party. We talked a bit about what he might say. He thinks they'll video it. Sorry — it's bringing it all back. At one point he said something like 'it's getting so bad I might take things into my own hands'. Yes, I asked him about harming himself. He said he would never actually do that. I believed him. What do you think? Is it worth going back to that next time I see him? What? What's it bringing back for me? Where do you want me to start?

Introduction

In earlier chapters, a number of dimensions of counselling skill were discussed. In order to explore these dimensions, it has been necessary to separate them out and examine them in turn. In practice, however, when actually working with someone engaged in the process of talking though an issue, all of these different aspects of counselling skill need to fit seamlessly together. On the whole, the best way to integrate different facets of counselling skill – as with any other skill – is just to do it. Each time that a counsellor enters into a helping relationship with a person is an opportunity for learning, and contributes to building up a reserve of practical knowledge. However, there are some specific issues that can emerge at the stage of moving from primarily learning about counselling to that of primarily practising it. These issues include: developing a counselling approach that is consistent with other professional roles within which it might be embedded; purposefully making use of consultation and supervision; developing a personal style in the form of an individual toolbox or repertoire of methods; engaging in continuing professional development; dealing with the stress of the work; and making use of research and inquiry.

Counselling embedded within other professional roles: integrating knowledges

A useful concept to have emerged in social science in recent years, that has been exploited by narrative therapists, is the idea of *knowledges*. Rather than thinking of 'knowledge' as a single, unitary body of concepts and information, which implies a fixed truth, it has been argued that it is more appropriate to recognize that different groups of people possess their own distinctive 'knowledges' around any topic. The idea of 'knowledges' implies that there can be different 'truths' on a subject or topic, reflecting diverse standpoints and perspectives. Narrative therapists have further developed this concept in their use of the term 'insider knowledges' to draw a contrast between 'expert' or 'objective' knowing, and the personal knowledge that is held by people who have actual first-hand experienced of a subject. For example, although textbooks can provide a wealth of expert knowledge on depression, this may not correspond to the 'insider knowledge' that is possessed by someone who has known depression in their life. Narrative therapists argue that the problems are often compounded by the tendency of professional helpers to impose 'expert knowledge' on them, and not take their personal 'insider knowledge' seriously. It is easy to do this, since expert knowledge derives authority from being based on research and contained in books on library shelves, while insider knowledge can only claim the authority of the voice of the individual person, or perhaps a group of service users speaking up collectively.

The concept of knowledges has a great deal of relevance for anyone involved in offering counselling within the context of another professional role, such as a nurse breaking off from wound care to allow a patient to talk through his feelings about the way that his disfigurement has impacted on his life, or a teacher finding time to explore a pupil's options in responding to bullying. In any such situation, the person offering counselling is required to take into account three different forms of insider knowledge:

- counsellor knowledge
- nurse or teacher knowledge
- personal knowledge.

These three sources of insider knowledge refer only to what is happening inside the awareness of the counsellor – in addition the counsellor will have an appreciation of the insider knowledge of the person seeking help.

Knowledges are inevitably complex, and consist of networks of ideas, concepts, memories, practices and so on. In order to highlight the potential for tension between knowledges, it can be useful to consider a 'knowledge' as comprising a specification for *how to understand* something, and *what to do* about it. For instance, the nurse in the example earlier, caring for a patient with a disfiguring facial wound, who has indicated that he wishes to talk about his feelings, might momentarily be aware of a range of potentially conflicting reactions:

- Counsellor response: 'How can I create a space for safe exploration of this issue?', 'He trusts me enough to open up how he is feeling', 'How much time do we have?', 'Is this a private enough place to talk?'
- Nurse response: 'Could this be a side-effect of the medication he is receiving?', 'Is he depressed?', 'Should I consider a psychiatric referral?', 'I don't have time for this right now'.
- Personal response: 'I would feel awful if that had happened to me', 'If I was in his situation I would just want to cry', 'I can't handle this – it's too heavy'.

Each of these responses is based on a different type of insider knowledge. One of the biggest challenges for anyone involved in providing counselling that is embedded within another work role is to develop strategies for acknowledging and making use of *all* of the knowledges that are available to them. As a nurse in a uniform, busy changing the dressing on a patient's wound, it would be impossible to move straight into a counsellor role and ignore the realities of the nurse–patient relationship. At the same time, a counselling conversation that was not informed by the personal experience of the counsellor would run the risk of being detached and distanced.

There is very little writing or research into the way that 'embedded' counsellors deal constructively with the challenge of conflicting knowledges. One of the most obvious strategies is *sequencing* by applying different knowledges in turn. For example, the wound care nurse could enter into a counselling conversation, close that conversation, then ask about side-effects and other possible symptoms of depression. In contrast, it seems likely that many people who work in human service occupations such as education and teaching, who may possess sensitivity and skill in counselling, find it virtually impossible to shift out of the dominant knowledge stance of their profession, and suppress any awareness they might have of the emotional needs of their clients, service users or patients.

Some practitioners choose to build opportunities for counselling into their work with clients by deliberately integrating counselling 'invitations' into their everyday practice. In this way, the practitioner can set the scene for counselling, rather than being in a position of being asked to respond to counselling needs at times when it is difficult to do so. For example, a teacher can let their students know that they are available for one-to-one consultation at a specific time each week, or a community nurse visiting patients in their homes can try to schedule time on a regular basis for a cup of tea and conversation with each patient, once nursing tasks have been completed.

Exercise 21.1: *Reflecting on your own personal and professional knowledges*

What are the areas of personal and professional knowledges that you posses that could be of potential value in your counselling? What do you do to integrate these knowledges into your counselling role with clients? Do you feel that you make sufficient use of these sources of knowledge? What might you do to acknowledge these sources more consistently?

Using supervision, consultation and support

One of the distinctive accomplishments of the counselling profession in Britain has been its insistence on the key principle that anyone who is involved in a counselling role must receive regular supervision from an experienced colleague who is not their line manager. This principle reflects an appreciation that the task of engaging on a one-to-one basis with the life difficulties of another person presents a set of challenges that cannot be effectively resolved alone. There is a lot happening in a counselling session, and it is invaluable to know that there is someone else available to act as a sounding board for questions such as 'have I missed anything?', 'is there anything else I can be doing to help?' and 'how can I make sense of the complex and confusing story I am hearing?' Supervision is also a place where the personal impact of the work can be explored, and the counsellor can receive support and develop strategies for self-care. Inevitably, the stories of some people seeking counselling will trigger memories and emotions in the counsellor, linked to similar types of experience in their own life. In addition, the emotional and relationship needs and patterns of some people who come for counselling can invite unconscious reciprocal responses on the part of the counsellor, which may not be helpful. For example, someone who copes with their difficulties by getting into arguments with other people, which reinforce a position that 'I need to deal with everything on my own because no one understands me', may talk about their concerns in a way that subtly irritates the counsellor, and leaves a strong residue of emotion at the end of the counselling session. Supervision provides a place for exploring this: 'what is happening that makes me feel angry every time that Ernie tells me about his problems?'

The separation of supervision and line management is important because the focus of line management supervision is usually on the performance of the individual in relation to organizational goals, whereas the focus of counselling supervision is more exploratory, supportive and personal. Effective counselling supervision requires that the counsellor should feel free to admit possible mistakes and disclose personal vulnerabilities – it is harder to do this with someone who may be responsible for continuing your contract or recommending you for promotion. There is obviously an overlap between management supervision and counselling supervision – for example, a counselling supervisor needs to be able to communicate their concerns, and have them acted on, if they believe that a supervisee is not working effectively – but on the whole it has proved most useful to keep these roles separate.

There are a number of different ways that supervision can be organized. Many people who work in counselling roles arrange to meet their supervisor for one 90-minute session each month, with the option of telephone or email consultations in emergencies. Some counsellors meet as a group with a supervisor, typically for a longer period, or on more occasions, each month to ensure that each member receives sufficient individual time. Other counsellors meet in peer supervision groups, while some belong to networks where they can call on other members as required for consultative support. Accredited counsellors operate within professional codes of conduct that specify the amount of supervision that is required, and the level of qualifications and experience of supervisors. At the present time, such guidelines do not exist for practitioners who provide counselling within the context of other work roles. This situation can lead to difficulties for such counsellors in terms of getting their managers to agree to the allocation of dedicated supervision time, or to reimburse supervisors.

When arranging supervision, it is important to recognize that different counsellors have different supervision needs. Just as people have different learning styles and coping strategies, they have different ways of engaging with supervision (see Weaks, 2002). The supervision style or needs of a counsellor may shift through their career; for example, as they become more experienced, or are faced with different client groups.

Box 21.1: *What happens in supervision?*

Just as a counsellor creates a space within which the person seeking help can explore and resolve a wide range of different types of problems in living, a supervisor provides a similar kind of space for a counsellor. There are many aspects of the work of a counsellor that may usefully be addressed in supervision. Hawkins and Shohet (2000) have devised a model of supervision that is widely used within the profession. They suggest that supervision can have three broad functions: *education, support* and *management.* The *educative* dimension of supervision relates to such aims as understanding the client better, and exploring methods of working with the client's problems. The *supportive* dimension refers to the task of becoming aware of how the emotions and needs of the person seeking help have had an impact on the helper, and avoiding burnout. The *management* dimension is concerned with ensuring that the highest standards of care and service are maintained. Hawkins and Shohet (2000) have observed that these functions can be explored by reflecting on, as necessary, seven distinct areas:

1   the content of what the person seeking help was talking about

2   the strategies, interventions and methods used by the counsellor

3   the relationship between the counsellor and the person seeking help

4   the counsellor's personal reactions to the person seeking help

5   the relationship between the counsellor and the supervisor

6   the supervisor's personal reactions to the counsellor

7   the organizational and social context of the counselling.

The relevance, in supervision, of areas 5 and 6 (what is happening during the supervision session) lies in the significance of a phenomenon known as 'parallel process' – the re-enactment in the supervision relationship of issues being played out in the counselling relationship. An example of parallel process might be if a person seeking help found it hard to talk about their problem, and then in turn their counsellor was vague or hesitant in describing the case within the supervision session.

Most supervision is carried out through talk – discussing the work that the counsellor is doing. However, as in counselling, supervision can be facilitated using a number of different methods. For instance, Lahad (2000) describes the use of expressive arts techniques within individual and group supervision contexts.

Underpinning all effective supervision is the establishment of a good working relationship between supervisor and supervisee. The evidence from research on supervision suggests that counsellors' experiences of supervision is polarized to a significant extent (Wheeler and Richards, 2007). There are some counsellors who find supervisors with whom they are able to form a strong, productive and supportive partnership, and from whom they never wish to part. There are other supervisor–supervisee relationships that seem almost to enter a downward spiral in which the counsellor becomes reluctant to share any evidence of difficulty or vulnerability with their supervisor, and the supervisor becomes more and more critical of the counsellor. This kind of experience can be highly damaging for counsellors, because it can take some time to decide to withdraw from such a relationship, given the authority of the more experienced supervisor, and the tendency to accept that their criticism might be soundly based. Lawton and Feltham (2000) provide a useful analysis of the factors involved in abusive or unhelpful supervision. Although the majority of experienced counselling practitioners are able to offer satisfactory supervision or consultation to colleagues, in recent years a number of supervision training courses have been set up, which are invaluable in enabling would-be supervisors to become aware of the complexities of the supervisor role and the issues involved in constructing appropriate supervision contracts (Page and Wosket, 2001).

When constructing a supervision or consultation system it is helpful to build in diversity and choice. Ideally, over a period of time, any person in a counselling role should be able to work with different supervisors, and gain experience of different modes of supervision and support (e.g. individual, group-based, face-to-face, online). Supervision and consultative support also need to be viewed in a broader context of continuing professional development and learning in which practitioners view themselves as *reflective practitioners*. Reflecting on practice is an activity that should be integral to practice in the form of thinking through different courses of action, keeping a personal learning journal, writing notes and attending training events. Formal supervision probably works best when it leads to self-supervision: the best supervisor is the one with whom one can carry out a conversation in one's head, and arrive at a productive answer to an immediate dilemma. It is also important to recognize that there can often be significant organizational barriers to the development of an effective supervision network. Particularly within a busy organization, such as a health centre in which counselling does not play a central role within the service that is provided for clients, but is embedded within other practitioner activities, it can be all too easy to argue that there is 'no time' for supervision, or that supervision is a 'luxury we can't afford here'. In other organizational settings, there may be a blame culture, or an overbureaucratic approach that makes it hard to achieve authentic supervision relationships. Hawkins and Shohet (2000) provide an excellent discussion of organizational barriers to supervision, and make a number of suggestions for ways in which supervision can contribute to the creation of a learning organization.

Box 21.2: *Supervision in action: a case example*

The cyclical model of supervision, developed by Steve Page and Val Wosket (2001), pays particular attention to the creation of a 'reflective space' in which the supervisee can explore dilemmas arising from their work, and to the crucial task of applying supervision insights in practice. Page and Wosket (2001) suggest that the work of supervision can be divided into five stages:

Stage 1: *Establishing a contract*. The counsellor and supervisor negotiate such matters as ground rules, boundaries, accountability, mutual expectations and the nature of their relationship.

Stage 2: *Agreeing a focus*. An issue is identified for exploration, and the counsellor's objectives and priorities in relation to the issue are specified.

Stage 3: *Making a space*. Entering into a process of reflection, exploration, understanding and insight around the focal issue.

Stage 4: *The 'bridge' – making the link between supervision and practice*. Consolidation, goal-setting and action-planning in order to decide how what is to be learned can be taken back into the counselling arena.

Stage 5: *Review and evaluation*. Supervisor and counsellor assess the usefulness of the work they have done, and enter a phase of recontracting.

Page and Wosket (2001) emphasize that this series of stages is cyclical with each completion of the cycle leading to a strengthening of the counsellor–supervisor relationship, and concluding with the negotiation of a new contract. The case example below illustrates how these stages can unfold in practice:

Helen is a social worker in a drug and alcohol service, and provides counselling to clients referred by the court system. Dave is her supervisor. The client she is taking to supervision is Anna, who is 32 years of age, single, and has a well-paid highly-qualified job in the laboratory of a commercial manufacturing company. Anna has difficulties in forming relationships, and feels anxious in social situations. She drinks too much and has had two suicide attempts (three years ago) that ended in A&E visits. Throughout her childhood, her mother was an alcoholic, and her father was frequently away from home on business trips. She has been coming to counselling for three months.

- *Establishing a contract*. Helen asks to devote most of the supervision session to her work with Anna. She says she feels stuck and does not know where the counselling is going. Dave agrees, but says that he wants to make sure there is some time to get updates on Helen's other cases.

- *Agreeing a focus*. Dave asks Helen what she would specifically like to look at in terms of her work with Anna. Helen says that the priority is to make sense of why it is so hard for Anna to talk in sessions.

- *Reflection on the content of the counselling session*. Dave asks Helen to describe what is happening in counselling sessions, specifically the most recent sessions. Helen outlines a pattern where Anna sends her emails almost everyday about how bad she feels, but then sits in on the session and will not speak. There are long silences.

- *Exploration of the techniques and strategies used by the counsellor*. Dave: 'What do you do when she doesn't talk? What do you do to encourage her to talk?' Helen: 'Initially, I would let the silence develop, but that is too uncomfortable'. Dave: 'Who is it uncomfortable for?' Helen: 'Me. Anna seems OK with it. What I have started to do is to remind her of what we have talked about before, and ask for more information. This doesn't have much impact, though. What else can I do?'

- *Exploration of the therapeutic relationship*. Helen describes the relationship as 'close but inconsistent'. She says that Anna often tells her how important the counselling is, and how helpful she has been. Helen says that she really cares about Anna. Dave asks Helen about how *empathic* she is with Anna. 'I think I am being empathic, but it is hard to tell. I don't know how much I'm getting inside her world. I think that I am maybe asking her too many questions, rather than offering empathic reflection'.

- *The feelings of the counsellor towards the client.* Dave asks Helen to say a bit more about how she feels towards Anna – whether she is able to *accept* Anna the way she is, and how *congruent* she is in respect of how she is feeling. Helen replies that she feels frustrated with Anna – it is hard to accept the part of Anna that holds things back and wants to go slowly.

- *Counter-transference of the supervisor.* Dave talks about his own recollection of the first time that he was a client, and how hard it was for him to tell his counsellor how he was feeling. This helps Helen to get some perspective on what is happening with Helen.

- *What is happening here and now between supervisor and supervisee.* Both Dave and Helen agree that their discussion about the case of Anna seems different from the other supervision sessions they have had. There seems to be a parallel process occurring, where Helen seems reluctant to talk, and keeps expecting Dave to come up with the answers and guide her in what to do.

- *The 'bridge' – making the link between supervision and practice.* Having discussed these issues, Helen acknowledges that she is better able to understand where her own frustration and stuckness with Anna is coming from in terms of her own style of dealing with things. This then enables the two of them to explore creatively the options open to Helen in relation to taking a different approach to Anna's silences. They agree that it might be a useful strategy for Helen to work more with the here-and-now process of what is happening in Anna, or in their relationship, at the moments when it is hard for Anna to talk.

- *Review and evaluation.* In wrapping up the session, they agree that it would be helpful to review the work with Anna at their next supervision meeting.

Exercise 21.2: *Reviewing your arrangements for supervision and consultation*

What opportunities do you have to talk about your counselling work, either with a formally contracted supervisor, or through consultation with colleagues? How satisfactory are these arrangements? In terms of the ideas about supervision outlined in the preceding section, what are the positive aspects of the supervision that you receive, and where are the gaps? What can you do to improve this situation?

Assembling a 'toolbox' of methods

The importance of counselling *methods* (what to do to achieve goals) has been highlighted throughout this book. Probably, when beginning to offer counselling to people who are seeking help, any practitioner will rely on a limited set of methods – some acquired during training, and others based on personal experience of life. Over the course of a career, one of the enjoyable aspects of continuing professional development can be that of acquiring awareness and competence in new methods. Perhaps one of the key messages of this book is that there are many, many things that a counsellor can do to be helpful. There are methods that have been devised by psychologists and psychotherapists, methods that are drawn from the arts, business, education, sport and many other fields. It may be valuable to accumulate a collection of 'counselling objects' – buttons, stones, driftwood, toys – that can assist the depiction of emotions and life situations. It can be useful to collect metaphors, images and stories that seem relevant to the client group with whom one is working.

Exercise 21.3: *What's in your toolbox?*

What are the ideas and methods that are currently in your counselling 'toolbox'? Which items would you like to add to your range of tools over the next two years?

Avoiding burnout

The practice of counselling is stressful. There are several factors that appear to be particularly associated with counsellor stress:

- Typically, counsellors work in settings where the potential need (i.e. number of people seeking help) is greater than the resource that is available to meet that need, and so there is a pressure to work long hours or find space to see another person.

- Quite a lot of the time counselling either appears to make little positive difference to the person seeking help, or the benefit that does result is hidden from the counsellor (e.g. following a helpful counselling session, a person may decide that they do not need to return to see the counsellor again, with the consequence that the counsellor never learns about their good news).

- Some people who engage in counselling have very harrowing and tragic stories to tell, or live in states of terrible emotional pain – being exposed to these realities inevitably has a powerful impact on a counsellor.

- Most counselling is carried out on a one-to-one basis, under conditions of confidentiality – this can lead to counsellor isolation and lack of social support, and a sense of being exposed ('I am responsible for what happens to this person') in comparison with other occupations where teamwork is possible.

The intensity and relative importance of each of these sources of stress will depend on the setting in which counselling is being carried out. For example, workers in agencies dealing with women who have been abused are regularly exposed to high levels of emotional pain, but can usually depend on strong collective support from colleagues. By contrast, a nurse in a busy hospital ward may be less likely to encounter stories of abuse, but will probably experience a high workload, time pressure, and lack of emotional support from colleagues.

There are two main patterns of stress that appear to be prevalent in people who do counselling work. The first of these can be described as 'burnout' (Leiter and Maslach, 2005; Maslach and Leiter, 1997). The theory of burnout was developed by the psychologist, Christina Maslach, to account for the effect on people of working in 'human service' or helping professions. Maslach suggests that people enter these professions with a passion to help others. Over time, the emotional consequence of always 'giving' to others results in the passion to help becoming 'burned out'. It is as though the energy and motivation of the person has become used up. The main symptoms of burnout are: a sense of emotional exhaustion; a tendency to treat clients in a detached way as objects or 'cases' rather than as people; and a deep disillusionment or lack of personal accomplishment ('it's all a waste of time . . . I have being doing this job for 10 years and nothing has changed . . .'). A counsellor who is 'burned out' is therefore merely going through the motions, and not really engaging with the people with whom they are working. This state also has serious negative implications for the private life of the person, and their capacity to sustain close relationships. Burnout is a type of stress that gradually accumulates day by day and week by week when people care for others without taking care of themselves.

A second form of stress that can occur in those involved in offering counselling relationships has been described as *secondary traumatization*. This type of reaction takes place when counsellors work with people who have themselves been traumatized (Morrissette, 2004). When a person has been through an awful event, such as torture, natural disaster, war and the like, a range of psychological consequences can occur. Often the sensory images of the event are so frightening that they cannot readily be assimilated into the person's memory. Images of the event continue to be intrusively re-experienced, and then locked away or avoided, as the person's cognitive processing struggles to integrate what has happened in their pre-existing understanding of the world. What this means for a counsellor is that when the person does begin to talk about these awful events in a counselling session, the images and re-experiencing and levels of fear are so strong that is almost as though the counsellor is some kind of witness to the original event. A counsellor may find that they cannot get the person's word, or their story, out of their mind. Another process that can take place arises from what Janoff-Bulman has called 'shattered assumptions'. When a person has experienced events that should 'never happen', then their basic assumption of trust in the world as a safe place, and people as good is shattered. A counsellor working with such a person is faced with having to overcome that person's basic lack of trust, and may also find that the person's story has in turn shattered or threatened their belief in a safe and good world. One of the hazards of counselling, therefore, is the danger of developing secondary traumatization, which can be expressed in a lack of trust in people, recurring images of cruelty and destruction, and general hyper-alertness to any source of potential threat.

Although there has been a considerable amount of research into sources of stress in counselling, and the ways that counsellors cope, the findings of these studies are contradictory and hard to interpret, and it is not easy to arrive at any generalizations. It seems likely that the process of stress in counsellors is often subtle and hidden. People who develop an interest in counselling, and readily offer counselling relationships to others, generally view themselves as possessing a good level of self-awareness and capacity to deal with stress. Probably this is true much of the time, and results in effective self-care in the majority of counsellors. But it may also lead to an unwillingness to acknowledge difficulty and vulnerability in the interest of maintaining a façade of competence. There are many strategies open to counsellors for keeping burnout hidden; for example, by adopting a detached, distanced approach to service users, becoming preoccupied with 'professionalism', or moving away from front-line work and concentrating on supervision, training and administration. A significant proportion of counsellors find they reach a point at which they cannot continue working, and undergo personal crisis, illness, time out and re-evaluation of personal goals at some point in their careers. Sometimes, these practitioners learn a great deal from their crisis, and return stronger and more resilient.

The studies that are available of stress in counselling have focused on the experiences of full-time specialist counsellors and psychotherapists. There has been no research into the stress and burnout in people whose counselling role is embedded in other work roles. In general, nursing, teaching, social work and other professions in which embedded counselling takes place are high-stress occupations. In these roles, it may be that the demands of responding to the counselling needs of clients and patients just cranks up the overall stress level another notch. On the other hand, it may be that at least some practitioners in these areas view the counselling dimension of their role as providing a degree of meaning and balance to their work, and therefore as something that acts as a buffer to other pressures.

The discussion of stress and burnout in this section has concentrated mainly on the impact of this kind of work on the counsellor. It is also essential to be aware of the effect of counsellor stress on the person seeking help from a counsellor. Spending time with a burned-out counsellor is unlikely to be satisfying. A very tired nurse in a casualty department can probably record blood pressure, and administer injections, at an acceptable level of reliability. A very tired counsellor, by contrast, is only minimally open to relationship.

Exercise 21.4: *Mapping your support system*

Take a large sheet of paper (A3 or bigger) and draw a map of your support system at work on it. In the middle of the paper draw a symbol or picture of yourself. Then around this picture or symbol draw pictures, symbols, diagrams or words to represent all things and people that support you in learning and being creative at work. These may be the walk to work, books you read, colleagues, meetings, friends, and so on. Represent the nature of your connection to these supports. Are they near or far away? Is the link strong and regular, or tenuous, or distant? Are they supporting you from below like foundations or are they balloons that lift you up? These are only suggestions; allow yourself to find your own way of mapping your support system.

When you are satisfied with your initial map, take a completely different colour and draw on the picture symbols that represent those things that *block you* from fully using these supports. It may be fear of being criticized or interruptions or the relative unavailability of these supports. It may be blocks within you, within the support or in the organizational setting. Draw whatever you feel stops you getting the support you need.

When you have done this choose someone with whom to share your picture. When you have shared your picture with them, they should first respond to the overall picture. What impression does it create? Then they can ask you the following questions:

- Is this the kind of support you want?
- Is it enough? What sort of support is missing? How could you go about getting such support?
- What support is really positive for you to the extent that you must ensure that you nurture and maintain it?
- Which blocks could you do something about reducing?

Your partner could then encourage you to develop some specific *action plan* as to how you might improve your support system. An action plan should include what you are going to do; how you are going to do it; when and where you are going to do it; and involving whom.

Personal therapy for counsellors

Over the course of their career, almost all specialist professional counsellors and psychotherapists undergo one or more episodes of therapy. For therapy practitioners, the experience of being a client is usually referred to as 'personal therapy'. While people in general go to see a therapist (counsellor or psychotherapist) because they wish to deal with a problem in living that is troubling them, counsellors go to see therapists not only to deal with troubles, but with the additional goal of learning about counselling. Being a client is one of the best ways to understand how the counselling process works (and does not work). In the client's chair, it is possible to watch what one's counsellor is doing. It is also possible to monitor one's own reactions to what the counsellor has said and done, both in the session itself and in the days or weeks following a session. A book that has been compiled and edited by Geller *et al.* (2005) includes a thorough analysis of the role of personal therapy in the development of practitioners. It also includes some very interesting and readable chapters by well-known therapists describing their own experiences of having received therapy. One of the contributors to this section of the book is Clara Hill, who is a leading figure in the area of counselling skills and in counselling research.

Exercise 21.5: *Reflecting on your use of personal therapy*

Take a few minutes to reflect on what being a client in therapy has meant for you and what you have learned from it. Specifically: what contribution has personal therapy made to your ability to offer an effective counselling relationship to clients? It can be useful to carry out this exercise in a group, and share experiences.

Making use of research and inquiry

In modern industrial societies, characterized by high levels of social and technological change, there are few occupations that are practised on a 'craft' basis through the application over a lifetime of knowledge and skills acquired during a period of apprenticeship. Instead, there is an expectation that new knowledge and information will constantly be generated by research, and that competent practitioners will continue to update their approach by being research-informed. The domain of practice-based research can be viewed as a continuum. On one end are large, theory- or policy-driven studies carried out by full-time researchers based in universities. There are also many smaller-scale studies that are carried out by practitioners. At this end of the continuum, which is concerned with knowledge generation, research is an activity in which a person is actively involved, a form of complex problem-solving. At the other end of the continuum, research is a product that is consumed. Detailed research reports can be read in research journals. Less detailed reports can be found in professional journals. Digested research knowledge finds its way into textbooks.

Within the counselling world, the tendency has been that the majority of practitioners admit to being not very interested in research. The products of research are viewed as boring, inaccessible, irrelevant, and too abstract or theoretical (Morrow-Bradley and Elliott, 1986). Counselling practitioners report that their work is better informed and updated through consultation with colleagues and supervisors, participation in skill-based workshops, and learning from clients than it is by reading or doing research. The depth of the research–practice 'gap' in counselling is surprising for practitioners from highly research-based professions such as nursing and medicine where being research-informed is a routine part of working life. It is important to bear in mind, however, that there is much less research into counselling in contrast to the vast amount of health research that has been carried out. Also, the fact that many medical interventions can be compartmentalized into separate elements (e.g. a drug, a specific surgical procedure) means that it is easier to carry out studies that produce results that can be 'slotted in' to everyday practice. It is rare that a research study in counselling yields knowledge that can immediately be applied in practice.

There exists a range of different research approaches that can be employed in looking at the process and outcome of the use of counselling skill in embedded situations. Making use of research and inquiry is a valuable way to stand back from practice, and engage in constructive and critical reflection. It is also a good means of learning about the ideas and methods developed by colleagues in other places – it makes it possible to keep abreast of best practice.

Conclusions

This chapter has discussed a number of themes that may appear obvious to many readers – there is nothing new about the idea that training and supervision are important in professional work, or that it is a good idea to develop strategies for coping with stress and avoiding burnout. What this chapter has attempted to do is to place these fundamental truths of good practice within a counselling context – in some respects people who open themselves to the distress of others do have distinctive training and support needs. There are perhaps two overarching ideas that provide a useful overview to the issues that have been discussed, not only in this chapter, but in the book as a whole. The first is the notion of *craftsmanship*. A good counsellor, no matter whether the context they operate in is high-end private practice or the corner of a busy inner-city health clinic, functions as a craft worker. The satisfaction of the job comes from making the best of the materials that are available, and in producing something that is valued by customers and fellow workers. The essence of craftsmanship is attention to the task in hand, the gradual deepening of skill over time, and pride in a job well done. The other important concept is *resourcefulness*. Throughout this book, the idea has been highlighted that people encounter problems in living because they lack the resources to resolve difficulties that arise in their lives. People seek help because their resources are not sufficient to cope adequately with the situation within which they find themselves. The same analysis can be applied to the role of the counsellor. Virtually anyone can be an effective counsellor to a limited set of people – those people whose problems and assumptions about change most closely match the helping resources of that practitioner. But in the longer term, anyone who hopes to offer counselling to a wide range of people needs to expand their repertoire of helping resources. Hopefully, this book represents an invitation to resourcefulness, and a gateway to thinking about, and trying out, some of the multitude of resources for counselling that exist within our culture.

Suggested further reading

A fascinating book that explores many aspects of 'doing good work' is:

Skovholt, T.M. and Jennings, L. (2004) *Master Therapists: Exploring Expertise in Therapy and Counseling*. New York: Allyn & Bacon.

Although this book is based on interviews with specialist psychotherapists, rather than practitioners whose counselling is embedded in other roles, it contains much that is applicable in embedded counselling settings.

A brief report on this study can be found in:

Jennings, L. and Skovholt, T.M. (1999) The cognitive, emotional and relational characteristics of master therapists, *Journal of Counseling Psychology*, **48**: 3–11.

Rothschild, B. (2006) *Help for the Helper: The Psychophysiology of Compassion, Fatigue and Vicarious Trauma*. New York: W.W. Norton.

Skovholt, T.S. (2008) *The Resilient Practitioner: Burnout Prevention and Self-care Strategies for Counselors, Therapists, Teachers, and Health Professionals*, 2nd edn. New York: Allyn & Bacon.

Various ways that 'knowledges' can influence professional practice are explored in:

White, C. and Hales, J. (eds) (1997) *The Personal is the Professional: Therapists Reflect on their Families, Lives and Work*. Adelaide: Dulwich Centre Publications.

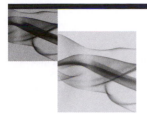

References

Adamsen, L. (2002) From victim to agent: the clinical and social significance of self-help group participation for people with life-threatening diseases, *Scandinavian Journal of Caring Sciences*, 16: 224–31.

Aldridge, S. and Rigby, S. (eds) (2001) *Counselling Skills in Context*. London: Hodder & Stoughton.

Allan, H. (2001) A 'good enough' nurse: supporting patients in a fertility unit, *Nursing Inquiry*, 8: 51–60.

Allan, H. (2007) Experiences of infertility: liminality and the role of the fertility clinic, *Nursing Inquiry*, 14: 132–9.

Ambady, N., Koo, J., Rosenthal, R. and Winograd, C.H. (2002) Physical therapists' nonverbal communication predicts geriatric patients' health outcomes, *Psychology and Aging*, 17: 443–52.

Angus, L.E. and Rennie, D.L. (1988) Therapist participation in metaphor generation: collaborative and noncollaborative styles, *Psychotherapy*, 25: 552–60.

Angus, L.E. and Rennie, D.L. (1989) Envisioning the representational world: the client's experience of metaphoric expressiveness in psychotherapy, *Psychotherapy*, 26: 373–9.

Argyle, M. and Kendon, A. (1967) The experimental analysis of social performance. In L. Berkowitz (ed.) *Advances in Experimental Social Psychology*, Vol. 3. New York: Academic Press.

Baker, R. (2003) *Understanding Panic Attacks and Overcoming Fear*. London: Lion Hudson.

Baker, S.B., Daniels, T.G. and Greeley, A.T. (1990) Systematic training of graduate level counselors: narrative and meta-analytic reviews of three programmes, *Counseling Psychologist*, 18: 355–421.

Barker, C. and Pistrang, N. (2002) Psychotherapy and social support: integrating research on psychological helping, *Clinical Psychology Review*, 22: 361–79.

Barker, M., Vossler, A. and Langbridge, D. (eds) (2010) *Understanding Counselling*. London: Sage Publications.

Barker, P. and Buchanan-Barker, P. (2005) *The Tidal Model: A Guide for Mental Health Professionals*. London: Brunner-Routledge.

Barkham, M. (1989) Brief prescriptive therapy in two-plus-one sessions: initial cases from the clinic, *Behavioural Psychotherapy*, 17: 161–75.

Barkham, M. and Shapiro, D.A. (1989) Towards resolving the problem of waiting lists: psychotherapy in two-plus-one sessions, *Clinical Psychology Forum*, 23: 15–18.

Barkham, M. and Shapiro, D.A. (1990) Exploratory therapy in two-plus-one sessions: a research model for studying the process of change. In G. Lietaer, J. Rombauts and R. Van Balen (eds) *Client-centered and Experiential Psychotherapy in the Nineties*. Leuven: Leuven University Press.

Barrett-Lennard, G. (1993) The phases and focus of empathy, *British Journal of Medical Psychology*, 66: 3–14.

Barrett-Lennard, G.T. (1981) The empathy cycle – refinement of a nuclear concept, *Journal of Counseling Psychology*, 28: 91–100.

Barrett-Lennard, G.T. (1998) *Carl Rogers' Helping System: Journey and Substance*. London: Sage Publications.

Bauman, Z. (2004) *Wasted Lives: Modernity and its Outcasts*. London: Polity Press.

Bedi, R.P., Davis, M.D. and Williams, M. (2005) Critical incidents in the formation of the therapeutic alliance from the client's perspective, *Psychotherapy: Theory, Research, Practice, Training*, 41: 311–23.

Bennett-Levy, G., Butler, M., Fennell, M., Hackmann, A., Mueller, M. and Westbrook, D. (eds) (2004) *Oxford Guide to Behavioural Experiments in Cognitive Therapy*. Oxford: Oxford University Press.

Berne, E. (1964) *Games People Play: The Psychology of Human Relationships*. Harmondsworth: Penguin.

Boal, A. (1979) *Theatre of the Oppressed*. London: Pluto Press.

Boal, A. (1995) *The Rainbow of Desire*. London: Routledge.

Bobevski, I., Holgate, A.M. and McLellan, J. (1997) Characteristics of effective telephone counselling skills, *British Journal of Guidance and Counselling*, 25: 239–49.

Bohart, A.C. (2000) The client is the most important common factor: clients' self-healing capacities and psychotherapy, *Journal of Psychotherapy Integration*, 10: 127–48.

Bohart, A.C. (2006) The active client. In J.C. Norcross, L.E. Beutler and R.F. Levant (eds) *Evidence-based Practices in Mental Health: Debate and Dialogue on the Fundamental Questions*. Washington, DC: American Psychological Association.

Bohart, A.C. and Tallman, K. (1996) The active client: therapy as self-help, *Journal of Humanistic Psychology*, 3: 7–30.

Bohart, A.C. and Tallman, K. (1999) *How Clients Make Therapy Work: The Process of Active Self-healing*. Washington, DC: American Psychological Association.

Bolger, E. (1999) Grounded theory analysis of emotional pain, *Psychotherapy Research*, 9: 342–62.

Bolwand, L., Cockburn, J., Cawson, J., Andreson, H.C., Moorehead, S. and Kenny, M. (2003) Counselling interventions to address the psychological consequences of screening mammography: a randomised trial, *Patient Education and Counseling*, 49: 189–98.

Bond, T. (1989) Towards defining the role of counselling skills, *Counselling*, 69: 24–6.

Bond, T. (2000) *Standards and Ethics for Counselling in Action*, 2nd edn. London: Sage Publications.

Boukydis, K.M. (1984) Changes: peer counselling supportive communities as a model for community mental health. In D. Larson (ed.) *Teaching Psychological Skills: Models for Giving Psychology Away*. Monterey, CA: Brooks/Cole.

Bower, P., Richards, D. and Lovell, K. (2001) The clinical and cost-effectiveness of self-help treatments for anxiety and depressive disorders in primary care: a systematic review, *British Journal of General Practice*, 51: 838–45.

Boyle, J., Kernohan, G.W. and Rush, W. (2009) 'When you are tired or terrified your voice slips back into its old first place': the role of feelings in community mental health practice with forensic patients, *Journal of Social Work Practice*, 23: 291–313.

Brammer, L. (1990) Teaching personal problem solving to adults, *Journal of Cognitive Psychotherapy*, 4: 267–79.

Branch, W.T and Malik, T.K. (1993) Using 'windows of opportunities' in brief interviews to understand patients' concerns, *Journal of the American Medical Association*, 269: 1667–8.

British Association for Counselling and Psychotherapy (2001) *Ethical Framework for Good Practice in Counselling and Psychotherapy*. Rugby: BACP.

Brown, L.S. (2005) Feminist therapy with therapists: egalitarian and more. In J.D. Geller, J.C. Norcross and D.E. Orlinsky (eds) *The Psychotherapist's own Psychotherapy: Patient and Clinician Perspectives*. New York: Oxford University Press.

Bryant, R.A. and Harvey, A.G. (2000) Telephone crisis intervention skills: a simulated caller paradigm, *Crisis*, 21: 90–94.

Buckroyd, J. (2011) *Understanding Your Eating*. Maidenhead: Open University Press.

Bunting, M. (2004) *Willing Slaves: How the Overwork Culture is Ruling our Lives*. London: HarperCollins.

Burns, G.W. (2005) *101 Healing Stories for Kids and Teens: Using Metaphors in Therapy*. New York: Wiley.

Burns, G.W. (ed.) (2007) *Healing with Stories: Your Casebook Collection for Using Therapeutic Metaphors*. New York: Wiley.

Burns, G.W. (ed.) (2010) *Happiness, Healing, Enhancement: Your Casebook Collection for Applying Positive Psychology in Therapy*. New York: Wiley.

Bylund, C.L. and Makoul, G. (2002) Empathic communication and gender in the physician–patient encounter, *Patient Education and Counseling*, 48: 207–16.

Bylund, C.L. and Makoul, G. (2005) Examining empathy in medical encounters: an observational study using the empathic communication coding system, *Health Communication*, 18: 123–40.

Cameron, D. (2004) Communication culture: issues for health and social care. In M. Robb, S. Barrett, C. Komaromy and A. Rogers (eds) *Communication, Relationships and Care: A Reader*. London: Routledge.

Campbell, H.S., Phaneuf, M.R. and Deane, K. (2004) Cancer peer support programs – do they work? *Patient Education and Counseling*, 55: 3–15.

Cardemil, E.V. and Battle, C.L. (2003) Guess who's coming to therapy? Getting comfortable with conversations about race and ethnicity in psychotherapy, *Professional Psychology: Research and Practice*, 34: 278–86.

Carkhuff, R.R. (1969a) *Helping and Human Relations, Vol. 1: Selection and Training*. New York: Holt, Rinehart & Winston.

Carkhuff, R.R. (1969b) *Helping and Human Relations, Vol. 2: Practice and Research*. New York: Holt, Rinehart & Winston.

Carrell, S.E. (2001) *The Therapist's Toolbox*. Thousand Oaks, CA: Sage Publications.

Carroll, M. (1996) *Workplace Counselling: A Systematic Appoach to Employee Care*. London: Sage Publications.

Carroll, M. and Walton, M. (eds) (1997) *Handbook of Counselling in Organisations*. London: Sage Publications.

Cash, R.W. (1984) The human resources development model. In D. Larson (ed.) *Teaching Psychological Skills: Models for Giving Psychology Away*. Monterey, CA: Brooks/Cole.

Coles, A. (2003) *Counselling in the Workplace*. Maidenhead: Open University Press.

Connolly, M., Perryman, J., McKenna, Y., Orford, J., Thomson, L., Shuttleworth, J. and Cocksedge, S. (2010) SAGE and THYME: a model for training health and social care professionals in patient-focussed support, *Patient Education and Counseling*, 79: 87–93.

Cooper, M. and McLeod, J. (2010) *Pluralistic Counselling and Psychotherapy*. London: Sage Publications.

Corey, G., Corey, M. and Callanan, P. (2007) *Issues and Ethics in the Helping Professions*, 7th edn. Pacific Grove, CA: Brooks/Cole.

Cornell, A.W. (1996) *The Power of Focusing: Finding your Inner Voice*. New York: New Harbinger Publications.

Cowen, E.L. (1982) Help is where you find it: four informal helping groups, *American Psychologist*, 37: 385–95.

Cowen, E.L., Gesten, E.L., Boike, M., Norton, P., Wilson, A.B. and DeStefano, M.A. (1979) Hairdressers as caregivers: a descriptive profile of interpersonal help-giving involvements, *American Journal of Community Psychology*, 7: 633–48.

Cowie, H. and Wallace, P. (2000) *Peer Support in Action: From Bystanding to Standing By*. London: Sage Publications.

Crandall, R. and Allen, R. (1981) The organisational context of helping relationships. In T. A. Wills (ed.) *Basic Processes in Helping Relationships*. New York: Academic Press.

D'Zurilla, T.J. and Nezu, A.M. (1982) Social problem solving in adults. In P.C. Kendall (ed.) *Advances in Cognitive-behavioral Research and Therapy*. New York: Academic Press.

Davies, L., Krane, J., Collings, S. and Wexler, S. (2007) Developing mothering narratives in child protection practice, *Journal of Social Work Practice*, 21: 23–34.

Davison, K.P., Pennebaker, J.W. and Dickerson, S.S. (2000) Who talks? The social psychology of illness support groups, *American Psychologist*, 55: 205–17.

De Board, R. (2007) *Counselling for Toads: A Psychological Adventure*. London: Routledge.

Degner, J., Henriksen, A. and Oscarsson, L. (2010) Investing in a formal relationship: support persons' view of treatment involvement regarding young persons in residential care, *Qualitative Social Work*, 9: 321–42.

den Boer, P.C.A.M., Wiersma, D., Russo, S. and van den Bosch, R.J. (2005) Paraprofessionals for anxiety and depressive disorders, *Cochrane Database of Systematic Reviews*, Issue 2, Art. No.: CD004688. DOI: 10.1002/14651858.CD004688.pub2.

Dickson, W.J. and Roethlisberger, F.J. (1966) *Counseling in an Organization: A Sequel to the Hawthorne Researches*. Boston, MA: Graduate School of Business Administration, Harvard University.

Doherty, N., Steffan, B. and Guyler, M. (2008) *The Essential Guide to Workplace Mediation and Conflict Resolution: Rebuilding Working Relationships*. London: Kogan Page.

Drewery, W. (2007) Restorative practices in schools: far-reaching implications. In G. Maxwell and J.H. Liu (eds) *Restorative Justice and Practices in New Zealand: Towards a Restorative Society*. Wellington: Institute of Policy Studies, Victoria University of Wellington.

Duncan, B.L., Miller, S.D. and Sparks, J. (2004) *The Heroic Client: A Revolutionary Way to Improve Effectiveness through Client-directed, Outcome-informed Therapy*, 2nd edn. San Francisco, CA: Jossey-Bass.

Duncan, B.L., Miller, S.D., Wampold, B.E. and Hubble, M.A (eds) (2009) *The Heart and Soul of Change: Delivering What Works in Therapy*, 2nd edn. Washington, D.C.: American Psychological Association.

Earle, S., Bartholomew, C. and Komaromy, C. (eds) (2008a) *Making Sense of Death, Dying and Bereavement: An Anthology*. London: Sage Publications.

Earle, S., Komaromy, C. and Bartholomew, C. (eds) (2008b) *Death and Dying: A Reader*. London: Sage Publications.

Easton, S. and van Laar, D. (1995) Experiences of lecturers helping distressed students in higher education, *British Journal of Guidance and Counselling*, 23: 173–8.

Egan, G. (1984) Skilled helping: a problem-management framework for helping and helper training. In D. Larson (ed.) *Teaching Psychological Skills: Models for Giving Psychology Away*. Monterey, CA: Brooks/Cole.

Egan, G. (2004) *The Skilled Helper: A Problem Management and Opportunity Development Approach to Helping*, 8th edn. Belmont, CA: Wadsworth.

Eide, H., Frankel, R., Haaversen, C., Vaupel, K., Graugard, P. and Finset, A. (2004) Listening for feelings: identifying and coding empathic and potential empathic opportunities in medical dialogues, *Patient Education and Counseling*, 54: 291–7.

Ellis, A. (1962) *Reason and Emotion in Psychotherapy*. New York: Lyle Stuart.

Engebretson, J. (2000) Caring presence: a case study, *International Journal for Human Caring*, 4: 211–23.

Eyrich-Garg, K.M. (2008) Strategies for engaging adolescent girls at an emergency shelter in a therapeutic relationship: recommendations from the girls themselves. *Journal of Social Work Practice*, 22: 375–88.

Fairburn, C.G. (1995) *Overcoming Binge Eating*. New York: Guilford Press.

Feltham, C. (1995) *What is Counselling?* London: Sage Publications.

Feltham, C. (ed.) (1999) *The Counselling Relationship*. London: Sage Publications.

Fennell, M. (1999) *Overcoming Low Self-esteem: A Self-help Guide Using Cognitive-behavioural Techniques*. London: Constable & Robinson.

Fineman, S. (1993) Organizations as emotional arenas. In S. Fineman (ed.) *Emotion in Organization*. London: Sage Publications.

Firestone, R.W. (1997a) *Combating Destructive Thought Processes: Voice Therapy and Separation Theory*. Thousand Oaks, CA: Sage Publications.

Firestone, R.W. (1997b) *Suicide and the Inner Voice: Risk Assessment, Treatment, and Case*. Thousand Oaks, CA: Sage Publications.

Fluckiger, C., Wueste, G., Zinbarg, R.E. and Wampold, B.E. (2010) *Resource Activation: Using Clients' own Strengths and Counseling*. Cambridge, MA: Hogrefe & Huber.

Frank, A. (1995) *The Wounded Storyteller: Body, Illness, and Ethics*. Chicago, IL: The University of Chicago Press.

Frank, A. (1998) Just listening: narrative and deep illness, *Families, Systems and Health*, 16: 197–212.

Frank, A. (2000) Illness and autobiographical work: dialogue as narrative destabilization, *Qualitative Sociology*, 23: 135–56.

Gabriel, L. (2005) *Speaking the Unspeakable: The Ethics of Dual Relationships in Counselling and Psychotherapy*. London: Routledge.

Gabriel, L. and Casemore, R. (2009) *Relational Ethics in Practice: Narratives from Counselling and Psychotherapy*. London: Routledge.

Gallacher, T.J., Hartung, P.J. and Gregory Jr., S.W. (2001) Assessment of a measure of relational communication for doctor–patient interaction, *Patient Education and Counseling*, 45: 211–18.

Gambrill, E. (1984) Social skills training. In D. Larson (ed.) *Teaching Psychological Skills: Models for Giving Psychology Away*. Monterey, CA: Brooks/Cole.

Geller, J.D., Norcross, J.C. and Orlinsky, D.E. (2005) *The Psychotherapist's own Psychotherapy: Patient and Clinician Perspectives*. New York: Oxford University Press.

Gendlin, E.T. (1984a) The politics of giving therapy away: listening and focusing. In D. Larson (ed.) *Teaching Psychological Skills: Models for Giving Psychology Away*. Monterey, CA: Brooks/Cole.

Gendlin, E.T. (1984b) The client's client: the edge of awareness. In R.F. Levant and J.M. Shlien (eds) *Client-centered Therapy and the Person-centered Approach: New Directions in Theory, Research and Practice*. New York: Praeger.

Gendlin, E.T. (1996) *Focusing-oriented Psychotherapy: A Manual of the Experiential Method*. New York: Guilford Press.

Gendlin, E.T. (2003) *Focusing: How to Open Up your Deeper Feelings and Intuition*. New York: Rider.

Gergen, K.J. (1990) Therapeutic professions and the diffusion of deficit, *The Journal of Mind and Behavior*, 11: 353–68.

Giddens, A. (1991) *Modernity and Self-identity: Self and Society in the Late Modern Age*. Cambridge: Polity Press.

Gilbert, P. and Irons, C. (2005) Focused therapies and compassionate mind training for shame and self-attacking. In P. Gilbert (ed.) *Compassion: Conceptualisations, Research and Use in Psychotherapy*. London: Routledge.

Glowa, P.T., Frasier, P.Y. and Newton, W.P. (2002) Increasing physician comfort level in screening and counseling patients for intimate partner violence: hands-on practice, *Patient Education and Counseling*, 46: 213–20.

Goldberg, C. (2000) Basic Emotional Communication (BEC) for intimate relating: guidelines for dialogue, *Journal of Contemporary Psychotherapy*, 30: 61–70.

Goldberg, M.C. (1998) *The Art of the Question: A Guide to Short-term Question-centered Therapy*. New York: Wiley.

Goleman, D. (2005) *Emotional Intelligence*. New York: Bantam Books.

Goodman, G. (1984) SASHAtapes: expanding options for help-intended communication. In D. Larson (ed.) *Teaching Psychological Skills: Models for Giving Psychology Away*. Monterey, CA: Brooks/Cole.

Goodman, J., Schlossberg, N.K. and Anderson, M. (2006) *Counseling Adults in Transition: Linking Practice with Theory*, 3rd edn. New York: Springer.

Gordon, K.M. and Toukmanian, S.G. (2002) Is *how* it is said important? The association between quality of therapist response and client processing, *Counselling and Psychotherapy Research*, 2: 88–98.

Gordon, T. (1984) Three decades of democratising relationships through training. In D. Larson (ed.) *Teaching Psychological Skills: Models for Giving Psychology Away*. Monterey, CA: Brooks/Cole.

Goss, S. and Antony, K. (eds) (2003) *Technology in Counselling and Psychotherapy: A Practitioner's Guide*. London: Palgrave Macmillan.

Grant, A., Mills, J., Mulhern, R. and Short, N. (2004) *Cognitive Behavioural Therapy in Mental Health Care*. London: Sage Publications.

Grayson, A., Miller, H. and Clarke, D. (1998) Identifying barriers to help-seeking: a qualitative analysis of students' preparedness to seek help from tutors, *British Journal of Guidance and Counselling*, 26: 237–54.

Greenberg, L.S. (1992) Task analysis: identifying components of intrapersonal conflict resolution. In S.G. Toukmanian and D.L. Rennie (eds) *Psychotherapy Process Research: Paradigmatic and Narrative Approaches*. Thousand Oaks, CA: Sage Publications.

Greenberg, L.S. (2001) *Emotion-focused Therapy: Coaching Clients to Work Through their Feelings*. Washington, DC: American Psychological Association.

Greenberg, L.S. and Geller, S. (2001) Congruence and therapeutic presence. In G Wyatt (ed.) *Rogers' Therapeutic Conditions: Evolution, Theory and Practice, Vol. 1: Congruence*. Ross-on-Wye: PCCS Books.

Greenberg, L.S., Rice, L.N. and Elliott, R. (1993) *Facilitating Emotional Change: The Moment-by-moment Process*. New York: Guilford Press.

Greenberger, D. and Padesky, C.A. (1995) *Mind Over Mood: Change How you Feel by Changing the Way you Think*. New York: Guilford Press.

Greenhalgh, T. and Hurwitz, B. (eds) (1998) *Narrative-based Medicine – Dialogue and Discourse in Clinical Practice*. London: BMJ Publications.

Grohol, J.M. (2004) *The Insider's Guide to Mental Health Resources Online*, 2nd edn. New York: Guilford Press.

Guerney Jr., B.G. (1984) Relationship enhancement therapy and training. In D. Larson (ed.) *Teaching Psychological Skills: Models for Giving Psychology Away*. Monterey, CA: Brooks/Cole.

Gulbrandsen, P., Krupat, E., Benth, J.S., Garratt, A., Safran, D.G., Finset, A. and Frankel, R. (2008) 'Four Habits' goes abroad: report from a pilot study in Norway, *Patient Education and Counseling*, 72: 388–93.

Hadfield, S. and Hasson, G. (2010) *How to be Assertive in any Situation*. London: Prentice Hall.

Haldeman, D.C. (2010) Reflections of a gay male psychotherapist, *Psychotherapy: Theory, Research, Practice, Training*, 47: 177–85.

Hall, B. and Gabor, P. (2004) Peer suicide prevention in a prison, *Crisis*, 25: 19–26.

Hall, E., Hall, C., Stradling, P. and Young, D. (2006) *Guided Imagery: Creative Interventions in Counselling and Psychotherapy*. London: Sage Publications.

Hall R.C. and Platt D.E. (1999) Suicide risk assessment: a review of risk factors for suicide in 100 patients who made severe suicide attempts, *Psychosomatics*, 40: 18–27.

Hart, N. (1996) The role of tutor in a college of higher education – a comparison of skills used by personal tutors and by student counsellors when working with students in distress, *British Journal of Guidance and Counselling*, 24: 83–96.

Harting, P., van Assema, P., van der Molen, H., Ambersen, T. and de Vries, N.K. (2004) Quality assessment of health counselling: performance of health advisors in cardiovascular prevention, *Patient Education and Counseling*, 54: 107–18.

Hawkins, P. and Shohet, R. (2000) *Supervision in the Helping Professions*, 2nd edn. Maidenhead: Open University Press.

Hecker, L.L. and Deacon, S.A. (eds) (2006) *The Therapist's Notebook: Homework, Handouts, and Activities for Use in Psychotherapy*. New York: Routledge.

Hecker, L.L. and Sori, C.F. (eds) (2007) *The Therapist's Notebook, Volume 2: More Homework, Handouts, and Activities for Use in Psychotherapy*. New York: Routledge.

Heron, J. (2001) *Helping the Client: A Creative Practical Guide*, 5th edn. London: Sage Publications.

Hill, C.E. (ed.) (2001) *Helping Skills: The Empirical Foundation*. Washington, DC: American Psychological Association.

Hill, C.E. (2004) *Helping Skills: Facilitating Exploration, Insight and Action*. 2nd edn. Washington, DC: American Psychological Association.

Hill, C.E. and Kellems, I.S. (2002) Development and use of the Helping Skills Measure to assess client perceptions of the effects of training and of helping skills in session evaluation, *Journal of Counseling Psychology*, 49: 264–72.

Hill, C.E. and Lent, R.W. (2006) A narrative and meta-analytic review of helping skills training: time to revive a dormant area of inquiry, *Psychotherapy: Theory, Research, Practice, Training*, 43: 154–72.

Hochschild, A. (1983) *The Managed Heart: The Commercialization of Human Feeling*. Berkeley, CA: University of California Press.

Hockey, J., Katz, J. and Small, N. (eds) (2001) *Grief, Mourning and Death Ritual*. Maidenhead: Open University Press.

Hofstede, G. (2003) *Culture's Consequences: Comparing Values, Behaviors, Institutions, and Organizations across Nations*, 2nd edn. Thousand Oaks, CA: Sage Publications.

Hofstede, G.J., Pedersen, P.B. and Hofstede, G. (2002) *Exploring Culture: Exercises, Stories and Synthetic Cultures*. Yarmouth, ME: Intercultural Press.

Holland, J. (2008) How schools can support children who experience loss and death, *British Journal of Guidance and Counselling*, 36: 411–24.

Hollin, C.R. and Trower, P. (eds) (1986) *Handbook of Social Skills Training. Vols. 1 and 2: Applications Across the Life Span; Clinical Applications and New Directions*. New York: Pergamon Press.

Holmes, J. (1999a) Narrative, attachment and the therapeutic process. In C. Mace (ed.) *Heart and Soul: The Therapeutic Face of Philosophy*. London: Routledge.

Holmes, J. (1999b) The relationship in psychodynamic counselling. In C. Feltham (ed.) *Understanding the Counselling Relationship*. London: Sage Publications.

Holmes, J. (2000) Attachment theory and psychoanalysis: a *rapprochement, British Journal of Psychotherapy*, 17: 157–72.

Holmes, J. (2001) *The Search for the Secure Base: Attachment, Psychoanalysis, and Narrative*. London: Routledge.

Honos-Webb, L. and Stiles, W.B. (1998) Reformulation of assimilation analysis in terms of voices, *Psychotherapy*, 35: 23–33.

Hopson, B. (1989) Life transitions and crises. In N. Niven (ed.) *Health Psychology*. Edinburgh: Churchill Livingstone.

Hopson, B. and Adams, J. (1976) Towards an understanding: defining some boundaries of transition dynamics. In J. Adams, J. Hayes and B. Hopson (eds) *Transition: Understanding and Managing Personal Change*. London: Martin Robertson.

Hunter, M. and Struve, J. (1998) *The Ethical Use of Touch in Psychotherapy*. Thousand Oaks, CA: Sage Publications.

Illich, I. (2001) *Medical Nemesis: The Expropriation of Health*, rev. edn. London: Marion Boyars.

Imber-Black, E. and Roberts, J. (1992) *Rituals for our Times: Celebrating Healing and Changing our Lives and Relationships*. New York: HarperCollins.

Ingham, C. (2000) *Panic Attacks: What they Are, Why they Happen and What you Can Do about them*. Glasgow: HarperCollins.

Ivey, A.E. and Galvin, M. (1984) Microcounseling: a metamodel for counselling, therapy, business and medical interviews. In D. Larson (ed.) *Teaching Psychological Skills: Models for Giving Psychology Away*. Monterey, CA: Brooks/Cole.

Ivey, A.E. and Matthews, M.J. (1984) A meta-model for structuring the clinical interview, *Journal of Counseling and Development*, 83: 237–43.

Ivey, A.E., Ivey, M.B. and Zalaquett, C.P. (2010) *Intentional Interviewing and Counseling: Facilitating Client Development in a Multicultural Society*, 7th edn. Belmont, CA: Brooks/Cole.

Jacobs, M. (2005) *The Presenting Past*, 3rd edn. Maidenhead: Open University Press.

James, R. (2012) *Crisis Intervention Strategies*, 7th edn. Belmont, CA: Wadsworth.

James, R. and Gilliland, B. (2001) *Crisis Intervention Strategies*, 4th edn. Belmont, CA: Wadsworth.

Jamison, K.R. (1999) *Night Falls Fast: Understanding Suicide*. New York: Vintage.

Jampel, J.B. (2010) When hearing clients work with a deaf therapist, *Psychotherapy: Theory, Research, Practice, Training*, 47: 144–50.

Jangland, E., Gunningberg, L. and Carlsson, M. (2009) Patients' and relatives' complaints about encounters and communication in health care: evidence for quality improvement, *Patient Education and Counseling*, 75: 199–204.

Jansen, J., van Weert, J.C.M., de Groot, J., van Dulmen, S., Heeren, J. and Bensing, J.M. (2010) Emotional and informational patient cues: the impact of nurses' responses on recall, *Patient Education and Counseling*, 79: 218–24.

Janssen, A.L. and MacLeod, R.D. (2010) What can people approaching death teach us about how to care? *Patient Education and Counseling*, 81: 251–6.

Jeffers, S. (2007) *Feel the Fear and Do it Anyway: How to Turn your Fear and Indecision into Confidence and Action*, rev. edn. New York: Vermilion.

Jenkins, A. (2006) Shame, realisation and restitution: the ethics of restorative practice, *Australia and New Zealand Journal of Family Therapy*, 27: 153–62.

Jenkins, P. (2007) *Counselling, Psychotherapy and the Law*, 2nd edn. London: Sage Publications.

Jennings, L. and Skovholt, T.M. (1999) The cognitive, emotional and relational characteristics of master therapists, *Journal of Counseling Psychology*, 48: 3–11.

Jennings, L., Sovereign, A., Bottoroff, N., Mussell, M.P. and Vye, C. (2005) Nine ethical values of master therapists, *Journal of Mental Health Counseling*, 27: 32–47.

Jevne, R.F. (1987) Creating stillpoints: beyond a rational approach to counselling cancer patients, *Journal of Psychosocial Oncology*, 5: 1–15.

Jevne, R.F., Nekolaichuk, C.L. and Williamson, F.H.A. (1998) A model for counselling cancer patients, *Canadian Journal of Counselling*, 32: 213–29.

Johnson, B. (2008) Teacher–student relationships which promote resilience at school: a micro-level analysis of students' views, *British Journal of Guidance and Counselling*, 36: 385–98.

Joseph, D.I. (2000) The practical art of suicide assessment: a guide for mental health professionals and substance abuse counselors, *Journal of Clinical Psychiatry*, 61(9): 683–4.

Josselson, R. (1996) *The Space Between Us: Exploring the Dimensions of Human Relationships*. Thousand Oaks, CA: Sage Publications.

Kagan, N. (1984) Interpersonal Process Recall: basic methods and recent research. In D. Larson (ed.) *Teaching Psychological Skills: Models for Giving Psychology Away*. Monterey, CA: Brooks/Cole.

Karp, M., Holmes, P. and Taubon, K.B. (eds) (1998) *The Handbook of Psychodrama*. London: Routledge.

Katz, J. (2001) Supporting bereaved children at school. In J. Hockey, J. Katz and N. Small (eds) *Grief, Mourning and Death Ritual*. Maidenhead: Open University Press.

Kenny, D.T. (2004) Constructions of chronic pain in doctor–patient relationships: bridging the communication chasm, *Patient Education and Counseling*, 52: 297–305.

Kettunen, T., Poskiparta, M. and Karhila, P. (2003) Speech practices that facilitate patient participation in health counselling – a way to empowerment? *Health Educational Journal*, 62: 326–40.

King, A. (2001) *Demystifying the Counseling Process: A Self-help Handbook for Counselors*. Needham Heights, MA: Allyn & Bacon

Kinman, C.J. and Finck, P. (2004) Response-able practice: a language of gifts in the institutions of health care. In T. Strong and D. Pare (eds) *Furthering Talk: Advances in the Discursive Therapies*. New York: Kluwer.

Kitchener, B. and Jorm, A. (2009) *Mental Health First Aid Manual*. Melbourne, VIC: University of Melbourne Orygen Research Centre.

Kitchener, K.S. (1984) Intuition, critical evaluation and ethical principles: the foundation for ethical decisions in counseling psychology, *Counseling Psychologist*, 12: 43–55.

Kleinman, A. (1988) *The Illness Narratives: Suffering, Healing and the Human Condition*. New York: Basic Books.

Kopp, R.R. and Craw, M.J. (1998) Metaphoric language, metaphoric cognition, and cognitive therapy, *Psychotherapy*, 35: 306–11.

L'Abate, L. (2004) *A Guide to Self-help Workbooks for Mental Health Clinicians and Researchers*. New York: Haworth.

Lago, C. (2006) *Race, Culture and Counselling: The Ongoing Challenge*, 2nd edn. Maidenhead: Open University Press.

Lago, C. (ed.) (2011) *The Handbook of Transcultural Counselling and Psychotherapy*. Maidenhead: Open University Press.

Lago, C. and Macmillan, M. (eds) (2000) *Experiences in Relatedness: Groupwork and the Person-centred Approach*. Hay-on-Wye: PCCS Books.

Lago, C. and Smith, B. (2010) *Anti-discriminatory Practice in Counselling and Psychotherapy*, 2nd edn. London: Sage Publications.

Lahad, M. (2000) *Creative Supervision: The Use of Expressive Arts Methods in Supervision and Self-supervision*. London: Jessica Kingsley.

Lakoff, G. and Johnson, M. (1980) *Metaphors we Live By*. Chicago, IL: University of Chicago Press.

Lakoff, G. and Johnson, M. (1999) *Philosophy in the Flesh: The Embodied Mind and its Challenge to Western Thought*. New York: Basic Books.

Larson, D. (ed.) (1984) *Teaching Psychological Skills: Models for Giving Psychology Away*. Monterey, CA; Brooks/Cole.

Larson, E.B. and Yao, X. (2005) Clinical empathy as emotional labor in the patient–physician relationship, *Journal of the American Medical Association*, 293: 1100–6.

Lawton, B. and Feltham, C. (eds) (2000) *Taking Supervision Forward: Enquiries and Trends in Counselling and Psychotherapy*. London: Sage Publications.

Lazarus, A.A. and Zur, O. (eds) (2002) *Dual Relationships in Psychotherapy*. New York: Springer.

Le Surf, A. and Lynch, G. (1999) Exploring young people's perceptions relevant to counselling: a qualitative study, *British Journal of Guidance and Counselling*, 27: 231–44.

Leahy, R.L. (2003) *Cognitive Therapy Techniques: A Practitioner's Guide*. New York: Guilford Press.

Leiper, R. (2004) *The Psychodynamic Approach to Therapeutic Change*. London: Sage Publications.

Lendrum, S. and Syme, G. (2004) *Gift of Tears: A Practical Approach to Loss and Bereavement in Counselling and Psychotherapy*, 2nd edn. London: Brunner-Routledge.

Leiter, M.P. and Maslach, C. (2005) *Banishing Burnout: Six Strategies for Improving your Relationship*. San Francisco, CA: Jossey-Bass.

Lent, R.W., Hill, C.E. and Hoffman, M.A. (2003) Development and validation of the Counselor Activity Self-Efficacy Scales, *Journal of Counseling Psychology*, 50: 97–108.

Levinson, D.J. (1986) *The Seasons of a Man's Life*. New York: Ballantine.

Levitt, H., Butler, M. and Hill, T. (2006) What clients find helpful in psychotherapy: developing principles for facilitating moment-to-moment change, *Journal of Counseling Psychology*, 53: 314–24.

Lewchanin, S. and Zubrod, L.A. (2001) Choices in life: a clinical tool for facilitating midlife review, *Journal of Adult Development*, 8: 193–6.

Lieberman, M., Yalom, I. and Miles, M. (1973) *Encounter Groups: First Facts*. New York: Basic Books.

Linden, S. and Grut, J. (2002) *The Healing Fields: Working with Psychotherapy and Nature to Rebuild Shattered Lives*. London: Frances Lincoln.

Lindgren, B.-M., Sture, A. and Graneheim, U.H. (2010) Held to ransom: parents of self-harming adults describe their lived experience of professional care and caregivers, *International Journal on Qualitative Studies of Health and Well-being*, 5: 1–10.

Loewenstein, G.F., Weber, E.U., Hsee, C.K. and Welch, N. (2001) Risk as feeling, *Psychological Bulletin*, 127: 267–86.

Luborsky, L., Barber, J.P. and Diguer, L. (1992) The meanings of narratives told during psychotherapy: the fruits of a new observational unit, *Psychotherapy Research*, 2: 277–90.

Luborsky, L., Popp, C., Luborsky, E. and Mark, D. (1994) The core conflictual relationship theme, *Psychotherapy Research*, 4: 172–83.

Lukas, C. and Seiden, H.M. (2007) *Silent Grief: Living in the Wake of Suicide*, 2nd edn. London: Jessica Kingsley.

MacCormack, T., Simonian, J., Lim, J., Remond, L., Roets, D., Dunn, S. and Butow, P. (2001) 'Someone who cares': a qualitative investigation of cancer patients' experiences of psychotherapy, *Psycho-Oncology*, 10: 52–65.

Machin, L. (2008) *Working with Loss and Grief: A New Model for Practitioners*. London: Sage Publications.

Madigan, S. (1999) Inscription, description and deciphering chronic identities. In I. Parker (ed.) *Deconstructing Psychotherapy*. London: Sage Publications.

Mahrer, A.R., Gagnon, R., Fairweather, D.R., Boulet, D.B. and Herring, C.B. (1994) Client commitment and resolve to carry out postsession behaviors, *Journal of Counseling Psychology*, 41: 407–44.

Mair, J.M.M. (1977) The community of self. In D. Bannister (ed.) *New Perspectives in Personal Construct Theory*. London: Academic Press.

Maisel, R., Epston, D. and Borden, A. (2004) *Biting the Hand that Starves you: Inspiring Resistance to Anorexia/Bulimia*. New York: W.W. Norton and Company.

Maiter, S., Palmer, S. and Manji, S. (2006) Strengthening social worker–client relationships in child protective services: addressing power imbalances and 'ruptured' relationships, *Qualitative Social Work*, 5: 161–86.

Mallon, B. (2010) *Working with Bereaved Children and Young People*. London: Sage Publications.

Maslach, C. and Leiter, M.P. (1997) *The Truth about Burnout: How Organizations Cause Personal Stress and What to Do about It*. San Francisco, CA: Jossey-Bass.

McAdams, D. (2000) *The Person*, 3rd edn. New York: Harcourt.

McAdams, D.P. (1993) *The Stories We Live By: Personal Myths and the Making of the Self*. New York: William Murrow.

McCluskey, G., Lloyd, G., Kane, J., Riddell, S., Stead, J. and Weedon, E. (2008) Can restorative practices in schools make a difference? *Educational Review*, 60: 405–17.

McGoldrick, M. (1998) Belonging and liberation: finding a place called 'home'. In M. McGoldrick (ed.) *Re-visioning Family Therapy: Race, Culture and Gender in Clinical Practice*. New York: Guilford Press.

McLellan, J. (1991) Formal and informal counselling help: students' experiences, *British Journal of Guidance and Counselling*, 19: 149–58.

McLeod, J. (1990) The client's experience of counselling and psychotherapy: a review of the research literature. In D. Mearns and W. Dryden (eds) *Experiences of Counselling in Action*. London: Sage Publications.

McLeod, J. (1997a) Listening to stories about health and illness: applying the lessons of narrative psychology. In I. Horton *et al.* (eds) *Counselling and Psychology for Health Professionals*. London: Sage Publications.

McLeod, J. (1997b) *Narrative and Psychotherapy*. London: Sage Publications.

McLeod, J. (1999) Counselling as a social process, *Counselling*, 10: 217–22.

McLeod, J. (2003) *Doing Counselling Research*, 2nd edn. London: Sage Publications.

McLeod, J. (2004a) The significance of narrative and storytelling in postpsychological counseling and psychotherapy. In A. Lieblich, D. McAdams and R. Josselson (eds) *Healing Plots: The Narrative Basis of Psychotherapy*. Washington, DC: American Psychological Association.

McLeod, J. (2004b) Social construction, narrative and psychotherapy. In L. Angus and J. McLeod (eds) *The Handbook of Narrative and Psychotherapy: Practice, Theory and Research*. Thousand Oaks, CA: Sage Publications.

McLeod, J. (2005) Counseling and psychotherapy as cultural work. In L.T. Hoshmand (ed.) *Culture, Psychotherapy and Counseling: Critical and Integrative Perspectives*. Thousand Oaks, CA: Sage Publications.

McLeod, J. (2009) *An Introduction to Counselling*, 4th edn. Maidenhead: Open University Press.

McMillan, D.W. (2006) *Emotion Rituals: A Resource for Therapists and Clients*. London: Routledge.

McNeill, B.W. and Worthen, V. (1989) The parallel process in psychotherapy supervision, *Professional Psychology: Research and Practice*, 20: 329–33.

Mead, N., MacDonald, W., Bower, P., Lovell, K., Richards, D., Roberts, C. and Bucknall, A. (2006) The clinical effectiveness of guided self-help versus waiting-list control in the management of anxiety and depression: a randomized controlled trial, *Psychological Medicine*, 36: 1633–44.

Mearns, D. (1997) *Person-centred Counselling Training*. London: Sage Publications.

Mearns, D. and Cooper, M. (2005) *Working at Relational Depth in Counselling and Psychotherapy*. London: Sage Publications.

Mearns, D. and Thorne, B. (2007) *Person-centred Counselling in Action*, 3rd edn. London: Sage Publications.

Meichenbaum, D. (1994) *Treating Post-traumatic Stress Disorder: A Handbook and Practical Manual for Therapy*. Chichester: Wiley.

Menchola, M., Arkowitz, H.S. and Burke, B.L. (2007) Efficacy of self-administered treatments for depression and anxiety, *Professional Psychology: Research and Practice*, 38: 421–9.

Menzies, I. (1959) A case-study in the functioning of social systems as a defence against anxiety: a report on a study of the nursing service of a general hospital, *Human Relations*, 13: 95–121.

Menzies Lyth, I. (1988) *Containing Anxiety in Institutions: Selected Essays*. London: Free Association.

Menzies Lyth, I. (1989) *The Dynamics of the Social: Selected Essays*. London: Free Association.

Merry, T. (2002) *Learning and Being in Person-centred Counselling*, 2nd edn. Hay-on-Wye: PCCS Books.

Miller, R.B. (2004) *Facing Human Suffering: Psychology and Psychotherapy as Moral Engagement.* Washington, DC: American Psychological Association.

Miller, W.R. and Rollnick, S. (2002) *Motivational Interviewing: Preparing People for Change,* 2nd edn. New York: Guilford Press.

Milne, D.L. (1999) *Social Therapy: A Guide to Social Support Interventions for Mental Health Practitioners.* Chichester: Wiley.

Milne, D.L. and Mullin, M. (1987) Is a problem shared a problem shaved? An evaluation of hairdressers and social support, *British Journal of Clinical Psychology,* 26: 69–70.

Mirsalimi, H. (2010) Perspectives of an Iranian psychologist practicing in America, *Psychotherapy Theory: Research, Practice, Training,* 47: 151–61.

Moleski, S.M. and Kiselica, M.S. (2005) Dual relationships: a continuum ranging from the destructive to the therapeutic, *Journal of Counseling and Development,* 83: 3–11.

Moodley, R. and West, W. (eds) (2005) *Integrating Indigenous Healing Practices into Counselling and Psychotherapy.* London: Sage Publications.

Moore, J. and Roberts, R. (eds) (2010) *Counselling and Psychotherapy in Organisational Settings.* London: Learning Matters.

Morgan, A. (2001) *What is Narrative Therapy? An Easy-to-read Introduction.* Adelaide: Dulwich Centre.

Morrissette, P.J. (2004) *The Pain of Helping: Psychological Injury of Helping Professionals.* London: Routledge.

Morrow-Bradley, C. and Elliott, R. (1986) Utilization of psychotherapy research by practicing psychotherapists, *American Psychologist,* 41: 188–97.

Mynors-Wallis, L. (2001) Problem-solving treatment in general psychiatric practice, *Advances in Psychiatric Treatment,* 7: 417–25.

Neander, K. and Skott, C. (2006) Important meetings with important persons: narratives from families facing adversity and their key figures, *Qualitative Social Work,* 5: 295–311.

Neimeyer, R.A. (2005) Growing through grief: constructing coherence in narratives of loss. In D. Winter and L. Viney (eds) *Advances in Personal Construct Psychotherapy.* London: Whurr.

Neimeyer, R.A. (2006) Complicated grief and the reconstruction of meaning: conceptual and empirical contributions to a cognitive-constructivist model, *Clinical Psychology: Science and Practice,* 13: 141–5.

Neimeyer, R.A., Baldwin, S. and Gillies, J. (2006) Continuing bonds and reconstructing meaning: mitigating complications in bereavement, *Death Studies,* 15: 715–38.

Neimeyer, R.A., Fortner, B. and Melby, D. (2001) Personal and professional factors and suicide intervention skills, *Suicide and Life-Threatening Behavior,* 31: 71–82.

Neimeyer, R.A., Harris, D.L., Winokuer, H.R. and Thornton, G.F. (eds) (2011) *Grief and Bereavement in Contemporary Society: Bridging Research and Practice.* New York: Routledge.

Newman, C.F. (2000) Hypotheticals in cognitive psychotherapy: creative questions, novel answers, and therapeutic change, *Journal of Cognitive Psychotherapy,* 14: 135–47.

Newnes, C., Holmes, G. and Dunn, C. (eds) (1999) *This is Madness: A Critical Look at Psychiatry and the Future of Mental Health Services.* Ross-on-Wye: PCCS Books.

Newnes, C., Holmes, G. and Dunn, C. (eds) (2000) *This is Madness Too: A Further Look at Psychiatry and the Future of Mental Health Services.* Ross-on-Wye: PCCS Books.

Nezu, A.M., Nezu, C.M. and Perri, M.G. (1989) *Problem Solving Therapy for Depression: Theory, Research, and Clinical Guidelines.* New York: Wiley.

Nezu, A.M., Nezu, C.M., Friedman, S.H., Faddis, S. and Houts, P.S. (1998) *Coping with Cancer: A Problem Solving Approach.* Washington, DC: American Psychological Association.

Nichols, K. (2003) *Psychological Care for Ill and Injured People: A Clinical Guide.* Maidenhead: Open University Press.

Norcross, J.C. (2006) Integrating self-help into psychotherapy: 16 practical suggestions, *Professional Psychology: Research and Practice,* 37: 683–93.

Norcross, J.C., Santrock, J.W., Campbell, L.F., Smith, T.P., Sommer, R. and Zuckerman, E.L. (2003) *Authoritative Guide to Self-help Resources in Mental Health,* rev. edn. New York: Guilford Press.

Oatley, K. and Jenkins, J.M. (1996) *Understanding Emotions*. Oxford: Blackwell.

Obholzer, A. and Roberts, V.Z. (eds) (1994) *The Unconscious at Work: Individual and Organizational Stress in the Human Services*. London: Routledge.

O'Connell, B. (1998) *Solution-focused Therapy*. London: Sage Publications.

Omer, H. (1997) Narrative empathy, *Psychotherapy*, 25: 171–84.

Orford, J. (1992) *Community Psychology: Theory and Practice*. Chichester: Wiley.

Page, S. and Wosket, V. (2001) *Supervising the Counsellor: A Cyclical Model*, 2nd edn. Hove: Brunner-Routledge.

Palmer, S. (2002) Suicide reduction and prevention, *British Journal of Guidance and Counselling*, 30: 341–52.

Palmer, S. (ed.) (2001) *Multicultural Counselling: A Reader*. London: Sage Publications.

Pavilanis, S. (2010) *A Life Less Anxious: Freedom from Panic Attacks and Social Anxiety without Drugs or Therapy*. Chicago, IL: Alpen.

Payne, M. (2010) *Couple Counselling: A Practical Guide*. London: Sage Publications.

Pedersen, P.B. (1991) Multiculturalism as a generic approach to counseling, *Journal of Counseling and Development*, 70: 6–12.

Pedersen, P. (1997) The cultural context of the American Counseling Association Code of Ethics, *Journal of Counseling and Development*, 76: 23–8.

Pedersen, P. (2000) *A Handbook for Developing Multicultural Awareness*, 3rd edn. Alexandria, VA: American Counseling Association.

Penn, P. and Frankfurt, M. (1994) Creating a participant text: writing, multiple voices, narrative multiplicity, *Family Process*, 33: 217–32.

Pennebaker, J.W. (1997) *Opening Up: The Healing Power of Expressing Emotions*, rev. edn. New York: Guilford Press.

Peters, H. (1999) Pre-therapy: a client-centered/experiential approach to mentally handicapped people, *Journal of Humanistic Psychology*, 39: 8–29.

Pierce, D. and Gunn, J. (2007) GPs' use of problem solving therapy for depression: a qualitative study of barriers to and enablers of evidence based care, *BMC Family Practice*, 8: 24.

Pilnick, A. (2002) 'There are no rights and wrongs in these situations': identifying interactional difficulties in genetic counselling, *Sociology of Health and Illness*, 24: 66–88.

Pistrang, N. and Barker, C. (1998) Partners and fellow patients: two sources of emotional support for women with breast cancer, *American Journal of Community Psychology*, 26: 439–56.

Pistrang, N., Barker, C. and Humphreys, K. (2010) The contributions of mutual help groups for mental health problems to psychological well-being: a systematic review. In L.D. Brown and S. Wituk (eds) *Mental Health Self-help: Consumer and Family Initiatives*. New York: Springer Verlag.

Platt, D. (2008) Care or control? The effects of investigations and initial assessments on the social worker–parent relationship, *Journal of Social Work Practice*, 22: 301–15.

Pope, K.S. (1991) Dual relationships in psychotherapy, *Ethics and Behavior*, 1: 21–34.

Prilleltensky, I. and Nelson, G.B. (2005) *Community Psychology: In Pursuit of Liberation and Well-being*. Basingstoke: Palgrave Macmillan.

Prochaska, J.O. and DiClemente, C.C. (2005) The transtheoretical approach. In J.C. Norcross and M.R. Goldfried (eds) *Handbook of Psychotherapy Integration*, 2nd edn. New York: Oxford University Press.

Prochaska, J.O., Norcross, J.C. and DiClemente, C.C. (1994) *Changing for Good*. New York: William Morrow.

Proctor, G., Cooper, M., Sanders, P. and Malcolm, B. (eds) (2006) *Politicizing the Person-centred Approach: An Agenda for Social Change*. Ross-on-Wye: PCCS Books.

Prouty, G. (2000) Pre-therapy and the pre-expressive self. In T. Merry (ed.) *The BAPCA Reader*. Hay-on-Wye: PCCS Books.

Prouty, G., Van Werde, D. and Portner, M. (2002) *Pre-therapy: Reaching Contact-impaired Clients*. Hay-on-Wye: PCCS Books.

Purton, C. (2005) *Person-centred Therapy: A Focusing-oriented Approach*. London: Sage Publications.

Qian, M., Gao, J., Yao, P. and Rodriguez, M.A. (2009) Professional ethical issues and the development of professional ethical standards in counselling and clinical psychology in China, *Ethics and Behavior*, 19: 290–309.

Quirk, M., Mazor, K., Haley, H., Philbin, M., Fischer, M., Sullivan, K. and Hatem, D. (2008) How patients perceive a doctor's caring attitude, *Patient Education and Counseling*, 72: 359–66.

Randall, R. and Southgate, J. (1980) *Co-operative and Community Group Dynamics*. London: Barefoot Books.

Read, S. (2007) *Bereavement Counselling for People with Learning Disabilities: A Manual to Develop Practice*. London: Quay Books.

Redding, R.E., Herbert, J.D., Forman, E.M. and Gaudiano, B.A. (2008) Popular self-help books for anxiety, depression, and trauma: how scientifically grounded and useful are they? *Professional Psychology: Research and Practice*, 39: 537–45.

Reeves, A., Bowl, R., Wheeler, S. and Guthrie, E. (2004) The hardest words: exploring the dialogue of suicide in the counselling process – a discourse analysis, *Counselling and Psychotherapy Research*, 4: 62–71.

Reid, M. (ed.) (2004) *Counselling in Different Settings: The Reality of Practice*. London: Palgrave Macmillan.

Rennie, D.L. (1994) Clients' defence in psychotherapy, *Journal of Counseling Psychology*, 41: 427–37.

Rennie, D.L. (1998) *Person-centred Counselling: An Experiential Approach*. London: Sage Publications.

Rogers, C.R. (1961) *On Becoming a Person*. Boston, MA: Houghton Mifflin.

Rogers, N. (2000) *The Creative Connection: Expressive Arts as Healing*. Ross-on-Wye: PCCS Books.

Romme, M. and Escher, S. (2000) *Making Sense of Voices: A Guide for Mental Health Professionals Working with Voice Hearers*. London: Mind Publications.

Ronan, K.R. and Kazantis, N. (2006) The use of between-session (homework) activities in psychotherapy, *Journal of Psychotherapy Integration*, 16: 254–9.

Ronnestad, M.H. and Skovholt, T.M. (2001) Learning arena for professional development: retrospective accounts of senior psychotherapists, *Professional Psychology: Research and Practice*, 32: 181–7.

Rothschild, B. (2006) *Help for the Helper: The Psychophysiology of Compassion Fatigue and Vicarious Trauma*. New York: W.W. Norton and Company.

Rowan, J. and Cooper, M. (eds) (1998) *The Plural Self: Multiplicity in Everyday Life*. London: Sage Publications.

Rowe, D. (2003) *Depression: The Way Out of your Prison*, 3rd edn. London: Routledge.

Sachse, R. and Elliott, R. (2002) Process-outcome research on humanistic outcome variables. In D.J. Cain and J. Seeman (eds) *Humanistic Psychotherapies: Handbook of Research and Practice*. Washington, DC: American Psychological Association.

Safran, J.D. (1993) Breaches in the therapeutic alliance: an arena for negotiating authentic relatedness, *Psychotherapy*, 30: 11–24.

Safran, J.D. and Muran, J.C. (2000) Resolving therapeutic alliance ruptures: diversity and integration, *Journal of Clinical Psychology*, 56: 233–43.

Saleebey, D. (2002) *The Strengths Perspective in Social Work Practice*, 3rd edn. New York: Allyn & Bacon.

Salkovskis, P., Rimes, K., Stephenson, D., Sacks, G. and Scott, J. (2006) A randomized controlled trial of the use of self-help materials in addition to standard general practice treatment of depression compared to standard treatment alone, *Psychological Medicine*, 36: 325–33.

Scheel, M.J., Hanson, W.E. and Razzhavaikina, T.I. (2004) The process of recommending homework in psychotherapy: a review of therapist delivery methods, client acceptability, and factors that affect compliance, *Psychotherapy: Theory, Research, Practice, Training*, 41: 38–55.

Scheel, M.J., Seaman, S., Roach, K., Mullin, T. and Mahoney, K.B. (1999) Client implementation of therapist recommendations predicted by client perception of fit, difficulty of implementation, and therapist influence, *Journal of Counseling Psychology*, 46: 308–16.

Schein, E.H. (2004) *Organizational Culture and Leadership*, 3rd edn. San Franciso, CA: Jossey-Bass.

Schoenberg, M. and Shiloh, S. (2002) Hospitalized patients' views on in-ward psychological counseling, *Patient Education and Counseling*, 48: 123–9.

Schut, M. and Stroebe, M. (2005) Interventions to enhance adaptation to bereavement, *Journal of Palliative Medicine*, 8: 140–7.

Scott, M.J. and Stradling, S.G. (2006) *Counselling for Post-traumatic Stress Disorder*, 3rd edn. London: Sage Publications.

Scott, S.G. and Bruce, R.A. (1995) Decision-making style: the development and assessment of a new measure, *Educational and Psychological Measurement*, 55: 818–31.

Seden, J. (2005) *Counselling Skills in Social Work Practice*, 2nd edn. Maidenhead: Open University Press.

Seiser, L. and Wastell, C. (2002) *Interventions and Techniques*. Maidenhead: Open University Press.

Sennett, R. (1998) *Corrosion of Character: The Personal Consequences of Work in the New Capitalism*. New York: W.W. Norton and Company.

Shafran, R., Egan, S.J. and Wade, T.D. (2010) *Overcoming Perfectionism: A Self-help Guide Using Cognitive-behavioural Techniques*. London: Constable & Robinson.

Sheehy, G. (1984) *Passages: Predictable Crises of Adult Life*. New York: Bantam.

Shelton, K. and Delgado-Romero, E.A. (2011) Sexual orientation microaggressions: the experience of lesbian, gay, bisexual, and queer clients in psychotherapy, *Journal of Counseling Psychology*, 58: 210–21.

Shiloh, S., Gerad, L. and Goldman, B. (2006) Patients' information needs and decision-making processes: what can be learned from genetic counselees? *Health Psychology*, 25: 211–19.

Shoaib, K. and Peel, J. (2003) Kashmiri women's perceptions of their emotional and psychological needs, and access to counselling, *Counselling and Psychotherapy Research*, 3: 87–94.

Silove, D. and Manicavasagar, V. (1997) *Overcoming Panic: A Self-help Guide using Cognitive-behavioural Techniques*. London: Constable & Robinson.

Silverstone, L. (1997) *Art Therapy: The Person-centred Way*, 2nd edn. London: Jessica Kingsley.

Singer, J. and Blagov, P. (2004) Self-defining memories, narrative identity and psychotherapy: a conceptual model, empirical investigation and case report. In L.E. Angus and J. McLeod (eds) *Handbook of Narrative and Psychotherapy*. Thousand Oaks, CA: Sage Publications.

Skibbins, D. (2007) *Becoming a Life Coach: A Complete Workbook for Therapists*. London: New Harbinger.

Skovholt, T.M. (2008) *The Resilient Practitioner: Burnout Prevention and Self-care Strategies for Counselors, Therapists, Teachers, and Health Professionals*, 2nd edn. New York: Allyn & Bacon.

Skovholt, T.M. and Jennings, L. (2004) *Master Therapists: Exploring Expertise in Therapy and Counseling*. New York: Allyn & Bacon.

Small, N. (2001) Theories of grief: a critical review. In J. Hockey, J. Katz and N. Small (eds) *Grief, Mourning and Death Ritual*. Maidenhead: Open University Press.

Sori, C.F. and Hecker, L.L. (eds) (2008) *The Therapist's Notebook Volume 3: More Homework, Handouts, and Activities for Use in Psychotherapy*. New York: Routledge.

Stadler, H.A. (1986) Making hard choices: clarifying controversial ethical issues, *Counseling and Human Development*, 19: 1–10.

Stein, T., Frankel, R.M. and Krupat, E. (2005) Enhancing clinician communication skills in a large healthcare organization: a longtitudinal case study, *Patient Education and Counseling*, 58: 4–12.

Stewart, I. and Joines, V. (1987) *TA today: A New Introduction to Transactional Analysis*. Nottingham: Lifespace Publishing.

Stiles, W.B. (1999) Signs and voices in psychotherapy, *Psychotherapy Research*, 9, 1–21.

Stokes, A. (2001) Settings. In S. Aldridge and S. Rigby (eds) *Counselling Skills in Context*. London: Hodder & Stoughton.

Stone, H. and Stone, S. (1993) *Embracing your Inner Critic: Turning Self-criticism into a Creative Asset*. New York: Harper.

Stroebe, M.S. and Schut, H.W. (1999) The dual process model of coping with bereavement: rationale and description, *Death Studies*, 23: 197–224.

Stroebe, W., Schut, H. and Stroebe, M. (2005) Grief work, disclosure and counselling: do they help the bereaved? *Clinical Psychology Review*, 25: 395–414.

Strong, T. and Zeman, D. (2010) Dialogic considerations of confrontation as a counseling activity: an examination of Allen Ivey's use of confronting as a microskill, *Journal of Counseling and Development*, 88: 332–9.

Sue, D.W., Capodilupo, C.M., Torino, G.C., Bucceri, J.M., Holder, A.M. B., Nadal, K.L. and Esquilin, M. (2007) Racial microaggressions in everyday life: implications for clinical practice, *American Psychologist*, 62: 271–86.

Sugarman, L. (2004) *Counselling and the Life Course*. London: Sage Publications.

Sugarman, L. (2009) Life course as a meta-model for counselling psychology. In R. Woolfe, S. Strawbridge, B. Douglas and W. Dryden (eds) *Handbook of Counselling Psychology*, 3rd edn. London: Sage Publications.

Syme, G. (2003) *Dual Relationships in Counselling and Psychotherapy*. London: Sage Publications.

Talmon, S. (1990) *Single Session Therapy: Maximising the Effect of the First (and often only) Therapeutic Encounter*. San Francisco, CA: Jossey-Bass.

Thompson, C. and Jenal, S. (1994) Interracial and intraracial quasi-counselling interactions: when counselors avoid discussing race, *Journal of Counseling Psychology*, 41: 484–91.

Timulak, L. (2011) *Developing your Counselling and Psychotherapy Skills and Practice*. London: Sage Publications.

Tolan, J. (2003) *Skills in Person-centred Counselling and Therapy*. London: Sage Publications.

Trower, P. (1979) Fundamentals of interpersonal behavior: a social-psychological perspective. In A.M. Bellack and M. Hersen (eds) *Research and Practice in Social Skills Training*. New York: Plenum Press.

Trower, P. (1988) *Cognitive-behavioural Counselling in Action*. London: Sage Publications.

Trower, P., Bryant, B. and Argyle, M. (1978) *Social Skills and Mental Health*. London: Methuen.

Tuckwell, G. (2001) 'The threat of the Other': using mixed quantitative and qualitative methods to eluci-date racial and cultural dynamics in the counselling process, *Counselling and Psychotherapy Research*, 1: 154–62.

Twentyman, C.T. and McFall, R.M. (1975) Behavioral training of social skills in shy males, *Journal of Consulting and Clinical Psychology*, 43: 384–95.

Uhernik, J.A. and Husson, M.A. (2009) Psychological first aid: an evidence informed approach for acute disaster behavioral health response. In G.R. Walz (ed.) *Compelling Counseling Interventions*. Alexandria, VA: American Counseling Association.

Ungar, M., Barter, K., McConnell, S.M., Tutty, L.M. and Fairholm, J. (2009) Patterns of abuse disclosure among youth, *Qualitative Social Work*, 8: 341–56.

Vanaerschot, G. (1993) Empathy as releasing several micro-processes in the client. In D. Brazier (ed.) *Beyond Carl Rogers*. London: Constable.

Varley, R., Webb, T.L. and Sheeran, P. (2011) Making self-help more helpful: a randomized controlled trial of the impact of augmenting self-help materials with implementation intentions on promoting the effective self-management of anxiety symptoms, *Journal of Consulting and Clinical Psychology*, 79: 123–28.

Walter, T. (1999a) A new model of grief: bereavement and biography, *Mortality*, 1: 7–25.

Walter, T. (1999b) *On Bereavement: The Culture of Grief*. Maidenhead: Open University Press.

Warren, B. (ed.) (1993) *Using the Creative Arts in Therapy*, 2nd edn. London: Routledge.

Weaks, D. (2002) Unlocking the secrets of 'good' supervision, *Counselling and Psychotherapy Research*, 2: 33–9.

Weaks, D., McLeod, J. and Wilkinson, H. (2006) Dementia, *Therapy Today*, 17: 12–15.

Weiser, J. (1999) *PhotoTherapy Techniques: Exploring the Secrets of Personal Snapshots and Family Albums*, 2nd edn. Vancouver, BC: PhotoTherapy Centre Press.

Wells, D. (2011) The value of pets for human health, *The Psychologist*, 24: 172–6.

Wertheimer, A. (2001) *A Special Scar: The Experiences of People Bereaved by Suicide*, 2nd edn. London: Routledge.

Westbrook, D., Kennerley, H. and Kirk, J. (2007) *An Introduction to Cognitive Behaviour Therapy: Skills and Applications*. London: Sage Publications.

Wheeler, S. (ed.) (2006) *Difference and Diversity in Counselling: Contemporary Psychodynamic Approaches*. Basingstoke: Palgrave Macmillan.

Wheeler, S. and Richards, K. (2007) *The Impact of Clinical Supervision on Counsellors and Therapists, their Practice and their Clients: A Systematic Review of the Literature*. Lutterworth: BACP.

White, C. and Hales, J. (eds) (1997) *The Personal is the Professional: Therapists Reflect on their Families, Lives and Work*. Adelaide: Dulwich Centre Publications.

White, G.L. and Taytroe, L. (2003) Personal problem-solving using dream incubation: dreaming, relaxation, or waking cognition? *Dreaming*, 13: 193–209.

White, M. (1997) *Narratives of Therapists' Lives*. Adelaide: Dulwich Centre Publications.

White, M. (1998) Saying hullo again: the incorporation of the lost relationship in the resolution of grief. In C. White and D. Denborough (eds) *Introducing Narrative Therapy: A Collection of Practice-based Writings*. Adelaide: Dulwich Centre Publications.

White, M. and Epston, D. (1990) *Narrative Means to Therapeutic Ends*. New York: W.W. Norton and Company.

White, V.E., McCormack, L.J. and Kelly, B.L. (2003) Counseling clients who self-injure: ethical considerations, *Counseling and Values*, 47: 220–9.

Wigrem, J. (1994) Narrative completion in the treatment of trauma, *Psychotherapy*, 31: 415–23.

Willi, J. (1999) *Ecological Psychotherapy: Developing by Shaping the Personal Niche*. Seattle, WA: Hogrefe & Huber.

Williams, G. (1984) The genesis of chronic illness: narrative re-construction, *Sociology of Health and Illness*, 6: 175–200.

Williams, M. (1997) *Cry of Pain: Understanding Suicide and Self-harm*. London: Penguin.

Williams, M. and Winslade, J. (2011) Co-authoring new relationships at school through narrative mediation, *New Zealand Journal of Counselling*, 30: 62–74.

Williams, M., Teasdale, J., Segal, Z. and Kabat-Zinn, J. (2007) *The Mindful Way through Depression: Freeing yourself from Chronic Unhappiness*. New York: Guilford Press.

Wills, F. (1997) *Cognitive Therapy*. London: Sage Publications.

Wills, T.A. (1982) Nonspecific factors in helping relationships. In T.A. Wills (ed.) *Basic Processes in Helping Relationships*. New York: Academic Press.

Worden, W. (2001) *Grief Counselling and Grief Therapy: A Handbook for the Mental Health Practitioner*. London: Brunner/Routledge.

Wortman, C.B. and Silver, R.C. (1989) The myths of coping with loss, *Journal of Consulting and Clinical Psychology*, 57: 349–57.

Wosket, V. (2006) *Egan's Skilled Helper Model*. London: Routledge.

Yalom, I. (2002) *The Gift of Therapy: Reflections on Being a Therapist*. London: Piatkus.

Yalom, I. (2006) *The Schopenhauer Cure*. London: Harper.

Yalom, I. (2008) *Staring at the Sun: Being at Peace with your own Mortality: Overcoming the Terror of Death*. London: Piatkus.

Yalom, I.D. (2005) *Theory and Practice of Group Psychotherapy*, 4th edn. New York: Basic Books.

Yip, K. (2005) A strengths perspective in working with an adolescent with depression, *Psychiatric Rehabilitation Journal*, 28: 362–9.

Yip, K. (2006) A strengths perspective in working with an adolescent with self-cutting behaviors, *Child and Adolescent Social Work Journal*, 23: 134–42.

Zuckerman, E. (2003) Finding, evaluating, and incorporating internet self-help resources into psychotherapy practice, *Journal of Clinical Psychology*, 59: 217–25.

Index

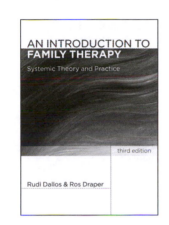

**Relationship Therapy
Systemic Theory and Practice
Third Edition**

Rudi Dallos and Ros Draper
9780335238019 (Paperback)
2010

eBook also available

The third edition of *An Introduction to Family Therapy* provides an overview of the core concepts informing family therapy and systemic practice, covering the development of this innovative field from the 1950s to the present day.

The book considers both British and International perspectives and includes the latest developments in current practice, regulation and innovation, looking at these developments within a wider political, cultural and geographical context.

Key features:

- Sections highlighting the importance of multi-disciplinary practice in health and welfare
- Includes chapters on practice development up to 2009
- Includes chapters on couple therapy

www.openup.co.uk

OPEN UNIVERSITY PRESS
McGraw - Hill Education

The Handbook of Transcultural Counselling and Psychotherapy
First Edition

Colin Lago

9780335238491 (Paperback)
Nov 2011

eBook also available

This fascinating book examines recent critical thinking and contemporary research findings in the field of transcultural counselling and psychotherapy. It also explores the effects of different cultural heritages upon potential clients and therapists.

Key features:

- Covers key issues such as: the implications of identity development for therapeutic work; ethnic matching of clients and therapists and working with interpreters and bi-cultural workers.
- Examines ways to overcome racism, discrimination and oppression within the counselling process.
- Provides an overview of current research within this field.

www.openup.co.uk

OPEN UNIVERSITY PRESS
McGraw - Hill Education

RELATIONSHIP THERAPY
A Therapist's Tale

Rosie March-Smith

9780335238927 (Paperback)
2011

eBook also available

"Rosie March-Smith has provided an insightful and rewarding journey into an area that we would all like to be better at – our relationships to others."
David Hamilton, Counselling student at South Kent College, UK

This fascinating book reveals what goes on in therapy sessions. It shows you how getting to the core of a painful issue or a relationship problem can be achieved within the first few sessions.

Key features:

- Offers invaluable learning tools for mental health professionals and trainees
- Contains case studies of different scenarios
- Includes post-therapy interviews

OPEN UNIVERSITY PRESS
McGraw - Hill Education

www.openup.co.uk

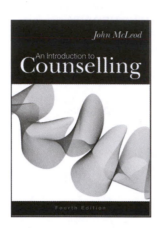

An Introduction to Counselling
Fourth Edition

John McLeod

9780335225514 (Paperback)
2009

eBook also available

This thoroughly revised and expanded version of the bestselling text, *An Introduction to Counselling*, provides a comprehensive introduction to the theory and practice of counselling and therapy. It is written in a clear, accessible style, covers all the core approaches to counselling, and takes a critical, questioning approach to issues of professional practise.

Placing each counselling approach in its social and historical context, the book also introduces a wide range of contemporary approaches, including transactional analysis, arts-based approaches and the use of natural environment in counselling.

Key features:

- Includes commonly used key terms and concepts
- Includes case studies and illustrations relevant to everyday practice
- Chapters covering the integrating of theory into practice

www.openup.co.uk

OPEN UNIVERSITY PRESS
McGraw - Hill Education

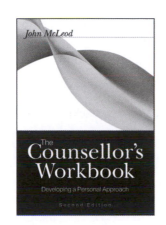

The Counsellor's Workbook
Developing a Personal Approach
Second Edition

John McLeod

9780335228713 (Paperback)
2009

eBook also available

This new edition of *The Counsellor's Workbook* offers you a personal exploration of the key issues that may emerge during your development as a therapist. It provides you with an opportunity to document and consolidate your learning and personal development. *The Counsellor's Workbook* can be used as a stand-alone resource or as a companion text with either the bestselling text, *An Introduction to Counselling 4e* or other key sources.

Key features:

- An entirely new section that focuses upon being a member of a learning group and developing self-awareness.
- New case studies that illustrate effective counselling in practice.
- Updated internet resources and further reading should you wish to explore subjects further.

www.openup.co.uk

OPEN UNIVERSITY PRESS
McGraw - Hill Education

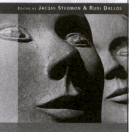

**Reflective Practice in Psychotherapy and Counselling
First Edition**

Jacqui Stedmon and Rudi Dallos

9780335233618 (Paperback)
2009

eBook also available

"This is a rigorously edited book that maintains consistency throughout, I found the concluding chapter 'reflections on reflections' particularly useful. This book captures what is current in reflective practice neatly charting its dissemination from education theory into the different therapy schools. Reflective practice is effectively illustrated within the different therapeutic schools. I will be recommending this book to other members of the multidisciplinary team where I work." BMA *Medical Book Awards 2010 – Highly Commended in the Psychiatry Section*

This book draws together conceptual and ethical issues regarding reflective practice, including the meaning and development of the orientation. More importantly, it connects theory to day-to-day practice in psychotherapy and counselling, addressing issues such as "What does reflective practice look like, in practice?", "How do we develop the skills in carrying it out?" and "What ways does it assist practice?"

www.openup.co.uk

⫸ OPEN UNIVERSITY PRESS
McGraw - Hill Education